D1287118

Unjustified texts

Robin Kinross

Unjustified texts

perspectives on typography

Hyphen Press . London

Published by Hyphen Press, London, in 2002
Copyright © Robin Kinross 2002

The book was designed by Françoise Berserik, The Hague. The text
was typeset and made into pages by Teus de Jong, Nij Beets, in Adobe
InDesign. This text was output in the typeface Arnhem, designed by
Fred Smeijers, Westervoort. Illustrations were scanned by Edith
Cremers, Amsterdam. Proofs of the pages in progress were read by
Linda Eerme, Montreal, and Henk Pel, Zeist. The book was made and
printed in the Netherlands by Koninklijke Wöhrmann BV, Zutphen

ISBN 0-907259-17-0

www.hyphenpress.co.uk

for Paul Stiff, fellow writer

Contents

An introduction   9

Examples   17

Elders, contemporaries

Marie Neurath   51
Edward Wright   56
F. H. K. Henrion   62
Jock Kinneir   65
Norman Potter   68
Adrian Frutiger   72
Ken Garland's writings   78
Richard Hollis   81
Karel Martens   87
MetaDesign   94
Neville Brody   99
The new Dutch telephone book   101
LettError   106

Evaluations

What is a typeface?   113
Large and small letters   131
Black art   143
Newspapers   150
Road signs   152
Objects of desire   158
Letters of credit   161
Two histories of lettering   164
Eric Gill   167
Herbert Read   170
Jan Tschichold   174
Fifty Penguin years   177

Teige animator   181
Adorno's *Minima moralia*   184
Judging a book by its material embodiment   186
The book of Norman   199
Adieu aesthetica   207
Best books   211
The Oxford dictionary for writers and editors   214
The typography of indexes   218

Stages of the modern

Universal faces, ideal characters   233
The Bauhaus again   246
New typography in Britain after 1945   264
Unjustified text and the zero hour   286
Emigré graphic designers   302

Signs and readers

Semiotics and designing   313
Notes after the text   328
Fellow readers   335

Acknowledgements & sources   372

Index   373

... ranged-left and open-ended ...

Norman Potter, from a position statement for the School of
Construction, Bristol, c. 1964

My position is that texts are worldly, to some degree they are events,
and, even when they appear to deny it, they are nevertheless part of the
social world, human life, and of course the historical moments in which
they are located and interpreted.

Edward Said, 'Secular Criticism', *The world, the text, and the critic*, 1983

The only way forward was to make a virtue out of the limitation:
the boundaries of legitimate knowledge are endlessly challengeable,
corrigible, movable, by God, by man, by woman. There is no rationality
without uncertain *grounds, without* relativism *of authority. Relativ-*
ism of authority does not establish the authority of relativism: it opens
reason to new claimants.

Gillian Rose, *Love's work*, 1995

An introduction: writing for publication

There is a presumption implied in this exercise of recycling what may be lesser writings on a topic that is itself already 'lesser', namely – typography (though the book's subtitle might have run on to 'graphic design, and design as a whole, with some dashes into architecture, and broad-brush cultural commentary here and there too'). In my defence: I have always tried to see typography in connection with the human world, and with the most important issues that can concern us; and I have always tried to write with full energy and seriousness, though appropriately, whatever the place of publication – magazine, academic journal, newspaper, company promotional publication, or photocopied circular.

Some further reasons for this collection: there is now a generation of people who know little of the things that we were caught up in even fifteen or twenty years ago. Our commentary from those times is scattered in hard-to-access publications. With this 'our' and 'we', I include a few colleagues who have made or wanted to make the same step of republishing their articles, and who have encouraged me in this venture. So there seems some point in this work of retrieval, even just on the level of documentary, whatever the status of these pieces as an unintended body of writing. And, in my case, much of what I have published has appeared in small-circulation journals; a few things have appeared only in languages other than English; and there are some texts that are published for the first time here.

After early forays into print in the school magazine, aged 16 or so (an article on jazz,[1] and a grim short story in the mood of Joseph Conrad's *The secret agent*), I began, after graduating from the course in Typography & Graphic Communication at the University of Reading, to pursue what must have been a deep urge for publication. That graduation happened in 1975. The next year, the then recently revived journal of the Society of Typographic Designers – *Typographic* – published a longish review I had written 'on spec' of Ruari McLean's book *Jan Tschichold: typographer*. McLean had been external examiner for our class at Reading, and I had written a final-year thesis on 'The idea of a new typography' in the work of Jan Tschichold, Max Bill and Anthony Froshaug. I was furious with Ruari McLean's book,

1. Somehow, in the mid-1960s and in my middle teenage years, already through with the Beatles and the Stones, and in a socially very confined English environment, I had found my way to such documents of deep human consolation, and liberation, as Miles Davis's *Kind of blue* and John Coltrane's *A love supreme*. Both discs were then quite recent: recorded in 1959 and 1964, respectively.

and the review was of a Leavis-like severity. (F. R. Leavis had figured large among my contradictory guiding stars – others were William Empson and Perry Anderson – while doing a degree course in English literature, unsuccessfully, before going to Reading.) McLean's book was too reliant, and without proper acknowledgement, on Tschichold's self-praising anonymous autobiographical essay of 1972; as well as slipshod, it was too genial, and without the moral attack and sometimes crazy concern for detail that its subject had always shown. My review, as it was published, had been clumsily edited. For example 'I feel that' and 'I say' were inserted in front of two of the blunter judgements. This grated especially because, at that time, the first person pronoun was forbidden in my writing: in great contrast to this present latest piece. So I became as angry with the magazine's editor, Brian Grimbly, as I was with the book's author. Some heavy correspondence between the three parties followed, both in print and privately. Publication of the review in *Typographic* had been set up by Anthony Froshaug, whom I was then getting to know – a master for Grimbly, as he was for me. The fall-out from this incident ran on for some years afterwards. In fact, these events resonate still, because they seemed to set a pattern for my writing: the argument in print with people whom you may know as colleagues; the tussle with the copy-editor; and the peculiar occasion of a new book being thrown into play – and the ensuing scrum, as the author, the publisher, and the reviewers, jostle and struggle for possession. The review of McLean's *Jan Tschichold* is not included here. A review of a further edition of that book is; it is a calmer and perhaps more interesting piece.

When Rob Waller started *Information Design Journal*, the first real platform for my writing came into existence. Rob had been a typography student at Reading, the year above me, and on graduating had gone to the Institute of Educational Technology at the Open University, to work as a theoretically informed designer (and vice versa). There, at Milton Keynes, he was spreading what we thought of as 'Reading values', chief among which was just this conjunction of theory and practice. Yet his decision to start this journal of the then almost unheard-of praxis of 'information design' was a personal declaration of independence, outside the nest, even if continuing much that he had learned as an undergraduate. (Later he returned to the Reading fold, by writing a PhD there, while continuing his work at the Open University.) At that time – 1979 – and two years overdue, I was finishing an MPhil thesis at Reading ('Otto Neurath's contribution to visual communication, 1925–1945: the history, graphic language and theory of Isotype'), and had also begun, almost by default, to teach part-time in the department. I wrote two book reviews for the first number of IDJ, and was also, in time for that first number, appointed 'book reviews editor'.

IDJ became a good platform because I was part of the inner circle of the journal, and could publish almost what I liked, unfettered by officious copy-editing. Most of my contributions to IDJ have been outside the main flow of information design. But, in the situation of a sometimes desperate lack of decent material, the stuff I submitted was welcomed. When in 1989, after a period as joint editors, Rob Waller handed over editorship of the journal to Paul Stiff, this situation of welcoming acceptance continued, and intensified. Paul and I had overlapped as undergraduates at Reading, and we had once made plans for starting our own journal.

In these years of postgraduate work and its aftermath, I latched on to the just starting Design History Society. This was formed officially in 1977, at the instigation of the architectural historian Tim Benton, at a conference at Brighton. The DHS was, for a time, a path out of what have always seemed to be the confines of typographic history. By contrast, the Printing Historical Society, formed in 1964, seemed too antiquarian, too focused on mere technics; it had a strong base at Reading, and two prime movers there in the persons of Michael Twyman (founder and head of the Department of Typography) and James Mosley (Librarian of the St Bride Printing Library, and part-time lecturer at Reading). Through the Design History Society I met people interested in all the other parts of the field of design, and for a time this Society's *Newsletter* (typewritten, small-offset printed, and redesigned by Ruth Hecht, in a project I supervised while she was an undergraduate at Reading) was a possible place for publication. When in 1988, after some long-drawn-out manœuvring, the DHS started its *Journal of Design History*, I became, in the journal's first years, its most frequent contributor.

In 1982, I left Reading to live in London and do freelance editorial and design work – trying to maintain the ideal of theory and practice, jointly pursued – and began to write more in earnest. For a time (1984–6) I also taught history of graphic design part-time at Ravensbourne College of Art & Design: an experience that made me resolve to stay away from formal (routinized, monitored) education. There now occurred what seems, in retrospect, a chain of events.

Starting work on the task in January 1983, I wrote some entries (eleven: more than a reasonable portion) for *Contemporary designers*, a 'who's who' work of reference. After the book had appeared in 1984, I began to agitate for payment from the publisher. The sum due was miserable. My only lever of influence was my typewriter. I wrote a review of the book for the *Design History Society Newsletter*, and then submitted another, different review – an interesting literary exercise, which I would do a few times again – to *Designer* (journal of the then-named Society of Industrial Artists and Designers: the SIAD). The first paragraph of that review ran: 'Authors should not review their own books, and so neither should contributors to large (658 pages) works of reference. But then who could review such a book sensibly? Who better than someone who has had a glimpse of how it was compiled, struggled with the job of writing 400 word "evaluative essays" on the complete works of several designers, and who further has no financial interest in the book (or at least, not until the publishers get round to paying).' The parenthetical clause was cut by the magazine's editor or sub-editor; but the review got me into *Designer* as a regular contributor. In March 1986, with the publisher still not paying, I wrote to them again: 'If nothing happens by Friday 21 March, I will make the matter public – I don't suppose I am the only still-unpaid contributor – with letters to *Industrial Design*, *Design*, *Designer*, *Designer's Journal*, the *Design History Society Newsletter*, and *Art Monthly*.' The next week a cheque arrived.

Just then, the middle 1980s, *Designer* was quite a lively publication, enjoying a period of flourish in the golden years of 'the eighties': there was lots of business to write about, and the magazine even had a 'financial section', printed on pages carrying a pink tint (after the *Financial Times*). The whole thing – the magazine and its topic – was altogether interesting. This flourish in the life of a professional society's bulletin was the creation of the editor Alastair Best, an experienced and literate journalist, who had read English at Cambridge, had memories of Leavis and was a Pevsnerite, much involved with architecture. He liked my writing. I knew this for sure when he once phoned on receipt of copy, to say how pleased he was: the piece was a caustic put-down of an overweening design-world figure. *Designer* – the SIAD – was also a chronically bad payer, and Alastair once showed his colours by sending me a cheque drawn on his own bank account; it bounced on first presentation.

I can remember vividly – it would have been 1987 – picking up the phone to hear, for the first time, the voice of Simon Esterson. He had seen my pieces in *Designer* – he was also part of that London circle of design-meets-architecture – and he asked if I would be interested in writing for *Blueprint*. Simon was the designer and one of the founding directors of *Blueprint*, and he played an editorial role on it too, commissioning pieces in his own spheres of activity and interest. I went to the offices of the magazine, at 26 Cramer Street in Marylebone, London W1, in what seemed a short-life occupation, but which in fact went on for years. There I was informally inter-viewed by Simon and the magazine's editor, Deyan Sudjic. I felt the door opening when Deyan laughed at a story I told (about a Dutch designer friend who wanted to write a book on Frank Sinatra). The first commission was immediately announced – I suppose now that this was what prompted the invitation: to write a piece about MetaDesign, Erik Spiekermann's graphic design practice in Berlin. I had just been to visit Erik in Berlin, and had already published (in *Information Design Journal*, the year before) a review of his 'typographic novel', *Ursache & Wirkung*; so it wasn't a difficult task.

Now my eyes were opened to the habits of journalism. When Simon Esterson read my copy for the MetaDesign article, he asked 'where are the quotes?': the staple ingredient of magazine writing. At first I thought it was a dumb question. This lack of quotations from the subject perhaps betrayed my academic upbringing – though the Leavis and Empson ap-proach required much quotation and intense consideration of verbal art;

certainly it showed a confidence in my own voice as a writer. In magazine articles, quotes from the subject tend towards mere ventriloquism, in the service of what the writer wants to say. I suspect them: they can be confections, plucked out of their context, tidied up, and changed in their meaning by their new situation within the journalist's prose. But in this case Simon was making a good point; he had spoken with Erik Spiekermann on the phone, and so knew first-hand about Erik's special powers of speech, and command of demotic English. Later (in IDJ, 1993) I made up for this lack by publishing a question-and-answer interview with Erik, in which my contribution was half-finished mumbles, with Erik in unstoppable flow. Just then, in the late summer of 1987, *Blueprint* was in some sort of race with *Designer's Journal*: who would publish a piece about MetaDesign first? I am not sure who won; but it can only have been by some days. Another insight into the practice of quick journalism came when I saw that the *Designer's Journal* writer (William Owen) had incorporated without acknowledgement passages from my review of *Ursache & Wirkung*.

After this article, I began to contribute to almost every issue of *Blueprint*, was put on the list of 'contributors', and became part of a loose group of writers associated with the magazine. We would see each other at the frequent parties that Peter Murray, the magazine's publisher, would throw in interesting locations, different each time, and with thoughtfully chosen wine. I suspected that these good parties were also a way of diverting contributors' attention from the company's shockingly slow payments. One always had to nag for cheques, which were anyway well below the proper rates for the trade. I remember Peter Murray and Deyan Sudjic rather sheepishly welcoming perhaps their star columnist to one of these receptions with an envelope: obviously containing a last-ditch cheque. But I felt I was part of some sort of intellectual scene, in conversation with writers (Jan Abrams, Brian Hatton, Rowan Moore, come to mind first) who were way beyond the hack journalists in powers of thought and expression, and in their intellectual reach, and yet were resisting the trap of full-time teaching.

The paradox of *Blueprint* in this, its first phase of existence, was intimately bound up with its subject. It was riding the waves of the extraordinary activity of the 1980s, of Britain under the governments of Margaret Thatcher – of deregulation, of Americanization, of the design boom. This provided the subject matter, and the advertising revenue. And yet the magazine was produced by some sharp people, who were able both to document these events and to put them into critical perspective. The magazine's large pages were often brilliant in their effects (photography, illustration). Simon Esterson and his assistant, then successor, Stephen Coates, had found a formula that carried very well the discovery of metropolitan life of that time in London: confidence and toughness; the feeling of relation to the other great world-cities, on which special issues were regularly produced. We all had qualms about the magazine's reliance on imagery: of the designers' own body and apparel (at an extreme in Phil Sayer's cover mugshots), of buildings as stage scenery, unexplained by plans. We wondered whether anyone read the words.

As a contributor to *Blueprint*, I learned much about compressed expression, speedily done. One wrote to a given length, with 100 words as the basic unit. Then when the pages had been designed, you were asked, or allowed, to come to the office. The copy editor (Vicky Wilson) would present you with the task of losing say 22 lines. On the paper proof, you then crossed out less necessary sentences or portions of sentences. Then you wrote captions to pictures. The design of the pages required that the captions run to an exact number of lines, no more, no less. My attempt was always to put the content I was losing from the main text back into the captions. And sometimes one had to spin out a caption to fill the required length, so then it was also a chance to say fresh things. All this one did at short notice, in two or three hours, often in the evening. For a home-worker, unused to offices and not (then) familiar with the Macintosh computers that they used at *Blueprint*, this was part of the challenge. Rick Poynor, who came then to work as assistant editor on *Blueprint*, once remarked to me that writing to length so exactly is one of the real buzzes of the business. I agree, and like to think that this simple craft or skill in writing is as with improvising musicians who can play seemingly effortless and varied successions of choruses, bringing the piece to a finish just as the licensing laws require the venue to close.

In 1990, Wordsearch Ltd, the publisher of *Blueprint*, launched a magazine about graphic design, called *Eye*. The idea had been mooted at Cramer Street for some time, years even. When it seemed that the project was being shelved, the intended editor, Rick Poynor, already *Blueprint*'s graphic design specialist, had even taken steps to join one of the competing magazines. In its first years, *Eye* was 'the international review of graphic design', with text in English, French and German. Before the name was settled on, research had been done on how the word 'eye' was received in continental European countries: there were doubts about how this assembly of letters would play, phonetically, in Italy. After some issues had been put out, it became clear that the great trouble and expense of producing text in three languages was not worth it: there was just a handful of subscribers in France, for example. Peter Murray joked that, but for *Eye*, he would have his helicopter by now. So first the French and then the German text was dropped.

I had switched from writing for *Blueprint* to becoming a regular contributor to *Eye*: with a sense of loss, because I had enjoyed the wide scope and the frequency and urgency of *Blueprint*. *Eye* was confined to 'graphic design' and always seemed too careful and sometimes even just precious. This was perhaps a reflection of Rick Poynor's great thoroughness; certainly it was a function of the magazine's relatively leisured schedule, and its high production values. Rick was on a mission, to create a culture of critical discussion of graphic design. I can respect this attempt, even now; but by then my own missionary zeal for graphic design had waned. I had had some zeal ten years previously, within the design history discussions, and in occasional encounters with art historians. But by 1990 I no longer really believed in the activity of graphic design or its critical discussion, though I was happy to play some variations on increasingly familiar personal themes. I enjoyed arguing with Rick, always marvelled at his fluency and cogency in discussion, and always remembered that he was the person at *Blueprint* who struggled to get a proper system for paying contributors.

In its trilingual period, the main copy-editor on *Eye*, chosen for his multilingualism, had that bleaching attitude towards text, very common in the newspaper and magazine trade, whereby all idiosyncrasies and subtleties of verbal expression are wiped out, regularized. Professional journalists must get used to such treatment, but I could not bear it. After one piece of mine had been published like this, I sent an annotated photocopy to the magazine. Two issues later, I wrote an anonymous letter to Rick at the magazine, pointing out that the German version of something I had written was a richer text than the English original. This was a piece in the issue (no. 5) that had dropped French text. I wrote this letter in the voice of an outraged poststructuralist, who suspected that this was a move against French thought, and who cursed the work of the Cranbrook school (recently published in *Eye*) as 'renegade' in its reported deviation from the path of deconstruction. Five years later, in 1996, I encountered a real-life French poststructuralist (Gérard Mermoz) who really did hold this opinion about the North American corruption of deconstruction: we had some exchange of views in the correspondence columns of *Emigre* magazine.

In 1992, despite a short engagement with a 'left-wing *Private Eye*' – the magazine *Casablanca*, which I had joined in a wish to escape from typography, and in the considerable political confusion of that time, post-1989 – my energies turned away from magazines and towards books. Resigning from the editorial group of *Casablanca*, exhausted, after its first two issues, I decided to put my energies into writing calmer material, with some prospect of making work of lasting value. In the autumn of that year my book *Modern typography* was published. When in 1993 I wrote two feature articles for *Eye*, on Edward Wright and Karel Martens, it felt like a signing off. These were both subjects dear to my heart, and whose work embodies values that live despite, and in opposition to, the consistent thread of nullity and false fronts in design culture. I was becoming sick of finding these tropes of opposition and lament being churned out so often in my writing.

The work of writing, editing and publishing books, on which I then began to concentrate, is difficult. Achieving anything in this world often seems impossible. With plentiful evidence of one's own mistakes and muddles now enshrined in print, one becomes kinder in assessing other people's efforts. Having published what seemed an endless succession of merciless book reviews, I began to be glad of the chance to celebrate 'contributors' – a word that Norman Potter used with special emphasis; he wasn't thinking of the people whose names appear on the imprint pages of magazines –

especially if they hadn't had much public notice. I hope that these pieces of appreciation bring some leavening to this collection.

Making this selection of pieces has been hard. I have selected to avoid too much repetition, and in favour of those pieces that have some function of imparting information, rather than just opinions. In a curious way, the writing that seems to survive best is that which is most of its moment – reporting on things that had just happened. The pieces are grouped here loosely by genre and mood, rather than by any strict system of order.

It seems best to let the themes of this collection speak for themselves, rather than attempt a grand summary here. I have added a note after each piece, giving information about the context of writing and publication. The question of payment, which I have emphasized in this introduction, could have been mentioned also in these notes. And it would be another way of categorizing these writings: those done for a fee, those not. One could not hope to make a living from this kind of writing – for that you need to write for newspapers and large circulation magazines, to be very productive, and to be prepared to write on any subject – but the question of payment is important, as a token of power. The fee gives some greater latitude to the editors of the publication: your words have been bought and are now at the disposal of the editor and sub-editor. A fee encourages the writer to fashion sentences that are worth buying, that play small tricks, that show off. I know this by contrast: from the relief, after a period of doing mostly paid journalism, of then writing without this pressure. Then one can find considerable satisfaction in exact description: passing on information or an experience without the need to amaze a reader.

In preparing the texts for this book, I have gone back, wherever possible, to the words I wrote, rather than to the words as they appeared in print. Sub-editors can certainly improve an article; and they can certainly damage it. Some of the *Blueprint* subs were especially good at writing titles (sharp titles went with the typography of the magazine) and two of these I have gladly retained. But in these pages, for the most part, and for better or worse, are the words as they came off a heavy Adler typewriter (to 1986), Amstrad PCW (to 1990), Macintosh SE/30 (to 1997), PowerMac 7300/200 (to date). I have standardized orthography, but otherwise made only minimal changes. Pictures have been included with the pieces only where necessary to the sense of the text.

The editor of a magazine or journal is a writer's first reader. One writes in the first place for that person. I am glad to thank the people who suggested or accepted these pieces, and especially those I have mentioned in the course of this introduction. In preparing this book, two readers have helped decisively with the choice and ordering of the pieces: Françoise Berserik and Linda Eerme. I thank them now formally, but very warmly too.

Examples

These images represent some of the leading themes and figures in this book. It is not a pantheon of 'good design'. Rather, these are things that I have acquired over the years, or have been able to borrow, so that direct scans could be made. Another factor in the selection is that, for the most part, these items have not been reproduced before. The size given is the size 'to view', with further explanation as necessary; in the case of books and brochures, it is the page size.

Here and throughout the book, in bibliographical references, place of publication is London unless stated otherwise.

Arjan, *Vítězný život: praktické náměty jak si zorganyzovat život*, Prague: Slunce, 1933.

Sewn in sections, cover, 68 pp, 210 x 148 mm. Letterpress. A stray document from the flourish of modernism in Czechoslovakia, whose title might be translated as 'Winning in life: practical suggestions for how to organize your life', and itself organized according to the principles of universal classification (0 to 9). The text is set entirely in lowercase, in an anonymous Grotesk. The front cover (in black and orange) reproduces fragments from the work of Otto Neurath's Gesellschafts- und Wirtschaftsmuseum in Wien, in tune with the themes of standardization and organization. The designer is Jaroslav Hošek.

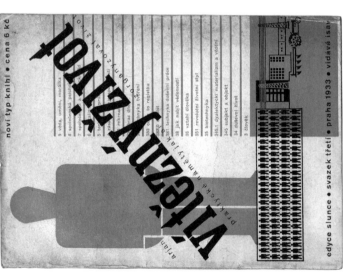

353 potrava vždyva všeobecně. první nezbytná životní potřeba. vířdbí energii pro všecki ostatní projevi.

353.0 vliv potravi na tělo.
353.1 vícena látek: trávení (příjem potravi a její zpracování v těle), vstřebávání a zažívání, vimšěování, přesícenost a hladovění.
353.2 hlavní živiny lidské: bílkoviny, tuki, uhlohidráty, minerální soli, vitaminy.
353.3 nápoje.
353.4 dráždidla, alkohol, kouření.
353.5 jídelní lístek.
353.6 úprava potravi.
353.7 vířiva nemocnych.
353.8 různé směri ve výživě: vegetářství, abstynence, prohibice.

354 předcházení nemocem, preventivní opatření, nezbitnost dostatku zdravého vzduchu.
354.0 hlgiena těla — tělo vilučuje nepořebné látki.
354.1 hlgiena ústa.
354.2 hlgiena kůži.
354.3 hlgiena oděvu.
354.4 hlgiena lásci.
354.5 hlgiena veřejných místnosti, ulic (zkažené prostředí kapit. výroboul).
354.6 hlgiena desinfekcí.
354.7 hlgiena očkováním.

355 355.0 dřsální zdravotní poměri.
355.1 medycína: léčení nemocí, boj proti nemocem.

356 odvy   misíta, účatelý odvy.

357 obidí   jak zatřít bit dostatečly prostor (viz č. 52).

358 různé
359 osobní hos-   životní prostředki: vliv utřídní stroju na dělníka: zdraví, nezdraví,
podářství   penize, vídíáává je těžko. musíš vlužít tedy jejich hodnotu. to není lakota, počítat penízi, za penize, které projdou mímа rukama, mají tobě, tvému hnutí, kamaridům přináší co nejvic užitku. proto počítej, hospodař a šetři.

36 vztahi   abych ukojil své životní potřebi. musím se účastnit společenského dění. jeho vztahů.
dělovka
nejsem celím človíkem, jako ruka nemůže žít odloučena od ostatního těla, nemohu ani já žít odloučený od společnosti. jako různé čásdí těla jsou zavíslé svím životem na společných orglánosti, tak i človík je zavíslý na společnosti, a to na živá. každý mislí pochopit své postavení, protože úspěch i neúspěch společenského dění velmi úzce se ho dotýká. nemní bit jen jeho objektem, částí, kterou druzí popostrkují, jak se jim zlibí, ale i subjektem, spolusmořhovatelem, znamená to boj, znamená to účastňovat se výáznýk akcí, elle-vědomí do něho zasahovat, chápat, podle lenina, že každý okamžik dá se rozložit na revoluční a kontrarevoluční možnosti, že tady v každém okamilku je možno revoluční jednat, zasvětit revoluci nejen několik volných

26

vedeni, ale celí život, pak teprve přestaneš bit otrokem a oprostíš se od špiny tebou nenávíděného, starého života. revoluční boj není nějakím romantyckím odbojem, heo radykalizující měštácké mládeže, ale vedomá tvorba, náplň života, životní úkol, ke kterému přístupuješ s plnou odpovědnosti, nadšením a radosti. bojuješ na všech frontách a žiješ tak mohutný život, tvoj život a síll nevíbují se v neplodných dyskurzích, vílece co mluvíš nejmíně, tak rozíř se nová osobnost. přesná znalá všech svích vztahů, její osobní život tvoří dokonalou jednotu se společnosti.

žijem, abichom mohli bojovat a víbojovat pro život novou zásladnu, dějiné nuříku, společnosti. bojujeme, abichom mohli žít, nebor jednak tak k lza dnes silní žít. chápeme, že otázka dokonalosti života není jen otázkou víle, ideologie, technyksí sebedokonaléjší, ale především otázkou společen-skou, polytyckou, kdo tohle přehlíží je naivstomec, nebo zaprodanec, kteří tak plete hlavu lidom. to ovšem neznamená, abichom zapomínali na život. život je nám nástrojem a proto nesmíme ztratit nikdy rovnováhu a stát se přece nakonec zralosí. o novém životě, o akutečné plném žití budeme moci mluvit, až vírobní prostředki vazmeme do vlastních rukou a tím všecki okromné vlastnosti techniky, vědy, prúmíslu, organyzace budou postaveny do služeb našeho života. ale zas je vílouženo, abi se nikdo stal dobrím re-voluzionářem, budovatelem nového pořádku, kdyř nepřikonal v sobě nej-horlí předsudki životní, sociální ideál nestačí, boj musí každého z nás za-sáhnout až na kořen bitosti a mění nás. to neznamená, že nové životní zviki získáme mímo boj a pak teprve až do toho pustíme. účasti na boji a neustá-lím sebezdokonalováním, sebepřekonáváním oprostíme se od měštáckého nefádu.

opustíme zatuchlé měštíon svích, jen osobních, životů, je v mladí níco radostnějšího a slíbújího, než to, bourat hranice, které náš tísní? náš je svět, budeme-li chtíti, abi jim bili.

vím, i ty jsi nespokojený, ale nechápeš, že kapitalismus je živí organyzmus, který chce si proctiouzzit život, proto je třeba tlut, hízet plenk do oči, za-tomfovat, abis nebel správnou castou. dokud míslíš, jsi hodným obcanem, dokud zaohovává kliid a pořádek, kterí pro tebe znamená vzdát se života. nikdo na tebe nesáhne, jakmile se hlásíš o své právo, hlásíš se o své právo je také přepsvátdovat druhé, postará se o tebe policejní pendrek.

to jest tvoje společenské zařazení ve viroibě a spotřebái.
hospodářská   to hospodářskím boji tvé třídy v odborovích, družstevních orga-
vztahi   nizacích. (viz č. 83).

chápeš, že změna hospodářského postavení tvého a všech prasoujících je
polytycké   možna jen změnou celého společenského řádu. jaká je tvá apoluúdast na
vztahi   tomto boji?

musíš ovládat abecedu polytycké vídy, abia mebil polityckimi šaríataný ed-váděn od správného řešení. tak jako ve škole nelze získat celé vzdělání, ale hlavně praktyckých životem, tak, neíza ani polityksí se víchovat z knih polytycké vídy, ale aktyvní účasti na polityckém životě. to je jedíná správná

360

361

27

Planvolles Werben: vom Briefkopf bis zum Werbefilm,
Basel: Gewerbemuseum Basel, 1934.
Saddle-stitched, without cover, 40 pp, 210 x 148 mm.
Letterpress.

Published to accompany an exhibition on 'planned commercial printing', this booklet shows the hand of Jan Tschichold, who had emigrated from Munich to Basel in 1933, yet it lacks his subtlety of control of detail. The cover, showing the DIN paper sizes, repeats the trope of the cover of Tschichold's *Typografische Entwurfstechnik* (1932). But the handling of the title lines is poorly considered. Note the way in which title and subtitle ('briefko|pf') are set, to accommodate the vertical rules. Inside, the Tschicholdian themes continue, in his own article on 'Die Gestaltung der Werbemittel' and elsewhere.

New year's greeting, Jan and Edith Tschichold, 1937–8.
Sheet folded once, 105 x 148 mm. Letterpress.

Without a strong organizing principle, this piece seems to reflect the moment when Tschichold made his notorious move from asymmetry to symmetry: 1937–8 was when this happened. But it is also a simple piece of printing, without much of the burden of 'design' that designers often impose on these items. The typefaces used are a Garamond and the then just issued Legende of F. H. Ernst Schneidler.

Ronald Davison, *Social security: the story of British social progress and the Beveridge Plan*, Harrap, 1943.
Saddle-stitched, without cover, 64 pp, 185 × 121 mm. Letterpress.

Designed and produced by the firm of Adprint, the booklet is a popular exposition of the history and future of social provision in Britain. It is of interest as a document of the plans for post-war reconstruction, already underway then, and for its use of specially commissioned Isotype charts, printed in carefully disposed colour, and interspersed as double-page spreads within the text. After their emigration to Britain in 1940 and after their release from internment in 1941, Otto and Marie Neurath had formed the Isotype Institute in Oxford, to resume their work as editorial designers. Adprint, pioneers of book-packaging and the integrated book, was another enterprise run by emigrés from Central Europe.

SOCIAL SECURITY

The Story
of British Social Progress
and the Beveridge Plan

by Sir Ronald Davison
visualized by ISOTYPE

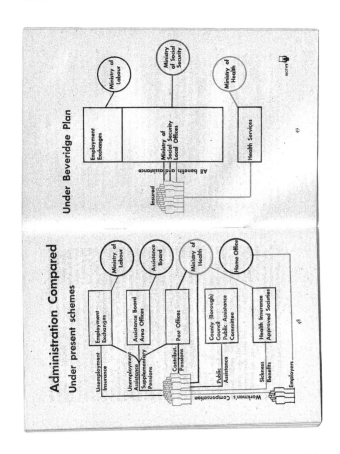

Administration Compared
Under present schemes

Unemployment Insurance — Employment Exchanges — Ministry of Labour

Unemployment Assistance Supplementary Pensions — Assistance Board Area Offices — Assistance Board

Contribut. Pensions — Post Offices

Public Assistance — County (Borough) Council Public Assistance Committee — Ministry of Health

Sickness Benefits — Health Insurance Approved Societies

Employers — Home Office

Workmen's Compensation

48

Under Beveridge Plan

Employment Exchanges — Ministry of Labour

Ministry of Social Security Local Offices — Ministry of Social Security

Health Services — Ministry of Health

Insured

All benefits and assistance

ISOTYPE

49

Association of Building Technicians, *Homes for the people*, Paul Elek, 1946.

Sewn in sections, cased, 184 pp + 16 pp plates, 184 x 120 mm. Letterpress.

A primer of housing for the post-war conditions in Britain, the book packs in much information, both visual and verbal. The person credited with the text design, Peter Ray, was among the handful of British typographers who showed some consciousness of the ideas of the 'new typography'. But the text typography of this book has the flavour of a printer's rather than a typographer's design, as if it was not quite in the designer's hands: an impression that Ray's pleasant and delicate cover image confirms by contrast. The publisher, Paul Elek, was an emigré from Hungary, who in these years began to develop a list of some distinction, both in content and design.

'Aid the wounded' poster, [Ministry of Information],
1943.
370 x 244 mm. Offset lithography.
British government departments and agencies
were main commissioners for designers during
the years of the Second World War and afterwards.
This sublime poster by Henrion, made for the
twenty-fifth anniversary of the Red Army, was part
of the government's campaign to confirm to the
public that it was fully behind the USSR's war effort.
The ordinary soldier is dignified – perhaps monu-
mentalized, in the Soviet spirit – through the device
of the greatly enlarged half-tone screen, suggesting
the coarse resolution of newspaper printing. This
conveys realism and ordinariness, rather than false
heroism. The simple, no doubt hurried, treatment of
the words plays its part here – especially in the use of
the banal script typeface. The poster was produced
in (at least) two sizes: the example shown here is a
half-size version of other surviving copies.

Stefan Schimanski & Henry Treece (editors), *Transformation four*, Lindsay Drummond, 1947.

Sewn in sections, cased, 306 pp, 215 x 134 mm. Letterpress. A characteristic example of British publishing of this time, immediately after the Second World War: materials were still scarce; paper was thin, often of poor quality; typesetting quality was poor too; publishers pressed the maximum content into the minimum page area. The content of this 'periodical in book form' (another phenomenon of the period) was of the moment: signs of cultural resurgence in Europe, with a stress on the visionary and the fantastic. The jacket illustration is appropriate indeed. A note on the inside flap reads: 'Book jacket and typography designed by John Heartfield'. This was the German John Heartfield then in unhappy emigration in Britain, doing small jobs for small publishers. One can guess that his intentions for the work were not exactly stated, and loosely interpreted by the printers.

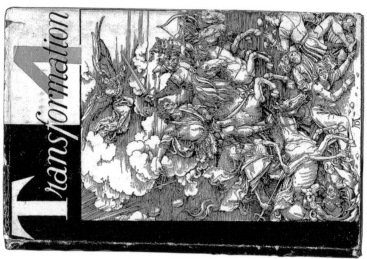

And rather transcendental verse:

> Fill the mountain
> With the names of life.
> Grow close to trees.
> Birds drink water.
> Man has his reason.
> O fill the mountain
> With the names of life.

And the recurring quasi-Biblical language for lost children who may yet hope:

> In thy falling bare flame
> May thy will O may the faces grow...
> On a body again and may thy will arise
> In the cold to be a cry and may thy flight
> The light of summits
> Seize the tents of my naked spirit
> To heal O to heal what toucheth
> Outside the animal.

No doubt, here is a Voice, *aut vincere aut mori*. Unlike Henry Miller who has bared himself, revealed his past and future in his *Cancer* and *Capricorn* books, the voice of Patchen seems to spring from out of nowhere. We know it belongs to the terrible years, but we search for the esoteric roots and find very few revealing clues. Some accidental, even seemingly slight esoteric reason might generate a Dracula or a saint. The powers of Patchen's sublimation are immense. Where and what are the esoteric causes of that sublimation? Perhaps knowledge of such roots, the genesis of his disguises, would damage the aura of the architect of the dark kingdom. We will leave it at that. For as the poet himself says, "It is enough to be innocent." The gates of the dark kingdom are open to those who are able and wish to enter.

Reflections on the Journal of Albion Moonlight

by KENNETH PATCHEN

To TELL YOU THE TRUTH, I have lost the way. I want to destroy all these stupid pages—what a miserable, broken-winded lot I am! What remains? Be assured—whatever happens, I won't lie to you.

One ends by hiding one's heart. I say: here is my heart, it beats and it pounds in my hand—take it! I hold it out to you . . . Close the covers of this book and it will go on talking. Nothing can stop it. Not death. Not life. Draw in closer to me. How small and frightened we are. Our little fire is almost out. What do we seek? I am smiling now. You will be told that what I write is confused, without order—and I tell you that my book is not concerned with the problems of art but with the problems of this world, with the problems of life itself—yes, of *life itself*. Does this astonish you? If you will listen to me, you will learn to create lives. You have none, you know. What did you get from Shakespeare's hooting and howling? A bit of stuff about an idiot and a king. And you threw up in sheer ecstasy. That won't do. The noble speeches aren't enough. The thread-bare and ridiculous plots aren't enough. Men were made to talk to one another. You can't understand that. But I tell you that the writing of the future will be just this kind of writing—one man trying to tell another man of the events in *his own heart*. Writing will become speech. Novelists talk about their characters. This is because they have nothing to say about themselves. You will ask, was this true of Dostoievsky? and sadly I must answer: yes, Dostoievsky made this stupid mistake—but I was wrong! I am right in what I say to you, *but it doesn't make sense*, it doesn't tell you what you should know. We must keep Shakespeare and Dostoievsky, because they talked above the clamour of their characters—they poked their bleeding heads through the junk-pile of literature, *and we saw their white, twitching faces*. We saw their lips moving. We heard their grunts and their sobs. Ah, but who did! I am full of danger when I think of the smug pigs who call themselves writers—the dirty, unthieveried fat boys fingering their mother's love letters off in the attic somewhere. What luck! Get that rubbish out of my way . . . you are damned right there, I am stewing in my own juices . . . don't turn away, I have bad habits. For one thing I never have money, I have no trade. There is money in novels but none at all in writing. Money is a necessity. Without it one starves. Then there is the matter of the landlord. Landlords care even less about writing than novelists do. It is hard to write in the street. People get the idea that maybe you are crazy. Writing is a difficult job. There is no trouble at all in knowing what you want to say; the trouble begins in keeping out the rest of it. I'd like to talk about God all the time. I know less about this than about anything else. I know that you encourage me to show my heart. I have never belonged to a political party. Please tell all your friends to read my journal. I have spent many lives learning to write. It would be a pity if no-one bothered to read this, wouldn't it? I feel that I have somebody to write to. I am not evil.

Das österreichische Fertighaus, Vienna: Österreichischen Produktivitätszentrum, 1953.

Comb-bound, covers, 182 pp, 205 x 318 mm [extending to 334 mm]. Letterpress.

This catalogue explaining a system for the prefabrication of houses shows what can happen when 'design for the user' and 'design from the content' meet: a slightly ungainly but wonderfully articulate document. The material is sorted into discrete parts, shown both visually and in the materials used: coated paper for the introductory, illustrated pages; grey cartridge for the pages on which costs can be calculated via highly considered tables; coloured paper for the tabbed dividing pages. For the designer, Ernest (Ernst) Hoch, who had emigrated from Vienna in 1938 to settle eventually in England, this was a rare job for his home country. He remembered that when something seemed wrong in the design, as he worked on this job, he checked with the client, who found that just here they had supplied him with false information. He felt that this was some proof that form could 'body forth' content.

28

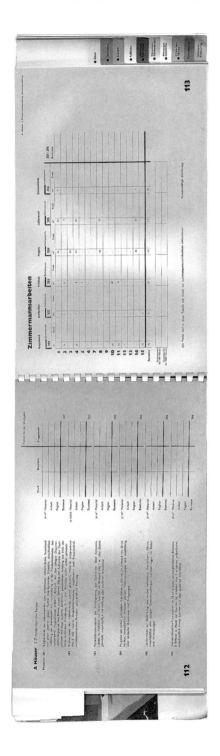

Zimmermannsarbeiten

A Häuser 3.7 Zimmermannsarbeiten

Paintings, drawings, and sculpture: a selection from the Arts Council collection, Arts Council of Great Britain, 1955. Saddle-stitched, 36 pp, wraps, 247 x 185 mm. Letterpress. A modest and straightforward catalogue, which plays some variations in its use of different papers: especially the brown paper of the cover, rough and full of wood particles on one side (the outside), and glazed on the reverse side. This, as well as some elements of the typography, are strong reminders of the Stedelijk Museum catalogues of Willem Sandberg: a master for Herbert Spencer, designer of this piece.

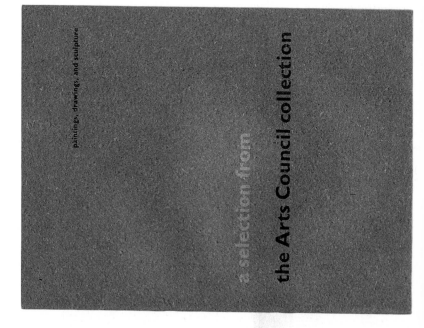

paintings, drawings, and sculpture

a selection from

the Arts Council collection

Peter Robinson store, London, 1959

This piece of architectural lettering by Edward Wright suggests ways in which signs can be integrated into buildings, given enough sympathy between architect and letterer. Such a collaboration also depends on the letter designer being brought into the project at an early enough stage. These are translucent plastic letters, internally lit, and placed within a recess that marks the division of the building: the shop on the ground and first floor, and offices on three floors above. The form of the letters feels exactly in tune with the restrained, geometric form of the building itself, which is on the Strand, one of the busiest through-ways in the centre of London. The sign and the shop have now gone; the building (designed by Denys Lasdun) made way for a piece of developer's postmodernism. (Photograph by Joseph Rykwert.)

Hochschule für Gestaltung Ulm,
new year's card, 1958.
148 x 105 mm. Letterpress.
As the caption on the reverse side explains,
in four languages, this image is a student
exercise, showing 'changes in tone-value
by deformation of a grid'. The student was
Hubert Zimmermann. The designer of this
very simple card is not credited – but it is
likely that Anthony Froshaug was the tutor
responsible for production (the asterisk for
the new year suggests his mind at work).
The pattern is printed in grey, the text be-
neath in red.

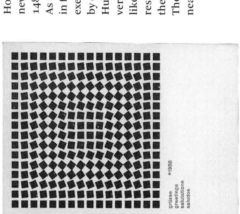

grüsse   *1958
greetings
salutations
saludos

Balding & Mansell, envelope, [1963].
105 x 216 mm. Letterpress.

One piece of the company identity designed by Derek Birdsall for the printers Balding & Mansell: this is a pocket window envelope, with opening and flap on the right-hand edge. The new logotype/symbol for the company acts out the process of printing. The overlapping blocks of colour are grey and orange, and the plus sign – more contemporary then than an ampersand – falls just where the colours are added to each other. The size of the envelope and placing of the window do not seem to conform exactly with any then current British size. This was done just at the point when British norms for stationery began to be adjusted to those of continental Europe.

3 Bloomsbury Place London WC1
Telephone Langham 6601
Telegrams Baldimentio London WC1

New Left Review, 1966.

Sewn booklet, covers, 96 pp, 225 x 154 mm. Letterpress.
Derek Birdsall's design for the *New Left Review* was that
journal's third visual identity (following those by Germano
Facetti and Brian Downes) and much the most durable
– accompanying the long editorships of Perry Anderson and
Robin Blackburn. It only disappeared finally in 2000, with
the 'New Series' that started then (designed by Peter Campbell). Birdsall's NLR had a classical restraint, with the life
provided by the surprising and memorable second colours
used on the cover (blue in this example), and by the clash of
typefaces: Monotype Garamond and the then-named Neue
Haas Grotesk (later Helvetica). Inside, the pages were de-
terminedly asymmetric and free of indentation. The feeling
was high-minded and 'European' – German or Italian, but
not British.

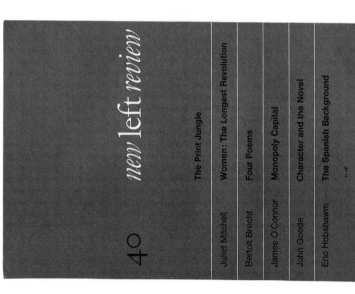

James O'Connor

Monopoly Capital

The late Professor Baran once remarked to the present writer that he was 'perfectly satisfied with the current state of orthodox economic theory' and considered further mathematical explorations of the properties of conventional economic models a waste of time and energy. A little reflection will suggest that this might be considered an unusual opinion for a Marxist to hold. Why, indeed, should Professor Baran have been satisfied with orthodox theory at all? *Monopoly Capital*, the final product of years of fruitful collaboration between our two leading Marxist economists, supplies an answer which will be helpful to many radical social scientists and offend many traditional Marxists.

Marxist analytic tools were developed to describe the transition from pre-capitalist to capitalist economies and to unravel the 'laws of motion' of competitive capitalism. An analysis of monopoly capitalism requires techniques which are more adaptable to their subject matter. These are nowhere to be found in the classic Marxist literature, although there have been attempts to stretch the labour theory to fit problems of monopoly pricing. The utility of the techniques

based on the labour theory nevertheless remains limited to explaining the origins of profits and the distribution of income between economic classes under a regime of competition. Mainly for this reason, the authors of *Monopoly Capital*[1] have been compelled to borrow most of their tools from economic orthodoxy.

It should be quickly added that the same thing cannot be said about the *method* which the authors use to study us monopoly capitalism. In their own words, Marxian social science focuses on 'the social order as a whole, not on the separate parts'. While American social science has discovered many 'small truths' about contemporary capitalism, 'just as the whole is always more than the sum of the parts, so the amassing of small truths about the various parts and aspects of society can never yield the big truths about the social order itself'. More concretely, what distinguishes the economic method from that of their orthodox rivals is the division of the total product, or gross national product, into 'socially necessary costs' and 'economic surplus'. For orthodox economists the cost of producing a given total product is equal to the value of that product, even when total product falls below the full capacity level. It will become clear that it is impossible to even identify the surplus unless economic society is viewed 'as a whole'. Thus the concept of the surplus is integral to the Marxian method and totally foreign to orthodox method.

Immediately there is apparent a striking asymmetry. Baran and Sweezy have welded techniques forged during the past few decades by academic economists to a methodological concept which in one form or another is as old as economic science itself, but which is presently associated chiefly with Marxian thought. As we shall see, the clash between method and technique is the source of some of the more troublesome theoretical difficulties which appear in *Monopoly Capital*.

Major themes

In order to convey some idea of the magnitude of Baran and Sweezy's achievement, as well as to prepare the reader for a critique of *Monopoly Capital*, we attempt below to summarize the book's major theses. Especially, the authors depart sharply from orthodox practice by placing monopoly at the very centre of their analysis. Today the typical unit in the capitalist world is not the small firm producing a negligible fraction of a homogeneous output for an anonymous market but a large-scale enterprise producing a significant share of the output of an industry, or even several industries, and able to control its prices, the volume of its production, and the types and amounts of its investments.[1]

Large-scale business is organized along corporate lines and is typical in the sense that a relatively small number of industrial giants own a large share of industrial assets. Controlled by a group of self-perpetuating professional managers, the big corporations retain the lion's share of their earnings and enjoy a great measure of financial independence. The

[1] Paul Baran and Paul Sweezy: *Monopoly Capital: an essay on the American economic and social order.* Monthly Review Press, New York and London, 61/-.

Iris Murdoch, *Under the net*, Harmondsworth: Penguin Books, 1960, 1962.

Cut & glued, covers, 256 pp, 181 x 110 mm. Letterpress.

After the purely typographic style that Jan Tschichold set for Penguin fiction editions in the late 1940s, there was, through the 1950s, a growing demand for the introduction of imagery. The first example, designed to a format of Hans Schmoller's, shows the state of affairs then: an illustration on the cover, but constrained by a given assembly of panels and rules. The illustration here is by the young Len Deighton, recently graduated from the Royal College of Art. Two years later, under the direction of Germano Facetti, the illustration is brought to the fore, the panels have gone, and the typeface changed from 'humanist' Gill Sans to 'industrial' grotesques. Another notable shift can be seen in

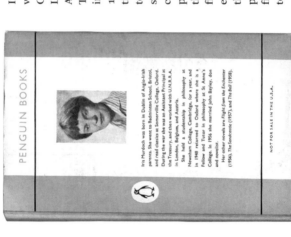

the setting of the title lines: from all-capitals to upper- and lowercase. The new British road signs, being designed just then by Jock Kinneir, showed the same progress. One may note also that, over the two years, the price of the item showed a rise of 40 per cent.

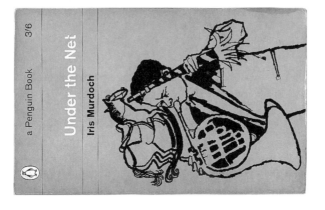

Ken Garland, *Graphics handbook*, Studio Vista, 1966.
Sewn in sections, covers, 96 pp, 196 x 165 mm.
Offset lithography.

In the strong 'through-design' of its material, Ken Garland's work seemed an exceptional item within the pleasantly relaxed series of handbooks on art and design that John Lewis edited for Studio Vista. Garland was concerned with ascertainable knowledge and definite procedures. Good style or inspiration were not discussed. This was a graphic design that had left the artist's sketchpad, and lived rather in the world of social interaction with a client or a printer. Itself organized into tabbed sections, the book contains much material on organizational themes. If these ideas could help architecture and industrial design, then why not graphics?

The telephone as a tool for the graphic designer

Why bother with technique?

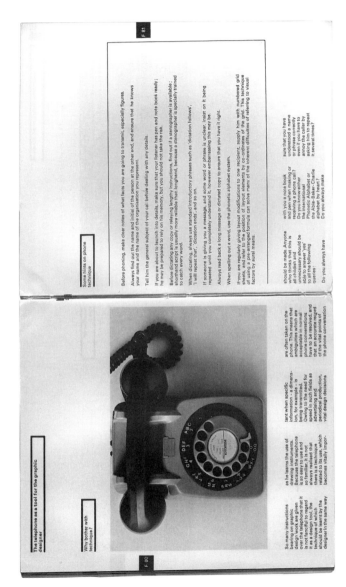

So many instructions bearing on graphic design work are given over the telephone that it is not fanciful to regard it as a design tool, the technique of which should be learnt by the designer in the same way as he learns the use of drawing instruments. Because the telephone is so easy to use and so familiar, it is not always realised that there is a technique related to its use, which becomes vitally important when specific information - a dimension, for example - is being transmitted. Owing to the need for speed in such fields as advertising and periodical production, vital design decisions are often taken on the phone. This means that ambiguities which are acceptable in normal phone conversations have to be resolved, and that an accurate record of the vital points of the phone conversation

Some hints on phone technique

Before phoning, make clear notes of what facts you are going to transmit, especially figures.

Always find out the name and initial of the person at the other end, and ensure that he knows your name and the name of the organisation you represent.

Tell him the general subject of your call before dealing with any details

If you are about to launch into details, make sure that your listener has pen and note book ready; he may be prepared to rely on his memory, but you should not take the risk.

Before dictating any copy or relaying lengthy instructions, find out if a stenographer is available; shorthand script is usually more reliable than longhand, because a stenographer is specially trained to catch every word.

When dictating, always use standard introductory phrases such as 'dictation follows', 'I will repeat that', 'dictation ends', and so on.

If someone is giving you a message, and some word or phrase is unclear, insist on it being repeated until you completely understand it, however embarrassing this may be.

Always read back a long message or dictated copy to ensure that you have it right.

When spelling out a word, use the phonetic alphabet system.

If you are regularly giving layout modifications to one recipient, supply him with numbered grid sheets, and refer to the position of layout elements by co-ordinates of the grid. This technique of using a pre-arranged formula can solve many of the inherent difficulties of referring to visual factors by aural means.

should be made. Anyone who thinks that this is all childish or unnecessary should be able to answer 'yes' to all the following queries:

Do you always have with you a note book and pen when making or receiving a phone call? Do you know either the International Phonetic Alphabet or the Able-Baker-Charlie alphabet by heart? Do you always make sure that you have understood a name or phrase correctly even if you have to annoy the caller by asking him to repeat it several times?

New Society, London, 1966.
Saddle-stitched, 34 pp, 333 x 236 mm. Letterpress.
In a time of modernization in Britain, *New Society* provided lively commentary on a huge range of topics. This issue is from the time (1966–9) in which Richard Hollis was art editor, working with a basic page layout and structure devised by Germano Facetti in 1964. The cover uses an illustration made by Edward Wright for the occasion. The spirit at work here – characteristic of these three designers, and following from Paul Barker's article on the Basques – is of the 'given', the documentary.

S. G. M. Lee & A. R. Mayes (editors), *Dreams and dreaming*, Harmondsworth: Penguin Education, 1973.
Cut & glued, covers, 512 pp, 199 x 129 mm. Letterpress.
The extensive series of 'Readings' that Penguin Education published in the 1970s was distinguished by a style for the covers (designed by Derek Birdsall's Omnific studio) that carried striking, simple images against a stark white background. On the spines the rule was that the title should be set in capitals in this grotesque typeface, in a size that would (to within a few millimetres) fill the spine. For this book, seizing on the serendipity of the words within the word, Anthony Froshaug took the laziest route and used just the title in the series typeface and a second colour.

PENGUIN MODERN PSYCHOLOGY READINGS

DREAMS & DREAMING

SELECTED READINGS

EDITORS: S. G. M. LEE AND A. R. MAYES

DREAMS & DREAMING

EDITORS: S. G. M. LEE AND A. R. MAYES

PUBLISHED BY PENGUIN EDUCATION   COVER DESIGN: OMNIFIC/ANTHONY FROSHAUGH

PSYCHOLOGY & PSYCHIATRY   0 14 08.0552 4

0 14 08.0552 4

Before the 1950s most investigations of dreams and dreaming were concerned with the content of dreams, in particular with their function and meaning. For those who remained unconvinced by the explanations of psychoanalysis and analytical psychology, the discovery in 1953 of rapid eye movement (REM) sleep seemed to hold out the possibility of a more 'scientific' theory being formulated.

This absorbing collection of papers draws together some of the most influential findings in the field. The first half of the volume includes accounts of some early dream theories, an investigation of the content of children's dreams, and an exposition of the classic theories of Freud and Jung. The second half offers a variety of papers on REM sleep, and the effects of its deprivation, and goes on to look at the question of the dream state in relation to visual perception, motivation, information processing, drugs and biochemical processes.

RE M

S. G. M. Lee was formerly Professor of Psychology and A. R. Mayes is Lecturer in Psychology, University of Leicester.

'Penguin Modern Psychology Readings should be of inestimable value to psychology students, to students in other social sciences, and for that matter to the educated general reader'
The Times Educational Supplement

United Kingdom £1.25
New Zealand $3.75
Canada $5.25

Australia $3.75
(recommended)

Bertolt Brecht, *Me-ti: boek der wendingen*, Nijmegen: SUN, 1976.

Sewn in sections, covers, 208 pp, 220 x 150 mm. Letterpress. Beginning his work for the Socialistiese Uitgeverij Nijmegen in 1975, this was among the first of the books that Karel Martens designed for the firm. The 'Sunschrift' series style was carried by the rules that bounded the front and back cover (and which encompassed the spine), and by the use of Franklin Gothic type – rubbed down in Letraset by the designer. Images followed from the nature of the particular title: here a pen-drawing by Paul Klee. The covers were printed (offset) on matt paper, unvarnished. Inside, the text is unjustified – as always in this series – and with centred display elements. The whole has a simplicity and modesty that matches Brecht's text.

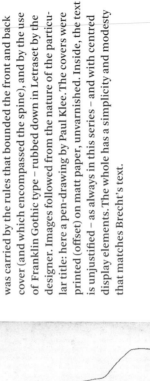

ME-TI
BOEK DER WENDINGEN
BERTOLT BRECHT
SUNSCHRIFT 108

MENEN EN WETEN

Keh Lan onderhandelde buiten medeweten van de vereniging en tegen
haar advies in met buitenlandse politici. Me-ti sprak: Keh Lan beroept
zich erop, dat hij vertrouwen waardig is. Het is mogelijk dat hij vertrouwen
waardig is. Wij menen niet dat hij ons vertraden heeft. Wanneer hij echter
verlangt dat we zeggen te weten, dat hij ons niet verraden heeft, dan
verlangt hij teveel. Tussen menen en weten bestaat een onderscheid,
hetwelk niet op te merken gevaarlijk is. Wanneer hij wil, dat wij weten,
mag hij geen beroep doen op ons vertrouwen. Hij zegt, dat we niet op de
buitenkant mogen afgaan, we moeten op het innerlijk afgaan. Waarom
wil hij ons niet toestaan, op de buitenkant af te gaan? De buitenkant kan
bedriegelijk zijn, maar ook beweten worden. Het innerlijk kan niet bewezen
worden, het moet eenvoudig geloofd worden. Wil hij ons leren te geloven,
terwijl hij ons ook in staat kon stellen te weten? Keh Lan zal misschien de
beste bedoelingen gehad en onze zaak naar best vermogen behartigd
hebben, maar hij zadelt ons op met een kwalijke gewoonte, wanneer hij
ons ertoe brengt menen als weten te beschouwen.

HET IS GEMAKKELIJKER HET GELOOFWAARDIGE
TE ZEGGEN DAN HET WARE

Men tracht dikwijls te doen geloven wat men niet bewijzen kan. Daarbij
beroept men zich op zijn waarheidsliefde. Helaas is het ware niet altijd het
waarschijnlijke. Dikwijls wordt het ware pas met behulp van kleine
onwaarachtigheden ook waarschijnlijk. Zo begint men dan te liegen op
het ogenblik, waarop men slechts door een beroep te doen op beproefde
waarachtigheid geloofwaardig is. Me-ti heeft gezegd: Het is voorzichtiger
van mij, ervoor te zorgen dat mijn vriend zichzelf geloven kan, in plaats
van mij.

SLECHTE GEWOONTEN

Naar plassen gaan, die door gaan onbereikbaar zijn, moet men zich afwennen. Praten over aangelegenheden, die door praten niet beslist kunnen
worden, moet men zich afwennen. Denken over problemen, die door
denken niet opgelost kunnen worden, moet men zich afwennen, heeft
Me-ti gezegd.

OVER DE DOOD

Me-ti bewonderde de wijze waarop onze vriend An-tse gestorven was.
Hij had stervend een paar gemakkelijke algebra-opgaven ter hand genomen.
Onder het oplossen daarvan stierf hij. 'Of hij was al klaar met het raadselen
over de dood of had althans besloten dat dat probleem niet oplosbaar is',
sprak Me-ti, en toen ik hem vroeg of men niet kon zeggen dat het deze
wijze van sterven aan diepte ontbrak, gaf hij ten antwoord: 'Wanneer men
de rivier over moet, zoekt men graag een ondiepe plek'.

106

107

The Springboard Educational Trust would like to acknowledge the support of the London Borough of Tower Hamlets

Frumkin's, Commercial Road, E1

3-21 August 1980

A series of audio-visual programmes presented by The Springboard Educational Trust in association with *The Jewish Chronicle*

THE SIGHTS AND SOUNDS OF THE JEWISH EAST END AT THE WHITECHAPEL ART GALLERY

Whitechapel High Street, London E1
Telephone 01-377 0107

Aldgate East

Open Sunday-Thursday 11am-9.30pm
Admission free

Whitechapel Art Gallery leaflet/poster, 1980.
297 x 420 mm, folding to 99 x 210 mm. Offset lithography.
The Whitechapel Gallery was not well-provided for in this period and full-colour posters were very rarely possible. The designer, Richard Hollis, makes the most of a wonderful photograph for this announcement, which doubles as a through-the-post (DL envelope) leaflet and something that could be displayed on a wall too. The size of type is delicately judged to allow for both situations, and is disposed along the folds, so that it reads coherently through the process of folding and unfolding. This is printed in just vermillion and turquoise – Hollis avoided black for such items – and further colours are found by screens and overprinting.

City Limits, 1981.
297 x 210 mm, saddle-stitched, covers, 88 pp. Offset lithography.
In 1981, after the London listings magazine *Time Out* had lost its co-operative status, some of disaffected staff started *City Limits* as a left-wing alternative to that increasingly 'establishment' paper. David King was the first designer of *City Limits*. His often strident, agit-prop graphic manner was certainly a style for that time of conflict in Britain. Later, the magazine was given a new format by Neville Brody, the young London designer of the moment. In 1990 the magazine went under, leaving the field open to its ever-expanding progenitor, *Time Out*.

45

FF Quadraat typeface specimen, Arnhem, 1992.
210 x 590 mm, folding to 210 x 118 mm. Offset lithography.
In the 1990s, with the rebirth of small-scale and even one-person type manufacture, printed specimens produced by the designer of the typeface reappeared. This one, in the clarity and fullness of its presentation, was an exceptional example. It was made by the small design office of Quadraat in Arnhem, whose members included Fred Smeijers, designer of the typeface Quadraat. The designer had had plans to issue the typeface himself, but eventually passed it to FontShop in Berlin. Nevertheless Smeijers went ahead with plans for his own specimen, giving it a degree of care that one does not find in company specimens (if they issue them at all). As appropriate to the conditions of DTP, it is assumed that the user will want to know the keyboard layout, especially for the ligatures and special characters that are a feature of Quadraat. Three colours are used: dark and light green, and rich blue.

(overleaf)
Berliner Verkehrs-Betriebe (BVG) bus & tram leaflet,
Berlin, 1992.

420 x 297 mm, folding to 140 x 50 mm. Offset lithography.
This modest and appropriate leaflet shows the high quality
of information provided, under the guidance of Meta-
Design, by the transport authority of the then recently unified Berlin. As in the *Fertighaus* catalogue (pp. 28–9 above),
content (the bus and tram lines) and form (the panels of the
folded sheet) are intermeshed wonderfully. This, and some
of the details, such as the use of organizing rules, suggests
a tradition of information design over forty years and more.
A friendly and direct letter to travellers explains that the
changes given in this leaflet are mainly about bus services,
which are assigned a prominent purple; tram lines are
given a recessive grey. A signature line reads: 'MetaDesign:
K. Lanz'.

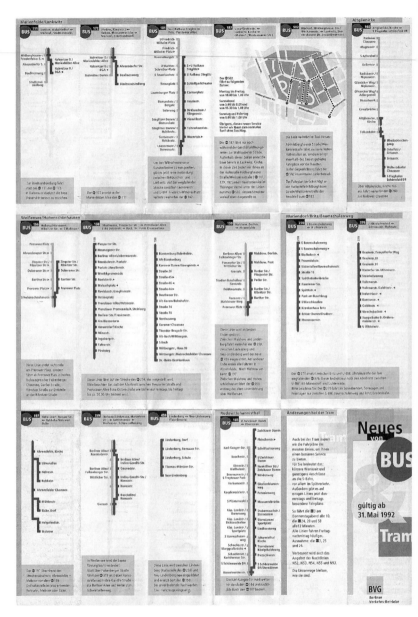

(See p. 47 for caption.)

Elders, contemporaries

Marie Neurath, 1898–1986

Marie Neurath died in London on 10 October 1986. Her work with Otto Neurath on what became known as Isotype is now well documented, not least by her own spare and lucid writings. The remarks that follow will not attempt a systematic description of her life and work, but are meant as an informal and personal statement.

In some of the autobiographical texts that she wrote, Marie Neurath fixed on the first moments of an experience or a relationship, as assuming special significance. The first occasion that I can remember is of her moving around a studio at the Typography Unit (as it then was) at the University of Reading. After she had given the materials of the 'Otto and Marie Neurath Isotype Collection' to the University, she came regularly to hold a seminar about Isotype with third-year students of typography. I was then only in the second year: that I could not go to the seminar (and that an 'ad hoc' student from the Netherlands sitting next to me could) was a source of considerable frustration and jealousy.

Marie's qualities were visible already from across the room: her uprightness, both in posture and, as one discovered, in the moral sense too; her natural dignity, and lack of pretension and ceremony; her sense of equality and her openness, so that there were never any barriers from difference of age. I wanted to get to know her. The first chance came in 1975, when we made an exhibition on Isotype at Reading. Then I wrote an MPhil thesis on the subject, and our contact continued with the cataloguing of the Collection. In the last years it was centred on the translation of and editorial work on Otto Neurath's writings, which was her major preoccupation after closing the Isotype Institute office.

Marie Neurath (née Reidemeister) came from Brunswick in the north of Germany. The decisive moment in her life came in September 1924, when, on a student trip to Vienna, she was introduced to Otto Neurath and decided – instinctively – that she wanted to work with him. There followed what one may see as her central years (1925–34), immersed in this work and in the life of the new Vienna of democratic-socialist reform.

Otto and Marie Neurath in Oxford, 1943.
(Photograph by their friend, Erna Braun.)

In her accounts of the history of Isotype, Marie tended to play down her own part – as we gradually came to realize at Reading. Though latterly she did hint that Otto Neurath would never have embarked on the project of a 'Gesellschafts- und Wirtschaftsmuseum in Wien' (social and economic museum of Vienna) without her. The history of their work, as it developed subsequently, supports this suggestion. When the Isotype Institute was set up in England in 1942, Otto and Marie were directors on equal terms. And, after Otto's death in 1945, Marie continued its work for nearly thirty years, concentrating on the production of educational books for young readers. The achievement of these books, seen in the context of their time, has yet to be properly assessed.

Otto Neurath was an encyclopaedist in the Enlightenment tradition, with multiple and academically unorthodox interests, of which Isotype was perhaps the strangest – especially to his associates who were respectably employed in universities, as Neurath was not. For Marie, this visual work was the leading activity of her life, and it perfectly suited her. She had wide cultural and social interests, and trained to be a teacher, specializing in mathematics and physics.

She also had a strongly visual side to her and had done a course in drawing at art school.

The character of Isotype – if one can personify it – followed from the interests and dispositions of the people behind it, Otto and Marie above all. It was concerned with the visual representation of things that needed to be said: not just any facts, but information worth presenting, and from which one could learn historical and social relationships, as well as facts. Isotype was not, as in the popular image of it, a simple method for turning numbers into pictorial statistics. Rather, and at its best, Isotype charts were intelligent visual statements, which were developed freshly on each occasion from a set of partly tacit principles. I tried to say some of this in an earlier contribution to *Information Design Journal* (vol. 2, no. 2). What I did not say there was that, despite Otto Neurath's wish for a widely diffused and perhaps international 'picture language', to think of an Isotype that was not a product of the collaboration of – most essentially – Otto Neurath, Marie Neurath, Gerd Arntz, is to imagine something different and probably something reduced in quality. The history of attempts by others to make 'isotypes' (as they are sometimes misleadingly called) shows this.

In Isotype terminology, Marie was the 'transformer': the person who made the visual statements, and the crucial intermediary between those with specialist knowledge, those who assembled the final product, and – in some respects the most important element – the public. Otto and Marie never used the term 'designer' (in English or in German equivalents). But this word has only in recent years resumed its special sense of someone who plans and gives material form to content; and when, at Reading, we used to speak of the transformer as a designer, Marie would be doubtful. She assumed that designers were visual decorators who changed the form of things every season, following fashion. (There are, alas, considerable grounds for this belief.) In contrast and as its name indicates, Isotype was standards-minded: if you have arrived, after considerable invention and experiment, at a satisfactory symbol or configuration of symbols, why change it? Marie stood for continuities, in spite of the tragedies of the times that she lived through. A story from her life illustrates this attitude. With Otto, she had left The Hague at the last moment in May 1940, in a small open boat.

Marie Neurath in London, 1984: in the garden
of the house in which she lived in a basement flat.
(Photograph by Gertrud Neurath, Otto's niece.)

After the war, she returned to The Hague on a visit, and there used
up the tram tickets that remained from a pre-war packet. They had
travelled with her through the escape, some months in internment,
and then an intensely busy and happy period (up to Otto Neurath's
death in December 1945) in Oxford, where the Isotype Institute was
first established.

Her life was extraordinarily productive. The Isotype Collection at
Reading includes many boxes of working materials, and I suppose
that similar small mountains of stuff got lost in the two forced
removals, from Vienna and from The Hague. She had a beautiful
economy of effort. In correcting translations, she would suggest the
minimum necessary changes, often finding one or two words which
then solved what had seemed an impossibly complicated problem.
In this translation and editorial work, her passion for accuracy was
vivid to those of us who knew her only in the last phase of her
life: looking at the products of Isotype, one can see this same quality informing them. And as well as her concern for accurate and
honest statement, she had a phenomenally exact memory: she was
an exemplary recorder of events.

The later years were enriched by new friendships with people who came to see her about Otto, but quickly became devoted to Marie. One by one, we came under her spell, and now form a still growing group of Neurath specialists in at least five countries. She was the very opposite of the tiresome widow who stifles free discussion of her husband's work. Though certainly a partisan of Otto Neurath's work, Marie applied no pressures. Our interest in Otto Neurath became a matter of common exploration with her. Another story: someone had published a selection of Otto Neurath's writings, prefaced by a long interpretative introduction, which he wrote without consulting her. She compiled a long list of points of query or disagreement. He came to discuss these. I asked her how the meeting had gone. She said, rather surprised, 'well, he agreed with me on every point'. They were soon on 'du' terms, and then he would come regularly to London, just because he loved her.

Her main regret, in her last days, was that further progress had not been made on the various editions of Otto Neurath's writings that are under way. These include a selection (in English) of his writings on economics, which was especially important for her. There is also an edition of the correspondence with Rudolf Carnap (in English and also in German), and the collected writings on visual education (in German). A short, well-illustrated book on Isotype is also planned, and the last text she wrote was for this. These books will appear eventually, and they will further confirm the significance of the life and work of Otto Neurath. This process of the discovery of Otto Neurath (he was never well enough known for it to be called a rediscovery) has been and will be one of Marie's great achievements. Those of us involved in these books will miss her especially. And, writing this now, it is hard to realize that I can no longer telephone her to arrange a visit for us to go through this text, drink coffee, and get on to talk about books, politics, people.

Information Design Journal, vol. 5, no. 1, 1986

Such a piece one could publish only in IDJ. Though perhaps the newspapers of the 'obituary culture' (*The Independent* and *The Guardian*) – in the mid-1980s just about to take off in Britain – would have accepted a short version. Of the books to be published, mentioned in the last paragraph, only Neurath's *Gesammelte bildpädagogische Schriften* has appeared (Vienna: Hölder-Pichler-Tempsky, 1991).

Edward Wright

His work slips free from the nooses of British culture. The man himself was like this too: nimble, shy but definite, informal but with grace and dignity, carrying the minimum baggage, taking risks but always landing on his feet. With good reason do his friends liken him to a cat. Now, five years after his death and scarcely present in the public record, it is necessary to explain almost everything about Edward Wright's work, and where, how and why it doesn't fit in.

'I suppose I had an acute sense of being uprooted', he wrote in an autobiographical essay. That is one of the keys. It joins Edward Wright to the considerable number of the exiled and emigré artists, who, it often seems, have provided Britain – and England in particular – with much of what has been of value in its culture in the twentieth century. He was born in 1912 in Liverpool, where his father was an Ecuadorian vice-consul. His mother was the daughter of the Chilean consul there. So the English-sounding name is misleading. Edward Wright was bilingual in Spanish and English: a fact that helps an understanding of his paradoxes. Some of his earliest years were spent in Barcelona, and his sense of uprootedness can only have been heightened by the years he spent in an English public school. Then in the 1930s he went to the Bartlett School in London, to train as an architect. He began to practise briefly, travelled, went with his family to live in South America, before returning to England in 1942. In the aftermath of the war, he emerged as a painter and maker of objects, who knew about typography and printing, was passionately interested in cinema, was a writer and a wide reader too. Later in life, he became a teacher of graphic design, but 'a culture-carrier who helped a lot of people' would be a more accurate description.

Letters in the city

It is hard to find a way in to discussion of such a wide field of activity: but Wright's public lettering provides a remarkable and still partially available body of work. Go to New Scotland Yard, the headquarters of London's Metropolitan Police. In this dull site, there is a small spark of life: in front of the architecturally banal building is a sign whose shining metal letters brighten even in the dirtiest weather. The triangular support echoes the shape of the site, where Dacre Street meets Broadway. And – revolving – the whole object engages in dialogue with its context. The lettering is one of Edward Wright's best alphabets. As usual with him, the forms were generated by a set of tough constraints: circles and lines only, the terminal points sheered off at right angles to the stroke. Geometric letters are often stiff and unusable, but these – characters subtly off centre and varied – sing with life. Wright wasn't so fond of the police and had doubts about the job, which included the signs throughout the building. But, having taken it on, he carried it out with full commitment, leaving London with this quiet surprise.

The New Scotland Yard alphabet was named Flaxman. At that time London's telephone exchanges had alphabetic codes, and this was the code for Chelsea. Wright was then overseeing an educational commune – known as the graphic design department – at the School of Art there. But the joke had some point: in its simplicity, the alphabet had the spirit of ancient Greek inscriptions. One might call it neoclassical, like the sculpture of John Flaxman.

Wright's signing and lettering work happened because he knew architects, especially the people who began in the mid-1950s to build modern architecture in Britain. More importantly, it happened because he understood spaces, and had no prejudices or difficulties in working with the materials of modern buildings: concrete, metal, glass, plastic. His letters become part of the fabric. One of his first jobs in this field was the lettering for the 'house of the future': Alison and Peter Smithson's project for the 1956 Ideal Home Exhibition. The expanded forms of the letters matched the long, low form of the structure, and followed a set of extreme constraints. A string of other projects followed. The highpoint was the painted mural-sign for Theo Crosby's building at the International Union of Architects Congress, put up on London's South Bank in 1961. The four languages of the event and the rough, provisional nature of the structure were the givens of the work, which Wright then let form into this long sign. Painted in primary colours, the bold forms rhymed with but also subdued the wall's grid of imperfectly joined rough planks. The structure was temporary and is known now only in photographs and memories.

Given the appalling and apparently incurable indifference of

Wright's letters as mural at the 'Turn Again' exhibition,
Manchester, 1955. (Architect: John Bicknell.)

architects to lettering, this part of Edward Wright's achievement is
very much worth rescuing and celebrating. It is far from the usual
tired routine of a typeface blown up big and stuck down on the
drawing, on the building. It is also far from the anaemic architectural efforts of the English letter-cutters. Here Wright exhibited his
foreignness and his value to us.

A cultural stream
'In the summer of 1952 Anthony Froshaug asked me if I would
outline a part-time course for his students of typography at the
LCC Central School of Arts & Crafts', Wright once remembered.
This conjunction of a place and some people was one of a series
of occurrences that happened in London in those years, and which
constituted a stream running outside and against the established
culture. Perhaps this stream was just a trickle, but it has had widely
dispersed, lasting consequences. At the Central School, 'we used a
hand press, wood type and rules for our exercises; this resulted in
a situation where the teacher could learn from the pupil as well as
vice versa, sometimes both were surprised at the results'. The visual
evidence remaining from that class is a handful of printed sheets.
These prints still look fresh today, and join the honourable modern
tradition of making it new with what is to hand.

So at the Central School then there was the typographer Anthony Froshaug, who, in brief, was Wright's opposite and equal
as a designer and teacher. Eduardo Paolozzi (textiles) and Nigel
Henderson (photography) ran contiguous classes. Among the students were Ken Garland, Derek Birdsall, Bill Slack, Philip Thompson, Ivor Kamlish, Colin Forbes, Alan Fletcher – and more. Some are
now well known, some hardly known at all. But they, with others
from other London schools, were the first generation of fully professional graphic designers in Britain. Wright's work was one available
element in their education, which in its cross-category drive, helped

to mean that 'professional' had none of the business-studies reductivism it has now taken on. Some of the full-time Central students came to Wright's evening classes. Outsiders who came included the designer Germano Facetti, the architect Pat Crooke, the cultural historians Joseph Rykwert and Bernard Myers. The architect Theo Crosby didn't come, but was around at the Central, and a little later, when he was editing the magazine *Architectural Design*, he began to pass work on to Wright.

This 'scene' had its most public centre at the Institute of Contemporary Arts. Edward Wright appears fleetingly in the comprehensive documentation of Independent Group, which grew up within the ICA He took part in 'This is Tomorrow', the IG's show at the Whitechapel Art Gallery in 1956, and designed its catalogue. But while he shared the spirit of curiosity and experiment with these others, there are clear differences between Wright and the Independent Group, especially as it shaded off into Pop Art.

Wright certainly had a vision of a democratic culture. 'We can't withhold feelings for rare occasions and at the same time keep them alive', he once wrote. This fires everything that he did. But where the Independent Group famously looked to the new world of the North American consumer, Wright's 'America' lay to the south. It was Hispanic, poor, old-colonial but liberating itself through resistance and rebellion, through secret codes, strange unexpected happenings, down-to-earth practical construction. Where Pop Art dreamed of listening to Elvis in a Chrysler car, Wright's vision was active: making something out of disregarded materials. All this has its aftermath in present cultural debates, now dominated by the pomo nihilism of 'cultural studies' theorists unable to make judgements of value. But in Wright's politically constructive vision, the poetry of Pablo Neruda, the old Argentinian tango, a balsa-wood raft, the flâneur who measures distance by the cigarette – these are all culture, and valuable because humanly valuable.

Public and private

The work that Wright made for the public sphere – architectural lettering and (very important for him) posters – had its dialectical counterpart in his long concentration on the book, as a tool for solitary thought and contemplation. In the late 1950s he worked at Rathbone Books, essentially a book-packaging firm, which had grown out of the wartime venture of Adprint. The firm was run by an emigré from Vienna, Wolfgang Foges, and in its early days gave work to many of the continental Europeans in England: among them John Heartfield, George Adams, Lewis Woudhuysen, Otto and Marie Neurath. One imagines that he felt easy enough there, among others who didn't belong, though the things that resulted – early exercises in the integrated book – now seem unremarkable. It was this kind of unapologetic employment in the commercial world that helped to seal his exclusion from the British art scene. The paintings he was then making – making with full command of his materials – have aged well. Often about and embodying the theme of communication, they need to be seen in public, as they could be, briefly, at his 1985 Arts Council retrospective. This was a 'regional' show, initiated by an ex-student (the designer Trilokesh Mukherjee), carried through by an independently minded curator (Michael Harrison), and largely unnoticed in the art press. Why aren't Wright's paintings in public collections? But there seems no point in asking. If they were there, then everything in Britain would be different.

The most private books that Edward Wright made were the sequence of notebooks that he wrote and drew in, from 1953. In these books – constant in their non-standard elongated format, rough hessian binding, pages made of detail paper or cheap yellowing paper – one finds a dialogue with himself about the things he was doing and making then. Of course the assembling of fragments is what notebooks are for, but this was also the system of much of his finished work. Wright himself traced this to his early years in his father's office. 'Liverpool in those days was a very busy port with a large trade in imported and exported merchandise. This meant that when the consulate was handling invoices, bills of lading and so forth, there was a variety of seals, rubber stamps and embossing dies being applied to the documents ...' He went on to describe the 'much more serious apparatus' of a press and a folio book of numbered blank pages, onto which written typewritten correspondence was copied, via dampened blotting paper.

From his first notebooks one can trace the slow formation of a work that embodies much of Edward Wright. This is the silkscreened fan-folded *Codex atorrantis*, printed in thirty copies. It was finished only in 1984. By this time he was living in retirement in

Cambridge, a small garden-shed acting as a workshop. He had a proofing press and some type. The codex – the precise description of its form – is quite roughly made and free of grand summarizing gestures. The chief subject is 'lunfardo', the slang of the vagrant people of Buenos Aires. This code was a medium that carried a human culture: in resistance to the mechanisms of official control. The book works as a kinetic construct. A single sheet of wrapping paper, printed on the rough side, is held between springy plywood covers. The paper is folded into facing pages that may make one spread of words or a pair of contrasting images. Vagrants ('atorro') face a state-issued postage-stamp bull, ironically labelled 'lastre': food. A truant boy drinking milk (from Truffaut's *Les quatre cents coups*) is labelled 'yirar' (roam) and faces some raft travellers ('yugo', work). The connections may be loose and dreamy, but – as usual – there's a pretty strict grid keeping the rough elements in place.

Edward Wright's work fizzes with energy and ideas. Disparate, sometimes mishandled in production, often done in collaboration and so visibly suffering the joys and despairs of that way of operating, much of it hidden or disappeared: it is far from the perfect œuvre that anyway only exists in the minds of unrealistic historians. Wright's work – all of it – badly needs to be taken away from the club of his friends and launched into the arena of public consciousness. Those in the know might regret losing the secret, but would be glad for him. He also needs to be seen in context, as part of the buried history of dissident modernism in Britain: a network of designers and makers who never made it to 'Sir' or 'Professor' or into the journalistic and academic record, and never wanted to. In their work, 'modern' means lively, improvising, anti-authoritarian, cosmopolitan, humane, modest, self-critical, regionally conscious and site-specific. It has nothing to do with the grey, centralizing modernism of the present myth. Maybe these claims are too loud for someone often quiet and withdrawing. But things have now gone so far and so cynically retrograde. Work made with such purity of heart comes to seem the more remarkable.

Eye, no. 10, 1993

Written at the suggestion of *Eye*'s editor – it was part of Rick Poynor's excavation of British graphic design of the 1950s and 1960s – this was a welcome commission.

F. H. K. Henrion, 1914–90

With the death of Henri Henrion, on 5 July, the design community lost an essential person, whose life and work helped to form present notions of 'design'. For someone who started out wanting to be a poster artist in pre-war Paris, this was some achievement. He had gone there from his family home in Nuremberg. Then, haphazardly, via Tel Aviv, he came to London, worked on the 1938 MARS exhibition, and fell in with the nascent profession of design in Britain. Henrion's progress exemplified a larger development: government work (posters and exhibitions) during the war, then through advertising and publishing, into commercial and corporate design; from Henrion the freelance commercial artist, to Studio H, to Henrion Design Associates, to HDA International, finally handing over the practice to former associates, as Henrion, Ludlow & Schmidt. Retirement was a constitutional impossibility, and over the past year or so, one heard reports that, despite cancer, he was carrying on his international activities, apparently with extra energy.

I met him first in 1974, as a student gaining work experience at his studio in London; or rather, in Pond Street, Hampstead. That location – Julian Huxley a few doors away, and an early job by Foster/Rogers to extend the back of the house – helped to define the aura that surrounded Henrion: looking to the Continent, in touch with books and ideas, just slightly bohemian, bow-tied and blouson-jacketed even in the age of sharp suits. In this he seemed more French than German (his mother's family had French roots); more Cassandre than Bayer.

By the mid-1970s the practice was HDA International, and the studio was rather empty – the country was more economically recessed than usual – although the British Leyland identity was going through in some confusion. I had righteous qualms about work for large corporate clients, wanted to get down to research for a dissertation, and so left after two weeks. Henri (at that time he was just 'Henrion' to his employees, although I found it hard to call him that in his presence, and 'Mr Henrion' would have been absurd) tried to persuade me to stay. He liked dissenters.

At that time I was getting to know the typographer Anthony Froshaug, who, about thirty years earlier, had also worked for him on a few jobs ('we've all worked for Henrion', Anthony explained). Henrion, I gathered, had dearly wanted to collaborate with Froshaug – a brilliant and bloody-minded designer, who refused to touch advertising or corporate work, for reasons of personal and political disposition. After Anthony's death, Henri wrote a pained obituary for *Designer*, revealing of both men. Later on, I showed him an ICA membership application form of 1948: cover image by Henrion, text typography by Froshaug. He eagerly photocopied it, as evidence that they had once collaborated.

Some moments I could recall from that relationship of the worldly generalist and the uncompromising purist: Anthony meeting Henri by chance on an underground train, and kissing him ('in vino veritas' yes, perhaps Henri had sometimes been a tough operator, but he was always warm); Anthony in public discussion at the London College of Printing rather baldly referring to a woman in whom they had once both taken an interest, in the loose days of the war, in the group around the Artists International Association ('interest', in all its meanings, might provide some key to an understanding of Henrion); and Henri's kindness and generosity when Anthony was dying from cancer, just up the road in the Royal Free.

The last encounter I had with Henri was in 1988, after writing a piece on British graphic design for *Blueprint*. In passing, I had clumsily likened him to the Vicar of Bray: the progression to HDA International seemed his most doubtful accommodation with the corporate world. Arriving back from a trip abroad, I listened to a succession of messages on the answering machine ('Henri here …') in that extraordinary voice. Guttural and as if from far down in his body, it gave one the sense that just a touch would put him into some other language-mode: German or French or … This led not to a rebuke, but to lunch and an invitation to help out with his history of the Alliance Graphique Internationale, a labour of love in which he had got bogged down. My bad conscience was brushed away with 'who was the Vicar of Bray? Oh well, no one will know.'

In the last few years, Henrion had come to see clearly enough where design in Britain was going. He spoke out against the meagre, money-driven ways of design-biz. Yes, he had pioneered design for the state and corporation, had worked tirelessly for design to see itself and be seen as a profession, had toiled in the unrewarding pastures of design education, but it was all done with a strong social and human motivation. He followed the logic of the modern movement: to plunge into the waters of industrial and social development, to order and make humane that process and its artefacts.

Henri Henrion in the 1980s.

Henrion's marvellous work was done when the cultural-political stream favoured these ideals: during and immediately after the war, especially for the Ministry of Information, and the Artists International Association. And then also in the 1960s, when it seemed for a short time that Britain might actually have some hope of becoming a modern country. As well as the corporate identity work, he did some jobs for the Labour Party and CND.

If hard-nosed, tubular-steel-chair critics have anything with which to reproach Henrion, it would be for compromising too much – not with the big clients, but with cosy English culture. To condense matters, this is the culture of the old *Punch*, of the honours system, the senior common room at the RCA, and sentimental ruralism – with all of which he had dealings. At the Festival of Britain, he took charge of the design of the Country and Agricultural Pavilions: hardly emblems of international modernism. But far from apologizing, he liked to point out that there were two tracks in his work: the hard, impersonal one, and the humorous, illustrational one. Whether or not one accepts the truth of this dialectic depends on

64

how unbearable one finds the English ancien régime. Coming from Germany in the 1930s, Henrion had good reason to value its best aspects.

Generous, wide in his views, curious about people – and his conversation could be uncomfortably direct (within a few minutes, one felt he could discover all the essential facts about someone) – he was a good motivator, driving on those around him. If other people looked after the details, he certainly had the broad vision. But then, against this partial description, I think of some pieces from the war years. His work for the AIA exhibition 'For Liberty' (1942), best seen in a set of hand-coloured photographs, was a quiet highlight of the recent 'Art in Exile' show, in Berlin and then London. And some of his war posters, such as 'Aid the Wounded' (that one especially), have a directness and graphic energy now departed from the sophisticated world of British graphics. They still take my breath away.

Blueprint, no. 70, September 1990

This was written with the encouragement and blessing of Marion Wesel-Henrion, who kindly provided the photograph reproduced here.

Jock Kinneir, 1917–94

The look of Britain owes much to the graphic designer Jock Kinneir. From the late 1950s, in partnership with Margaret Calvert, who had been his student at Chelsea School of Art, Kinneir designed all the major public signing systems: for roads, airports, railways, the army and hospitals.

Jock Kinneir's career followed a familiar path for designers of his generation. In the 1930s at Chelsea his interests were engraving, illustration and painting. While still a student he produced a poster for Shell, with a second following just as war broke out. After active service, he worked on exhibition design at the Central Office of Information. Then in 1950 he joined the 'finishing school' of British design: Design Research Unit, a major player in the Festival of Britain. In 1956, Kinneir set up his own practice, in Knightsbridge, also teaching part-time at Chelsea. Acquaintance with the architect David Allford, of Yorke, Rosenberg and Mardall, who was working on the new Gatwick Airport, led to a commission to do the signing there. A luggage labelling system for P&O led to his appointment as designer to the Anderson Committee on signing for the new motorways. This, in turn, led to his appointment as designer to the Worboys Committee on signs for the whole road network.

The Committee's brief required that British road signs be brought into line with Continental protocols, particularly in the use of pictorial elements. It also required a system of configuration in directional signs, which could be implemented by local authorities and signmakers with only a manual to follow. Kinneir started from scratch, not as a designer but as a driver. 'What do I want to know, trying to read a sign at speed?'

His system, which lets the signs design themselves according to the information they have to convey, has wonderful elegance and practicality. And the whole project was a rare model of the role that design could play in public life. Kinneir learned then that design depends on political circumstance. In the 1960s, the ideal of public service was still alive, and this, combined with an official will to modernize the public infrastructure, made the achievement possible. In recent years, the road signs have fallen into neglect. The Department of Transport is now working on an overhaul. But, without significant public consultation and without design advice, it threatens to ruin an existing system of great resource.

After the road signs, Kinneir/Calvert had signing as a staple job, but undertook work of all kinds. Their identity for Rymans (red, sanserif, geometrical) lingers in the memory, unbudged by weaker successors. The firm took its place in the flourishing graphic design culture of London in the 1960s. Kinneir was appointed head of graphic design at the Royal College of Art in 1964 and was there for five years.

In 1980 on the day his book *Words and buildings* was published, Jock Kinneir was in hospital, where a second operation failed to save the sight of his right eye. In 1981 he moved from the house he had designed himself in Ham Common to a new home in Oxfordshire. This house, which he designed and partly built himself, is calm, open, and delightful to be in. Together with his wife Joan, he lived there far removed from the brash design world of the 1980s. Children and grandchildren visited frequently. Among the activities that absorbed him were his painting, including a series of pictures of winter flowering plants. He grew vegetables and fruit according to the Henry Doubleday philosophy, worked on a long 'Chaucerian' novel about politics, and he researched his ancestry.

Jock Kinneir in the 1970s.

Jock Kinneir was a man of principle. To meet him, one felt both his reserve and warm straightforwardness. He was naturally democratic and unstuffy, and had a deserved reputation for brevity. He said what he thought, and then stopped. This was well conveyed by his given name, Jock; though he had only distant Scottish ancestry. These 'British' characteristics complemented a wide, thoughtful outlook. He was European-minded, and worked on the Continent, in the near East and in Australia. The sign systems were modern and international, but they have the inevitability of plain common sense. They have 'common sense' too, in that they benefit all of us, every day.

Revised from the obituary published in *The Guardian*, 30 August 1994, this fuller and corrected version was published in the newsletter of the Sign Design Society: *Directions*, no. 7.

Norman Potter, 1923–95

The designer Norman Potter has died of a heart attack, while cycling in Falmouth on a gleaming machine built to his own specification. Potter, as he recognized and elaborated at length in his book *Models & Constructs*, belonged to the margins of English design culture. He pictured himself – truly – as a tightrope walker, always going the bloody hard way.

Potter became a designer gradually and informally. It was within the British anarchist movement that he brought himself to a set of ideas and beliefs that would last him his life. This was the cultured, internationalist anarchism of figures such as John Hewetson, Marie Louise Berneri, Vernon Richards and George Woodcock. Too young to have fought in Spain, Potter was then old enough to resist call-up in the Second World War. Coming up to London from his family home in Essex, he became part of a group of dissidents that included Anthony Froshaug (the brilliant typographer whose life and work was to run parallel with Potter's) and George Philip, with whom through the 1950s Potter was to run a construction workshop. Much of the activity of this group – improbably lodged in Mayfair – centred on some government-funded research and development of an anti-frostbite machine. This project was led by Geoffrey Bocking, who with Froshaug and Potter, formed a sometimes fraught trio of buddies. It was indeed like an episode from a book that Potter loved, E. C. Large's delightful novel *Sugar in the air* (1937): a story of young outsiders reaching for the moon.

Of this group of dissidents, it was – typically – only Potter who saw the inside of a prison cell: first a brief detention under suspicion of 'hostility to the state', then a month at Chelmsford for refusing an ID card. Then in 1948 he spent six months in Wandsworth and Wormwood Scrubs as, in his own words, an 'on-the-run-hitherto-undetected-conchie'. From his family background of fallen gentility, this experience must have opened his eyes finally to the realities of the English system of social class. And prison became one of his great themes, especially in the poetry he was then beginning to write. Here really was the zero point: existence minimum and maximum, both at once.

Norman Potter in formal dress for a lecture at the North East London Polytechnic (1981); on the table is a copy of *What is a designer*. He had brought some iconic images: Le Corbusier and Mies van der Rohe at the Weissenhof, Stuttgart 1926; the Bauhaus strip-film of the future of furniture (mostly obscured); Le Corbusier's Dom-Ino skeleton; Alexander Graham Bell in his tent; the Chamberlain House of Gropius & Breuer (Weyland, Massachusetts, 1939).

Norman Potter became hugely skilled as a workman: through, I suppose, patience and stubbornness. Anthony Froshaug once referred to his 'immense sensibility to tools'. These were the ordinary hand-tools of cabinetmaking and also the powered machinery that the English Arts & Crafts movement then still shunned. Potter was reluctant to remember dates, as a point of modernist, anti-historicist principle. But around 1949, his construction workshop was established: first in Cornwall, then Melksham and then Corsham in Wiltshire. They made modern furniture and fittings, hoping to work like a garage, for the local community; though much of the work came through London connections. In the look and spirit of the work, the nearest comparison would be with Gerrit Rietveld, the great Dutch cabinetmaker, designer and architect.

At the end of 1950s Potter was called by Hugh Casson to teach full-time at the Royal College of Art, on the interior design course. Questioning both 'interior' and 'design', he tried to touch the roots of design practice. In his view, the human processes of getting the work done were vital. Image and the whole foolish magazine-culture of design was a distraction. And all of this in the publicity-conscious, star-obsessed RCA. Yet, despite his low-church plainness and seriousness, Potter did like this brush with the establishment. He welcomed being let briefly into the warm.

In 1964 Potter left the RCA with a nucleus of fellow teachers to set up a Construction School within the West of England College of Art and Design at Bristol. This, like all of Potter's work, was infused with the highest ideals and yet realistic in accepting the given situation. He was very good at just talking with people, especially young people. He was also an intense listener. His prime inspiration was music, which fed his abstraction. A breakfast conversation with Norman might turn into a seminar on Schnabel's Beethoven. Latterly he became preoccupied with Glenn Gould, as a figure of the brilliant misfit.

In 1968, when the revolt came, Potter joined the students at Hornsey and Guildford, and left teaching for 'an open-ended future'. After this he never really found or was given good use for his talents. But in the aftermath of 1968 he wrote the book *What is a designer* (a proposition as much as a question). This unassuming work is remarkable in its seamless mix of high dreams and plain speaking. Bloody-mindedly, it does without pictures. Think for yourself, question, go, seek out, strip away, relate, make: these are the Potter imperatives.

By 1979, *What is a designer* had fallen out of print. I knew Potter only through that book, and had heard about him through the grapevine of dissenting design in Britain. I wrote to him about the need to get the book back into print: c/o the Royal Cornwall Yacht Club at Falmouth (another claim on insiderdom). Later he was brought to live entirely on his beautiful boat, moored with near-wrecks on the only rent-free bay at Falmouth.

By Christmas 1980, I had become a publisher, and we had made a new edition of *What is a designer*, twice the original length and nearer to our ideals of book production: stern, undecorated, joining the European tradition, and turning our backs on cosy England. For me, this project was the start of a long dialogue with Norman Potter, whose next significant public issue was his book *Models & Constructs* (1990). This is his 'magnum opus', containing most of what he thought worth saving of his work, including the poetry.

Norman had an intense presence: having him around demanded all your attention. But he could be light, sometimes astonishingly off-hand, and he was very ready to laugh: often in huge peals. He was an internationalist, finding England just awful, especially in recent years, which were marked by his forays to a succession of run-down properties in France. Yet he was constitutionally incapable of speaking anything but English. Just as he was far too concrete and literal to manage a computer. (But with a typewriter, he was a virtuoso.) In writing, he deliberately resisted easy meaning: he had a kind of short-hand that you had to get to know. Yet he could speak and write about objects (a tool-rack, say) in ways that did full justice to simple material construction, and, in the same paragraph, put forward metaphysical views that – without pretension – share thoughts with Gestalt psychology, with Martin Buber and Simone Weil.

In the circle of friends and colleagues there would always be fallings-out, with people who couldn't stand the commitment. *Models & Constructs* is dedicated to Potter's four children (including the filmmaker Sally Potter and the musician Nic Potter): the offspring of his marriage to Caroline Quennell and a succession of later relationships – intense, searching, unresolved. The women often had to put up with confined and hard situations: only an Aalto chair for comfort. His students, if they didn't reject his ideas at once, would become followers on a testing journey. Even after fifteen years of co-operation and friendship, I hesitated before opening his letters: knowing the blasts that sometimes arrived. But England has lost an awkward, indispensable man, whom it should have known much better.

The Guardian, 29 November 1995

Under the headline 'Designer always on the edge', and this photograph of Norman Potter – looking questioningly at the camera – *The Guardian* ran this as their lead obituary that day, adding a piece by Sally Potter (their normal practice forbids notices written by relatives of the subject). Quite severe cuts made in the published text have been restored here.

Adrian Frutiger

Trying to explain the mysteries of letterforms, he resorts to analogies. It's like architecture, he suggests: columns seem to need terminating elements, top and bottom. Serifs do that job too. And, like buffers on railway wagons, they keep the verticals apart, setting up a rhythm of spaces. Without serifs, you are playing a more difficult game, and one that requires some courage. Adrian Frutiger is speaking to an audience in London, promoting his latest attack on the problem of sanserif.

He is not the first to make such explanations. The paradoxical nature of typography breeds them. Its components are entirely abstract forms, which, in combination, carry meaning. Typographers, and especially the select fraternity of type designers, deal simultaneously in the esoteric and the familiar, the rarified and the banal.

And why do typefaces need to be different? Why so many? Again the analogies pour out. It is like the clothes that men wear, changing every few years according to cultural and technical shifts. (Women's fashion moves more frenetically.) Or take shoes. Modern life multiplies the categories: football, skiing, jogging. Just as you may wear football boots only once a week, so even ugly display faces may have a use. (He is no dictator.) Or think of spoons ... By this time one may think that even the dullest listener will have got the point. But, as he confides later, these days he gives talks to desktop publishers. And it's clear that Frutiger could do better than most in persuading those visual bunglers that typography matters: that typographic quality could just be the key to success in the present extraordinary explosion of text and image technology.

Adrian Frutiger makes an unlikely design star. He is too serious and straightforward about his work to be capable of personality-flashing. He listens to questions, answers them, and then stops speaking. But he enjoys the challenge of explanation, and has a realistic awareness of the powers of the few companies that now dominate type production, and their need to present the people behind the typefaces. By now, just reaching sixty, he has a secure and privileged niche: a wool-knitted exception in a world of sharp suits.

He was born in Interlaken, speaking Swiss-German, and still feels slightly distant from formal German, as well as from his now everyday environment of French. One supposes that this distance may help him to see his material more clearly: and his concern has been very much with material. His father was a hand-weaver, who at first contemplated a pâtisserie apprenticeship for his son, then felt that was not quite appropriate. So Adrian Frutiger became a printing compositor's apprentice, rounding this off with three years at the Zurich Kunstgewerbeschule.

Switzerland in the late 1940s: a country and a culture that had come through the battles neutral and intact, gaining a few years' start in the post-war economic race. That was the ground from which the phenomenon of 'Swiss typography' grew and, in the late 1950s, conquered the Western world. It was fertilized by a strong craft tradition that (unlike the pallid British equivalent) was able to accept technical innovation – and modern design. By this time Frutiger was on Christmas-card terms with Emil Ruder, head of typography at the Basel school and a chief of the movement. Never a paid-up subscriber to their dogmas, he was a respected, rather distant colleague, but one who was to supply Swiss typographers with a trump card.

At Zurich, as a student project, Frutiger made a set of wood-engravings showing the development of Western letterforms. An amazingly assured piece of work, it won a government prize and was printed in an edition of 3,000. Frutiger sent copies to likely employers, eventually getting an invitation to join Deberny & Peignot in Paris, then still a flourishing typefoundry.

After some learning jobs, now more or less forgotten, Frutiger's break came in 1954, when Deberny & Peignot started construction of Lumitype machines (called Photon in the USA), which used the then very new technology of photocomposition. As well as adapting classic faces for the machine, he designed two new ones. First, Méridien, a variation on traditional, serifed themes. Then, on his own initiative, he began a sanserif. When drawing a typeface, one starts, typically, with 'm' and 'n' (to establish the verticals), then 'o', then – combining these – 'd'. After that, all you need are some diagonals. So, with these letters in front of him, Frutiger called it 'Monde'. Then, trying for a less French-based name, he proposed 'Univers'.

Taking advantage of his 'tabula rasa' situation (basic forms, a new technology), Frutiger planned the typeface from the outset as comprising a family of graduated weights, widths and slopes (twenty-one variants in all). In complement to this systematization, the letters were drawn (by hand, it seems astonishing now) with considerable subtlety. They may look simple and regular, but that is achieved by countless small adjustments of thickness and direction. The result was a typeface that did indeed have some claim to universality: at home on different composing systems, in different languages, even in visual translation to other scripts.

Thirty years on, Frutiger makes no claims for timelessness, and is quick to place Univers in its historical context: when TV was new (those rounded corners), when internationalism and systems were in the air, when typographers were hungry for such a product. At that time, as the Monotype Corporation was wondering whether to buy the typeface, Frutiger met Stanley Morison in his London club; the arch-traditionalist, by then in retirement, gave his blessing to it, as the 'least worst' of the new sanserifs.

The Monotype version of Univers, released in 1961, was especially important in ensuring the commercial success of the typeface. Since then, Frutiger's career has unfolded with great solidity and consistency. In 1964, after leaving Deberny & Peignot, he started a consultancy with IBM, working especially on a version of Univers for the IBM Composer. This souped-up typewriter, at the time a wondrous instrument of print-democratization, now seems a half-remembered bad dream. Another exercise in working with heavy constraints was his alphabet for optical character reading – OCR-B, still an international standard – which showed the benefits that a designer, on behalf of the reader, could bring to the domain of the computer engineer.

Since 1968, Frutiger has been retained by the Linotype group, in a fruitful collaboration that has allowed him to build up a formidable œuvre. His designs have been predicated on new needs, usually on developments in typesetting or printing techniques. Stylistic and technical considerations are then explored together, and synthesized. All his typefaces have been made primarily for text composition, which – rather than display text – is the really tough and interesting sector of letterform design.

In 1962, Frutiger set up a design practice, starting his long collaboration with the graphic designer Bruno Pfäffli. 'When it comes to putting more than one letter on a page, type designers are inept.' One might find some exceptions to this maxim, including its coiner (Erik Spiekermann: though he is a typographer-turned-type-designer). Frutiger now feels that his foray into whole page design (mainly with books) was useful in allowing him to see what the problems were for the graphic designer, the first users of his letters. But, beyond type design, his principal field of exploration has been in signing. Here the major jobs have been for the Paris Métro and at Charles de Gaulle airport. For the latter, he refused the easy solution of just adapting Univers, instead attempting a more organic and super-legible alphabet. Subsequently issued as the typeface 'Frutiger', this was his second major sanserif. Looking back on it now, he draws another analogy: if Univers was a shiny, chromey face of regular forms, then Frutiger was matt and organic, like the sucked-sweet cars that were then coming onto the market.

In the 1970s, a new factor entered the type designer's life: digitization. Minute subtleties of swelling and contraction had to be plotted onto crude either/or rasters. At first, existing typefaces were simply forced into digital moulds. For Frutiger, seeing what happened to his own letters came as a nasty shock: one of the mistakes of his life. What had been smooth slopes became jagged staircases. So, with the new typefaces of the early 1980s, he learnt to incorporate the processes of digitization into his drawings – and into his mental conception of letters. Thus Icone is a 'rubber face' that will suffer any distortion; Breughel consists of forms that correspond to the sweep of the scanner.

Now, rather suddenly, greater refinements have been introduced into text composition, especially through laser technology. Looking recently at some proofs from a lasersetter, Frutiger realized that his 'long journey through the desert' – the thirty years' war with technology – was at an end. 'This new kind of letter-reproduction was so good, that its curve formations could bear comparison with the contours of the original hand-drawings. It was a breakthrough – a glimpse into the future.'

He no longer believes in 'designing down' for the limitations of a particular machine. In ten years' time, if not quite yet, such coarse systems will be obsolete. And now he is back on his own, no longer in daily attendance at the partnership, just drawing letters by hand. Would he work directly on a screen? No: too set in the paper-and-pencil mentality. And, raising the philosophical stakes, he suggests that 'computers can't understand deep feeling. That comes through drawing.'

One might think that this is too mystical to be true. But two stories that Frutiger tells are suggestive here. Some years ago, as a spin-off from a research project, he took each letter 'n' from his typefaces, translated them into (rotated) parallel lines, and then overlaid these. The blurry ur-form that emerged – his own deep structure – was a Univers 'n'. This letter, which he first drew as a student project, has, it seems, haunted all his subsequent work. Then recently he joined a sculpture class. The task was to make a face, without a model. He worked obsessively, with no thought of eating. In the evening, in a certain light, he caught sight of the stone, and was shocked to see that it was his mother's face.

This is the sensibility – and sensitivity – that tempers Frutiger's logic. He admits to a puritanical streak. He would, for example, like 'locks' in composing machines to prevent letterspacing that is too tight or too wide. Without such constraints, even good ingredients have no protection against their designer cooks. And why has information design been so bad, so undeveloped in France? In the last analysis, he thinks, it is a question of culture. The Latin-Catholic mentality just can't understand. A Northern-Protestant severity of approach is required. While there is a continuing tradition of the graphic artist (exemplified by Cassandre or, more recently, Roger Excoffon) most of the few good graphic designers in France have been Swiss, German or Dutch. Isn't this changing? He doubts it.

Yet, Frutiger has always been active as an illustrator and especially as a sculptor, carving pieces that have no direct reference to alphabets. And this artist's sphere has joined to complement his highly constrained work with types and sign-alphabets: as a recent critic has shown, by juxtaposition of his free drawings and his letters, the two spheres have surprising qualities in common.

Looking back over the body of Frutiger's work, one can see that he has designed typefaces in most of the major style-categories. It is perhaps like an actor taking on the great parts, working up to Lear. But, as the superimposition experiment suggests, one can better construe Frutiger's career as showing a recurrent interest in one problem: his sanserif-Hamlet. First, and most brilliantly, as a young man (Univers). Next, Hamlet in strange costume (Serifa, which seems to be Univers with serifs). Then, showing greater maturity (Frutiger). And now there is Avenir: a reworking of the 'constructivist' sanserifs of the 1920s. We might take this as the older man's wistful search for childhood: his own (he was born the year after Futura), and also that of the roman alphabet. He wanted, he says, something of the feeling of the ancient Greek inscriptions, of an even-thickness line scratched into stone.

Floating a theory, I suggested to him that one could divide typeface designers into calligraphers and cutters. The former see and generate strokes, as if with a pen. The latter work by cutting away, seeing rather the space within and around letters. Hermann Zapf, the leading German type designer, obviously belongs to the first group. We wondered about Eric Gill: in between, but more towards the second pole. And Frutiger himself? The man who might just have been a pastry cook? Unquestionably a cutter.

Blueprint, no. 54, February 1989

Ken Garland's writings

Ken Garland, *A word in your eye: opinions, observations and conjectures, from 1960 to the present*, University of Reading,
Department of Typography & Graphic Communication, 1996

In conjunction with a retrospective exhibition of the work of his design practice, this book was made to mark Ken Garland's retirement from part-time teaching at the University of Reading's Department of Typography & Graphic Communication. The retirement is not yet quite complete: ways have been found of re-employing him. Neither does *A word in your eye* claim completion or completeness. Some writings have been extracted; some have been omitted, especially those that would have required extensive illustration; some illustrations have had to be left out of those pieces that are here. And, frustratingly for completist scholars, there is no bibliography of all his writings and no chronology of his doings. But the book does present a genuinely interesting collection. Garland is one of the handful of graphic designers who can write for publication and who find interesting topics about which to write. Though firmly based in North London, he is notably peripatetic and curious about what is going on in the world. The everyday urban scene is a recurring topic of this book. Ken Garland's voice is strong and pervades every sentence. The texts he writes for printed publication are hardly less spoken than the transcripts of talks or discussions that are also published here.

Ken Garland belongs to the first generation of fully-fledged graphic designers in Britain. As he describes here in some invaluable retrospective pieces, these were the designers who emerged from the London art schools in late 1940s and early to middle 1950s. They began to inhabit a territory that went beyond that of the previous 'commercial artists', who, since the end of the nineteenth century, had struggled to reach the parts of design – the social and visual/verbal whole – that printers could no longer deal with. Some of these new graphic designers tried hard to make a pact with the printing trade: by understanding the limitations and possibilities of production, rather than by just blindly imposing 'designs' and hoping for the best. For example, Derek Birdsall, one of Garland's fellow students at the Central School, spent some years working as a consultant designer to the printers Balding & Mansell. The slightly older Herbert Spencer had, since the late 1940s, been performing a similar role at Lund Humphries. But these were exceptional firms. The general, pervasive feeling among the graphic designers was one of considerable frustration with the dreary culture of the British printing trade, circa 1955.

One can detect some such feeling in Garland's article 'Structure and substance', with its sideswipe at the Monotype Corporation, still extolling the virtues of 'decorative borders, arabesques, and fleurons'. This was published in 1960, in Lund Humphries' *Penrose Annual*, and is the first piece in *A word in your eye*. The thirty-year-old Garland presents two rich sources of contemporary graphic culture: Switzerland ('structure') and the USA ('substance'). Both are attempts to continue the modern movement of Central Europe between the two world wars. He sees the qualities of each approach, and notices the characteristics that are local to Basel and Zurich, and New York. Then he calls for British designers to use their advantages: not to copy, but to make their own synthesis – of structure and substance.

Garland was himself just then beginning to find his own true themes, both as designer and writer. In his time (1956–62) as art editor on *Design*, the magazine of the Council of Industrial Design (later, the Design Council), he encountered the 'human factors' or ergonomic approach to design practice. (*Design* in this period, under the editorships of Michael Farr and then John Blake, was a good conjunction of the serious and the lively: remote indeed from the utter flimflam of present-day British design magazines.) How things actually work, rather than merely what they look like, is central to the ergonomic approach; as is the attempt to test and measure the product at prototype stage. Instructional material, tabular displays, maps and diagrams, are of central interest in this view of graphic design. Yet Garland never got bogged down in any skeletal purity. In the ergonomic years he gave his services as a designer to the Campaign for Nuclear Disarmament, and elsewhere spoke up for an emphatically non-bureaucratic democratic socialism. Glad to work with small and humane firms, his best clients have been those, such as the toy-makers Galt, who are making real products that are useful and pleasurable.

Garland wants a design that is of use in the world, that isn't locked in the chains of fashion and style. As a writer he has celebrated two inventors who have put professional designers to shame, with work that orders useful content to great effect. Henry C. Beck, deviser of the London Underground diagram, is the clearest exemplar here. After a tip from Anthony Froshaug, one of his teachers at the Central School, Garland got to know Harry Beck, eventually (1966) dedicating his first book to him, then (1969) writing a long article on the diagram for the *Penrose Annual*, later (1975) making a travelling exhibition and giving lectures, most recently (1995) publishing a monograph. The second exemplar is Alfred Wainwright, whose walker's guides to the Lakeland Fells do, more imaginatively and more straightforwardly, with pen and paper, what countless professional designers have not quite dared to do with high-technical equipment. Elsewhere Garland praises William Blake: another driven, cranky, one-person producer. The same description could apply to the printer and poet Ken Campbell, whose book *Broken rules and double crosses* (1984) Garland rightly describes as 'the most powerful and moving he has yet produced'.

In a brief piece not reprinted here, Garland chose Campbell's *Broken rules and double crosses* as his book of that year, 1984, for *Designer*: journal of the then-termed Society of Industrial Artists and Designers, the professional body of designers in the UK, which Garland has never joined. That Orwellian year came right at the moment when design in Britain was having quite disproportionate expectations placed upon it; when the service sector, and design at the heart of it, was fancied to be the new motor of national progress. A Minister for Design had been appointed, within the Department of Trade & Industry. Some designers puffed themselves up in response to this political stroking and to incoming cash flows; a number of the largest firms were floated for public quotation on the London stock market. Garland began to speak against this current, attacking corporate identity schemes, which fattened these design firms as well as the companies for whom they were made, as the most nebulous but unfortunately most real manifestations of his trade. But however sympathetic his arguments were and are, one has the sense that they can't be more than pin-pricks. We can only hope that someone with enough time, funding and inquisitiveness, and the pen of a Christopher Hitchens or a Paul Foot, can investigate this process by which a decent and occasionally noble activity has turned so bloated and empty.

Meanwhile, this unassuming book can be recommended. It provides authentic accounts that simply can't be found elsewhere in print. And, especially in our present context of incipient death by cultural studies, Garland's no-messing directness is unusual and affecting.

Printing Historical Society Bulletin, no. 44, 1997

Richard Hollis

In talks to students about his work, Richard Hollis sometimes shows a slide of his desk: the jumble of tools and materials encapsulates the miscellaneous and humble basis of the job. It is an unfancy view. The life of the one-person designer is necessarily jumbled and fragmented too, and this quality gets enacted in conversations with him. The topics switch rapidly: good clients and bad ones; typesetters, printers (he hesitates before disclosing the current favourites); the extraordinary things that colleagues say (done in different voices); then a messenger arrives with proofs, or he has to rush to an appointment.

A year or so ago the conversation always seemed to circle back to the explosion of design into big business; though now that the bang has happened, he seems happy enough with his clearly defined position outside this new sector. It has been a development that has left some graphic designers of the 'heroic generation' – now in their fifties – rather stranded. Those that have not metamorphosed into company directors or heads of department have found the going tough. Clients tend to send letters saying that they are now 'taking advice from a design firm'; as if needing the reassurance of a receptionist and a fax machine. Jobbing graphic design in Britain, with its high tension and low fees, is a young person's game. On the Continent, say in the Netherlands or West Germany, a designer of Hollis's accomplishment would be heading towards a calm retirement, picking and choosing from prestigious commissions, garlanded with prizes and medals. He does not worry about the lack of official recognition, believing that the number of letters after a name is no index of talent. And it may be just the visual pollution resulting from this development that is painful. 'If you want a quote, I would say that marketing design is kitsch.' His friend David King sums it all up, visually and spiritually, as 'cocktail graphics'.

When he came out of art school, in the late 1950s, Richard Hollis was a painter. His move towards typography and graphic design was made gradually. As one had to do in Britain then, when design education was still so undeveloped, he picked up knowledge just by looking. He remembers Toni del Renzio's jobs for the ICA, for the uninhibited handling of different weights of type, as among the instructive work of that time. He did attend typography evening classes at the Central School, which had been set up by Edward Wright, but by then were being taught by George Daulby. At this stage he was interested in 'action typography', in the Wright spirit, and was in fact dismissed from the course at the Central – not by Daulby – for using type that was too large. Wright's work for the exhibition 'This is Tomorrow' (1956) was an important inspiration.

Hollis got into design through his own silk-screen printing: doing posters as well as art prints. The make-it-yourself approach has remained as a strong thread; given a cloth to clean a lorry, during National Service, he made a rag book. At this early stage he was doing abstract 'concrete' work and, in the Swiss spirit, was able to imagine a unified sphere of visual activity, without differentiating design from art. Like a few others of his generation, he did the 'grand tour', going to the HfG Ulm and inviting himself to visit some of the great figures elsewhere on the Continent, or 'just anyone who really cared about their work'. It is a practice that, like the great figures, has died out. In the early 1960s, working from London, he went on other forays. A trip to Cuba was reported and self-published as a broadsheet. He also lived for a year in Paris, working for Galeries Lafayette with art directors such as Peter Knapp: Swiss by nationality but not by graphic alignment – and in Paris for that reason. Returning to Britain in 1964, Hollis led the graphics course within an experimental 'school of design', established precariously at the West of England College of Art at Bristol. Here briefly there was an attempt at a modern design education, of the kind that has never had a chance in Britain: cross-departmental mixing (between graphics and 'construction'), sign-theory a decade or so before it got popularized, and visiting teachers such as Paul Schuitema and Emil Ruder.

These were formative experiences which helped to set Hollis firmly in the modernist, internationalist camp. His work was then fairly straight 'Swiss': sanserif, ranged left, images and text bowing to the dictates of the grid. The intriguing turn came as he realized the inadequacy of this approach for articulating content. Towards the end of the 1960s one sees a search for other principles of organization: the large indent (of the first line of a paragraph) through which another axis of alignment could be found; or the intelligent use of axial symmetry. A tension between freedom and constraint, between experiment and respect for meaning and technical necessity: this is the dialectic, helped out by a nice sense of humour, that runs through his work since then. And this is what distinguishes it from the mindlessness of the merely 'innovative' (the term so loved by creative people). 'Inventive' is rather the word to characterize Hollis's production: accepting and playing with the constraints of process and budget. Thus the posters with text disposed around the folds, which can be cut for use as leaflets, and whose camera-copy is correspondingly small enough to fit in his cycle pannier. Sometimes, as he is eager to point out, a job seems unresolved, probably due to lack of time: see the messengers in the first paragraph. Occasionally he seems to be trying too hard and falls into over-complication, but, given a sympathetic client, better to be a little sorry than safe.

The inventive approach has been encouraged by long years of working for poor clients who can afford only two-colour printing. So that out of red and blue are squeezed, by screens and over-printing, lighter tones, purples, and rich almost-black. Here a painter's

83

sensibility gets coupled with attention to the meaningful use of typographic detail: he cares about italic, small capitals, and – perhaps most of all – non-lining numerals.

Two customers especially have provided Hollis with the conditions for good work: the Museum of Modern Art in Oxford, and the Whitechapel Art Gallery. He designed posters, catalogues and leaflets for both galleries, and was house designer for the Whitechapel, first under the directorship of Mark Glazebrook in the early 1970s, then later under Nicholas Serota. Glazebrook, for whom he still works, would be an example of a 'good client': collaborative and keenly interested, and once even suggesting a reprint of a poster ('well, if you aren't happy with it ...'). Just as he remembers the pleasure in the 1950s of getting Anthony Froshaug's cards for St George's Gallery through the post, so Hollis's lessons in visual organization came free every other month to anyone with eyes to see. When the Gallery was reopened in its upmarket guise in 1985, Hollis was replaced by a design group. The new graphic style, in tune with the building, went white and expensive. After some muddled efforts with the leaflets, they have returned to Hollis's format, but done without his zip and loving care.

Given his interest in folding and his painterly concerns, it might come as a surprise to find Hollis confessing that book design is what he likes above all. Perhaps not so surprising if you regard a book as a three (four?) dimensional matter of sequence and movement. The stories of two of his publishing employments of the 1970s point a moral about the English situation. The negative lesson came in the year of the hot summer (1976), when he was appointed production director at Faber & Faber, some years before the firm was Pentagrammed. Here he encountered genteel literariness in quite extreme forms (a production controller reading proofs at a lectern). One weekend, symbolically and in good modern-movement spirit, Hollis installed a preconstructed office within the building. The job was terminated after six months.

By contrast Hollis's work for Pluto Press, as designer and de facto art director, proved long-lasting and productive. Pluto was then a small and radical publishing house, whose books – both the covers and their often complex texts – fell readily into this design approach: there were no problems over modernity. It was around

Pluto, especially, that the 'Graphic Ring' formed: a group of designers (Hollis, Robin Fior, Ken Campbell) who never got round to formal meetings, but found this means of putting a growl (GrR!) after their names. A particularly energetic and angry younger colleague, Clive Challis, became an 'AGrR' – though later got the sack. David King was close, but never joined. The common link, apart from shared political outlook, was a commitment to experiment, including an acceptance of honourable and educative failures. The now celebrated 'constructivist' influences in their work were exactly appropriate to the content of those books and the campaigns of the time. But, especially in Hollis's case, inspiration also came from less obvious sources: tabloid journalism (the 'bullet' mark indicating discrete chunks of text), magazine work (he had been art director of *New Society* in the late 1960s), as well as certain books that were not particularly 'designed', but – perhaps for this reason – could develop fresh approaches (he remembers especially a book of commentaries by the French film director Chris Marker).

From this period also, the books that Hollis designed for and with John Berger – *G*, *Ways of seeing* (both 1972), and *The seventh man* (1975) – are further confirmation of the conditions that allow good work: texts and images of real content, and a sympathetic author prepared to sit down and help sort it out page-by-page, line-by-line. Here his interest in process, in the unfinished and the interim, can find scope for expression. He is at his best with texts and images that tell about the material reality of something. It is not a very fashionable attitude, and it provides a fundamental explanation for his distance from marketing graphics. Hollis, and designers who share this approach, are in the business of explaining, not of image or façade. In *Ways of seeing*, as in some of his leaflets and catalogues of the time, one sees the beginnings of Hollis's preoccupation with placing pictures just where they are discussed. The best example of this, to date, may be the design of Colin MacCabe's *Godard: images, sounds, politics*, published by the British Film Institute (1980), which was set and pasted up as MacCabe wrote, chapter by chapter. 'Design is a question of finding a graphic language for the particular client, not of imposing the designer's hieratic', he says, apologizing for the pompous tone. In this content-determined, anti-formalist approach, he is very different from designers whose work always looks the same; one of the constructivist comrades comes to mind.

In such labour-intensive taking of pains lies the economic extravagance of this work; and also in such things as the cutting-up and respacing of photoset headlines and in the ancient craft of Letrasetting, which Hollis still practises. The studio-hands of the big design companies can't allow themselves the time for this, even supposing that they are conscious of the importance of fine tuning. With the technical constraints of text composition now more or less gone, so the notion of standards has collapsed. 'It's as if all we feared would happen with photocomposition has actually come true', Hollis admits. Recently he acted as adviser to Phil Baines for the graphic design of the Craft Council's 'New Spirit' exhibition, and could feel some kinship, across the generations, with Baines's experiments with the old technology of letterpress printing. His attitude to Neville Brody's work is equivocal: admiring the experimental approach, questioning the results. While understanding the French enthusiasm for Brody – he makes an eloquent French gesture – one is more likely to find Hollis talking with Joseph Brodsky. (He was a director of the magazine *Modern Poetry in Translation* as well as its designer.)

Richard Hollis thus finds himself in a paradoxical position, though he is by no means alone in it: of a modernist defending some traditional, craft virtues. The computer, if he could get his hands on a good one for layout and page make-up, might offer prospects of ways forward. But the best help would come in the form of an enlightened publisher needing design direction. Given present conditions, it is not very likely to be an English-language firm.

Blueprint, no. 46, April 1988

This was published in a special 'British graphics' issue of *Blueprint*, to which I also contributed a small history of the development of the profession of graphic design in Britain ('From commercial art to plain commercial'). Hollis was a little behind in acquisition of machines, but before long he had got a fax machine. By the middle 1990s he had begun to use an Apple Macintosh.

Karel Martens

How to group text and images in ways that make sense? What size of type? How much space between the words, between the lines? What length of line? The basic problems of typography don't change: human beings go on reproducing themselves in similarly sized and constrained bodies. One could write the history of typography, from 1450 on, as a struggle between texts and designers, whose whims and vanities have often lead them to butchery, indifference, ego-driven overemphasis and profligacy.

Just now this struggle is nowhere more evident than in the Netherlands. A rich country still, with a well-provided cultural super-structure: its predominant ethos of a high valuation of social use has benefited its designers, even as Dutch fine artists have suffered from the new economic stringencies. A particular mixture of social application and individual license has given birth to the phenomenon of 'Dutch design', largely fostered by swooning Anglo-American spectators. In understanding typography – this above every other area of design – knowledge of the language makes all the difference. When you begin to read Dutch graphic design and the native debates around it (if they aren't in English, or certainly when they are), then it loses its otherness. Then this Dutch design becomes mundane, like things back home.

Any discussion of decent treatment of text and Dutch typography should start with a salute to a glory of the culture: the matchless and apparently endless stream of book typographers at work for their publishing houses. To name just some older ones, one thinks of Wim Mol, Harry Sierman, Alje Olthof, Karel Treebus, Joost van de Woestijne. But then there are a few typographers now in middle age who have worked across the range of tasks, who started out as grid-obeying modernists, and who have matured into a typography that respects and uses traditional values, but which explores and risks, while cleaving to the meaning of texts and images. Among the first names that come to mind: Kees Nieuwenhuijzen, Walter Nikkels, and Karel Martens. Within the Netherlands, these designers have some reputation; outside the country they are more or less unknown. Indeed Martens might be cited as an exemplary instance of someone whose work is rooted, not interested in fashion – and fresh.

On finishing as a student at the Arnhem school of art in 1961, Karel Martens became a freelance graphic designer, as he has remained ever since. One should qualify this: although able to work over the whole field, he has specialized in typography, for books especially; and he is also a committed and prolific maker of free graphic work. The juxtaposition – and separation – of these two activities is a vital, enlivening factor in his total production.

His first major client was the publisher Van Loghum Slaterus. Martens designed cool, geometrical images for the covers and left-ranging text inside. If it suited academic and often abstract books, it also ended in a cul-de-sac. This was also the general crisis of post-1945 modernism, which by the late 1960s was finding that blind pursuit of the economic miracle and of bureaucratic rationalism was not enough. In keeping with the times, the small firm of Van Loghum Slaterus was incorporated into the large combine of Kluwer.

Designers are dependent on their 'commission-givers' (opdrachtgevers: the Dutch word is better than our sleazy 'client'). This is a banal truth, but it becomes even truer in the case of a designer as sensitive and socially minded as Martens. In 1975, however, he found the client through and with whom he could develop out of the cul-de-sac. This was the SUN publishing house. As its full name indicates – the Socialistiese Uitgeverij Nijmegen – the SUN has a clear commitment. It grew out of the Dutch student movement of the late 1960s, at first publishing stencil-duplicated texts. Now Martens had the chance to work on a stream of books of real substance, with a consistently socialist alignment and produced on minimum budgets: ideal conditions in which to work out his critical modernism. There was a geographical factor too: Karel Martens has always lived in the province of Gelderland that includes Nijmegen and Arnhem, and one might make a case for him as a 'critical regionalist', in the term of the architectural critic Kenneth Frampton. (Although books travel, as buildings don't.) The editor at the SUN who spotted him also played a role in the work, as a lively, questioning partner. This was Hugues Boekraad, whose progress has intertwined with that of Martens ever since.

The SUN book-covers designed by Martens are marvellous instances of how to achieve much with very little. He set up a simple set of elements and then, with each new cover, played variations: author and title in Franklin Gothic caps (rubbed down in Letraset by the designer himself), thick rules around certain edges, and then just space and sometimes an image. Here, as throughout his work, the choice of colours was delicate and remarkable. Inside the books, there was no budget to do more than a standardized format; text was usually set on an IBM golfball-composer. But anyway a large part of the SUN list were reprints, whose pages were those of another publisher's edition. Here the covers played a vital part in linking together wildly varying insides.

There is a thesis to be written about graphic designers and the socialist publishers of that time in Europe. In Britain, the radical Left, particularly in its more intellectual manifestations, had since the mid-1960s used some of the best designers (Robin Fior, Ken Garland, Derek Birdsall, Jerry Cinamon). And just when Karel Martens was working for the SUN, Pluto Press, once the publishing arm of International Socialism, had Richard Hollis as its de facto art director. Indeed the paths of Hollis and Martens run quite closely parallel to each other, especially in this turn from dry geometry into a richer, more flexible, but still clearly modern approach. A more demanding thesis still would be a dissertation on the use of typographic indentation to articulate text, in relation to social and political change, as deployed in the typography of Martens and Hollis, 1965 to 1993.

In 1977, Martens began to teach part-time at the school of art at Arnhem. He is still there (two days a week), and this has helped to keep him and a family afloat, supplementing the poorly paid but otherwise rewarding work that he does. His teaching has helped to consolidate what one might now speak of as a school of 'Arnhem typography'. Before him, Jan Vermeulen, Kees Kelfkens and Alexander Verberne had helped to establish a serious interest in typography at the school. Now there are about twenty-years' worth of Arnhem students, a few from each class, who have picked up an engagement with typography as a serious, life-absorbing activity, concerned with making texts accessible without the interposition of a designer-ego. The starting point is always: is this text worth publishing anyway?

Talk to Verberne and you may see him ironically wiping some pretentious piece of graphic design on the dirty café table top. Talk to Martens, and you will find him throwing things down – even work that bears his name – with the comment 'another superfluous book!'

Karel Martens stopped working for the SUN in 1981. His fiery editor Hugues Boekraad left a little later, and in 1986 was launched as a critic and theorist of graphic design, with a remarkably thorough and penetrating essay on the SUN and Martens. Since then the cultural sector has provided work for Martens: stamps and booklets for the PTT, exhibition catalogues, and books, but no longer any consistent engagement with a publishing house. Or not until he became the designer of *Oase*, the architectural journal.

Oase had been an undistinguished A4, staple-stitched production. Its editors were preparing for a new phase of life under a new publisher. This was the SUN, which by now, like all successful left-radical houses, is publishing a more general, less political list. Karel Martens was approached, with the assumption that he would not want the job himself, but maybe he could find a student? Martens, who has always taken architectural theory as one source of guidance in his work, decided to take on the job himself. As this story implies, the designer's work is not well paid, and the journal is produced by a group of people in their spare time. But already, after a handful of issues, something remarkable has been created, recognized in this year's Werkman Prize award to Martens. He is back with a public place in which to work out his typography.

So what could it be, this socially committed, critical typography? Without a connection to explicitly radical content, and with the eclipse of left politics through the 1980s, it isn't obvious. In the last few years, 'radical' has meant radical in form, or in fact radical in image. Architects and designers have borrowed the false prop of poststructuralist theory, in which the airy abstractions of language become everything – and material reality is displaced and denied. (Jean Baudrillard on the Gulf War was the clearest instance of this.) Text is unsettled and deconstructed, to become just image. And when this stuff is reproduced in magazines and annuals, its fate as mere image is sealed forever. The critical and subversive possibilities of this wild and 'radical' work are then zero.

A few designers have stood against the reduction to image. Here is the power and the resonance of the deep commitment to material in Karel Martens's typography. His preference is for materials that are a bit rough, not so perfect. If they wear visibly in use – well, that is what happens in life. You won't find any heavy varnishing on his covers; unless, as with *Oase* no. 33, it is there as an ironic comment on that number's special theme: the metropolis. Take the simplest case, of a single sheet of paper for a letterheading. Printing some text on the reverse side, to let it show through to the front, provides another way of coding information; it also demonstrates that the sheet is a three-dimensional thing in the world.

Another area of exploration is the edge of the sheet. Bleeding elements off the page, and the rejection of the frame, have always been a prime device of modern design: in its refusal of self-engrandisement, its effort to seek relation to the world, to assert a social connection. Especially in his recent work, and where it is appropriate for the job in hand, Martens has taken edge exploration further. Elements straddling the fold on a flap of a booklet carry the reader in, or the cutting of the folded sheets is left to the reader. This last device is used in *Oase* no. 34, whose theme is 'the interior'. The reader is indeed then an active participant, physically so; but uncut pages are also just the old, cheaper way of making books.

Here one can refer to the free work that Karel Martens has always made alongside the design work. For some years in the late 1970s and 1980s, the leading theme was paper. In the simplest works, a pile of printed sheets was sliced through: this cut edge then provides a face, its blurry and random-but-determined marks struggle to say something about the world. These are, after all, slices of reality, as their titles say: 'Karl Marx, *Das Kapital*, first volume', '*Financial Times* 15.08.80–20.12.80', 'Walt Disney's *Donald Duck and other stories*'. More recently, Martens has been making monoprints from bits of metal, especially Meccano. In one series, many overprintings result in extraordinarily intense and deep colour effects – from which a white slot shines out – as well as in three-dimensional accretions of ink.

The free work with paper, with ink, with found elements, informs a special distinction of Martens's typography. This is its quiet sensuality – that more powerful sensuality which the protestant imagination allows itself – achieved without indulgence and within the terms of mass production for everyday use. In both areas of his work, the drive for economy in materials and processes is notable. Thus the reuse of old Stedelijk Museum cataloguing sheets in recent prints. Thus the very comfortable format of *Oase* (24 x 17 cm), which was chosen because it uses a 70 x 50 cm paper sheet without waste.

In one of Martens's current jobs – the monograph on Wim Crouwel, marking Crouwel's retirement from the Boijmans Museum at Rotterdam – he proposed a format that would use the press economically and also enable the material of the book to be organized in manageable units. But the book must be larger, to conform to the format of a series subsidized by the government money of the Prins Bernhard Fonds. Although the writers (Frederike Huygen and Hugues Boekraad) are critically minded, the project is inexorably turning into a monument, contradicting material economy and usability. But Martens's arguments here illustrate some basic assumptions of any critical typography.

It is the task of any such critical typography to turn on itself and doubt. Karel Martens, in conversation, is questioning and modest about his own production. Yet he once wrote that 'form is the condition through which a common life becomes possible ... design determines the quality of our common life'. But where really could the social meaning lie, in a journal of architecture or a booklet for the PTT? And this painstaking work, made with the help of hand-drawn visuals and without a computer in the studio – what sort of example is this for designers who have to hurry through large workloads in large offices? What example is it to the armies of non-designers, working with DTP? And if designers look at this work, won't they just rip off its apparent mannerisms?

Modesty forbids an answer from Martens, so let me try an explanation. The mannerisms are apparent, they don't stay still: the work develops, responds appropriately to each new task, observes and accepts the constraints of the job. There is no style, only an approach and an attitude: unapologetic intelligence and unbeatable moral integrity. Drive hard for content and for the real object, refuse the delusions of the image: that is the lesson this work offers. It won't be accepted into the culture of empty designerism, of slide-shows on the international conference circuit, because in its spirit and in every detail, it resists that culture.

And yes, a book printed in a thousand copies, whatever its distinction, cannot have the 'social effect' of a newspaper, a social-security form, or a logo for a transnational company. Martens has been happy to taken on public-sphere commissions – stamps or signs on buildings – but the point is that that the social cannot be estimated merely in terms of numbers produced or numbers of people who see and use. It is a question of human spirit and of human culture. One finds an 'aesthetics of resistance' here: a rich but meaning-constrained surplus, beyond and against the expectations of societies ordered by narrow accounting-economics and by flagrant material and human waste.

At this point in the argument we are back with the tasks of typography. Multiplication of text is a social act that provides a forum for dialogue and exchange: making text deliberately hard to read is thus a public offence. So: a page of words that actually say something of interest, maybe set in Grotesque 215 (an ordinary typeface, without pretensions), word-spaces equal so that the lines range freely from the left, paragraphs and headings organized by easy 5 and 10 mm indents, spaces that distinguish line from line without over-isolation or dazzle. The page reads effortlessly. In its freedom and its order, it is a model for social arrangements too.

Eye, no. 11, 1993

Stimulated by seeing Karel Martens's work for *Oase*, this was one of the few articles that I proposed to *Eye*. It was also a farewell to trying to write feature articles for the magazine. In 1994, Martens took up a position in the design department at the Jan van Eyck Akademie, Maastricht, and acquired an Apple Macintosh. (Like many teachers at that school, his stay was brief.) In 1996, he was awarded the Heineken Prize for Art, and I collaborated on a book in celebration of his work. In 1998, with Wigger Bierma, he set up the Werkplaats Typografie in Arnhem, as an experiment in practical education. The monograph on Wim Crouwel referred to here was to go through some further mutations. It was eventually published in 1997, designed by Martens and Jaap van Triest, and in a format smaller than the one preferred by the Prins Bernhard Fonds. I published a long review of that book in *Typography Papers*, no. 3, 1998.

MetaDesign, Berlin

The lack of standards by which to judge graphic design is widely admitted. If architecture, at another extreme, is overburdened with debate, graphic design suffers from an almost complete absence of discussion and of common ground. The profession is young, its field is wide, purposes and budgets vary enormously, and the products are abundant and often necessarily ephemeral. What could 'quality' in graphic work mean? If you try it in German – 'Qualität' – meanings change and sharpen. Then one has the watchword of the Deutscher Werkbund, and the implication of something thoroughly considered and tested, made of the best materials and to the best standards, for which you will certainly have to pay, but in the knowledge that this outlay will be well rewarded in years of good performance.

The German idea of quality lies far from the frothy world of design business that has developed in Britain in the 1980s. This froth has been nowhere more evident than in the graphics sector, where styles and mannerisms have seemed to change as often as the spectacle frames of creative directors, the names of whose firms have rivalled each other in silly whimsicality.

Someone immersed in the London scene, coming across a German practice with the name of MetaDesign, which specializes in complex information work, might assume that it must be devoted to the production of reports and analytical memoranda (numbered paragraphs and matrix tabulations), in the tradition of the HfG Ulm at its most methodolatrous. They would be surprised. Certainly MetaDesign's work does bear out some of the implications of the name. It has a tendency to step back to question the first (client's) assumptions about a job, to be interested in the means by which the product is made, to incorporate this awareness into the product itself. This gives the work a dimension that is of special interest and instruction to other designers: it has didactic possibilities. And among their customers are other people in the design business: the type manufacturer H. Berthold AG, the Internationales Design Zentrum in Berlin, the Bund Deutscher Grafik-Designer, Herman Miller. But the work, in its liveliness and clarity, consistently escapes the trap of design-world self-referentiality.

MetaDesign was established in Berlin in 1983, though only Erik Spiekermann, its elder presiding genius, continues from that time. He, with three others (Hans Werner Holzwarth, Jens Kreitmeyer, Theres Weishappel), comprise the present core of the group, which is more of a concept than a limited company. Spiekermann's background suggests where some of the intelligent idiosyncrasy of the work derives from. He took up design after doing art history at the Free University in Berlin. For most of the 1970s he lived in London, becoming a graphic designer by the most painful route: the type composing room, briefly with metal, then with photocomposition.

From this shop-floor experience comes Spiekermann's recognition of the need to understand the processes and capacities of any machine. In the face of rapid innovation in composing technology, designers have separated into two polarized camps. Conservatives have – as the American writer Stanley Rice once observed – tended to treat a new machine exactly as they treated the last model that they fully understood, thus closing themselves off from the exploration of new possibilities. The radicals (though 'fashionables' might be more a more accurate term), and the merely ignorant, have dropped everything in excitement and accepted all the tricks and distortions of which the new photo- and digitized composition is capable. The genuinely radical course would seem to lie in a conscious exploration of this technology, with eyes open to the needs of readers, as well as to old metal standards that might be improved upon.

In his London years, Spiekermann began to acquire the metal type that was then being junked from composing rooms, intending to set up business as a specialist printer: not in any antiquarian spirit, but out of sheer love – or mania, as he would put it – for type, and the wish to get close to his material. The whole lot was destroyed in a fire: something for which we can perhaps be grateful, if it forced him to work in wider, more public contexts.

The strong thread that runs through MetaDesign work is a sense of proper typography: a respect for the meaning of a text, and for the fine adjustments of space that allow letters to cohere into readable words. The successful achievement of this quality of typography depends on technological capacity, which is now quite widely available, and – what is much rarer – intelligent specification by designers and sympathetic interpretation by machine operators. Meta-

Design tends to rely on just a few known and trusted typesetters and printers, who can provide a real partnership, in which designer, compositor and printer are working for the same goal.

A principal means by which this is achieved is the grid sheet on which layouts are specified. The setting process can then go straight to pages, bypassing the gummy and hair-raisingly imprecise stage of paste-up, so love-hated by designers still hankering after craft satisfactions. These grids, for setting on Berthold machines, are millimetric along both x- and y-axes ('measure' and linefeed, respectively) and typesize is also specified in metric units. In this practice, MetaDesign honours the promise of its name, demonstrating a fully conscious approach, which abolishes the archaism of 'artwork' and the employment of two or more unrelated systems of measurement (Didot points, Anglo-American points, millimetres, inches ...). Their machines, which also include Apple Macintoshes for drawing and in interface with typesetting, are thus really used, unobtrusively, rather than fetishized.

This approach finds full scope for employment in the redesign

MetaDesign with computers in 1987. Around the table, clockwise: Erik Spiekermann, Inken Greisner, Theres Weishappel, Robert Hummel, Christoph Preussler, Jens Kreitmeyer, Petra Mader, Anke Jaaks. Prominent on the table is a copy of *Blueprint*.

of forms for the Deutsche Bundespost (German Post Office), on which Erik Spiekermann has been working, as consultant to Sedley Place Design in Berlin. The job arose from the Bundespost's wish to change the language of the forms, from one of command to one in which the user feels that she or he is a partner in the transaction. With the change in the words, there could come a correspondingly more open and accessible visual treatment. So, for example, where there were long lines of justified text, there are short, unjustified columns; typesize is increased where possible; where there had been boxed areas, there is space and only horizontal rules; instead of black on grey paper, colour is meaningfully deployed. The programme is still in its early stages, but the first results do seem to achieve the aim of 'Bürgerfreundlichkeit' (citizen-friendliness), and this by means not of any visual 'speaking down', but rather by a more systematic approach. One might consider these forms as evidence for the argument that democratic openness is best served by an uncompromisingly modern approach; though – as for example in Norman Foster's work – there is a difficult line to be drawn between this politics of liberty-equality-fraternity-sorority and its sometimes disingenuous imitation by the large corporate or state organization.

Political questions have also been raised by another element of the Bundespost work. As part of the redesign programme, Spiekermann has proposed a new company typeface. This would attempt to meet the special needs of post office printed matter (legible in small sizes, able to stand up to very variable production conditions), as well as providing the products of a huge organization with a sense of unity and identity. The typeface has now been fully developed and tested, but has not – so far – been accepted by the client. Meanwhile, the Bundespost continues with Helvetica: the typeface which, if it claims to signify 'Switzerland', suggests only the Switzerland of multi-lingual, transnational conglomeration. The Bundespost typeface is a sanserif, though a distinctive one. And elsewhere in their work, Spiekermann and MetaDesign, far from adhering dogmatically to sanserif, often use quite unlikely seriffed typefaces, without apology. In the same spirit, illustration is consistently used, as well as, not instead of, photography. Here may lie the elements that appetize the wholesome diet of well-composed text.

MetaDesign have established a nice balance. Their current work includes the most demanding tasks of graphic design – a 'city in-formation' system for the Berlin transport authority is one such major project – as well as lighter jobs for smaller customers, includ-ing some on the local 'alternative' scene. And now, with a full-scale typeface design under his belt, Erik Spiekermann seems to be enter-ing the ranks of the international heavyweight typographers.

As if in further confirmation of this status, Berthold is this year issuing Spiekermann's treatise on typography. The book was first published in German as *Ursache & Wirkung: ein typografischer Roman*, and will appear in English under the slightly different rubric of *Rhyme & reason*. A Dutch reviewer has compared it favourably with Stanley Morison's *First principles of typography*. And one sus-pects that, unlike Morison's dull text (which lives merely on its reputation), the book could prove really effective in its purpose of explaining principles – and also mysteries and delights – of typo-graphy. Bored first-year graphics students might begin to be per-suaded that designing with words can be actually exciting.

As even a glance at *Rhyme & reason* will suggest – it takes the form of an illustrated novel (but the novel of Sterne or Queneau rather than of Dickens) – 'heavyweight' is a misleading term for Spiekermann and his fellow MetaDesigners. Their work is too nimble and witty for that. Returning to cultural generalization, one might say that it combines the English virtues, of an interest in meaning and a light touch, with German tough-minded vigilance in the preparation and production of a job. This particular version of the Berlin-London axis provides one demonstration of quality in graphic design.

Blueprint, no. 40, September 1987

From 1990 MetaDesign was expanded, with Erik Spiekermann being joined by other partners, and sister companies were set up in San Francisco (1992) and London (1995). In the summer of 2000 MetaDesign became a publicly listed corporation; by then it had 200 employees in Berlin. In that year also Erik Spiekermann resigned from the company. In 2001 MetaDesign was sold to Lost Boys, the Dutch new media company ('we create brand experi-ences you'll never forget'). In this new manifestation, it could boast 550 employees and offices in eight countries. The Deutsche Bundespost never used the typeface designed for it; Spiekermann then developed it, releasing it as Meta, through FontShop.

Neville Brody

'The Graphic Language of Neville Brody': exhibition at the Victoria & Albert Museum, London, 27 April to 29 May 1988

Writing once about cities, John Berger likened London to 'a teenager, an urchin'. It is a thesis that finds direct confirmation any weekend at Camden Lock market, or any night in the clubs of Soho. Neville Brody's graphic design work provides further proof: in its unruly vitality and in its present limitation to the culture that is 'credible' on London streets.

The display at the Victoria & Albert Museum, with its accompanying book, presents a retrospective of ten years' work since leaving college. During this time Brody has become almost synonymous with a new style of graphic design (or a set of mannerisms?), through his art-direction of *The Face* and *Arena* magazines, his covers for the London listings weekly *City Limits*, and a large output of covers and ephemera for independent record companies. Emerging from the Punk Rock world of the late 1970s, he has maintained an iconoclastic approach. For example, in the frequent use of images degenerated by photocopying or TV screen projection, which carry the suggestion of urban Angst; in the exhibition, this is reinforced by edgy background sounds.

A main problem for dissident artists in the West is that of incorporation into the commercial world; of seeing devices that carried a charge of rebellion transmuted (appropriately softened) into the fascias and packaging of the shopping arcades. In his interviews Brody has shown himself to be much preoccupied with this. Thus he explains his use in *Arena* of the sober Swiss typeface Helvetica as a way of escaping from the attentions of his imitators, just now catching up with his more expressive work for *The Face*.

This exhibition and its accompanying commentary are certainly a coup for their subject, but they will bring him new problems. Those who may have enjoyed Brody's images, week by week as they appeared on the magazine racks, are now confronted with a set of intentions. The elements of a philosophy behind the work are presented in writings by his colleague Jon Wozencroft; for example, in aspersions against dark forces such as 'the post-colonialism of air travel and pop music', bumped out with quotations from George Steiner, Susan Sontag, and others. Whether the work can support this load of fuzzy theorizing is doubtful. Designing carrier bags for Bloomingdale's (a recent job) hardly suggests a biting critique of consumerism. Rather, one would think that for as long as he works as the willing fox to the commercial hounds, Brody's position is one of connivance at the culture of appearance and consumption.

Though hailed in the blurb as a 'pioneer of modern typography' for the 1980s, inside Wozencroft's book, Neville Brody engagingly admits that he still feels in some respects 'totally incompetent at typography'; he finds book-design too much work for 'a small re-turn' and would rather just do the cover. Brody is a member of the first generation to have escaped instruction in the habits of the now departed metal typography, and this fuels both the sense of freedom his work gives off, and its severe limitations. Words are treated as material for pattern-making, without much regard for sense or for readers. His approach is intuitive and every job carries his stamp: something that can only work for a tightly defined set of clients. In this attitude and in some of the devices used – especially the frequent impulse to symmetry – these images recall the commercial art of fifty years ago, before the advent of impersonal, problem-solving design. Then designers were valued for their signatures, and exhibited their work in galleries.

The Times Literary Supplement, no. 4442, 20–26 May 1988

The new Dutch telephone book

Since privatization, the Dutch PTT has tried to resolve its strong tradition of support for art and design with the new commercial imperatives. These forces led PTT Telecom to a reconsideration of its phone book, which since late 1994 is being issued in a new format. The pure list of subscribers is now combined with a commercial section (on pink paper) and these two parts are prefaced by an extensive information section. The whole becomes a quality reference work, rather than a meagre list. Fifty regional books cover the country. Advertising is being sold by TeleMedia, a daughter-company of the Swedish telecom business, Telia. With these new 'combined books', PTT Telecom now competes on superior terms with the Dutch Yellow Pages (published by ITT), and is in a position to sell elements of its new design internationally.

The Dutch must have been the first to use professional designers for the page layout of phone books. These were Wim Crouwel and Jolijn van de Wouw, working within Total Design, who for the first fully automated books (of 1977) radically rethought the typographic conventions. Numbers were placed before names: the two vital components were then next to each other, and no dot leaders were needed to join them. The typeface was a condensed Univers: a real designed letter in place of the vernacular grotesques that had been the norm. And – most astonishing of all – no capital letters were used. Crouwel argued that the very limited character-set of the CRT-typesetting machine left a choice of either capitals or punctuation, and he preferred the latter. So the modernist dream of single-alphabet typography could at last be authentically realized. There were complaints about the small size of type, and whines from people 'who didn't want to be known as numbers'. A few years later, some of this was softened in a redesign by Crouwel and Total Design. Type-size was increased, three rather than four columns per page were used, a set of more open numerals was designed (by Gerard Unger and Chris Vermaas), and phone numbers were put at the end of lines. But, strangely, the all-lowercase typography was maintained.

Since privatization, there was a growing feeling within PTT Telecom that something needed to be done about the phone book. But the project of redesign started informally in 1992, as an initiative of two designers: Jan-Kees Schelvis and Martin Majoor. Schelvis had been designing covers for the phone books for some years, and realized that the whole book needed a rethink. Majoor said to him jokingly, 'then I'll make a typeface for it'. They went to R. D. E. ('Ootje') Oxenaar, then head of the Art & Design department at the PTT, to explain their ideas: inclusion of postcodes, capital letters at the start of proper names, space rather than punctuation, numbers before names again, and a typeface that would both save space and offer new features. Oxenaar, very open to all this, asked them to put their thoughts on paper. After doing that they got a budget and three months to develop these ideas into workable visual form.

Although the new books are new in respect of every design element, they are most interesting for their microtypography: the letters, word spaces, and organization of text within the line. Here Martin Majoor played the leading role, finding that the design of the characters and their treatment in the lists had to go hand in hand. Majoor, aged thirty-four and one of the horde of 'young Dutch type designers', broke into typeface design with Scala, the first serious text typeface to be issued by FontShop – and now one of its best sellers. That was in 1991, and two years later he followed it up with Scala Sans. The new phone book typeface, Telefont, continues this line of thinking. 'Humanist sans serif' is the best technical description for these last two typefaces. This means that the forms of the letters follow the lines of pre-industrial romans, that the italic is a real italic (not a sloped roman), that the character set includes small capitals and has non-lining numbers as a norm. One could see Gill Sans as an early and partial essay in this category, which has recently begun to flourish. Lucida Sans and Stone Sans provided examples, and, with Scala Sans and Telefont, one would add Meta and most recently Thesis. Caecilia, the 'humanist egyptian' designed by Peter Matthias Noordzij, sits next door to this grouping.

We are dealing here with a new spirit in typography. Let us call it – taxonomists take note! – Modern Traditionalism. This means that traditional values, of skill, subtlety, and an embrace of the full resources of typography, are deployed in thoroughly modern

Groenekan (03461)

Remu NV Regionale Energiemij Utrecht (03438) 2 53 11
Regio Heuvelrug, tijdens kantooruren
Voor doorkiezen (03438) 2 53 - -
Voor storingen binnen en buiten kantooruren (03438) 3 18 70

Riemens J Beusichemsewg 41 3997 MH 21 13
Rietveld H Tiendwg 1 3997 MN 25 32
Roel R A M Wickenburghsewg 81 3997 MT 19 89
Roffelsen Ch G De Eng 21 3997 MD 16 31
Rooms-Kath Pastorie Beusichemsewg 102 3997 ML 13 31

Rooij, de
Transport- & Garagebedrijf Tankstation
Beusichemsewg 58 3997 MK **20 24**
fax > 15 24

Rijken A J G Tuurdk 1 3997 MS 20 03
Rijn J W van Beusichemsewg 36 3997 MJ 18 67
Saaleman P H Tuurdk 7 3997 MS 22 80
Salad Salarisverwerkingen Wickenburghsewg 79 3997 MT 22 85
Sandwijk H van Wickenburghsewg 59 3997 MT 14 43
Schaberg J Wickenburghsewg 32 3997 MV 18 61
Schaik J C van Tiendwg 15 3997 MN 15 72
Schaik-Hooijman J B P van Beusichemsewg 94 3997 ML 12 19
Schild Barth en Lilian Wickenburghsewg 76 3997 MX 19 90
Scholman W G M Beusichemsewg 26 3997 MJ 23 19
Smorenburg R P Tiendwg 5 3997 MN 15 10
Spithoven G A M Beusichemsewg 68 3997 MK 15 01
Spithoven M A J De Eng 52 3997 MG 14 83
Spithoven Fa Gebr A en H Tuurdk 12 3997 MS 14 76
Spithoven A W Fruitteler Tuurdk 18A 3997 MS 14 36
Spithoven H A M Tuurdk 20 3997 MS 15 26
Spithoven A J Tuurdk 18 3997 MS 13 20
fruitteler
Spithoven-Van Rijn A G Tuurdk 12 3997 MS 14 76
Steenbakkers E A M De Eng 58 3997 MG 18 06
Stokbroekx J M E Keramiste Wickenburghsewg 35 3997 MT 20 89
Stork C J Beusichemsewg 112 3997 ML 17 26
T&D St Kruisw Gezinsverz Alg Maatsch Werk
Het Kant 3 3995 DZ HOUTEN (03403)7 70 04
districtskantoor Houten/Nieuwegein (03403)7 70 04
Timmeronderhoudsbedrijf N S van Dort Groenedk 5 3997 MZ 18 48
Toekomst Vastgoed de Beusichemsewg 44 3997 MJ (06)52 87 21 76
mobiele telefoon
Transportbedrijf Rooy de Beusichemsewg 58 3997 MK 20 24
Tweede Alarmnummer Te UTRECHT (030)33 22 22
Uijtewaal C Beusichemsewg 84 3997 MK 22 08
Uytewaal Hugo De Eng 1 3997 MD 22 52
Uytewaal Eddie De Eng 45 3997 ME 22 42
Uijtewaal H J Fruitteler Tiendwg 8 3997 MN 15 36
Uyttewaal J A Fruitteler Kapellewg 20 3997 MP 16 36
Vecht W C M vd Fruitteler de Knapschinkel Beusichemsewg 39 3997 MH 19 91
Vera H L M Beusichemsewg 112 3997 ML 17 26
Verbeek J H Wickenburghsewg 62 3997 MX 15 33
Vermeulen D H H De Eng 15 3997 MD 25 47
Vermeulen H M Metsel Wickenburghsewg 71 3997 MT 16 16
Vernooy W M Beusichemsewg 32 3997 MJ 13 41
Vernooy A H E Beusichemsewg 130 3997 ML 16 15
Vernooy A H Beusichemsewg 138 3997 ML 13 44
Vernooy Gebr E en H Veefokk Beusichemsewg 146 12 05
Vernooy E J H Beusichemsewg 146 12 05
Vernooy G A Groenedk 3 3997 MZ 13 42
Vernooij J H Kapellewg 25 3997 MP 13 24
Vernooij W J H Wickenburghsewg 23 3997 MT 21 88
Vernooy J H Wickenburghsewg 58 3997 MV 26 14
Vernooij A G M Groenedk 7a 3997 MZ 22 29
Vernooy Gzn W M Wickenburghsewg 39 3997 MT 14 60
Vernooy H G J Veehoud Beusichemsewg 49 3997 MH 12 46
Vernooy-Van Rijn C M Beusichemsewg 140 3997 ML 17 28
Vernooy-Verhoef G J Th Wickenburghsewg 21 3997 MT 14 55
Verplancke Management Partner Wickenburghsewg 67 3997 MT 18 87
Verwey A C H Beusichemsewg 78 3997 MK 18 77
Verweij J G M Tiendwg 9 3997 MN 19 66
Voetbalvereniging Goy 't Kantine Tuurdk 19b 3997 MS 17 21
Vonk J C De Eng 13 3997 MD 17 81
Vorderman C C G De Eng 49 3997 ME 21 20
Vos v J E M Groenedk 8 3997 MZ 14 12
Vossen L J M Wickenburghsewg 54 3997 MV 18 37
Vreeswijk C J Tiendwg 7 3997 MN 12 60
Vreeswijk C J Wickenburghsewg 7 3997 MT 13 74

Wilt u adverteren in deze gids?
Bel TeleMedia 06-0025

Waterleidingbedrijf Midden-Nederland WMN
Reactorwg 47 Postbus 2124 3500 GC UTRECHT (030)48 72 11
hoofdkantoor
fax > (030)41 49 55
voor klachten en storingen (dag en nacht) (030)48 72 81
m.i.v. 10-10-1995 telefoon (030)248 72 11
m.i.v. 10-10-1995 fax > (030)241 49 55
m.i.v. 10-10-1995 voor klachten en storingen (030)248 72 81
Weert Jan en Diny De Eng 51 3997 ME 21 57
Weverwijk J M van Groenedk 2 3997 MZ 20 48
Weijden G C vd Tuurdk 15 3997 MS 13 04
Wieman J B Nachtdk 19 3997 MR 14 68
Wieman J G Wickenburghsewg 63 3997 MT 24 29
Wieman A C Wickenburghsewg 85 3997 MT 15 73
aannemingsbedr gebr Wieman BV
woonh J Wieman 14 68
Wieman & Zn J P Beusichemsewg 136 3997 ML 14 32
loonwerkbedrijf
woonhuis john wieman (03403)4 14 75
Wind E Wickenburghsewg 43 3997 MT 12 50
Winkel G P J Tuurdk 19A 3997 MS 17 82
Wit J M de Tuurdk 3a Postbus 35 3998 ZR SCHALKWIJK 22 70
Wttewaall A G A Fruitteler Wickenburghsewg 9 3997 MT 13 86
Wttewaall J Wickenburghsewg 19 3997 MT 13 02
Wttewaall G W Wickenburghsewg 19A 3997 MT 19 21
Wttewaall O J Wickenburghsewg 19b 3997 MT 20 15
historicus fotograaf
Wijngaarden C J van Tuurdk 10 3997 MS 15 20
Zumbrink T H J De Eng 53 3997 ME 22 67
Zutphen M van Tuurdk 25 3997 MS 25 91
Zwambag Wim en Ina Tuurdk 6 3997 MS 21 36
Zijl H N A van Beusichemsewg 112 3997 ML 12 82

Groenekan (03461)

Aannemersbedrijf Berg A P vd Voordorpsedk 10 3737 BK (030)73 24 42
Aannemersbedrijf Douze BV J C Kon Wilhelminawg 513 3737 BG 26 39
Aannemersbedrijf Engelsman den Kon Wilhelminawg 451 3737 BE 32 22

Aannemersbedrijf Nagtegaal bv
Groenekansewg 112 3737 AJ **33 99**
fax > 35 60

Aannemingsbedrijf Beek E C vd Voordorpsedk 41 3737 BM (030)20 00 35
Accountantskantoor Nieuwenhuizen BV Groenekansewg 17 3737 AA 37 36
fax > 12 77
Advocaat W Veldln 18 3737 AP 16 28
Advocaat J Versteegln 40 3737 XA 42 21
Agterberg A M Voordorpsedk 30 3737 BK (030)20 16 37
Agterberg A Th Voordorpsedk 32B 3737 BK (030)20 36 56

Agterberg BV A
Voordorpsedk 34 3737 BK **(030)20 15 82**
aannemingsbedrijf van grond, water, wegenbouw- en cultuurtechnische werken
kantoor
fax > (030)20 15 82
werkplaats Biltsestrwg 76 (030)71 97 67
Agterberg A Th (030)73 52 47
Agterberg T B J (030)71 04 04
Agterberg A A (030)71 23 45
Agterberg F G (03404)3 38 02
Riet Th M Van, adm (03436)16 56
Zeeuw G Th De, calc (03439)11 31
Haaksman C (030)20 04 63
woonhuisaansluitingen uitvoerders
Agterberg J A (030)94 31 20
Agterberg M M (030)28 07 35
Bie M de (03436)30 66
Duyst H (03499)8 43 40
Meulen A Vd (030)88 75 62
Rooyen O Van (030)73 23 72
Smid F (03449)25 65
Woudenberg A Van (03435)7 65 03
woonhuisaansluitingen chauffeurs
Barneveld G Van (03465)6 68 51
Wildt A De (03406)6 36 87

Alarmnummer (06)11
Alberts H Vyverln 19 3737 RG 33 08
Alem G A M van Copynln 47 3737 AV 30 01
Alfen F W Versteegln 6 3737 XA 35 89
Alfrink J C Copynln 10 3737 AW 16 50
Alink Drs E J Berkenln 30 3737 RN 36 57
Alvarez Prof Dr G E Eikln 10 3737 RL 14 20
Ambulance Te UTRECHT (030)33 22 22
Ambulance Alarmnummer (06)11
Arends G Kon Wilhelminawg 381 3737 BC 22 14
Arinfo Kon Wilhelminawg 461 3737 BE 32 04
Arissen G J Econ Groenekansewg 218 3737 AL (030)20 55 49
Aristos Beheer BV Kon Wilhelminawg 461 3737 BE 32 04
Aristos Grafische Service BV Kon Wilhelminawg 461 3737 BE 32 04
Asperen K van Oranjeln 13 3737 AS 21 42
Asselt M van Voordorpsedk 31A 3737 BL (030)72 22 59
Asselt T van Kon Wilhelminawg 472 3737 BJ 25 68
Atteveld C P M Vyverln 5 3737 RE 29 66
Auto Taxibedrijf Beerschoten Groenekansewg 166 3737 AK 15 73
Automagazine 4wd Kon Wilhelminawg 441 3737 BE 31 54
Automatiseringsbureau Groenekan BV Kon Wilhelminawg 383 3737 BC 25 04

Autoschadebedrijf Markus BV van
G v Prinstererwg 43 3731 HA DE BILT **(030)20 01 37**
idem Leeuwerikln 6 3704 GR ZEIST (03404)6 13 01

Autoverhuurbedrijf J G van Deutekom Groenekansewg 104 3737 AJ 40 81
Baars R Kon Wilhelminawg 397 3737 BD 40 03
Baas H S Copynln 3 3737 AV 29 43
Baas A W J Voordorpsedk 28A 3737 BK (030)20 04 73
Baelde I Nw Weteringsewg 95 3737 MG 26 67
Baelde I Nw Weteringsewg 97 3737 MG 38 55
loonbedrijf
Baggerman R Veldln 33 3737 AM 25 97
Bakker J C C Grotheln 2 3737 RK 42 45
kunsthistorica
Bandenhandel Dijk BV J J van Kon Wilhelminawg 497 3737 BG 13 73
accu- en oliehandel
Bantzinger M G J Veldln 21 3737 AM 38 41
Barneveld C van Copynln 37 3737 AV 17 27
Barneveld Ing H van Groenekansewg 58 3737 AH 38 30
Barneveld G Kastanjeln 20 3737 RB 27 40
Barneveld P van Nw Weteringsewg 151 3737 MG 20 44
Barneveld Dr A Dierenarts Ruigenhoeksedk 123 3737 MR 15 71
Barneveld A Ruigenhoeksedk 123 3737 MR 47 11
Barneveld C Veldln 10 3737 AP 24 56
Barneveld W Versteegln 50 3737 XA 14 95
Barneveld N J van Vyverln 8 3737 RH 15 81
Baron E Versteegln 14 3737 XA 42 46
Bartels J A C Kon Wilhelminawg 319 3737 BB 35 97
Basten F D Lindenln 30 3737 RD 17 05
Bax J Kon Wilhelminawg 313 3737 BB 40 75
Bedrijfsverzorgingsdienst Aav Groenekansewg 90a 3737 AH 21 14
fax > 17 64
Beek O J vd Vyverln 9 3737 RE 19 51
Beek Aannemingsbedrijf E C vd Voordorpsedk 41 3737 BM (030)20 00 35
Beerschoten W J van Café Kweekzicht Groenekansewg 168 3737 AK 13 36
Beerschoten Arnold en Corine van Nw Weteringsewg 39 3737 MG 36 47
Beerschoten H van Veldln 6 3737 AP 19 18
Beerschoten Auto-taxibdr Groenekansewg 166 3737 AK 15 73
Beerschoten Mr H J van Ruigenhoeksedk 5 3737 MP 14 76

Begrafenis- en Crematieonderneming Tap BV
Soestdijksewg Z 265 3721 AE BILTHOVEN **(030)28 37 41**

Begrafenis/Crematie Uitvaartcentr Barbara
Egginkln 51 3527 XP UTRECHT **(030)94 76 45**
miv oktober 1995 (030)296 66 66

Begrafenis en Crematieondern Agterberg BV W Heukelsln 50 (030)51 09 82
dag en nacht bereikbaar
Begrafenisverzorging Bruyn de Schutmeesterwg 14 (03469)17 11
Beltman J J Groenekansewg 85A 3737 AC 29 03
Berendsen T H W J Groenekansewg 102 3737 AJ 24 20
Berg S vd Kon Wilhelminawg 429 3737 BD 12 95
Berg D vd Putterln 123 3722 WR BILTHOVEN (030)29 32 16
directeur schildersbedrijf peperkamp bv
Berg A P vd Aannemersbedryf Voordorpsedk 10 3737 BK (030)73 24 42
fax > (030)73 24 42
Berg G vd Ruigenhoeksedk 15 3737 MP 23 34
Bergh G vd Kon Wilhelminawg 403 3737 BD 16 63
Beste Vof ten Kon Wilhelminawg 470 3737 BJ 40 99
Bevama Tuinbemesting B van Maanen Nw Weteringsewg 51 3737 MG 20 75
Beyleveldt A R Oranjeln 10 3737 AT 27 67
Beyloo D P M Cafebdr Kon Wilhelminawg 435 3737 BD 13 08
Bicker A J Kon Wilhelminawg 483 3737 BG 27 56
Biggelaar J A M vd Copynln 26 3737 AW 20 99
Blaauwendraad, ds. B.J. Copijnlaan 30 3737 AW AMERONGEN (03436)17 31
Blauwendraad G Nw Weteringsewg 26 3737 MD 13 88
Blauwendraat J C Nw Weteringsewg 42 3737 MD 17 08
Bleijenberg H Lindenln 22 3737 RD 37 44
Bloemers H Groenekansewg 2 3737 AG 34 71
Boekhout J Ruigenhoeksedk 16 3737 MN 27 51
Boerrigter T J Vyverln 37 3737 RG 30 62

Telefoonnummers 225

A page (290 x 210 mm) from the first of the new directories: for Nieuwegein, Utrecht, Zeist, October 1994.

contexts. It also means that the old dichotomy of 'modern' versus 'traditional' is swept away: any means are used, as appropriate. No wonder that this approach should get along so well in the liberal and open Dutch society. At the back of Martin Majoor's typography is the painstaking and critical spirit of his most important teacher at the Arnhem school of art, Alexander Verberne. It is in the work of Verberne and several of that generation of Dutch typographers (born around 1930) that one can find the first flourish of this 'Motra' typography: something to place against the shallowness of 'Pomo' and the up-its-own-arseness of 'Decon'.

Having got the go-ahead to work up their ideas, Schelvis and Majoor worked intensively to meet a March 1993 deadline. A trial printed specimen from that time shows their early ideas intact. Numbers were still before names; though this idea was later reluct- antly discarded, at the wish of the client. Final approval came at the end of 1993, after a presentation to PTT Telecom and TeleMedia.

For the typeface design, Majoor relied significantly on collab- oration with his 'Motra' buddy, Fred Smeijers, another Verberne- student and designer of the full-blooded sixteenth-twentieth- century Low-Countries typeface Quadraat. Schelvis worked on the overall 'information-wayfinding' design of the book.

True to his education, Majoor first drew the letters in pencil on paper: still the best way to think visually. Smeijers helped with digitizing the letters and so naturally provided Majoor with neces- sary critical dialogue. A leading feature of the new design was the wish to maximize the difference of weight between names in bold and addresses in medium. Majoor interestingly cut a corner here by testing degrees of weight with another typeface: the Adobe Multiple- Masters font Myriad. From satisfactory experiments with this type- face, he could read off stroke widths and apply them to his new design.

Here we should step back and contrast this project with its predecessors in the Netherlands and elsewhere. There is one large difference. Martin Majoor was working in Ikarus and then Fonto- grapher to produce PostScript Type 1 outline fonts – for typesetting on Scitex machines that also use PostScript. So there was nothing in between the designed and the output forms. The last landmark in phone book typefaces, Bell Centennial (designed by Matthew Carter in 1978), is a low-resolution bitmap typeface for CRT typesetting machines. It incorporates all the 'spikes' and 'inktraps' necessary to appear untouched by the double ordeal of this typesetting process and high-speed web-offset printing on short-life paper. After tests, Majoor found that such compensations for formal distortion were hardly necessary. This and the effectively unrestricted character set – by contrast to the severe constraints that Crouwel suffered and enjoyed – gave Majoor and his colleagues much greater freedom. But now some new constraints of content appeared: post codes, fax and mobile numbers, advertisements.

The new phone book typography follows a complex, double-pronged course. For the list itself, Majoor made a robust and sim-plified 'industrial' typeface (Telefont List), which does without the refinements of small caps, non-lining numbers, ligatures and kern-ing pairs. Initial capital letters and word-spaces are deployed, rather than the lowercase and punctuation of the Crouwel design. Turn-over lines are indented: a procedure that helps meaning, but of-fends tidy-minded modernist dogma. Post codes are set in reduced-size capitals. But in the typically flexible 'Motra' spirit, for the introductory pages Martin Majoor designed a variant typeface for continuous text: Telefont Text. Here characters are a little expanded in width, capital height is larger, x-height less, and the full resources of small caps and non-lining numbers are provided.

The typography of the new Dutch phone book certainly possess-es an air of visual assurance that is lacking in books still conceived in the vernacular-grotesque tradition (this includes the British Tel-ecom redesign of 1989). Any doubts that one has are connected more with its editorial conventions. Thus, the heavy visual emphasis given to names and initials runs counter to the habitual Dutch prac-tice of ordering strings of the same name alphabetically by street-name, rather than by a person's first names. Could punctuation have helped to sort out and clarify the letters that follow on from a surname, especially complex in Dutch orthography? In these condi-tions of space-scarcity, and given the boldness of the typeface here, one can understand the designers' wish to do without extra marks. Majoor's intentions are set out in a specification that runs to 60 pages of A4.

The issue of the first book, for the Utrecht region, has met with some criticism from users. People and businesses have been left out of the book, and there is considerable inconsistency in the conventions of presenting and ordering entries in the list. This is a data preparation and coding fault, and will be corrected by the PTT and its partner TeleMedia.

The new phone books will survive these teething faults: a very workable typographic foundation has been laid. And while all this was going on, Karel Martens (one of Majoor's teachers at Arnhem) was working on a marvellous set of standard phone cards for the PTT, issued also in 1994. So it is clear that responsible and lively public design is still possible in the age of privatization. At least it is in the Netherlands.

Eye, no. 16, 1995

This piece was suggested to Rick Poynor at *Eye*, who was happy to publish it. I conducted a formal, taped interview with my friend Martin Majoor, to get the quite complex details of the story right. I was happy to make propaganda for Martin's 'Motra' idea – though the acronym was lost in *Eye*'s publication of the text.

LettError: Nypels Prize 2000

The latest Charles Nypels Prize for typography was awarded last November to Erik van Blokland and Just van Rossum – together, 'LettError' – at the Jan van Eyck Akademie in Maastricht. This was the sixth award of the prize, which is given in recognition of a significant body of work. The previous recipients have been Diter Rot (1986), Walter Nikkels (1989), Harry Sierman (1992), Pierre di Sciullio (1996), and *Emigre* (1998). Charles Nypels was a printer and publisher in Maastricht, and a notable contributor to the 'fine printing' culture of the Netherlands in the first half of the twentieth century (he died in 1952). The prize given in his name followed the establishment in 1985 of the Nypels Foundation, by William PARS

Graatsma, then director of the Jan van Eyck Akademie. The prize is very much tied in with the local politics of that school, and with its situation in Limburg: that finger of Dutch territory that extends down into the Catholic and French-inflected heartland of old Europe, between Germany and what is now Belgium.

Just van Rossum (born in 1966) and Erik van Blokland (1967) now have ten years of work behind them. Soon after finishing at the Royal Academy at The Hague, they jumped into the headlines of the typographic world with their randomized font Beowolf. When it was presented at the Type 90 conference at Oxford, it was already causing some stir in the normally placid typographic waters, and was seen as a provocation, a Dada joke, but with a serious core. Beowolf and other early typefaces from Van Rossum and Van Blokland – Trixie, Just LeftHand and Erik RightHand, Advert – were among the first typefaces to be published, on the FontFont label, by FontShop, the distribution company that Erik and Joan Spiekermann had established in Berlin in 1988. Through the 1990s, the progress of FontShop and LettError was intertwined: Van Rossum and Van Blokland did much behind-the-scenes work for the company, as well as for Erik Spiekermann himself and for MetaDesign. At the Nypels award ceremony this was acknowledged by Spiekermann in a touching and powerful encomium.

As their work developed it became clear that Van Blokland and Van Rossum – or better, Erik and Just (the least pretentious people I know) – are more than type designers. One can say that they are systems designers, and type has been just one of the systems that they have designed. The small book published to mark the prize gives the first overview of their œuvre, and it lets us distinguish one from another. Just is more interested in type design, and has done some quite straightforward and assured work in this field. It is clear that, if need be – and thank goodness it needn't – he could make yet another humanist sanserif or the fortieth Garamond. Erik is less of a type designer, more of an illustrator. One suspects that his great gift for drawing would flourish if he had time for it: perhaps it is something for his retirement. Both are programmers, who came out of the culture of teenage-bedroom computer fascination, but went on to do something more serious with their skills. Their greatest quality is that they are sharp thinkers. It is this intelligence that

Erik van Blokland and Just van Rossum at the Nypels Prize ceremony in Maastricht, 3 November 2000. The two puppets Typoman and Crocodile (held by Erik and Just, left and right, respectively) are the stars of one of their inventions, the live-animation system called PoppeKast. (Photograph by Carry van Blokland-Mobach.)

sets their work apart from the many digital graphic designers who emerged through the 1990s with claims to be doing something new. It is clear now, if it was not already at the time, that much of what was published in the 'new typography' anthologies and surveys of the 1990s was very dull work: because merely formal, without a genuine idea in its head.

What are the ideas of LettError? Their attempt has been to take a step or two back and ask what the tools could do. While typography and design more generally has loved the definitive statement – the defined, described achievement – LettError has investigated how things might change, and how you might set up a system that accommodates and provides useful change. One can see this even in the progression from Beowolf, which had an excess of variation and to no great effect, to the Flipper fonts that followed. In these a limited set of alternative characters is deployed, just enough to give the impression of infinite variety; variations of position, just as important as character form, can be introduced. There is a pleasing economy to the way they think. This shows itself not just in the will to routinize drudgery – every computer geek proclaims this – but in such gems as the map of the characters of LettError fonts, sorted from narrowest and tallest to widest and shortest. With colour coding of fonts, one can see how the fonts cluster in their physical properties.

The Nypels award is a celebration, and an occasion for reflection. My sense is that Just and Erik have not yet found the material to match their intelligence. They have been good inventors, and often very funny deadpan critics. For example their 'Stamp Machine' is both a system for designing stamps (or any graphic item with those particular needs), and I take it also as a joke about the endless production of stamps in the designed-to-death culture of the Netherlands. The potential for a system like this could be great, but the immediate application is slight. One can say the same about Erik's Federal fonts: pleasant, but very small beer. The real thing here is the scripting that makes possible this customized shading of imitation Americana, and one day it must find more worthwhile applications.

Designers only exist in the context of their culture, their social circumstances, which they both help to make and are made by. If these remarks about a failure of application have any truth in them, then this must be partly a consequence of the larger culture, and especially the clients who might commission the work. Is this a request for Erik and Just to put on suits and ties and bury themselves in forms-design work for the Ministry of Social Security? Maybe they should go a little way in that direction, though without the neckwear. But it's a perilous business, and the culture has shifted over the ten years of their activity. In this period the very serious endeavour of MetaDesign has gone from a local involvement with public sector design, to a dispersed and hardly tangible servicing of international corporations. LettError is well out of that. But one hopes, very much, for their good client to materialize.

Eye, no. 39, 2001

Evaluations

What is a typeface?

If you were to ask 'what is a person?', I might assume that you were a philosopher exploring notions of identity and selfhood, or perhaps someone who has been unsettled into questioning the assumptions through which we unthinkingly live our lives. People with a radical loss of certainty on this question tend to fall out of expected routines and then we call them mad. There is less at stake in the question 'what is a typeface?' We are talking not about the abyss of our selves, created by God or by accident or some other unknowable factor, but merely about a class of things that we make and over which we thus have some control. But if this question is more open to reasoning and seems simple enough at first glance – after all, as designers we use typefaces all the time, and even more so (in another way) as readers – the more one thinks about the question of what a typeface is, the less simple it becomes. This brief consideration will not provide any single straightforward answer to the question: what it will attempt is a tour through some of the issues, hoping to bring to light difficulties that may not have been recognized, and thus to clarify a situation of considerable muddle.

Problems of definition

A dictionary definition runs as follows: 'Typeface: the design of, or the image produced by, the surface of a printing type' (*Shorter Oxford English Dictionary*). This looks helpful: at once we can separate 'the type' from 'the face'. And, now that metal composition in printing is all but extinct, the early and precise meaning of the word 'type' can be recovered: 'a small rectangular block, usually of metal or wood, having on its upper end a raised letter, figure, or other character, for use in printing'. But the definition refers to just 'a' printing type: it has no conception of the set of related images that goes to make up, say, the typeface Baskerville. (Let us agree for the moment that 'Baskerville' is an example of a typeface.) The word most commonly used to describe this set of images is 'fount' or 'font' (American spelling, but it seems to be gaining acceptance everywhere else), which the dictionary defines as: 'a complete set

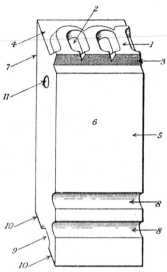

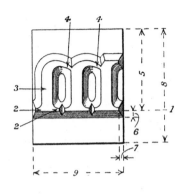

Fig. 3.—*Isometric view of type.*
(2½ times full size.)

1. The face.
2. The counter.
3. The neck (or beard).
4. The shoulder.
5. The stem or shank.
6. The front.
7. The back.
8. The nicks.
9. The heel-nick or groove.
10. The feet.
11. The pin-mark or drag.

Fig. 4.—*Plan of type.*
(2½ times full size.)

1. The line.
2. Serifs.
3. Main-stroke.
4. Hair-line.
5. Line-to-back.
6. Beard.
7. Side-wall.
8. Body.
9. Set.

The body-wise dimension of the face is called the gauge.

1   A type in the days of metal composition and certainty: a rectangular piece of metal, with its own topography and highly developed nomenclature. On the face of the type lay an image: the typeface.
(From: Legros & Grant.)

of type of a particular face and size'. The word 'font', even more than 'type', belongs to the days when molten metal was poured into adjustable moulds in type foundries. But that need not forbid its transference to the technology of light and electrical pulses, for it suggests the idea of a reservoir of images, ready to flow when the keyboard is tapped. (As an aside, one may observe that it is hard to find any excuse, apart from laziness, for carrying over a term like 'leading' to non-metal printing.) There is, however a problem in the dictionary's specification of size: that made sense in the days when

114

Tonight's big match

Edward Woodward v the KGB.

2   When is Bembo not Bembo? When it has a Baskerville 'g' in it?
     Typefaces put through the wash by manufacturers of photocomposing
     machines do not always come out as you knew them in their metal days.

a font of 8 point type was bought by weight and came wrapped in
brown paper, and when the 8 point images were subtly different
from the 10 point images of the same typeface, but hardly applies to
composing from a single or limited set of master images to be projected to any desired size. Perhaps we could keep the word 'font' but
loosen its definition, to become just 'the complete set of characters
(not 'type' any more) of a particular face'.

At this point, when one is in danger of becoming bogged down
in terminology, it might be helpful to remind ourselves that not
everyone conducts their lives in English, and that there are other
words for the concept of typeface. In Dutch, for example, the word
'lettertype' is in current use: this sounds at first like a duplication
of sense, if one still assumes that 'type' means visual images (as
in 'Baskerville is one of my favourite types'). But if we remember
the deeper meaning of 'type', as a pattern or model or something
typical, then 'lettertype' begins to make sense. The concept is of a
set of letters that are models, from or after which reproductions
are made: thus the idea of printing is inherent in the word 'type'.

If 'letter' (in Dutch and in English too) means any alphabetic sign, however produced, then 'lettertype' describes those letters that are composed, for printed reproduction, rather than uniquely written. The German word 'Schrift' works similarly, in that it encompasses both writing and printing: one just has to specify 'Handschrift' or 'Druckschrift'. Similarly the French word 'caractère' can refer to both written forms and those designed for composition. It begins to seem as if English-speakers are rather handicapped in having this word 'typeface' that demarcates so strongly between letters for composition (and printing) and written letters. How often has one heard uninitiated speakers groping for the words: having to stretch 'writing' to cover composed letters, or making 'printing' describe any kind of text or perhaps letters that are written with extra care.

Faces and families

Despite the seemingly fortuitous, purely English-language nature of the connection between type 'faces' and human ones, it is hard to resist some attempt to follow the implied analogy. It might be that a typeface is made up of elements (its letters or characters) which are like the parts of the human visage: ears, eyes, nose, mouth, and perhaps finer sub-divisions. The parts have their own expected formal properties: we know what a mouth is, and – taking an enormous leap into the particular – we know what her mouth is like. And, so the analogy would go, we know what a 'g' is and – again jumping to the particular – we know what a Baskerville 'g' is like. This analogy could be pushed a little further. The parts, though formally different, should fit together: the 'g' should look as though it belongs with every other character; her mouth sorts with every other element of her face, becoming part of a whole that is unique (thus the photograph on her passport, or in her lover's wallet). At this point one introduces ideas of value and perhaps beauty. Do some mouths fit their faces better than others? Do some faces launch more ships?

At this level of direct comparison the analogy soon becomes absurd. One descends into arguments about the conceptual integrity of the nostrils (separate from the nose? as a pair or individually?) and other such diversions. Anthropomorphism has its uses and its pleasures, but has severe limits too: letters are made by human beings, but are not human outgrowths.

3   It is hard to resist an analogy between the faces on types and those on human bodies: theories of form in letters have been built on it, especially by the Renaissance humanists. But if metaphors using the human body are inevitable, one should remember that letters are constructions and not outgrowths. (From: Tory.)

Proceeding from the face to larger categories, there are further and stronger analogies to be made, which are validated at least by custom. Faces belong to families: daughters look like mothers; nephews may bear some resemblance to aunts; one might guess that he comes from Scotland (pale skin, red hair, and the features of a diet of much sugar and not much vitamin C). So we might speak about the family relations between variations of Monotype Baskerville: series 169 (medium), series 312 (bold), and series 313 (semibold). Or we could discuss resemblances between English and German branches of the family: say Monotype Baskerville and Stempel Baskerville. Or we might speak of affinities between the Baskerville families and other members of the category of eighteenth-century transitional typefaces (the products of a certain set of historical factors and circumstances, over and above the contributions of individual punchcutters). Many attempts at the classification of typefaces have been made in this latter spirit: the structuring of knowledge in tree-form is by now an ingrained habit of human thought and it works well enough with typefaces, as with any historically developing collection of human artefacts.

Family members

This attempt to identify members of the Baskerville dynasty raises some awkward questions that it will now be as well to tackle head on. John Baskerville of Worcester and Birmingham (1707–75) designed some sets of types (rectangular pieces of metal ...), both uppercase (or capitals or majuscules) and lowercase (or small letters or minuscules), both roman (upright?) and italic (or cursive). All these letterforms had a similar weight and a similar lateral proportion: he designed no bold or light, no expanded or contracted versions. Additions to the family, notably bold versions, came later. The concept of a bold typeface arose during the nineteenth century, when heavier typefaces began to be used for differentiation and emphasis within text set in letters of what now became 'medium' weight. At first these letters were necessarily of a different style: of another typeface. Typically this bold typeface was a Clarendon, and for some printers 'Clarendon' and 'bold' were still synonymous years after the first related bolds had been designed. With the advent of machine-aided punchcutting, mechanical typesetting, and the designer (as against the humble punchcutter), there could develop the idea of a family of related variants of weight, contraction/expansion, and other formal mutations. Cheltenham (designed by Bertram Goodhue, c. 1900) is often cited as an early instance of such a type family.

This development of an auxiliary for variations on a norm can also be seen early on in the history of printing, in the gradual recognition of italic as a complement to roman. The first italic printing types (those used by Aldus Manutius) were cut in the attempt to recreate the handwriting of contemporary humanist scholars. The idea behind the first italics, so Harry Carter argued, was not mere utilitarian space-saving, but rather that the new type 'savoured of learning and was intimate'. Though, by the middle sixteenth century in France, one begins to see italic being used within roman text for purposes of differentiation. Success in this function depended on the design of italics that married well with their roman norm: of a matching height and weight, and sharing certain formal properties (thus not too 'cursive' or handwritten in appearance), but nevertheless a different set of forms. And were italics thus different typefaces?

There is an interesting cultural difference that has survived

Sur quoy vous me permettrés de vous demander en cette occaſion , ce que, comme i'ay des-ia remarqué, [a] S. Auguſtin demande aux Donatiſtes en vne ſemblable occurrence : *Quoy donc ? lors que nous liſons , oublions nous comment nous auons accouſtumé de parler ? l'eſcriture du grand Dieu deuoit-elle vſer auèc nous d'autre langage que le noſtre?* Puis que Ieſus Chriſt dit clairement

---

4   Italic, though it may have started life as an alternative to roman, soon came to be used as a necessary complement to roman (upright) letters, for purposes of differentiation. (From: Updike.)

even into our present homogenized and multinationalized world of typography. In German-language countries, italic is still termed 'Kursiv': the implication is of a letter that circulates, fluently, and thus – head into the wind – of necessity has those typical forms and that characteristic slope. And German and Swiss type manufacturers still give a 'Kursiv' its own series number, different from that of the upright norm: as if in response to the essential otherness of italic letterforms, seen from a cultural perspective in which the norm was for so long a letterform (blackletter) that had no cursive partner.

It is a question of the assimilation of the foreigner. For the parts of the world that have been using roman (i.e. derived from Italy) typography for all or most of their printing history, roman (upright) and italic (into the wind) are inseparable partners and combine to form one typeface. Bold, the dark newcomer with a doubtful background in commerce, has staked a claim. But in traditionally minded circles, where voices are not raised, his face is still

Type, cost of, per pound, 301–02
  delivery-knives, pivotal caster, 306
  description, 10–11
  design, 24–33, 118–20
    accurate inaccuracies, 24, 28–29
    classification by form of serif, 29–33
    illusions, 24–28
    influence of body-size, 118, 120, 121, 122, 123
      illusion on form of characters, 28–29
    new, essentials of, 118–20
    totally new letter, 36
Type, direction of movement in Paige compositor
    383–84
  distribution by hand, 7, **316**
  dot, 10, 11
  earliest movable, 6
  edge-upon-edge in magazine, Paige, 378
  ejecting in Monotype, 261
  enlargements of, 123
Type faces, 82–120, 685–86
  absence of standard nomenclature, **33**
  accuracy of, 116–18
  a–z lengths of, 90–92
  classification, 29–33, 82–83, 86–88

5   In the nineteenth century, thicker typefaces flourished and were increasingly used with those of medium weight, for purposes of emphasis. As previously with italic, bold variants began to be designed as part of the armoury of a typeface. (From: Legros & Grant.)

rather an aberration and numbered as separate. Light has risked a converse fate among traditionalists: altogether too weak, his manhood in doubt. Though here one ought to add that the whole question of traditionalist attitudes to bold and light is undercut by an initial unease with sanserif, whose rise has so much enabled the development of these variants.

    History and technology have forced the issue of what sets of letterforms may be considered to constitute a typeface. The concept of the type family, as it was developed in typefaces such as Cheltenham and Gill Sans, received a systematic overhaul with the design of Univers in the 1950s. It is clear that 'Univers' is the typeface, and that 'Univers Medium', 'Univers Medium Condensed', and so on, are variants within the overarching concept: fonts perhaps, depending on whether or not a font ('complete set of type') includes both capitals and lowercase. Since the appearance of Univers, and with the further development of photocomposition and then of digital processing of letters, the idea of the typeface as a large family of variants has become normal. A single set of master patterns – the patriarchal metaphor is significant – may now provide the basis for theoretically limitless variants of weight, expansion/contraction,

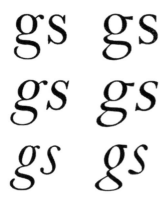

6   Italic means more than just inclined to the right: if a 'sloped roman' is more logical than an italic, is it as satisfying visually and semantically?

slope, and other formal deviations. If this opens up ideal vistas – for example, we might think that, at the press of a button, a true 'sloped roman' can be generated – it has also brought much unhappiness. To return to the family metaphor, the situation has become one, not even of incest and inbreeding, but of self-generation (perhaps parthenogenesis). The family members have become grotesque mutations of the father: forcibly reduced or enlarged, or distorted by genetic manipulation. No longer the dialectic of sheer difference and extraordinary complementarity that one may find in a well-matched roman and italic. In an 'italic' produced by deforming a roman master, the wife can be no more than a subservient echo of the husband. This has been true of the most simple-minded and cheapest photocomposition systems of recent years. But with further technical development and with the incursion of typographically enlightened designers into machine-systems design and typeface production, there is the prospect of a recovery of quality.

Here one should mention the development of computer-aided design systems: the Ikarus system, under Peter Karow in Hamburg, and Meta-Font under Donald Knuth at Stanford (California). In particular, the debate over Meta-Font provides much food for thought

The LORD is my shepherd;
    I shall not want.
He maketh me to lie down
            in green pastures:
        he leadeth me
            beside the still waters.
He restoreth my soul:
        he leadeth me
            in the paths of righteousness
            for his name's sake.
Yea, though I walk through the valley
            of the shadow of death,
        I will fear no evil:
    for thou art with me;
        thy rod and thy staff
        they comfort me.
Thou preparest a table before me
            in the presence of mine enemies:
        thou anointest my head with oil,
            my cup runneth over.
Surely goodness and mercy
            shall follow me
            all the days of my life:
        and I will dwell
            in the house of the LORD
            for ever.

7   Donald Knuth's Meta-Font, a system for designing families of fonts,
    has upset notions of what a typeface is. Here a font is put through its
    paces, by a continual variation of parameters.
    (From: Knuth, 1982.)

on the question of what a typeface is. As its name indicates, this is
not a typeface in the sense of a font or a family of fonts, but rather
'a schematic description of how to draw a family of fonts'. Knuth
aims to give designers the tool (in the form of computer software)
with which to design a family of fonts, along any desired lines. One
should make clear that he has disclaimed the suggestion that Meta-
Font could somehow be the generator of all possible fonts. Knuth's
own experiments in font design have taken Monotype Modern Extended 8A, long familiar to him in mathematical setting, as a basis

for re-creation and variation; though the variations go some way beyond this style model. The first results of Meta-Font were crude and a shock to sensitive palates, but greater sophistication has been achieved. It is clear that Knuth's experiments have the power to unsettle many assumptions about letterforms and their design.

Identity and value

One argument provoked by Meta-Font concerns the sufficient conditions for a particular letter to be recognized as such: what does an 'A' need to possess in order for it to be seen as an 'A'? It is an argument with an ancient pedigree, but one given new impetus by the need to write descriptions of letters for computers. So, what is an 'A'? Is there some ghostly Platonic form that lies behind every 'A', however wild or improbable the typeface? To take a very simple example, consider a stencilled capital A, in which the cross-bar does not (of necessity) touch the main vaulting strokes. How large can the gaps become before the 'A' ceases to be recognizable? Or can we perhaps recognize it (particularly in the context of a word) without any third stroke? Such matters of minute visual distinction come into play at every point, with every character, and there is no need to indulge in any West-Coast celebration of Creativity to see that what constitutes the identity of a letter is an extraordinarily complex matter, informed by history and culture as well as by the particular context of perception. To write all that into a computer program would be a long job.

The identity of letters was earlier discussed by a less sophisticated argufier than Knuth or his critics: Eric Gill. Without much hesitation – though resisting dogmatism – Gill decided on the principle of norms, which, it transpired, approximated to those of Edward Johnston's sanserif letters and his own Gill Sans in their medium weights. With norms come values: for Gill, some versions of a letter might be 'decent', others 'comic' or 'vulgar', and another 'a poor thing, but might be worse'. Gill thought, and we might agree with him, that fancy letters were a consequence of the pressures of advertising and the search for incessant novelty. But whatever the motivation behind letterforms, what one judges first of all is their appearance: their visual performance.

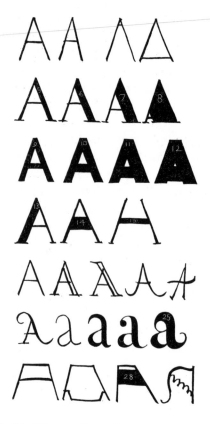

8 Eric Gill struggled to define 'the A-ness of A': he decided that there
   were norms (roughly those of Gill Sans medium) and that other forms
   were deviations, some more acceptable than others. (From: Gill.)

Property rights

Dismissing notions of essences, we may confidently state that sets
of letterforms only exist as particular visual manifestations. Yes, but
where do they exist? To return to metal type, is it in the drawings for
characters, or in the punches, or the matrices, or the types, or the
printed images? Similar conundrums arise in the case of other composition techniques and are real problems, because at each stage
of the process the image is slightly different. They are also real
problems for any designer or manufacturer trying to register the
copyright of a typeface. It does seem to be an indication of the col-

124

lective uncertainty over what a typeface is that no really satisfactory protection has been devised for typeface designs, even allowing for some measure of bad faith among manufacturers and the difficulties of enforcing international law.

When does a reworking of an established style model (say 'Garamond') qualify as new and original, and thus become eligible for copyright? The 'fancier' the typeface (to use Gill's word), the more obviously 'original' it becomes. Though even in the field of decorative display letters, it must be getting hard to find novelty. There is some paradox in the axiom, so frequently asserted, that the best (most readable) typefaces are those that are least noticeable, least eccentric, least new and original. Perhaps typeface designers should content themselves with the compliment that imitation or copying constitutes, or else give up drawing and devote themselves to writing computer programs for typeface production, which can be scrambled and which seem to be more open to copyright legislation (at least in the USA).

Here one might mention very simple typefaces: typewriter faces or, even more clearly, dot matrix letters. At what point do they become so simple as to cease to have any interesting identity? At some point, the constraints become so great, and the scope for formal invention so restricted, that the element of conspicuous originality will disappear. Are these fonts typefaces? Does the concept of typeface imply a certain level of formal complexity?

Identity in action

There are grounds for adopting a roughly existentialist view of the identity of a typeface: lying there passively in its font disc, or arrayed in twenty-six character equally-spaced strings of nonsense in a specimen book, it hasn't really started to live. Only when composed and printed as text does it begin to take on some recognizable identity. On this view, a typeface has no definite identity. It merely exists differently (though perhaps characteristically) in innumerable different contexts: as composed in words of a particular language, printed with a particular quantity of ink on a certain paper, viewed under particular conditions.

These may be quite minute distinctions, especially nowadays in the age of litho. But letterpress printing in the era of the hand press and hand-made paper provided clear instances of the difference between the typeface in its first state (as cut) and the typeface in action. The typefaces from those years, up to around 1800, cannot be properly understood without seeing them as printed. The fate of Caslon typefaces in the era of powered printing on machine-made paper provides a notorious instance of misunderstanding: spindly forms, which had been designed to blossom when sunk into damp paper, remained spindly on dry, smooth paper. To a lesser extent, one can observe the misunderstanding at work in the transfer, without adjustment, of hot-metal faces to photocomposition and litho printing. Monotype Garamond works, but Monophoto Garamond does not.

All this implies an enlarged sense of the 'design' of a typeface: to understand by this just the forms in their unsullied, pre-printed or pre-transmitted state, is to have a false idea of design. The design job – as any reasonable designer knows – includes an anticipation of the thing in use: this has to be built into the drawings or the computer program.

At least as important as printing process for this view of a typeface is the typographic treatment of the text: how long is the measure, how much space between the words and between lines. All this affects our perception of the typeface, though these factors lie outside the sphere over which the typeface designer can have any influence. But there is one area of space that the designer of a typeface may dispute with those in charge of the composition of the letters, and which has a vital effect on the appearance of the typeface: between the letters. One can state without much fear of contradiction – certainly not from any typeface designer – that the space around the letter, between one letter and the next, is an essential factor in defining the appearance of those letterforms. Beauty and recognizability depend on an intricate interplay of space and form: a balancing act that requires enormous attention to set up (one might consider every possible combination of characters) and which can be ruined by the press of a button on a composing machine.

For our purposes here, in trying to clarify the concept of a typeface, consideration of the space between letters is helpful in differentiating a typeface from a mere collection of letterforms. Not only is a typeface a set of letterforms designed for repetition and reproduction, but it is a set that is designed to be composed. The letterforms must become types, units for combination in planned ways: so the space between the letters is part of the design. This view casts some doubt on the status of dry transfer lettering as typeface: certainly the letterforms are unit-types and do come with a system of letterspacing indicated (though not in the early days). It is just that the system of spacing is in the hands (literally) of the compositor, without physical constraint. This is an ambiguous benefit. But, as well as much naive setting (it is certainly easier to butt them all up together), one has seen impoverished back-bedroom designers (pencils in a jam-jar, cat lolling on the desk) rubbing down whole pages of text with marvellous sensitivity.

Size and scale

There was once (1972) a dispute in the correspondence columns of *The Times* that ran under the headline 'London's type face'. A complaint about the apparent predominance of sanserif on shop and street signs was answered by defenders of that letterform, as being appropriate for display purposes, if not for books. The exchange was concluded by a firm statement from Nicolete Gray: 'Sir', she wrote, 'type faces are designed for printing on paper and reading at close quarters. Street lettering, whether directional or architectural, for shop fascias or for advertising, is required to be executed in totally different materials, on a different scale, and for a different sort of reading'. This broad distinction is clear and one that most people would recognize, though any attempt to draw an exact boundary between 'typefaces' and 'street lettering' would soon run into difficulty, especially if one includes, within the category of 'typeface', (small) letters not for printing, but, say, for screen projection. The more decisive criterion for this distinction seems to be not size but space. Thus one returns to the distinction between letters standardized as types for composition – this could include large neon displays – and letters that are not types but mere 'lettering', without any inbuilt systems of inter-character spacing or horizontal alignment.

The extreme case of street lettering does however help to illustrate clearly a point that is true for all sizes of letter: that a particular form has an appropriate size. Just as we feel that a certain painted

Caslon Caslon Caslon Caslon

9 Sets of letterforms have their own optimum size, and so forms of letters need to be modified for composition at different sizes. One can see
traditional optical scaling at work by bringing different sizes of a metal
typeface to a common size (here 72, 48, 24, 8 point, from: Williamson).
Photocomposition has encouraged the neglect of this subtlety.

image has an optimum size, so – more subtly, but even more decisively – it is clear that a certain letterform composes well at a certain
size: the size at which the forms were designed to compose. For
example, the smallest sizes of Monotype Times were designed with
special care, for the special purposes of newspaper setting (classi-
fied advertisements, and so on), and are clearer and nicer (and more
legible?) than the rather gross forms of 10 point and upwards. Thus
one may speak (as Harry Carter did) of an 'optical scale' in typeface
design. The logic of this, as every punchcutter knew, and as every
good software designer is trying to reassert, is that the letterforms
of a typeface must be adjusted for every size at which they are to
be used. So, again, the simple, single typeface comes into question.
The best, most sophisticated typefaces cannot be represented by a
single set of drawings or images, but consist of a series of modula-
tions on some perhaps notional standard. Not only may a typeface
then consist of a family of variants (italic, bold, and so on), but, if it
is to work properly at every size, it should consist of sets of variants
of these variants.

Uncertain times

If difficulties over the concept of typeface are to some extent just a
problem of the English language, they cannot be dismissed as nothing more than that. Out there in the real world, there is a referent
for the concept, and a referent that is subject to the pressures of
human dealings and history: it is not fixed or immutable. One might
sketch an analogy: the more stable, nineteenth-century, Western
world of men and women with a home, a family, a trade, a network
of continuing relationships, is being lost under the pressures of
suburbanization, migration, transnational capitalism. Human identities become uncertain in these conditions. So too the identities of

typefaces, and the very concept of them, have been undermined, most obviously by the demise of metal composition and letterpress printing; though it is clear that, throughout the history of printing, typefaces have never been stable entities (witness the development of italic and bold). But when typefaces were cast on metal bodies, it was certainly easier to think that one had a framework for those images. Now that these faces are fragmented into digital bit-maps, and enjoy only a half-life through screens or ink-jet printers, such delusions are less possible to maintain. Recognition of this state of affairs may bring consolation: there is some pleasure to be taken in the dissolution of myths. If the concept was imprecise from the start, it has now become so vague as to be dangerous. It is good to be clear about that, and say exactly what one means.

Bibliography

Bigelow, Charles, 'Technology and the aesthetics of type', *The Seybold Report*, vol. 10, no. 4, 1981

—, 'The principles of digital type', *The Seybold Report*, vol. 11, no. 11 & no. 12, 1982

Carter, Harry, *A view of early typography*, Oxford: Clarendon Press, 1969

—, 'Optical scale in typefounding', *Typography*, no. 4, 1937

Gill, Eric, *An essay on typography*, Sheed & Ward, 1931

Knuth, Donald, 'The concept of Meta-Font', *Visible Language*, vol. 16, no. 1, 1982; and further discussion in vol. 16, no. 2 (1982) & vol. 17, no. 4 (1983)

—, 'Lessons learned from Meta-Font', *Visible Language*, vol. 19, no. 1, 1985

Legros, L. A. & J. C. Grant, *Typographical printing-surfaces*, Longmans Green, 1916

Tory, Geofroy, *Champfleury* [Paris, 1529], English translation: New York: Dover Books, 1967

Updike, D. B, *Printing types*, 2nd edn, Oxford University Press, 1937

Williamson, Hugh, *Methods of book design*, 2nd edn, Oxford University Press, 1966

Baseline, no. 7, 1986, pp. 14–18

This was the second of two articles that I wrote for Baseline, published by Esselte Letraset and edited – for just these two issues – by Erik Spieker-mann. (The first article was 'Universal faces, ideal characters', pp. 233–45 below.) Contributors were paid by the page, and this factor, together with the friendly and sympathetic editor, encouraged this ramble. The passage that discusses whether dry-transfer letters can really be type was cut by the editor: too obviously a swipe at the hand that was feeding us. It is reinstated here. A note of acknowledgement ran as follows: 'Some of the ideas put forward here were first raised for me in discussions in the seminar room at the Department of Typography, University of Reading, England (c. 1978); further help was given by Jane Howard, Paul Stiff, and Erik Spiekermann.'

Large and small letters:
authority and democracy

Hierarchies

Forget for a moment the precedence of speech and say that in the beginning was a single set of characters: ideograms becoming letters and numerals. In Greek and Roman antiquity these were developed into the familiar forms we know in English as 'capitals' (or in other languages as 'Großbuchstaben', 'majuscules', 'kapitalen' ...). The word brings with it the suggestion of being at the head ('caput' in Latin): the chief city of a country or the crowning feature of an architectural column. One might suppose that the application of the word to these letterforms is connected with this latter sense, for capital letters were to be found, most publicly and formally, in inscriptions placed 'at the head of' columns in built structures. Columns of stone and of text: the analogy with architecture is here, as elsewhere in typography, hard to resist.

The capital letters of Rome and its empire entered into the consciousness of Western cultures as *the* forms for letters. Think of the first letter of the alphabet and you probably think of two diagonals meeting at a point, with a cross-bar. Try to describe the lowercase 'a' in words, and you are in trouble, even before getting to the problem of whether it is a two- or single-storey form. Nicolete Gray once observed that the lack of a positive term (in English) for this other category of letters supports the idea that capitals are the essential forms.[1] And now that metal type is almost extinct, 'lowercase' may need to be explained: capitals (or majuscules or large letters) were kept in the upper of a stacked pair of cases, the minuscules or small letters lived below. That the old terms live on may be due to the upstairs/downstairs class distinction that attaches to the two kinds. Certainly for traditionally-minded people there are capitals – proper letters – and then, as a secondary matter, these other forms. This view was clearly expressed in one of the gospels of traditionalism, Stanley Morison's *First principles of typography*. Writing about title-pages, he insisted on capitals for book title and

1. Nicolete Gray, *Lettering on buildings*, Architectural Press, 1960, p. 53.

author's name, adding: 'As lower-case is a necessary evil, which we should do well to subordinate since we cannot suppress, it should be avoided when it is at its least rational and least attractive – in large sizes.'[2]

The most celebrated and influential public letters of Roman antiquity were proportionately square capitals, as on the Trajan column. At the same time another set of forms was in use: rustics. These letters were distinguished by narrow proportions and more flowing strokes. Rustic letters were used in less prominent situations and for less formal messages. For private, ephemeral communication there were free scripts, rather formless to our eyes. The coexistence of different forms for different purposes has persisted. Whether or not capitals are seen as the essential forms of letters, they are still generally accepted as the most suitable variety for public declarations, or in displayed text. Small letters are for quieter, more intimate uses: from one person to another.

This broad distinction may be true, but the matter becomes complicated by the fact that, for a millennium or so, we have been using large and small letters together, and this is where the game of 'upper or lower?' really starts. For typographers who are not traditionalist nor postmodernist, the difficult issue is not whether to set a whole word in capitals – the need for that may rarely arise – but whether to set its first letter with a capital. What are the conventions that help us to decide?

Rules of style

Capitalization could begin to become an issue from the time when texts were printed. With this multiplication in identical copies, the transcription of languages began to be standardized. Although manuscript production could be, and was, highly organized, the process of writing a text allowed a certain indeterminacy about how the language was to be orthographically 'dressed'. The very nature

2. Stanley Morison, *First principles of typography* (1930), 2nd edn, Cambridge: Cambridge University Press, 1967, p. 14. The arguments in Britain in the early 1960s over road-sign alphabets raised this question very publicly: seriffed capitals versus upper- and lowercase sanserif. The victory for the latter seemed to be a landmark for the late arrival of modernism in this country.

of printing, as a succession of distinct processes (copy preparation, composition, proofing, machining) encouraged a more detached attitude to the product, and allowed a much greater ability to control consistency of 'dress'. It took some centuries after Gutenberg for the issue of consistency to emerge clearly, in manuals laying down rules of style. But by the end of the eighteenth century, in the major Western languages, the wildest variations in spelling and capitalization had been brought to cultivated order.

The conventions for presenting printed language are specific to a language-community at a particular time; but within the community there may be subgroups following different practices. To take just the English language as printed in the late twentieth century, rules for capitalization may be outlined as follows. We agree that words should have initial capitals at the start of sentences and when they are proper names. The first category is clear; the second is not. There may be no argument over 'London', 'Mary' or 'Easter'. But what about 'Marxism', 'Gothic' and 'God'? The question of whether the deity (Deity) should be capitalized points to the strong cultural pressures at work here. Logic can only go so far. Even in a largely secular community, we still hesitate to set 'god' (a concept that can be disbelieved) and not 'God' (an undisputed primary being).

English-language practice shows some significant differences with that of comparably developed languages. The French seem more reasoned in their approach to capitalization. Thus in setting titles of books, say in a bibliography, the standard French style is 'first word and proper names only': *The life and adventures of Robinson Crusoe*; while an unenlightened English-language text would have *The Life and Adventures of Robinson Crusoe*. Applying this system to titles of periodicals brings some problems: one has *Illustrated London news* or *The guardian*, both of which may look odd. So perhaps this category of title should be regarded as a proper name and capitalized throughout.

The German case

German orthography is different and requires lengthier discussion. Like the history of its speakers – one is inclined to say – German is especially problematic. In all the politically and culturally various communities that constitute the German-speaking world, nouns are

1   Jakob Grimm, *Deutsche Grammatik*, 1st edn, 1819. (Same size.)

capitalized. In one doubtful respect this makes life easier. Evange-
lists and card-carrying atheists will treat 'Gott' (god) and 'Hund'
(dog) equally, for purely grammatical reasons. Yet there are many
fine judgements to be made over what exactly is a noun, especially
when in another context the same word might be an adjective or a
verb. See the long lists of rules and exceptions concerning this question in any manual of German orthography. Or consider such silly
sentences as 'Ich habe in Moskau liebe (Liebe) Genossen (genossen)', where the capitals tell the difference between what has been
found in Moscow: comrades (capital G) or something more intense
(capital L).

The convention of capitalizing nouns in German seems to have
been formally instituted in the eighteenth century. As in other lan-

fennen, kénden erweiflich, da henden auch auf bewun-
den (9ᵇ) reimt und fo verhält es fich mit einer menge
ungenauer reime in Roth. fragm. und kaiferchr., die
durch herftellung fcheinbarer niederd. formen genau werden würden. Ein näheres ftudium der freieren reim-
kunft kann aber grundfätze an hand geben, - nach wel-
chen fich mancher zweifel zwifchen hoch - und niederd.
urform in diefen gedichten löfen wird. Ähnliche dun-
kelheit, doch geringere, fchwebt über Heinr. v. Vel-
decks werken, den die mittelh. dichter felbft als den
gründer ihrer meifterfchaft anfehen, und deffen êneit
(oder ênêd im reim auf wârhêd 4ᵃ 102ᵃ) mir die haupt-
quelle mittelh. fprache fcheint. Dichtete er in niederd.
fprache und wurden feine arbeiten nachher in hochd.
umgefchrieben? oder bequemte er fich felbft zum hochd.
fo, daß er eigenheiten der angebornen mundart dabei
freien lauf ließ? Anders und in näherer beziehung auf
unfere buchftabenlehre ausgedrückt lautet diefelbe frage
fo: find eine menge ungenauer reime in Veld. werken
in genaue niederdeutfche zu verwandeln? oder als un-
genaue hochd. beizubehalten? Beiderlei anficht läßt
fich vertheidigen. Dafür daß der dichter in reiner mut-
terfprache dichtete, redet 1) feine herkunft aus weftpha-
len, fein aufenthalt am clever hof, wo er die êneit be-

2 Jakob Grimm, *Deutsche Grammatik*, 2nd edn, 1822. (Same size.)

guages, words were then heavily but rather indiscriminately capitalized. (One imagines that this was sometimes affected by the arbitrary factor of what was available in the typecase at that moment.)
While in other countries the rationalization of that time was towards a minimum of capitals, in German the opposite direction was
followed. Some enlightened voices spoke out against this convention. The most famous of these were Jakob and Wilhelm Grimm,
who formulated the criticisms that were to emerge again in the
twentieth century: the German language was written and printed in
ugly scripts that were hard to read, especially for foreigners, and
it suffered from irrational, wasteful capitalization. In his *Deutsche
Grammatik*, Jakob Grimm practised a reformed orthography, using
capitals just at sentence openings and for proper names. While

Schon war der raum gefüllt mit stolzen schatten

Die funken sprühten in gewundnen dämpfen

Es zuckten die gewesnen widerscheine

Bei edlen holden die urnächtig frühen.

Ihr zittern huschte auf metallnen glänzen

Begierig suchten sie sich zu verdichten

Umringten quälend uns und wurden bleicher..

So sassen machtlos wir im kreis mit ihnen...

Wo ist des herdes heisse erdenflamme

Wo ist das reine blut um uns zu tränken?

Neblige dünste ballet euch zu formen!

Taucht silberfüsse aus der purpurwelle!

So drang durch unser brünstiges beschwören

Der wehe schrei nach dem lebendigen kerne.

3   Stefan George, *Der Stern des Bundes*, Berlin: Georg Bondi, 1914.
     (Same size.)

the first edition of this text (1819) was set in blackletter with all
nouns capitalized, the next (1822) and succeeding editions used roman type with this reduced use of capitals (figures 1 & 2). Later, in
the *Deutsches Wörterbuch* (first volume 1854), Jakob and Wilhelm
Grimm took this further, using capital letters only at the start of
paragraphs; within paragraphs sentences were marked off only by
full points and a slightly increased word space.

The Grimms were philologians and wrote in a spirit of gentle
rationalism. As conducted a hundred years later, the argument took
on sharper overtones. A reform of orthography and of letterforms
was embodied in the work of the poet Stefan George (1868–1933)
as part of a larger project of a simplification and aestheticization

of life. (The architect Adolf Loos's lowercase preferences would be another contemporary instance of the attitude.) The later books of George's verse, designed under his direction, use a specially modified sanserif typeface and capitals only for opening words; punctuation is also simplified (figure 3). Early, pre-humanist and pre-capitalized German literature may have provided some inspiration here.

Some of these arguments were made by others at this time for quite different reasons: those of business efficiency. Walter Porstmann's book *Sprache und Schrift* (1920) proposed a total abolition of capital letters, together with the use of a phonetically more accurate orthography and modified punctuation (figure 4). Porstmann had written a doctoral dissertation on measuring systems and had a scientist's sense of good order, but this book was aimed at the world of administration. His ideals were exactly those of the Taylorist theories of conveyor-belt production, then at the height of their influence: 'quick, clear, positive, fluent, economical'.[3]

These arguments were quickly taken up by modernist typographers in Germany and incorporated into their more aesthetically and also socially conscious vision. *Sprache und Schrift* was cited as the source for the single alphabet argument, as developed by (among others) Moholy-Nagy, Herbert Bayer and Jan Tschichold. In 1925, the Bauhaus cut its expressionist roots in conservative Weimar and moved to industrial, Social-Democratic Dessau. And, confirming this shift, capital letters were now abolished at the school (figure 5). In the heightened atmosphere of Germany at that time, the social-political implications of 'Kleinschreibung' (lowercase typography) began to emerge clearly.

The debate over 'Kleinschreibung' can be traced in the pages of *Typographische Mitteilungen*, the journal of the Bildungsverband der Deutschen Buchdrucker (educational organization of German letterpress printers). The extent and seriousness of concern with the question among printers – not just typographers – is suggested by a poll that was carried out by the organization, announced in a special issue on the theme in May 1931. Members were asked to

3. Walter Porstmann, *Sprache und Schrift*, Berlin: Verlag des Vereins Deutscher Ingenieure, 1920, p.84.

4 Walter Porstmann, *Sprache und Schrift*, Berlin: Verlag des Vereins Deutscher Ingenieure, 1920. (Same size.)

read the articles carefully and then vote for the approach that they supported:

(1) capitals for sentence openings and proper names;

(2) complete abolition of capitals;

(3) continuation of the present rules.

The result was a clear majority for the first option: 53.5 per cent of the 26,876 members who voted; with 23.5 per cent and 23.0 per cent for the second and third approaches. The organization then adopted this moderated 'Kleinschreibung', as a campaigning policy. But the argument was soon forgotten, displaced by an intensification of the blackletter/roman debate. And when the National-Socialist party seized power in 1933, the burning typographic issue was the matter of letterforms, not orthography.

The discussion in *Typographische Mitteilungen* did produce one unambiguous statement of the political associations that could be attributed to lowercase. An editorial statement in the special issue concluded: 'write small! no letters with powdered wigs and class-coronets / democracy in orthography too!'[4] So lowercase was adopted by people who felt that egalitarian principles should extend to letters. For example, Bertolt Brecht habitually wrote and typed 'small' in his letters and diaries.

This debate was resumed in Germany after 1945. As after the First World War, the context was a society starting again from zero: basic assumptions were open to question.[5] Socially critical writers such as Günter Grass and Hans Magnus Enzensberger went lowercase in their poems, and capitals were dropped for much internal communication at the Hochschule für Gestaltung Ulm (figure 6). But, despite some persuasive advocacy of the moderate reform, German-language orthography remains out of step with all other Latin-alphabet languages.

Meaning and articulation

The German debates raise the problem of upper- and/or lowercase in rather extreme forms: a process that helps to illuminate the issues. The argument put by Porstmann, and taken up by Moholy-Nagy, Bayer and the other new typographers, was 'one sound, therefore one alphabet': we pronounce 'Dog' and 'dog' identically, so why write them differently? And – to raise a slightly different question – if we can manage with only one set of numerals, why do we need two sets of letters?

In reply one might pose another question. If written language must follow speech, then should not every word be an exact transcription, responding to regional dialects and even personal idiolects? You say 'tomarto', I say 'tomayto'. And if I came from Tasmania or Singapore, then further spelling adjustments might be necessary; and all spellings would have to be continually reviewed, to make sure that pronunciation had not changed. But written lan-

4. *Typographische Mitteilungen*, vol. 18, no. 5, 1931, p. 123. The contrast with Stanley Morison's view (note 2) could hardly be greater.
5. See, for example, the articles for and against 'Kleinschreibung' in the 'Sprache und Schrift' issue of the journal *Pandora*, no. 4, 1946.

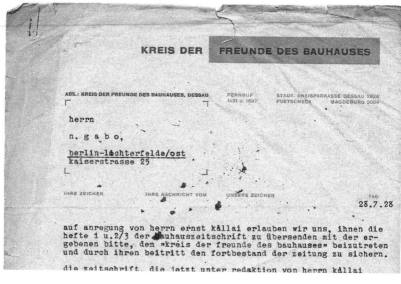

KREIS DER FREUNDE DES BAUHAUSES

ABS.: KREIS DER FREUNDE DES BAUHAUSES, DESSAU

FERNRUF 1431 u. 1587

STADT. KREISPARKASSE DESSAU 2826
POSTSCHECK MAGDEBURG 2084

herrn

n. g a b o,

berlin-lichterfelde/ost
kaiserstrasse 25

IHRE ZEICHEN   IHRE NACHRICHT VOM   UNSERE ZEICHEN

TAG
28.7.28

auf anregung von herrn ernst kállai erlauben wir uns, ihnen die
hefte 1 u.2/3 der bauhauszeitschrift zu übersenden mit der er-
gebenen bitte, dem »kreis der freunde des bauhauses« beizutreten
und durch ihren beitritt den fortbestand der zeitung zu sichern.

die zeitschrift, die jetzt unter redaktion von herrn kállai

5   A letter from the Kreis der Freunde des Bauhauses to Naum Gabo (28
July 1928). Note all-capitals in the heading, all-lowercase in the letter
itself: a common thread of 'one-track' joins them. (Reduced to 52% of
original size.)

guage does not merely transcribe the spoken. It is a fabricated system with an independent existence and its own conventions. If this
unsettles the single-alphabet view, it does not prove a need for capital letters.

The argument must then back out of the dead end of sound-
transcription and concentrate on the visual forms of text and what
they mean. Let us agree that a requirement to capitalize all nouns
is indefensible. But why stop short at proper names and sentence
openings? Concerning the first category, the defender of capitals
would say that it can actually make all the difference, in some contexts, to know that 'Reading' means the town in Berkshire or Penn-
sylvania, while 'reading' means the activity you are now engaged in.
Or that 'END' is not 'end', but the group campaigning for European
nuclear disarmament. Capital letters are part of the typographic
repertoire and can articulate text in many ways, including those
still undiscovered. Consider how clumsy a British or Canadian post-

hochschule für gestaltung

rektoratskollegium

ulm (deutschland)

herrn
anthony fröshaug
im hause

telefon 3 73 39

11.dezember 1959

sehr geehrter herr fröshaug,

das rektoratskollegium hat ihren antrag vom 8.dezember 1959
positiv beschieden und beurlaubt sie hiermit für die dauer von
zwei monaten (15.januar – 15.märz 1960) zur durchführung eines
gastkurses an der norwegischen technischen hochschule in trondheim.
zu ihrer vertretung im unterricht haben sich ihre kollegen bereit
erklärt.

nach mitteilung von herrn risler ist eine finanzielle vereinbarung

6 An internal letter from the HfG Ulm: Tomás Maldonado to Anthony
   Froshaug (11 December 1959). Lowercase tended to be used at the HfG
   for internal communications, upper- and lowercase for external communications. (Reduced to 52% of original size.)

code is when set just in lowercase (especially with capital-height
numerals).

The justification for capital letters to open sentences would
follow this last line of argument. It is not so much that capitals
give meaning here, more that they give subtle assistance to the reader's assimilation of text. We may not be able to measure it, but reading does seem to be made more comfortable by seeing sentences
demarcated by initial capitals. The advocates of a radical 'Kleinschreibung' recognized this when they suggested the mid-position-
ing of full points or oblique strokes, to make up for the loss of the
capital. The tendency for capital letters to stick out of text too noticeably has long been countered by the practice of designing forms
that are just short of ascender-height, and by the development of
small (x-height) capitals. But this close-grained typographer's view
has hardly been noticed in a debate dominated by philologians and
visionaries.

Seen in this more complex light, the absolute demand for lower-case seems mistaken: a product of utopian thinking in extreme conditions, but not a real option now, except in special cases. There are, however, still reforms to be fought for, in the German-language countries above all. Even in relatively enlightened English-language communities, capitalization often seems to go too far: in bibliographical lists or in display setting, where every noun is capitalized, if not whole words. We are still under the sway of a traditionalist-authoritarian view, which demands obedience to the 'three-line whip' of capitalization. The opposing attitude, which values informality and equality, and which sees small letters as the norm and capitals the exception to be deployed carefully and meaningfully, is not yet widely shared. A further push towards letter-democracy is still required.

Octavo, no. 5, 1988

This was commissioned by the editors of the design group 8vo's magazine *Octavo* for a special 'lowercase' issue.

Black art

Sebastian Carter, *Twentieth century type designers*, Trefoil, 1987
Walter Tracy, *Letters of credit: a view of type design*, Gordon Fraser, 1986

More than five hundred years on from its first practice, some mystery still surrounds the 'black art' of printing. And now, when the secure identity of the printing trade is threatened by instant printers, desktop publishers, and women compositors, the mystery has been displaced and further confused. Typographers feel this every time they are asked what exactly it is that they do. 'Oh, newspapers?', someone will hazard (this is the first connotation of print for many people). 'No, books, leaflets, that sort of thing.' 'You print them?' 'No, design them.' 'You make the illustrations?' Then one tries to explain the function of editorial and visual decision-taking that should intervene – or may happen by default – between the writing of a text and its composition and multiplication as printed pages. The other familiar conversation is of insiders talking together: the obsessive discussions of the visual forms of text matter, of line-lengths and letterspacing. Between these two worlds, of the reader and of the designer of text, the gap may sometimes feel impossibly wide, and yet each depends on the other.

This gap can be traced to the essential workings of printing. Although the labour of producing manuscript books may be, and was, divided up, writing is a unitary process. Printing, however, consists of two stages – composing the text and then multiplying it – and those performing these separate tasks may well know nothing of each other. The process of writing with a pen is easily comprehended and practised. The business of assembling the characters to generate printed words belongs, however, to the realm of the machine, and has never been very easily accessible: this has been ensured by the barriers of cost, religious and political censorship, and the closed shop. Another twist to the mystery is added by the fact that these characters must be mirror images of the letters they engender.

The history of the typographer is a story of emergence. At first the function was performed by the master printer, who oversaw the workshop of compositors and press operators. But with the development of power-driven presses and (from around 1900) the mechanization of composition, the designing or planning function fell out of the hands of the printer. This role began to be picked up by outsiders to the trade, who came to appropriate the old term of 'typographer'. Coinciding with and confirming this shift came a reintroduction of the aesthetic element into printing, which was seen to have been squeezed out by the rise of mechanized processes and of merely economic calculation. William Morris's Kelmscott Press represented this new impulse most forcefully. Its immediate legacy was the diversion (not at all wished for by Morris) of private press printing: unwanted texts, preciously dressed for the investor's market. But the more important consequence of the Kelmscott books, for those who could get beyond imitation of their appearance, was a new understanding of typography. As against simple 'printing', typography now came to be a practice that infused elements of visual and tactile pleasure into the meaning-governed organization of text. What form this aesthetic element took, and how inseparable and necessary was its place in the whole product, was the great question, to be argued out in the new journals of typography that began to appear alongside the printing trade press (which was, and is, limited to merely instrumental considerations).

The material conditions determining the forms of printed letters or characters were fundamentally altered at this time. In 1885 a machine for cutting 'punches' (the product of the first stage in the process of making metal type) was patented by Linn Boyd Benton. With this device, the design of letters was removed from the hands of the punchcutter, who had cut in metal at the size at which a letter would eventually be produced. Responsibility for the final form of letters now passed to a person (either the 'designer', or more usually an anonymous technical draughtsman) who made large-scale drawings that were then reduced, by pantography, to produce the necessary punches. The extraordinary and hard-won skills of the punchcutter could then be bypassed, and the design of type was open to those who simply had an interest in letterforms, and some drawing talent.

This new production method coincided with changes in the

economy of printing. There were greater demands for novelty of form in letters, as printers responded to the pressures imposed by their customers, and especially those in the commercial sphere, outside the quiet preserves of book-production. So the image on the face of the type began to be treated as a commodity, and was sold separately from its material embodiment. Thus arose the greater differentiation of these types: where letters for printing had been rather loosely described in terms of their size and style ('Pica Old Style'), there now began to appear 'typefaces', distinguished by trade-names: 'Ringlet', 'Cheltenham', 'Mikado', and so on. (A count made in 1974 found there to be 3,621 such named typefaces.) In the years of aestheticism and free-market capitalism, and up to the First World War, one sees a rather wild growth of new letterforms in Europe and the USA: chasing novelty and not restrained by any noticeable formal propriety. But in the 1920s a movement of historical revival got under way, in the USA and – where it was pursued with most enthusiasm – in Britain.

The recurring issue for this movement was that raised by the composing machine: could good work be done with it? William Morris had not engaged with the problem, though by implication had answered 'no'. The first generation of typographers, several of whom had been seduced by the astonishing sight and touch of the Kelmscott books, now began to enter into the worlds of publishing and print-design. In several cases also these typographers professed a Morrisian socialism, but without Morris's sense of the human damage wrought by machine production.

In Britain, the most important and certainly the most vociferous figure was Stanley Morison, who, in his role as consultant to the Monotype Corporation, was able to agitate for or instigate a number of new interpretations of pre-industrial types for that company's composing machines. So, for example, the Monotype-owning printer could purchase a type called 'Garamond', derived circuitously from the style of letter defined in the work of the sixteenth-century French punchcutter Claude Garamond. With a fast-talking blend of scholarship and salesmanship, Morison, assisted by Beatrice Warde (in charge of publicity at Monotype), raised the typographic consciousness of the English-speaking printing world. In a few golden years of desperate activity, historical research in the libraries of Europe and the USA went hand in hand with business deals: persuading type manufacturers to issue these re-creations, printers to buy them, publishers to issue the discussions and reproductions of old ('fine') printing and also of the work that was then being done in a spirit of 'new traditionalism'. In Britain there grew up the network of publications, institutions, and enlightened businesses, which came to constitute a culture of typography: the *Monotype Recorder* and *Newsletter*, the Curwen Press, the *Fleuron*, the Double Crown Club, the Nonesuch Press.

The books by Sebastian Carter and Walter Tracy are products of this culture in its present mutation, after the revolution of offset lithography and photocomposition, and in the middle of the diffusion of computer-assisted and digital typesetting. The travails of Fleet Street have dramatized this change of process and the degradation of the compositor's work that is entailed by the application of computer technology. Less widely noticed have been the visual changes allowed by the new machines, especially in their cruder and earlier versions. Standards in the forms and spacing of letters, which had been ensured by the very material of characters (lead, with carefully admitted additional elements), were lost in the new, unbounded technology of light. One might draw an analogy with change in the material of a simple hand-tool, when wood is replaced by a synthetic substance: it may do the job as well, but one misses the incidental sensual pleasures of a slightly idiosyncratic, slightly malleable material. This is not to argue any special case for the items that now trickle from the hand-presses of California and New England; though one might do well to take more notice of the letterpress printing that is still common in Eastern Europe and the Third World.

Tracy's book is an attempt to explain what one might mean by quality in the forms of letters for text composition: why some characters or sets of characters are of greater 'credit' than others. It is written out of the author's long experience of typeface development for the British branch of the Linotype company, and has the benefits of internal knowledge of production processes, clearly expounded in lucid prose and appropriate illustrations. This writer has managed to escape from the usual pattern for such books, which is that of a short history of Western (roman) letterforms. Instead he considers basic elements of type design and production (measurement, spacing, variants of style, and so on), with historical perspectives drawn where necessary. This is followed by five essays on typeface designers, which contain a good deal of practical criticism of letters.

Carter's *Twentieth century type designers* might seem to duplicate this part of *Letters of credit*, though the two books are largely complementary in their treatments. Tracy is drier and more interested in the letters than their designers. Carter reproduces drawings or photographs of his subjects, and is attentive to the men (as they all are, with one minor exception) behind the letters. This might be misleading, because, as in any process of industrial production, these designers worked within contexts shaped by a complex of factors: the policy of the commissioning company and its economic fortunes, the constraints and opportunities offered by their machines, the skills of the technical staff. This last factor was particularly important in the Monotype Corporation's recutting of historical types, the forms of which owe more to the skills of their draughtsmen and workshop overseer than to their initiating consultant (Morison), distanced from 'the works' by a train journey and with several other irons in his typographic fire.

Carter does show some awareness of the multi-determined complexity of any design process, and prefaces his essays on individuals with discussion of the conditioning factors, as well as with basic information about the making and assembly of type. The predominant mode of the book, however, is that of appreciation, conducted in the rather fruity tones of a Double Crown Club discussion. (A separation of the work from its creators, such as is sometimes possible in academic discourse, has not yet been entertained in the sphere of design, where you will soon find yourself sitting down to dinner with the people responsible for the artefacts you have discussed in print.) Beatrice Warde founded her theory of typography on an analogy with a 'crystal goblet': she wanted a transparent but just noticeable container that lent refinement to the meaning of a text. The same ethos of good food informs *Twentieth century type designers*: 'In many ways types are like wines: one can learn to discriminate between the varieties of Garamond as produced by Monotype, Linotype, ATF or Stempel, just as the wine taster can detect the Chardonnay grape, whatever vineyard it comes from.'

Among Sebastian Carter's subjects are Eric Gill and Jan Tschichold: outsiders who posed awkward questions, though the posthumous reputations of both have been shaped so as to allow assimilation into the old boy's club of British typography. Both gave addresses to the Double Crown Club. In the course of his, in 1926 (a few weeks before the General Strike), Gill remarked that he felt 'like a miner before a court of mandarins'. This was the time of his first engagement with the activity of designing typefaces for machine composition, and the involvement led him to think out the problems at some length in his *Essay on typography*. Although the principles of the Arts & Crafts movement had been formative for him, Gill was critical of its later mutations, and his position came to be an amalgam of Catholic-anarchist-pacifist beliefs, expressed in a fluent (sometimes logorrhetic) discourse that bears some comparison with that of D. H. Lawrence. (Lawrence's last piece of writing was a review of Gill's *Art nonsense*: it sorts out the one 'great truth' from the pub-bore element in Gill.) 'The machine' and 'industrialism', for Gill – as for Ruskin and Morris – were the devils to be wrestled with. But, by this time, the battle was over. Gill could only point to the loss, and to the evasions and lies involved in designing as if mechanization had not happened: 'what I ask of machine-made books is that they shall look machine-made'. Gill Sans, the typeface designed, under Stanley Morison's prompting, for the Monotype Corporation, was Gill's best expression of this belief; though, in the subtlety with which its characters were drawn and in their avoidance of simple geometry, it was far from the elemental machine-age typeface that the 'Zeitgeist' might seem to have demanded.

At that time, on the Continent, Jan Tschichold was the most articulate practitioner of the 'new typography': the typographic counterpart to the new architecture. In Tschichold's work, especially of the early to mid 1930s, this approach to the design of text surpassed in visual subtlety and responsiveness to meaning the more celebrated typography that was practised at the Dessau Bauhaus. By the time that Tschichold came to talk at a Double Crown Club dinner, in 1937, he was living in exile in Switzerland and was on the point of renouncing his modernism for a return to a traditional manner (quite strongly inflected by the British 'new traditionalism'. The depth of ignorance of modern typography that he would have encountered then in Britain is well indicated by the menu designed for that dinner: an anthology of misunderstandings. Fifty years later, Sebastian Carter writes appreciatively of Tschichold in both the 'modern' and 'traditional' phases of his career. But the old difference is not so easily smoothed over, and a sour remark about the title-page of *Typographische Gestaltung* (1935) – the clearest and most beautiful statement of Tschichold's modern typography – betrays the distance that still persists between the clubbable English manner and the hard, elegant rationality of Continental modernism.

In 1947, Tschichold was called to work in Britain, to supervise an overhaul of the typography of Penguin Books. He had by this time condemned modernism, as a passed phase (if perhaps a necessary purgative of nineteenth-century ornamental dross). He argued, very doubtfully, that in its ordering zeal it had shared in the spirit that informed National-Socialism. At Penguin, in the face of the post-war lassitude of the British printing trade, his ordering zeal did not diminish, though was now directed towards more reader-friendly traditional configurations. The books from this reform, which was continued by another Continental import (Hans Schmoller), are now to be found yellowed and tattered, but the intelligence and assurance of their typography remains unsurpassed. Their success lay in the achievement of high standards of typographic detail, applied to a large list of titles. Faced with the hyped-up but typographically dismal outpourings of the Anglo-American publishing industry, one is inclined to protest that really what we need to do is learn again the lessons of those books.

London Review of Books, vol. 10, no. 7, 1988

Written on spec, after some exchanges with the editors of the *London Review of Books* about their own typography, and, about a year after submission, they published this piece. The heading 'Black art' was supplied by the LRB. The mere fact of publication in a journal of general interest seemed the most important thing about this piece. It resumes themes of my book *Modern typography*, which I had by then written, but which was languishing in unpublished limbo.

Newspapers

When you tell someone that you are a typographer and have to do with printing, the response is often 'newspapers?' For some people, printing and newspapers are more or less synonymous, and certainly for many of us in Britain, this is the category of printed matter that we know most intimately.

Every day the paper erupts through the front door, at a time when we may still be dreaming. We collect it in a state of undress and digest the words along with the other first stimulants of the day. Any changes in format are deeply felt. Letters to the editor pour in when the crossword gets moved to another page or, even worse, removed altogether. And when the typeface is changed, the most unlikely people have views on the matter. I remember the earnest debate among clergymen and retired soldiers on the qualities of Times Europa, when it was introduced in 1972. I remember also, as an irregular and reluctant *Times* reader, first noticing that something was different and thinking it was just the beer. (The problem of what to read in a pub – reading books seems too studious and antisocial – is most happily solved when you alight on a disowned newspaper, or better, strike up contact by borrowing one.) On that occasion the typographers' prize was won by Hans Schmoller; he had spotted the new typeface in trial settings, sneaked into the paper some days before the official launch.

Radio and television may have eroded the command that newspapers have: no politician bothers much with newspaper interviews (perhaps they are less easy to manipulate); B-movie gangsters on the run no longer buy the latest editions through the day. But for people who – existentially – are readers, the newspaper is still a necessary daily intake. If the quality of the product is now often very low, both typographically and in content, we still turn to the famous titles in hope.

Newspaper production is special too: the extreme pressures of time and space, and of finance. That newspapers should always have attracted such bizarre owner-executives speaks for itself. The axiom that wicked proprietors and devious trade unionists breed and deserve each other seems true enough. One longs for the experiment of a paper produced by a journalist–printer co-operative to be successful in this country. And, in post-Shah conditions of viable small-circulation papers, this begins to seem less unlikely.

Looking to the Continent (or just to Leicester Square) one sees publications that seem to be models of their kind: *Le Monde*, *Neue Zürcher Zeitung*, *El Pais*, *Corriere della Sera*, the *Frankfurter Allgemeine*, *Die Zeit*, *Vrij Nederland*, NRC *Handelsblad*. In comparison with these titles, the *Guardian* is too erratic and messy, the new *Times* too shrill and strident, the *Telegraph* just sleep-inducing. The posh Sundays are disqualifying themselves in a down-market drift. The *Financial Times* is attractive, but marginal for non-specialists. These judgements apply both to content and design. Content is made visual in a newspaper in a very direct way, through layout and perhaps even, as Paul Luna suggests, through typeface. The phrasing and tone of a headline and its typographic treatment interact to produce one effect. This would help explain our sense of seeing national characteristics in newspapers: the ordered and 'seriös' Germans, the rational but slightly dotty French, the informal down-to-earth Dutch. Negative evidence is provided by the recent English-language *Pravda*, which seems to lack any clear identity: neither Soviet nor English. It is, of course, set in a degraded Times Roman. But the game is too easy: one should remember that these countries also have their *Suns* and their *Stars*. And we may ponder the horrible vision of some lowest-denominator transnational tabloid, with pop star and Royal Family stories written in Americanized Euro-speak.

Designer, October 1986

Designer published a 'special' on newspapers to mark the launch of the *Independent*, and this was part of a symposium in that issue. 'Post-Shah' refers to the proprietor Eddie Shah, who in March 1986 had launched *Today*, predicated on the fullest use of computing in print-production. Paul Luna had written an article on newspaper typography for this issue of the magazine.

Road signs: wrong turning?

Recent moves over public signs in Britain suggest that something is up with this specialized but also commonplace aspect of our built environment. On the roads, the Department of Transport has been concerned for some years to review and update the system of directional signs. A pilot scheme for new road signs has been installed at Guildford by the Department of Transport. British Rail is engaged in a review of its signs, and signs on the London transport systems have also been the subject of recent adjustments.

It is in the nature of human affairs that design systems should deteriorate, however well formulated initially. Consider the London bus destination boards: the old specification for upper- and lower-case names, set in Edward Johnston's transport alphabet, has recently been subverted in some areas by all-capital displays in a crude, thick sanserif. Horrible departures from the rules are everywhere evident on the road signs: illegitimate layouts betray the muddled hand of wilful local officials and their contractors.

The signs that we place in the public arena are indeed telling political indicators. These days in Britain such signs often seem to function only on the political level, failing in their primary duty of guiding us around the kingdom. Messages whose sense depends on delicate positioning are easily negated by changes in the topography to which they refer. Or, in their un-coordinated proliferation, they confuse each other through visual noise. The urban context is one of filth, queues, overcrowding, and disfunction. A political diagnosis isn't hard to make.

The sweeping explanation is that of a retreat from public life and civic concerns, into screen-illuminated private interiors. The English-British have always had a distaste for planning, and over the last decade the idea has become unmentionable. Local government has suffered political and financial attrition, the public services have been fragmented and sold off. Design has found a role in all this – has flourished as never before – but as a lubricant to the mechanisms of disintegration, creating identities for the bodies of the new disorder.

Thirty years ago, design played its part in shaping adequate systems of signs in Britain: on the roads, the railways, in airports, in hospitals and throughout the public realm. The new road signs of the 1960s, in particular, provide an instance of a structural rather than image-making use of design, enabled by a civilized if unremarkable political context: design in a proper sense.

The story of these new signs centres on the unglamorous work of two government committees. These tools of policy-making seem now to have been discarded, as wasteful obstacles to the implementation of political conviction. But such bodies were then a respected accessory of government. In 1957 an advisory committee on signs for the motorways was set up, under the chairmanship of Sir Colin Anderson, an enlightened and visually aware industrialist. This new category of road was just then beginning to be built in Britain, and, to cater for the faster speeds, a fresh approach to signing was needed. The committee appointed a designer to act as consultant: Jock Kinneir, who had worked on a baggage-labelling system for the ships of the P&O Line, of which Anderson was a director.

Kinneir had had an art school education in the late 1930s, and, after the war, he worked mainly in exhibition design before setting up in private practice in 1956. He thus came to this job without any formal typographic or design training. Looking back now, in retirement and at a considerable mental distance from the London design world, Jock Kinneir suggests that this innocence had its advantages. He had to start from first principles. 'What do I need to know, sitting in my driving seat, from this angle of vision, at that speed?' The alphabets that he and his associate Margaret Calvert designed, and the rules for their configuration as signs, reject formalism at every turn, at every avoidance of a meaningless alignment or blandly regular curve. The aim was simply rapid intelligibilty.

A key figure behind the road sign redesign was, in Kinneir's description, 'a far-sighted civil servant' at the Ministry of Transport (as it was then) – T.G. Usborne – who realized that one had to use 'the salami approach' in relation to the Treasury purse-holders and to public opinion: slice by slice. First a stretch of motorway at Preston, then all the motorways, then the whole road network. So the Anderson Committee (whose report was signed in 1960) paved the way for the Worboys Committee report of 1963, which recommended

This sign, probably photographed in 1963, shows Jock Kinneir's new system for British road signs well implemented – and suggests some of the complexity of information with which that system would have to deal.

a system of signs for all-purpose roads. (Sir Walter Worboys was another industrialist with design connections, and he came to the task after seven years as Chairman of the Council of Industrial Design.) This longer perspective wasn't disclosed at the start – and, as Kinneir now points out, it was by good fortune rather than forethought that the motorway system lent itself to this extrapolation.

The process of this design work was to a significant extent open to public discussion, to amendment and rational justification. To point a contemporary moral again, this is something that has been lost in the recent cult of the designer, who reveals expensive master-creations to a boardroom, as a 'fait accompli'. So when in 1959 letters appeared in *The Times*, expressing worries about the new signs at Preston, a debate was started. The main challenge came from the lettercutter David Kindersley, with the support of luminaries of English typographic traditionalism (including Stanley Morison). Kindersley's proposal – uninvited, but respectfully heard out – was for an alphabet of seriffed capital letters, as against the upper- and lowercase sanserif of Kinneir. It was a striking instance of the squabble between ancients and moderns that has been a feature of recent English life. (The Prince and the architects is just the latest episode in this saga.) Kindersley suggested that his own letters would be more legible and nicer to look at too. The Road Research Laboratory ran tests, reported in conscientious detail in *Design* magazine (those were the days!). No significant difference in legibility was found. And so it came down to looks, in which respect the Kindersley signs were thought by the committee to be – in the words of a witness – 'just so ugly'. Scrutinizing the published photographs of them, and contemplating the extraordinary rightness of a properly executed Kinneir sign, one must agree with the committee.

One might wonder, too, how the Kindersley alphabet could possibly have sat alongside the new abstract-pictorial symbols, which the Ministry of Transport was anxious to adopt, following the 'Protocol' devised at a United Nations World Conference at Geneva in 1949. These symbols, which Kinneir could redraw but had to accept in essential respects, were a fundamental constituent of the redesign, and were – together with the new alphabet – a recognition of the facts of modern road transport, and of the need for an internationally intelligible sign system.

In another minor clash of cultural values, the Worboys commit-tee debated the background colour to be used for the primary route signs: blue was reserved for the motorways, black was thought to be too 'funereal', though it was supported by the four architectural rep-resentatives on the committee. So it came to green: the architects wanted a dark near-black (Hugh Casson described such a green as 'you know, the colour of old dinner-jackets'); Kinneir wanted a bright, highly visible green (such as one now sees on some more re-cent plastic signs). The final choice was in between these extremes: British Standard colour 2660, no. 6-074, familiarly known as 'Slough green' (after the location of the Road Research Laboratory).

The real beauty of the new signs was the system dictating their layout, spelled out in Appendix VIII of the Worboys report. Taking as a module one stroke-width of a capital I in the basic alphabet (Transport Medium), rules were given for the spacing and dimen-sions of all the visual elements in any sign. Here the language of the report has an Old Testament assurance: 'Internal angles at the junction of route symbols shall be radiused one stroke-width / Side turning route symbols shall extend to two-thirds of the distance from the forwards symbol to the border ...' Letters were placed on space-incorporating 'tiles' and only needed to be butted up against each other for good spacing to be ensured. Layout and overall di-mensions of the sign thus followed from the needs of the informa-tion. Local authorities could then, without design help, make de-cent signs, consistent with each other and with the MoT signs on major roads. This approach of 'set up a system and let the thing design itself' was also, a historian might add, in the very best mod-ern movement spirit, as not too much else in these islands has been. Ask a typographer from a country with otherwise much better public design than ours (Germany or France) and you will find that the Kinneir signs are a cause of jealous admiration.

The road signs system has an inbuilt flexibility of response, which could be turned to meet the new needs that have arisen over the last thirty years. There have been doubtful additions, such as the brown 'tourist' signs. Jock Kinneir has always said that it should be overhauled: to correct certain weaknesses, and generally to cater for new conditions resulting from a fast-changing road network. But now there is a danger that this updating will be forced on the system by the Department of Transport, without any design consultation. The new signs at Guildford show all the marks of the crassness that can occur when engineers and civil servants are left in charge of visual semantics. The letters and the symbols may be the same, but their sense has been disrupted by the attempt to combine signs, in an otherwise laudable attempt to reduce clutter. The scheme is said to be only an experiment and a basis for discussion. A group of designers, under the auspices of the Design Business Association, is submitting criticisms. So there is some prospect of the Department being made to understand just what they are tampering with, and being encouraged to take positive measures to develop the system in ways that respect its fundamental principles. But, as everyone acknowledges, the matter is 'political', in the fullest sense of this word. It will be worth keeping an eye on these indexes of the nation-state.

Blueprint, no. 61, October 1989

In preparation for this article I went to meet Jock Kinneir for the first time, and he corrected a draft of my text. Since 1989, the state of Britain's roads and of the signs has become ever more incoherent and unmanaged.

Adrian Forty, *Objects of desire: design and society 1750–1980*,
Thames & Hudson, 1986

'To represent design purely as the creative act of individuals ...
temporarily enhances the importance of designers, but ultimately
only degrades design by severing it from its part in the workings of
society.' Adrian Forty's thesis might seem to suggest that designers
are just idiot-puppets, their movements controlled by the forces of
capitalism. This is an ultimate extension of his argument, but *Objects of desire* is not so simple-minded. The 'purely' in the sentence
quoted is characteristic of his approach, which, while forceful, is
also notable for its careful formulation.

In a set of ten essays Forty argues that designing is the resolution of two fields: the economic and the ideological. Designed artefacts embody ideas and ideologies, and, in doing so, they serve the
interests of their manufacturers and marketers. A strong sub-plot
of the book, which emerges as the main theme of the final chapter,
is an argument about design history. Most historians have concentrated on the designer as quasi-artistic creator; some have regarded
design rather as a matter of ingenious invention in a context of
glorious technical progress. *Objects of desire* constitutes an effective
rebuttal of both of these views, and does so partly through its own
construction. It is a discontinuous series of explorations of such
themes as 'The first industrial designers' (Wedgwood in the eighteenth century), 'Design and mechanisation' (textiles, garment manufacture, cabinetmaking in the nineteenth century), 'Hygiene and
cleanliness' (ways in which these notions have motivated design in
the modern world). Forty shows that one need not tell stories to do
history (and especially not stories in which things get better and
better).

Unlike so many surveys of design, the book contains no concluding hymn to the new technology. Rather, Adrian Forty observes
that the computer has brought greater dullness and monotony to
office work. Here design has performed an ameliorating function,

in the creation of soft, semi-domestic interiors. In this discussion, as in its treatment of the home interior and domestic appliances, the book shows the benefits of feminism: a concern with how it is; a disbelief in glossy images of good design, which falsify, if they do not exclude, the realities of most of us, and women especially.

In support of his thesis, Forty has turned away from the existing design literature. Instead he makes discriminating use of a wide range of material, including some period novels, as well as his own archive research. The book is painstakingly documented and thus – despite its rather flashy main title (redolent of 1983?) – an entirely different thing from the written-in-a-weekend jobs that are just now choking the bookshops.

One of the clearest instances of Forty's thesis is in his discussion of Wedgwood. He suggests that the factory's turn to a neo-classical style, away from more florid motifs, was not just a matter of stylistic expression: they were following public taste, for marketing reasons. Nor was it just to do with mechanization: processes of manufacture did not change much at this time. Rather, he argues that the new style allowed greater scope for standardization of pattern and form, and variation through combination. There was a technical element, but one subsumed within the larger motive of profit-making. This explanation coherently connects the formal, the ideological (the complex meanings of neoclassical style), the technical, and the economic, while positing this latter as the prime factor. Forty does not parade his credentials – there are no footnote genuflections to Althusser – but this is an essentially Marxist view: everything is, in the last analysis, motivated by economic interest.

Suppose we accept that this is true of the developed, capitalist world. How would the thesis work out in the socialist countries? or in independent, only partly developed Third World countries? Is there somewhere the possibility of a design process that does not always come down to base drives for profit? Is there not, even within capitalism, the prospect of design that resists myth-making and which suggests, however faintly, some better vision. It is sad that Forty – who can see the truth of William Morris's views – has apparently no hope. But, given the persistent pattern of hopes defeated (one thinks of Chile, China, or Lucas Aerospace, or the Greater London Enterprise Board), it may be that he is right.

On the historical ground covered by the book, I feel that Adrian Forty does sometimes over-extend his case. This is most clear in the discussion of corporate identity, which takes London Transport as its example. In what is the thinnest and sketchiest of his essays, Forty is driven to see the London Underground map as part of an all-encompassing plot to encourage people to use the tube. Thus the map's standardized interchange symbols disguise the difficulties of transferring from the Northern to the Circle Line at Kings Cross ('two escalators, staircases and some hundreds of yards walking'), while the fact that the stations are placed at equal intervals distorts 'the actual length of the journeys, making a trip from, say, Ruislip to Leytonstone seem very much less formidable than it actually is'. Here his argument seems fanciful and not materialist enough: it shows no understanding of the process of designing network diagrams (it is in their proper logic to have these features), and neglects the designer. The fact that the designer of the map (Harry Beck) was not a 'designer' (in the sense of ideology-imparting stylist), but rather an engineering draughtsman who proposed the diagram on his own initiative, does throw some light on the matter. Though, of course, one would then have to consider the reasons for management's acceptance of the proposal. But against Forty's suggestion, I would argue that the map is a case of design that is genuinely useful, and which escapes the mythologies of – to use another of his examples – Raymond Loewy's Lucky Strike pack. One begins to think that the denial of the designer may lead to a false idealism, just as much as can exclusive concentration on the personal agent.

At one point, Forty suggests that the 'only previous attempt to relate design to the history of society in a comprehensive way' was Giedion's *Mechanization takes command*. That is a bold claim, with some truth in it. Certainly the book is effective within the limits of the ground it covers. However, one is loathe to grant the comparison with Giedion, who had a vision and wrote to change the world. But history went wrong. Forty has little hope of a better world: he writes, like the rest of us, just to change design history.

Designer, May 1986

Letters of credit

Walter Tracy, *Letters of credit*, Gordon Fraser, 1986

Changes in the conditions of printing over the last thirty years
have been immense. The workshops of the 'black art' (molten metal
and grime) have metamorphosed into carpeted offices, where the
main physical danger comes from visual display units. The means
by which text is composed have been transformed. From 1450
to 1900 nothing much changed; then came machine composition
(Linotype, Monotype). In the 1960s, printed letterforms began to
be more usually produced not from types (lumps of metal), but
by means of rays of light. In the most recent phase – which may
amount to a third era of composition – letterforms have been stored
not as photographic master images but as information in the memories of computers. Where, in the days of metal, the rights of letters
were protected by the laws of their material, now letterforms are
subjected to endless acts of violence: crammed together, forcibly
enlarged, blown to one side. Along with these changes in the material nature of typography has come a break-up in traditional patterns
of work and employment. And there has been the incursion into
the trade of visually innocent computer scientists, executives with
eyes only for stock-exchange quotations, and designers indifferent
to the meaning of words. If you add to all this the various crises of
the western economies, then the problems of typography will hardly
seem surprising.

Yet the discussion of typography, especially in books and within
education, has hardly begun to face up to these changes. So we still
talk about typefaces as timeless entities, divorced from the method
of their generation. For example, the typeface in which these words
are set would still commonly be referred to as just 'Garamond', the
name of a punchcutter in sixteenth-century France, who helped to
define the style of a long tradition of roman letters. The relation
between Claude Garamond's letters and these of a Linotron composing machine can be usefully compared to that between the first
performance of a Shakespeare play and a modern-day production.
(Compugraphic Garamond would be the musical version.)

In this situation of general ignorance and of loss of confidence among specialists, Walter Tracy is concerned to make clear that some letterforms are better than others: thus the otherwise rather awkward title of his book. *Letters of credit* has two parts. The first contains discussion of fundamental topics, such as nomenclature, measurement, manufacture, spacing of letters. The second part is devoted to studies of the work of twentieth-century typeface designers: Van Krimpen, Goudy, Koch, Dwiggins, and Stanley Morison's one real design contribution – Times Roman. The subject is typefaces for continuous text, rather than display: by far the more substantial and rewarding area of work and study.

The approach of the book is very refreshing: we are spared another run through the history of letterforms, and are instead plunged straight into the tough basic issues (but treated with a strong sense of history) and then given extended considerations of examples, in which Tracy educates us in the values he finds in letters. This second part amounts to practical criticism (in the I. A. Richards sense): with the material adequately reproduced, we look on as the author unerringly homes in on an inept set of numerals or a W that is too narrow. He is appreciative too, and one of the services of the book is its revaluation of received opinions. None of the typefaces of Jan van Krimpen is judged to be wholly successful: beautiful as the individual letters may be, they never quite work together as text matter, which is the acid test. Conversely, W. A. Dwiggins's very inventive approach is upwardly valued. It is good to see a reconsideration of Rudolf Koch's work, too easily put aside as teutonic and strange, and it is a sign of Tracy's open-mindedness that he should undertake this essay. One knew by now that Stanley Morison's type-design adventures were marked by considerable muddle, accompanied by studiously anonymous trumpeting of the products. In a cool account of Times Roman, Tracy reinforces this more realistic assessment.

Tracy writes out of long experience as the manager of the typographic department of Linotype in both its metal and its photocomposition days. (This involvement may have set him slightly apart from the centres of the old-boys club of British traditionalist typography: Linotype means newspapers not books.) He knows that machine constraints have the last word in the argument with aesthetics, and that shop-floor managers and drawing-board artisans can teach designers about the finer points of the job. Thus the thesis, which he now backs up with character-width measurements, that the primary source for Times Roman was a previous Monotype typeface (Plantin) and not some more ancient original; because that would be the obvious and most practical course for the factory draughtsmen (Morison only did rough sketches).

Despite its ubiquity, typography, and devising typefaces above all, is a rather hermetic field of design. It seems characteristic that, while most designers draw small for production on a larger scale, designers of typefaces draw large for production at a size of a millimetre or so. Typographers often become passionate about their small products, and this may be baffling to outsiders. So explanations to the lay audience are badly needed. Tracy writes in his preface, with typical precision and modesty, that it has occurred to him to set down his thoughts 'in the hope that they may be useful to a reader who is fairly new to the subject, has an interest in type and perhaps some acquaintance with it, thinks (as I do) that it is more important to judge the quality of designs than to have an encyclopaedic knowledge of them, but does not yet feel sufficiently equipped to make a confident assessment of the merits of a type'. I have some reservations about his treatment. Though it might have disfigured the book, it would have helped his educational purposes to have shown and discussed some of the many uncreditable letters of recent years. His attitude towards nomenclature (the language of typography is a nightmare of imprecision) and towards reform of typographic measurement seems too resigned. And, in general, despite its scepticism and rationality, the book is unmistakably a product of the still largely traditionalist British typographic culture. But the achievements of that culture are real ones, and this book is a notable case in point.

Designer, June 1986

As the discussion in the second paragraph suggests, *Designer* magazine was set in a Garamond.

Two histories of lettering

Nicolete Gray, *A history of lettering: creative experiment and letter identity*,
    Phaidon, 1986
Alan Bartram, *The English lettering tradition: from 1700 to the present day*,
    Lund Humphries, 1986

Lettering is well provided for in Britain: both in its native materials, as Alan Bartram's new book demonstrates, and in its historians of the subject, the doyenne of whom is Nicolete Gray. It was she who first opened up the subject in articles for the *Architectural Review*, republished in *Lettering on buildings* (1960). This book, together with her further articles and some seminal essays by James Mosley, established a clear map of the development of public lettering over two and a half millennia. Subsequent contributions came from itinerant designers with cameras, such as Alan Bartram and Jock Kinneir. Now Nicolete Gray has returned to provide a concise summary of the whole field – both the public and the more intimate – in *A history of lettering*.

Gray's book is concerned with the Roman or Latin alphabet, in the broadest sense, the vagaries of whose forms it plots in fourteen chapters, from their immediate progenitors in Classical Greece, to their present passage through the grid of computer digitization. By 'lettering' she means letters that have something 'over and above bare legibility': 'letters used as a medium of expression and design'. Her sub-title of 'creative experiment and letter identity' introduces the dialectical opposition that propels the argument of the book: individual expression against agreed or perhaps regulated form. These poles of opposition compare interestingly with the contrast of 'authority' against 'freedom' that Stanley Morison employed in his summarizing work on the subject, *Politics and script* (1972). Both authors write as Roman Catholics, but where Morison's treatment of church politics was heavily argumentative and much attached to 'authority', Gray's touch is light, and, while recognizing the claims of 'identity', she consistently celebrates the drive to experiment.

As Gray suggests, lettering history can be represented as a story of continual struggle with the Roman 'norms' (most famously, those of the letters on the Trajan column), which return to favour with any revival of classical culture. Her great contribution has been to notice and explain letters that are left out by the narrowly Roman view. Thus her attention to the other Roman letters (especially rustic) and to the centuries-wide gaps of darkness between the classical cultures. We can now see that between Charlemagne and the Renaissance there were indeed splendid things (Romanesque and Gothic lettering). Here, as in her dazzling first book, *Nineteenth-century ornamented types* (1938), Gray's method is to accept what was produced, without preconceptions, and to understand it in its social and cultural context. Unlike Morison, with his aversion to modernism, Gray has always written out of real sympathy for the attempt to 'make it new'. Thus her concluding chapters on 'Experiment unlimited' and 'Yesterday and today' maintain the tone and themes of the rest of the book. But it is not an entirely permissive view, and one important discrimination recurs: between experiment that follows from real thought and feeling, and the merely formal and clever. Whether eleventh-century Romanesque or twentieth-century Constructivist, the genuinely experimental is serious and personal; the other thing is done for cynical motives.

This raises questions of the aesthetics and morality of craft production, which both these books illuminate. Edward Johnston was a central figure for the craft revival of lettering, and Nicolete Gray makes some criticism of his followers, whose work has been 'largely divorced both from the requirements of everyday life and from individual expression' (p. 202). She writes as herself a hand-producer of public lettering, which gives the discussion a welcome dimension of inside knowledge, and this criticism is made from an expressionist position. By contrast, Alan Bartram is a typographer and he betrays the designer's typical dislike of art-production. His book leads off with quotations from Ruskin on Gothic and David Pye on 'things which can give ordinary life a turn for the better', and then, in his own vigorous prose, goes on to celebrate the production of anonymous signwriters and lettercutters. Of his 378 splendid photographs (the majority newly published here) only one is perhaps the work of a conscious artist, included for its un-art-like decent suitability. This culminating book in Bartram's pursuit of the

'English vernacular' letter does provide some evidence to suggest that the form is still alive, despite the ravages of the plastic fascia.

As one might expect of a book on a simple theme, designed by its author, *The English lettering tradition* works well for the reader. Nicolete Gray's immensely larger subject has posed considerable problems of editorial organization. The main divisions by chapter are clear and helpful, and examples are shown in good photographs, mostly drawn from the Lettering Record at the Central School of Art & Design. But no indication of the scale of these items is given: an important point, when examples vary so greatly in size, and when scale is a crucial element in their functioning. By failing to place their numbers by each illustration, the book's designer has given readers extra labour. So too the editorial work is less than immaculate. The author has been allowed to misremember bibliographical details (especially those of her own writings) and to misidentify the designer of the magazine *Wendingen* (illustration 271); the appendixes, supplementary charts and bibliographies are puzzlingly jumbled. One mentions these blemishes in the hope that they will be corrected in further editions, which the book certainly deserves.

Crafts, no. 85, March/April 1987

Crafts is the magazine of the (British) Crafts Council.

Eric Gill

Fiona MacCarthy, *Eric Gill*, Faber & Faber, 1989

Eric Gill (1882–1940), though primarily an artist and designer (he would have refused both terms), was also a lesser example of those loud, self-contradictory sages, who figured prominently in English culture of the first half of the twentieth century. One thinks of G. B. Shaw, H. G. Wells, or (closer to Gill) Hilaire Belloc and G. K. Chesterton. Active in several fields, they had strong views on everything. Celebrities in their own time, they have generated a succession of biographies, which become increasingly candid. Great men some of them may have been, but, one often feels, quite unbearable to know.

Fiona MacCarthy's *Eric Gill* is the fourth full-length study. The books by Robert Speaight (1966) and Donald Attwater (1969) were respectful accounts by younger contemporaries of Gill, from within or on the fringes of his social-religious orbit. Malcolm Yorke's *Eric Gill: man of flesh and spirit* (1981) was written by an artist-academic of a younger generation. More about the work than the life, Yorke's new information was a detailed description of Gill's erotic and anatomical drawings, said to be unsafe for publication.

MacCarthy's book is a simple biography. Indeed, advocates of Gill's work – one awaits a Peter Fullerish revival of interest – may feel that she gets too much absorbed in the life. The lead story of her text is the account of Gill's sexual activities. One knew, or could have guessed, that there had been a string of infidelities, put up with by his infinitely suffering wife, Ethel Mary. Now we know the names. Here the biographer's task was simple enough: a trip to Los Angeles to read Gill's diaries, in which he noted these occasions, along with much mundane description ('haircut 8d.'), and the facts of his professional life, necessary for invoicing clients and making tax returns. But these affairs were not, except in a few cases, matters of the heart. The picture that we are given is of a mildly pathological character: a voyeur-patriarch, trying to keep jealous tabs on his extended family. There were incestuous episodes (sisters and daughters), experiments with prostitutes, even with a dog.

Gill announced his difference immediately, in his dress. His standard garment came to be a pre-modern, penis-freeing smock, the rationale for which he advanced in several essays and pamphlets. And his attitude to women was quite consciously medieval. He wanted them simple and undecorated, covered-up in public, and confined to domestic and agricultural activities. Despite himself, he did fall for the provocation offered by several modern or 'new' women of his acquaintance. As MacCarthy points out, the missionary trait ran in the Gill family – a grandfather and a brother served in the South Seas. For Eric, 'missionary' can be understood in every sense of that word. His saving graces seem to have been a sense of humour and a canny realism: he could compromise and admit mistakes, at least in public.

Do these revelations matter? Do they affect our understanding of the work? 'It all goes together', Gill used to proclaim, and one can – more than Fiona MacCarthy does – make connections. At one point she remarks that his large public sculptures are 'overwrought and ponderous, they have a certain deadness'. On largely photographic evidence, I would agree – and extend the judgement to the small sculptures, most of the wood engravings, some of the drawings. The overworking in these things seems to belong with the unpleasantly obsessional in him: the essentially Calvinist (despite his Catholic conversion) drive for perfect order. Thus his very assured, instinctive 'line' – which seems bound up with his sexuality – gets polished to death. What is still alive are the things that were made in a hurry, particularly the less formal drawings. He was endlessly repetitive in his writing, but the *Autobiography* (done in a rush, just before he died) and the *Essay on typography* still bear reading. His correspondence is lively, especially the postcards.

Gill's lettercutting and his typefaces are another matter. There his obsessions, his energies, the material, and the task, do all come together. It was lettercutting that (in 1903) let him escape from the drudgery of an architectural apprenticeship, into the independent life of the 'workman'. Then, towards the end of the 1920s, it was type design that took Gill into useful engagement with mass-production, despite his previous rejection of it. Most typographers would now dismiss his first typeface, Perpetua, as a failure. Rather than anything Gill wanted, it was an attempt to prove Stanley Morison's dogma that good types had first to be cut in metal, not just drawn; the design process was a messy improvisation. But with the next types, Gill Sans and Joanna, his impulse to over-polish found a proper object. Typefaces have to be worked intensively, in a process of proposal and adjustment that involves several people, not least the draughtsmen who make the finished drawings. MacCarthy skates over these matters. But, as the sardonic chronicler of the British design establishment, she does better than previous biographers in sketching the conditions of Gill's design work: his relations with clients, with apprentices, and the peculiarities of the workshop life.

Eric Gill is a gift to the strongly literary-biographical culture of his country: and despite his taste for theological-philosophical argument, he was very English. After some time in his company, the Continent seems far away, and the USA even further. He was a 'character', an English eccentric. He couldn't stop producing, from instinct and from necessity (he charged only artisans' fees, on principle). His doings can be documented in great detail. It makes an engrossing, depressing tale. Such biographies have their uses, but the more interesting and more difficult task would be to relate the life of Gill to the culture that nourished him and which he in turn – under protest – sustained. This would be a study of retardation, of a protracted adolescence in despite of the modern world: a larger pathology.

Blueprint, no. 54, February 1989

James King, *The last modern: a life of Herbert Read*, Weidenfeld & Nicolson, 1990

> Herbert Read begs to thank you for your letter, but has to inform you that he has retired from all unsolicited correspondence, from lecturing, attending meetings and conferences, joining committees, writing prefaces and introductions, visiting studios and opening exhibitions, reading unsolicited manuscripts and books, offering his opinion on drawings and paintings submitted to him through the post, and generally from all those activities which render his present existence fragmentary and futile.

This postcard, which Read had printed in the 1940s, is one of the more telling documents quoted by James King (though he cuts it clumsily; the full text was given by Vernon Richards in his memories of Read, in *Anarchy*, no. 91). In the struggle to support a family, country house and town flat, to meet school fees and alimony payments – on the base of just part-time employments, mainly as a publisher's editor – Read took on a horrible load of odd jobs.

King's biography is an efficient catalogue or annotated engagement diary of a life. It feels like not much more than a passing stop in the career of a busy academic author: one of a series of 'lives' (first William Cowper, then Paul Nash, now Read, next year William Blake). And the game is given away by its five-page index entry on 'Read, Herbert' which puts all the facts on display, for super-rapid consumption. Although the book may serve to reintroduce Read to us as a cultural phenomenon, it does him little service as writer or thinker. For that there are two better books: George Woodcock's *Herbert Read: the stream and the source* (1972) and David Thistlewood's *Herbert Read: formlessness and form, an introduction to his aesthetics* (1984). Those who want a quick introduction to Read's politics should turn to chapter 7 in Woodcock's book, which, as Thistlewood remarked, 'cannot be improved upon'. A distressing feature of King's account is the continual turn to Read's writings to pick out merely those passages in which Read seems to writing surreptitiously about himself (for example, in the book on Wordsworth) – as if his work had or has no independent value.

The chief theme of the book is the fragmentation of Read's life: as if he was defeated both by his immediate circumstances and by the larger forces of the society in which he lived. The battle for coherence must be a leading motive in many lives, but in Read's case this took an acute form. His father – a 'gentleman-farmer' in North Yorkshire – died after a riding accident, when Read was ten years old. From the rural idyll of early childhood (at least, that was how he came to construct it), Read was thrown into the harsh society of an orphanage, then a bank clerk's job in Leeds. But through energetic self-education, with the help of an unusually lively local culture in Leeds – and via war service in the army – he found a way out of this predicament and into the world.

Herbert Read's reputation may now be as various as his interests: a writer on art and a promoter of modern art and design in Britain; a literary critic and poet; an 'unpolitical' but politically conscious writer. Or, in this third respect, maybe just as the anarchist who (in 1953) accepted a knighthood. With all of these components of Read, the Canadian James King deals impartially, neither as an uncritical partisan for his subject, nor with the axes to grind that a trueborn British person has. For example, about the incident of the knighthood, King puts the matter in the context of Read's life at that time, and demonstrates that biography can sometimes explain things. Thus, it was Margaret ('Ludo') Read – his second wife – who especially wanted this honour, with its spin-off of turning 'Mrs' into 'Lady'. Their marriage had always had its tensions and agreements to differ (she was a strong Catholic, he an atheist) and had just been through a difficult passage over Read's friendship with another woman. So, in accepting this title, Read made a domestic peace offering. King quotes a beautiful excuse that Read made to an acquaintance – 'I didn't feel important enough to refuse' – and, knowing all this, even British dissenters might now be prepared to forgive him.

The other famous public incident in Read's life was his active engagement in the Freedom Defence Committee, during and immediately after the war, which centred on the trial and imprison-ment of leading anarchists around Freedom Press. Witnesses of his public appearances during this campaign have vivid memories of Read, white with anger and overcoming his marked shyness to deliver a forthright attack on the government and its war conduct, and to call for resistance. That mood of blunt statement was always present in Read – it seems to have been quite frequent in his private remarks and letters – but one could wish that he had been able to channel it more usefully into a public political engagement.

Read's political radicalism was formed in his Leeds days and stayed with him, in various registers, throughout the rest of his life. Like others in his generation, it was the events of the 1930s, and particularly those in Spain, which brought him to a more explicit concern with political issues. The titles of his books from those years showed him 'coming out' politically: *Art and society* (1937), *Poetry and anarchism* (1938), *The philosophy of anarchism* (1940), *To hell with culture* (1941). Big themes rumbled through his work: the human and cultural damage entailed almost equally by capitalism and by socialist totalitarianism; the possibilities of resistance to these processes, within small centres of human endeavour, and through the fostering of imagination – especially visual imagina-tion – in education. Occasionally he could be direct and precise in his cultural-political formulations. But through most of Read's intellectual production there is a pervading sense of vagueness and generality, so that it is hard to recall any exact arguments, and a hasty inspection might see him as just another English man of let-ters. Thinking back to an extended reading of his critical work some years ago, I remember especially the citations and recommenda-tions: Jung, Kierkegaard, Buber, Kropotkin, Lao-Tzu, Coleridge ... After a while one longs for something tougher, more analytical. Yet, imagining oneself back into his context, it may be that in a cultur-ally barren situation there was no other course for him but to work in this generous way. And one could add that Read was quite largely forced into criticism and theory by the need to earn cash, and his work in these forms inevitably suffers from the speed and frequency of its production: he wanted, much more, to write poems and im-aginative prose. There are exceptions to this verdict: especially his one novel, *The green child* (1935). And *Education through art* (1943), is a sustained and thorough discussion of its subject (written with a two-year university fellowship), and one that brings together the major themes of his work.

The special interest of Read's life and work now is as that of an exception to the patterns of British culture – to the assumption that ideas and politics don't mix, that parliamentary sovereignty is unquestionable good sense, that literary culture is dominant and is unrelated to visual culture. Read's endeavour, which had its heroic aspects, was to transgress and question these patterns. In the latter part of his life he became a totem-figure – the knighthood reinforced this – representing an established modernism in culture. In the inevitable revolt of the sons, younger critics began to distance themselves from him. King quotes one of them (Lawrence Alloway): 'There was nobody much else to attack ... Herbert was really all there was.'

Nowadays, although conditions have changed, the deep structures of English-British culture continue to make Read's kind of boundary-breaking very difficult. It is hard to think of individuals carrying on in the same spirit. John Berger may be the best candidate – and no accident that he has chosen Continental exile. The British climate isn't kind to wide-ranging freelance artist-intellectuals: the ground is occupied by academics and journalists, both categories being hampered by limited vision. As to the cross-disciplinary meeting ground – the ideal community that Read wanted to found (in 1932 he made a proposal to set up a Bauhaus-type centre for arts – in Edinburgh!) – this has been allowed to suffer only brief and intermittent forms of life. The Institute of Contemporary Arts was his best attempt, and though never living up to the best hopes for it – King provides an account of the involvement of the CIA, and of the English aristocracy, in the early life of the ICA – it has proved to be a notable legacy. Within formal education, the Construction School at the West of England College of Art, Bristol, was another, more concerted experiment in cultural bridge-building. Norman Potter reported on it in his book *What is a designer*, itself an attempt to locate and continue the tradition in which Read worked. These have been fragments, isolated endeavours; they are also signs that Herbert Read's struggles still have their after-effects.

Solidarity, no. 27, 1991

Jan Tschichold

Ruari McLean, *Jan Tschichold: typographer*, Lund Humphries, 1990

Typographers have to be fussy about details, the good ordering of which largely makes for good typography. Jan Tschichold (1902–74) was one of the fussiest of typographers, both in the conduct of his own work, and also (while still alive) in tending to the accuracy of his historical reputation. Apart from fussiness, the Tschichold phenomenon can be summarized as being that of a designer of quite exceptional assurance in giving visual and material form to words and images, who also had the ability to give lucid explanations of what others have been content to leave untheorized as 'good typography'. This didactic labour was carried out in the large numbers of articles (well into three figures) and books (well into two figures) that he published. He used to annotate the lists of his publications: which items were still in print, how much they cost. Of one unauthorized translation he remarked: 'Hundreds of mistakes. Anyone who owns this sorry effort should throw it in the waste-bin.'

The son of a Leipzig sign-writer, Tschichold was born into the heart of German typographic culture, and this provided the terms and assumptions of his earliest work (he started very young). In 1923, seeing the Bauhaus exhibition at Weimar, he underwent a conversion to modernism, apparently almost Pauline in its suddenness. He also picked up the radical socialist sympathies that were part of the modernist deal (or perhaps just their Bolshevik aura: his family had Slav roots on both sides). Tschichold soon became the most convincing exponent of typographic modernism, and of the proposition that this 'new typography' was the way in which all printing could – should – now be designed. Then in January 1933, the National-Socialists seized power in Germany. In the spring of that year, Tschichold was detained in custody for six weeks (he had worked for left-socialist organizations), and suffered what seems to have been the shock of his life.

On release, Tschichold at once emigrated to Switzerland, with his wife and their son. Through these years of turmoil he produced his most serene exercises in the new typography: freely placed elements that also seem to respect semantic and technical reason (though, persuaded by its beauty, one can overplay the rationality of his work). Then, around 1937, he turned to another approach: the old typography of symmetry, of pre-industrial typefaces and unstandardized paper sizes. This astonishing change came to dog Tschichold's career. When, in 1946, he first explained it publicly (in a highly-charged exchange with Max Bill), his reasons were of two kinds: that his modern typography had been authoritarian and militaristic and so imbued with the spirit that also drove German National-Socialism; and that modernism in typography was limited to publicity work (as opposed to book design), could not properly articulate content, could be practised only by an initiated élite.

These arguments – a tangle of true perceptions and ingenuous special pleading – inform what may be the only decent attempt at postmodernism in typography, done for the most serious moral-political reasons. After the war, Tschichold settled into a life of relatively quiet production. Though not so quiet was his stay in England in 1947–9, where he worked on 'my reform of Penguin Books' (the title of an article he wrote about his application of enlightened traditional principles to the typography of mass-produced texts).

These few paragraphs may be enough to suggest that Tschichold's work is important and deserves to be properly documented and accounted for. Ruari McLean's *Jan Tschichold* is the main English-language attempt at a 'life and work'. First published in 1975, it has now been reissued in paperback. There are some tiny revisions: four new items in the bibliography, and a missing diagram provided on page 129. The 1990 press-work (done in Singapore) improves on the 1975 printing (Bradford). When the book first appeared, I was shocked by what seemed a too casual if innocent piece of compilation, and said this in a review published in an obscure typographic journal. Some rather acrid exchanges between author and reviewer followed, in public and in private.

Among my objections was that McLean's chief source of information, inadequately acknowledged, was an article, full of praise for its subject, which Tschichold himself wrote and published pseudonymously. (Only the chapter on Tschichold at Penguin Books has the feeling of a fresh account.) And, like the author's way with historical evidence, the treatment of illustrations was less than scrupulous: many being derived from existing reproductions, thus producing flat simulacra several times removed from original artefacts (and this for a designer so concerned with material qualities!). And that the design of the book itself (not McLean's work) was a muddle, which Tschichold, in any phase of his career, would have thrown into the waste-bin. The title-page, with its jam-packed letters, now has the feel of a period piece, as certainly as any pair of flared trousers.

At the root of this argument there seems to be a large difference of attitude. Ruari McLean, though a Scot, is a good pillar of the English typographic establishment, towards which the older Tschichold looked with some affection (removed from the storms of Central Europe, it seemed reassuring). This 'establishment' is in fact quite various in its tastes and social composition: though, as elsewhere in English life, there is a marked distaste for anything too intellectual or intense. In this spirit of gentle consensus, McLean writes here: 'There is good typography and bad typography, but not modern typography in any significant sense'. For others of us – outsiders to the old-boys' club of English typography – it still seems important to practise a modern typography, and to trace its history. This book may have some function as a primer, but it shows scant feeling for the adventure of the modern movement in design, and is written and illustrated with too little fussy concern for detail. In these ways it is no match for its complex subject.

Blueprint, no. 72, November 1990

Fifty Penguin years

An exhibition at the Royal Festival Hall, London, 21 September to 27 October 1985, with accompanying book: *Fifty Penguin years*, Penguin Books, 1985

History is always written with a purpose, and this is nowhere more clearly the case than with histories produced to celebrate the anniversary of an institution or a company. It has been the peculiar quality of Penguin Books to be both 'company' and 'institution'. Thus anyone whose reading habits were formed before about 1975 must feel that they have a stake in Penguin: then it might have seemed that the Penguin Stock List could reasonably define the horizons of one's reading. After Allen Lane's death in 1970, and with the immediate acquisition of the company by the multi-interest conglomerate of Pearson, Penguin went through a stormy passage, in that time of general recession and economic crisis. This reached a climax in 1978 with the arrival of a new chief executive, Peter Mayer. Under the direction of this rude, brash American, Penguin embarked on a policy of hard-sell marketing, throwing away their standards of seriousness of content and good design, in favour of airport books wrapped in embossed and gold-blocked packaging.

This is one version of the latest episode in the story of Penguin Books, and it is attractive to Penguin watchers of long standing, who feel personally grieved to see the publisher of Leavis, Edward Thompson, Pevsner, and Dorothy George now making so much of (and out of) Shirley Conran and Audrey Eyton. The recent anniversary celebrations have been marred by one such expression of outrage: from Richard Gott, who edited the Penguin Latin American Library, one of the casualties of the rationalization of the 1970s. His attack on Penguin under Pearson and Mayer (*The Guardian*, 19 September 1985) carried the headline 'Pulp fiction and pots of money ... Pick up a Penguin? I'd rather have a chocolate biscuit'.

But the story is not so simple. The dispelling of the myth of glorious high standards collapsing into pulp was one of the tasks successfully accomplished by the fiftieth birthday exhibition, its accompanying publication, and the other presents-to-itself that

Penguin Books have indulged in. It is to the credit of those producing this company-sponsored history that they have achieved this by resisting hype (though some of that has inevitably crept in) and by presenting what looks like the whole face of Penguin with frequent stops to point out the warts.

The ambiguities of the enterprise of Penguin Books – the balance of cultural philanthropy and shrewd calculation were there from the start. The famous first ten Penguins (now reprinted in a boxed set) were no more than a rather arbitrary cross-section of the popular literature of 1935, whose rights happened to be affordable. The educational impulse came later (1937) with the success of the first Pelicans. One's impression of Allen Lane – a man blessed with frank biographers – is not so much of a missionary of cultural enlightenment, but of a rather unliterary entrepreneur who somehow found himself riding on the crests of a succession of waves that encouraged a near insatiable appetite for good cheap books. A key to this success was Lane's gift for acquiring the services of scholarly but business-minded editors. (One of the pleasures of the exhibition was the painting by Rodrigo Moynihan of the editors in 1955: frozen in silent limbo.)

The story of the company is a complex one of shifts and ruptures, not of smooth progress. The publications produced in celebration of previous anniversaries did not really admit this, as their titles indicate – *The Penguin story* (1956), *Penguins progress* (1960) – though much of the company's trouble was then still to come. The changes of the 1960s, especially those instigated by Tony Godwin, were in their way as drastic as those overseen by Peter Mayer. Certainly the covers produced under the art-editorship of Alan Aldridge rivalled in bad taste those of the last few years. But whereas Penguin in the late 1960s was operating in a climate conditioned by the Robbins Report and Labour in power, the present context is utterly different. So that instead of the Latin American Library we have the *F-Plan diet*. In the oedipal drama of the 1960s the father was still around to disapprove and dismiss (the case of Tony Godwin), but now, with Allen Lane transmuted into Pearson plc, the only sanctions on the unruly son seem to be financial ones.

The anniversary exhibition took the form of thirty-four large panels, each the format of a standard Penguin book: on one side a blown-up cover of landmark titles; on the other side an assembly of text and images with a square glass-covered cut-out section in which were placed books and other documents. This arrangement worked well: a strong sense of real artefacts was conveyed, balanced and put in context by the surrounding commentary. Though the sequence of panels was essentially chronological, within this scheme special themes or categories were picked out, and throughout good use was made of comparative juxtaposition. Perhaps the strongest point of the exhibition's approach – and what lifted it above mere publicity – was the inclusion of non-Penguin material. Thus there were examples of the predecessors – Tauchnitz, Benn's Sixpenny Library, Albatross – and the imitators (Toucan, Jackdaw, and so on). At various stages the rivals that have prompted Penguin to changes of direction were shown and discussed. It was good to see the section on the process by which the books get produced, from typescript to bound copy. And there were a few treasures: pages from Pevsner's fieldnotes for the 'Buildings of England' *Sussex*; a jacket proof with corrections ('8 points more space') by the late Hans Schmoller, whose contribution to Penguin typography has been perhaps unfairly overshadowed by that of his celebrated predecessor. In these and other ways the exhibition lived up to the best Penguin tradition of enlightened and enlightening self-interest.

The publication produced to accompany the exhibition contains fully illustrated texts on the publishing history by Linda Lloyd Jones and on the design history by Jeremy Aynsley. These contributions largely correspond to the structure of the exhibition and the issues it presents, and they do not escape the problems of doing history with the subject looking over your shoulder. This difficulty becomes most acute in the final sections on 'the present', where the pressure to turn into a company spokesperson must be intense. Jeremy Aynsley struggles valiantly against it in his essay. Included with this survey is a sequence of 84 colour reproductions of covers, with details of size, date, designers, then tabulated. For its illustrations especially this publication will be a useful document, though one misses a bibliography of writing about Penguin and about paperbacks in general. The book is designed in the best Tschichold–Schmoller tradition by Jerry Cinamon and Tony Kitzinger; as if to show that Penguin can still do it when they try.

By way of conclusion, and for the wider issues that it raises – so that what might seem just a matter of design in fact entails every other aspect of the operation – it is worth mentioning one piece of muddle in the book. Jeremy Aynsley suggests that the coming of filmsetting ('photocomposition' would be a more accurate term) has reduced the range of available typefaces. But this new process of text composition (by no means confined to Monophoto) has greatly increased the repertoire of typefaces, while at the same time radically undermining their quality and even their identity. Indeed the very concept of a typeface now makes little sense: such has been the effect of the redrawing of master images, the distortions of optical generation, the disruption of spacing norms. It is all, one is tempted to observe, and for some of the same reasons, rather like the destruction of the individual subject in late-capitalist society. So where the old splendidly informative Penguin colophons explained that the book was 'set in Monotype Bembo' or 'set in Intertype Times', now we are lucky if they admit to the useless information of 'set in Bembo', 'set in Times'. What variety of Bembo or Times we, and probably Penguin too, do not know. But where, as is often now the case (for reasons of economy), the text has not been reset for the Penguin edition and is the setting used for a hardback edition, then there is little likelihood that anyone knows what typeface was used, if it ever had any identity in the first place.

In the early 1970s, Hans Schmoller produced a proposal of guidelines for design of hardback texts so that they could be reduced to paperback size without the losses entailed in the unplanned reduction of text setting. The proposal came to nothing: as usual, rational co-ordination of design did not appeal to competing enterprises. But, since that time, publishers – not least Penguin Books – have been swallowing each other up with increasing pace. The prospect is now of a few giant conglomerates, irritated (one hopes) by a swarm of small publishers. Perhaps, as John Sutherland suggested in a penetrating article on Penguin (*Times Literary Supplement*, 27 September 1985), this could lead to a breakdown in the traditional division of the Anglo-American book trade into hardback and paperback. Such a dissolution would have its effect on the design of books. The paperback and hardback editions of these new conglomerates could be co-ordinated, and it might even be that we could return to sober covers with decent letterspacing. Without the fetish of the compulsory hardback, we might be free to emulate the standards, both of content and of design, of publishers on the European continent: one thinks of Suhrkamp, Einaudi, Gallimard. But the matter is more complicated, and, before believing in such dreams, the very different cultural traditions of these countries would have to be considered. As case studies in such an investigation, one could well take the designers who contributed so much to Penguin: Tschichold, Schmoller, Facetti.

Design History Society Newsletter, no. 27, 1985

Teige animator

An exhibition at the Stedelijk Museum, Amsterdam, 4 February to 3 April 1994, with accompanying booklet: *Teige animator*, Teige Genootschap, 1994

A compact and suggestive exhibition on the work of Karel Teige was shown at the Stedelijk Museum in Amsterdam earlier this year. Until recently, Teige has been a footnote figure of Central European modernism in its heroic years. For example, I knew of him as the man who attacked Le Corbusier from the left flank in the debate of 1928–9 over the Mundaneum project; and then also as a designer of books reproduced in anthologies of the 'new typography'. Teige was born, with the new century, in Prague. He moved rapidly into orbit as an 'animator' across the whole cultural field, but especially in architectural criticism, before sinking into obscurity in the later 1930s. He died in Prague in 1951, in politically charged and doubtful circumstances.

Teige was and *did* – more than he created material products. Certainly the spirit of his work proclaims this. He is for life, activity, change, process: and against the production of self-satisfied objects. This is the force of his Poetism ('free and without limits, it knows no inhibitions'), which coexisted with his advocacy of a tough, political

Constructivism. The former is then a wild 'superstructure' on the solid 'base' of the latter. So, given this double-pronged refusal of the static glorified object, it is hard, perhaps even perverse, to make an exhibition of Karel Teige's work.

At the Stedelijk, two small rooms contained cases of books, pamphlets, periodicals, photographs. Short explanatory texts had been photocopied onto sheets of detail paper. The architectural section, under the guidance of Czech-born Netherlands-residing Otakar Máčel, presented Teige's strong judgements on the buildings of his time. On the walls were hung pictures, especially the photo-montages that Teige made from the mid-1930s to the end of his life. These works use images of women cut from soft-pornographic pub-lications, often in juxtaposition with photographs of cool modern architecture. If there is always an element of contradiction in Teige, it is clearest in these private fantasies, made in political hiberna-tion. It is only since 1989 that they have been widely published and discussed.

The exhibition was launched on 6 February with a delightful event in the museum's lecture theatre. This comprised an intro-duction to Teige by Koosje Sierman (critic and ring-leader behind the exhibition), a view of the photomontages from the Czech-born Switzerland-residing architect Hana Císařová, a speech by the Czech cultural attaché in the Netherlands, and a performance of the 'ABC Ballet'. Two women danced out the letters of the alphabet, in accom-paniment to a reading (in the original Czech) of Vítězslav Nezval's poem on this theme. This was published in 1926 as the book *Abece-da*, designed by Teige. We saw the corresponding page projected as a backdrop to these letters made flesh – and were again reminded that heroic Modernism was stranger than is allowed by the present myth of grey constraint.

To accompany the exhibition, a 24-page booklet (in Dutch only) was produced. This is well illustrated with some images not repro-duced before, and has three short critical essays on aspects of Teige, two texts by Teige himself, and an interview that he recorded in 1935 with Mart Stam about architecture in the USSR. If your Dutch is bet-ter than your Czech – or even if it isn't – this document is worth get-ting hold of. It takes its place with a number of recent or forthcom-ing publications about Teige. These include some English-language items: an issue of *Rassegna* (no. 53) on 'Karel Teige: architecture and poetry', an article by Koosje Sierman on Teige's book design work in *Eye* (no. 12, 1994), and a selection of Teige's architectural writings due for publication by the Getty Center. But the main event in this process of rediscovery must be the first large-scale exhibition on Teige, which was shown earlier this year at the Galerie Hlavního Města Prahy (Gallery of the City of Prague). This show was accompanied by a well-produced 208-page A4 catalogue that deals with the whole span of Teige's activity – in Czech, but with English resumés.

Finally, there is a moral to be drawn from the Amsterdam show. It was the work of a group of enthusiasts, mainly self-employed and outside the academy. In just under a year, they came together to form a 'Teige-society', held meetings, got a letterheading printed, opened a bank account, raised 30,000 guilders in subsidy, persuaded the Stedelijk Museum to put on the show, borrowed material from National Literature Archives in Prague and from private sources in the Netherlands, compiled and published a booklet, and arranged an opening in which it was hard to find even room to stand. In other words, it was a splendid demonstration of 'civil society' in action – that thing which is being rediscovered in the East, and which sometimes in the liberal West is in danger of being squeezed out by the rigidities of institutional and academic life.

Design History Society Newsletter, no. 62, 1994

For a typographer, reading books can be difficult. If the page numbers are clumsily positioned, then the story has to be very good – to soak up the constant irritation of this mishandled detail. There is a special pleasure that comes with a book that is good in both content and typography. And I think you can often judge a book by the space between its lines.

A little book that I encountered first as a student has some claims to biblical status: it certainly changed my life. This was Norman Potter's *What is a designer*. The mix of down-to-earth practicality and high-flown ideas appealed to me, as did the 9/12 point Times Roman unjustified setting (Monotype, printed letterpress). Later I got to know the author, became his editor and publisher, and put out two further editions of the book. The second edition is the best typographically: still letterpress and still 9/12 point Times; but now A5 format and paper-bound with flaps (in the French manner). We tried to make it look like a standard book: a prototype for a series of hundreds, in the best modern spirit.

But my real secular bible would be a more difficult work than this. To tell the truth, it is a text that I still haven't quite finished (the closing pages are very hard). Theodor Adorno's *Minima moralia* bears the subtitle 'reflections from damaged life'. It was written in 1944–5, while the author was in Los Angeles, exiled from his language and from the culture of the old world, which had anyway been shattered by German National-Socialism. The damage that the book acts out, even in its own form of fragments and aphorisms, is both personal and world-historical. History had gone horribly wrong, and Adorno looks unblinkingly at the very worst, while still hanging on to some forms of reason and modernity.

Adorno's meditations take a form that isn't known to the empirical English: they are philosophy, but written in a dense, taut language that is certainly 'literature', and, while addressing the familiar issues of philosophy, the book's examples often come from everyday life in the modern world. Adorno works through details: 'the whole is the false' is one of his mottos, and it could stand as a reproach to all those sweeping theorizers who never stop to look at anything in particular.

I liked the book in its original German-language edition, without being able to understand much of it, but admiring the sober Suhrkamp typography. In 1974, New Left Books published a brilliant English translation by Edmund Jephcott. Their books were printed letterpress then, and were still being designed by a good typographer (Jerry Cinamon); they came to club members in hardback and without a dustjacket. The sombre, unsentimental content of the book was given appropriate form.

So what could this book mean for designers? At that time a few of us were beginning to conceive some notion of a 'critical approach'. We thought of a theory that would inform practice, and a practice that would work good effects on theory. Our heroes were the Weimar intellectuals: Walter Benjamin, Adorno, Ernst Bloch, Siegfried Kracauer. They were just 'writers', resisting the academy, and not disdaining the 700-word newspaper column. In architecture, critics such as Kenneth Frampton were showing the way: and Frampton had after all been a practising architect (witness the apartment-block in Craven Hill Gardens, London w2). We had some dream of sitting at marble-topped tables in Central European coffee houses, composing texts or layouts on cigarette-packets. As well as his writing, Adorno's form of practice was music: he could play his way through a Schubert piano sonata and composed some pieces of his own.

Despite – or especially because of – the loss of faith in modernity and rationality, Adorno's work seems just as necessary now as when I encountered it twenty years ago. His long paragraphs anticipate and consider the doubts, act out the contradictions and inconsequences – and yet, just through this endeavour of critical thought, leave the reader with the sense of something won, and with the need to go on thinking.

Design Review, no. 2, 1991

Commissioned by Deyan Sudjic for a column in the relatively short-lived *Design Review*, published by Wordsearch Ltd for the Chartered Society of Designers. Designers were asked to write about their 'bible'.

Judging a book by its material embodiment: a German-English example

'... the ideal reader, whom books do not tolerate, would know something of what is inside when he felt the cover in his hand and saw the layout of the title page and the overall quality of the pages, and would sense the book's value without needing to read it first.'[1] Thus Theodor Adorno concluding the series of reflections, 'Bibliographische Grillen' ('Bibliographical musings'), which, his editors explain, he developed from an article first published in the *Frankfurter Allgemeine Zeitung*, 16 October 1959. I quote it now as a salute to the marvellous Adorno, who for much of his life wrote journalism of the most serious kind – short critical essays, feuilletons – and I quote this because it gets straight to the heart of what I want to talk about.

Adorno opens these reflections by explaining that he has just been at a book fair. This was October, so I suppose it was the great Buchmesse at Frankfurt. The book fair experience is dizzying. In a few hours you may pass by thousands of books, and look in some detail at hundreds of them. Nowadays at Frankfurt each of the huge halls is provided with stalls around the edges, where you can buy energy foods and drinks, to keep you going, in a kind of pit-stop. If you are there for professional reasons, say as a publisher looking to acquire titles for a list, or a bookseller looking for books to stock in your shop, you will make many instant judgements of the value of a book, on the basis of picking it up, balancing it in your hands, flipping through the pages. This is the initial screening of the text: the decision about whether to take a closer interest in it, as a business proposition.

In this essay, Adorno laments the fate of the book. He writes: 'I realized that books no longer look like books. Adaptation to what – correctly or incorrectly – is considered the needs of consumers has changed their appearance. Around the world, covers have become

---

1. In the translation by Sherry Weber Nicholsen: Theodor W. Adorno, *Notes to literature*, vol. 2, ed. Rolf Tiedemann, New York: Columbia University Press, 1992 (at p. 31).

advertisements for their books. The dignity that characterizes something self-contained, lasting, hermetic – something that absorbs the reader and closes the lid over him, as it were, the way the cover of the book closes on the text – has been set aside as inappropriate to the times.'[2]

This perception of the book, and of the printed product more generally, as suffering a fall, is one that has been widely held, if variously applied and variously understood. For example, you can understand William Morris's endeavours in the field of printing and publishing as a protest against this situation of the fall, and as an attempt to provide a little model of how printing could be decently done. Morris's example was taken up quite widely then, the last years of the nineteenth century, in many western countries. The familiar account, which I think has much truth in it, is that out of the Arts & Crafts rebellion emerged the figure that we call the designer – the typographic designer, the book designer. This person attempted to order the processes of production in printing, and attempted to reinfuse the aesthetic element, the dimension of material and visual surplus – pleasure – which printers could no longer provide as an inbuilt part of what they were making.

This complex of forces – technical change, changes in component materials – has set the terms of what has happened since that moment at the end of the nineteenth century. It is a struggle that has gone through many turns, and still continues. Thus in the 1950s in the UK or in Adorno's Federal Republic of Germany, for a hardback book, cloth was still a normal material to use as a cover for the case. Cloth has an inherent material quality: you don't have to add 'design' to make it look good. Though, of course, some cloths are better than others. As cloth began to be replaced by paper-derived or other rather obviously synthetic materials, it became necessary for a design/production person to intervene. Previously a specification for binding might have been lazily stated by an editor in the publishing house and then more precisely implemented by a printer. But now one definitely needed someone with experience and constantly updated knowledge to search for good materials among the diminishing suppliers of cloth, or to discriminate be-

2. 'Bibliographical musings', *Notes to literature*, p. 20.

A timeline of British publishers

A simplified history of the main trade publishing groups

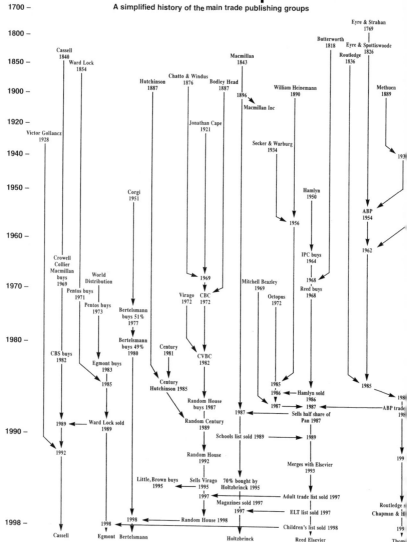

1   From: Christopher Gasson, *Who owns whom in British book publishing*,
    Bookseller Publications, 1998, pp. 12–13. (Copyright © Bookseller Publications / CG 1998.)

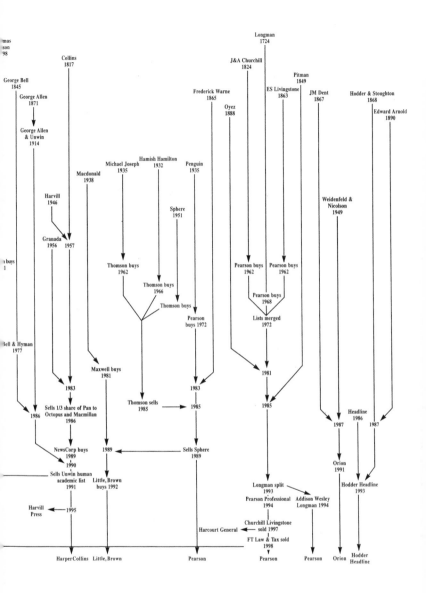

See also the listing of ownerships (primarily North American and transnational) compiled by Laura Miller and published in 2002 at
<http://people.brandeis.edu/~lamiller/publishers.html>.

tween the other materials. This is the hard battleground of design, and one could talk about every aspect of a book in just these terms of search, discrimination, negotiation: in paper, binding techniques, typesetting, picture reproduction.

This is not the occasion to argue it out, but I want to state firmly here that I do not see the situation of book production, in the twentieth century, or in any other century, as one of 'fall'. It is much more complex than this. With paper or with typesetting, the development has been one of progress and regress, both, and – both at once. With colour printing, you might argue that there has been only progress.

There is one fundamental dimension of book production that exhibits relentless progress, which you might well call regress, and in the diagram reproduced here, it is shown as a vertical drop (figure 1). This tells what we all know, but which is not often brought together so precisely and so vividly. One can see that 1959, the year of Adorno's visit to the Buchmesse, came just at the end of the stable years. The middle 1980s were when things really fell apart – or came together, under a diminishing number of corporate roofs.

In January 1985 a new publishing imprint was launched in the German Federal Republic, 'Die Andere Bibliothek' ('the other library'). It was a collaboration between the printer and publisher Franz Greno, working from Nördlingen (Bavaria) and the writer and editor Hans Magnus Enzensberger, living in Munich. Franz Greno already had a publishing and book-packaging company, the Greno Verlag, and also had a printing business. As a printer, trained as a compositor in the 1960s, he had become devoted to letterpress printing and Monotype (hot-metal) composition, which by the 1980s was for most intents and purposes extinct. The Andere Bibliothek was, and still is, an attempt to publish books of real content in a form that had distinct material quality, and which, in sum, resisted the apparently irresistible processes of commodification. Books would be set on the Monotype machine, printed letterpress on good paper, case-bound with patterned or in other ways distinguished paper, without a jacket and with no more than the name of the author and the title on the spine, usually as a 'label' or an embossed plate.

The list of the Andere Bibliothek is varied; indeed here, as in the form of its books, it exhibits a radical otherness. It includes some straight fiction, but not so much; it has much informal writing – travel reports, letters, diaries, and other texts that defy categories more completely. There is much translated work. To give you an idea: from the English language are books by George Gissing (*Zeilengeld*), Laurence Sterne (*Yoricks empfindsame Reise durch Frankreich und Italien*), Walter (*Viktorianische Ausschweifungen*), Nancy Mitford (*Liebe unter kaltem Himmel*), Ian Buruma (*Der Staub Gottes*), John Aubrey (*Lebens-Entwürfe*), Henry Mayhew (*Die Armen von London*).

The Andere Bibliothek has elements of the book-club: just one new title is issued every month, in a limited and numbered edition, for which one can subscribe. In the first period of the life of the series, a monthly newsletter was published. But the books are also available through the ordinary book trade, and in the first years they were sold with a flat and rather low cover price: 25 Deutschmarks. In 1988, the Andere Bibliothek published an international bestseller, Christoph Ransmayr's *Die letzte Welt*, which sold over 150,000 copies in the Federal Republic in its first year. Despite such successes, the next year, 1989, Greno Verlag found itself in financial trouble. The Greno Verlag was wound up, and, in October of that year, its Andere Bibliothek series was sold to Eichborn Verlag, a large general publisher based in Frankfurt. The series continues to this day, essentially unchanged in concept: still edited by Enzensberger, production still in the hands of Franz Greno.

The rest of this discussion will be given over to a close look at one of the books of the Andere Bibliothek: *Die Ringe des Saturn* by the German teacher and writer W. G. Sebald, since 1970 resident in Norwich and teacher at the University of East Anglia. *Die Ringe des Saturn* was published in October 1995, as number 130 in the series.

In what follows my sources are the books themselves, the occasional report in the book trade press, and catalogues and leaflets picked up over the years at the Frankfurt Book Fair. They tell us that Sebald's first book was *Die Beschreibung des Unglücks* ('the description of unhappiness'; Residenz Verlag: Salzburg, 1985). Then *Nach der Natur* ('after nature'), was published in 1988 by the Greno Verlag, whose catalogue described the work as having the character of a

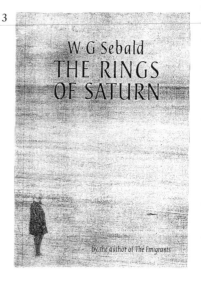

long poem, though without rhyme and metre, the text being accompanied by photographs by Thomas Becker, which, the catalogue
says, 'suggest thoughts of the deepest melancholy – that the world
would be better without human beings in it and would be in order
only as a world without meaning.' In addition to *Die Ringe des Saturn*
(1995), two other books by Sebald have appeared in the Andere Bibliothek: *Schwindel, Gefühle* (1990) and *Die Ausgewänderten* (1992).
Sebald became known to the reading public in the UK in 1996, with
the translation of *Die Ausgewänderten*, as *The emigrants*, published
by The Harvill Press.

For information here, one can turn back to the *Who owns
whom* diagram. Harvill began to publish in 1946. It was established
by two women – Manya Harari and Marjorie Villiers – thus the
name: Har-vill. They specialized in translations of literature into
English – high-minded and occasionally finding big sellers (Pasternak, Lampedusa). Translated literature is the Harvill specializa-
tion that still continues, despite the changes of ownership that have
seemed absolutely in tune with the times. The progression is as fol-

4

beinahe ein Vierteljahr. Erst am Weihnachtstag läuft die Mont Blanc, schwer angeschlagen von den Winterstürmen, in Le Havre ein. Unbeirrt von dieser strapaziösen Initiierung in das Seeleben, macht Konrad Korzeniowski weitere Reisen zu den Westindischen Inseln, nach Cap-Haitien, nach Port-au-Prince, nach St. Thomas und dem wenig später von einem Ausbruch des Mont Pelée zerstörten St. Pierre. Hinüber

werden Waffen gebracht, Dampfmaschinen, Pulver und Munition. Herüber kommt tonnenweise Zucker und das in den Regenwäldern geschlagene Holz. Die Zeit, in der er nicht zur See ist, verbringt Korzeniowski in Marseille sowohl mit seinen Berufsgenossen als auch mit vornehmeren Leuten. Im Café Boudol in der Rue Saint-Ferréol und im Salon der majestätischen Gattin des Bankiers und Reeders Delestang gerät er in eine aus Adeligen, Bohemiens, Geldgebern, Abenteurern und spanischen Legitimisten seltsam

120

gemischte Gesellschaft. Die letzten Zuckungen der Ritterlichkeit vereinigen sich mit den skrupellosesten Machenschaften, komplizierte Intrigen werden gesponnen, Schmugglersyndikate gegründet und undurchsichtige Geschäfte abgeschlossen. Korzeniowski ist vielfach verstrickt, verbraucht weit mehr als er hat und erliegt den Verführungen einer geheimnisvollen, mit ihm etwa gleichaltrigen, aber nichtsdestoweniger bereits im Witwenstand sich befindenden Dame. Diese Dame, deren wahre Identität nie mit Sicherheit festgestellt werden konnte, war in den Kreisen der Legitimisten, in denen sie eine prominente Rolle spielte, unter dem Namen Rita bekannt, und es wurde behauptet, daß sie die Geliebte des Bourbonenprinzen Don Carlos gewesen sei, den man, auf die eine oder andere Weise, auf den spanischen Thron bringen wollte. Später ist von verschiedener Seite das Gerücht ausgestreut worden, daß es sich bei der in einer Villa in der Rue Sylvabelle residierenden Doña Rita und bei einer gewissen Paula de Somoggy um ein und dieselbe Person gehandelt habe. Dieser Geschichte zufolge hat Don Carlos, als er im November 1877 von einer Besichtigung der Frontstellungen des russisch-türkischen Krieges nach Wien zurückkam, eine Mme. Hannover gebeten, ihm eine junge Choristin namens Paula Horvath aus Pest zuzuführen, die ihm, wie man annehmen muß, ihrer Schönheit wegen in die Augen gestochen war. Von Wien aus fuhr Don Carlos mit seiner neu aquirierten Begleiterin zuerst zu seinem Bruder nach Graz und von dort aus nach Venedig, Modena und Mailand, wo er sie als Baronin de Somoggy in die Gesellschaft vor-

121

5

and thirty-seven guilders and seventy-five groschen. He took with him no more than would fit into his small case, and it would be almost sixteen years before he returned to visit his native country again.

In 1875 Konrad Korzeniowski crossed the Atlantic for the first time, on the barque Mont Blanc. At the end of July he was on Martinique, where the ship lay at anchor for two months. The homeward voyage took almost a quarter of a year. It was not until Christmas Day that the Mont Blanc, badly damaged by winter storms, made Le Havre. Undeterred by this tough initiation into life at sea, Konrad Korzeniowski changed for further voyages to the West Indies, where he visited Cap-Haitien, Port-au-Prince, St Thomas and St Pierre, which was devastated soon afterwards when Mont Pelée erupted.

210

On the outward sailing the ship carried arms, steam-powered engines, gunpowder and ammunition. On the return the cargo was sugar and timber. He spent the time when he was not at sea in Marseilles, among fellow sailors and also with people of greater refinement. At the Café Boudol in the rue Saint-Ferréol and in the salon of Mme Delestang, whose husband was a banker and ship owner, he frequented gatherings that included aristocrats, bohemians, financiers, adventurers, and Spanish Legitimists. The dying throes of courtly life went side by side with the most unscrupulous machinations, complex intrigues were connived at, smuggling syndicates were founded, and shady deals agreed. Korzeniowski was involved in many things, spent more than he had, and succumbed to the advances of a mysterious lady who, though just his own age, was already a widow. This lady, whose true identity has not been established with any certainty, was known as Rita in Legitimist circles, where she played a prominent part; and it was said that she had been the mistress of Don Carlos, the Bourbon prince, whom there were plans to instate, by hook or by crook, on the Spanish throne. Subsequently it was rumoured in various quarters that Doña Rita, who resided in a villa in rue Sylvabelle, and one Paula de Somogyi were one and the same person. The story went that in November 1877, when Don Carlos returned to Vienna from inspecting the front line in the Russo-Turkish war, he asked a certain Mme Hannover to procure for him a Pest chorus girl by the name of Paula Horvath, whose beauty had caught his eye. From Vienna, with his new companion, Don Carlos travelled first to see his brother in Graz and then onward to Venice, Modena and Milan, where he introduced her in society as

211

2 & 3   *Die ringe des Saturn* (212 x 120 mm) and *The rings of Saturn* (210 x 147 mm) from the front: the original edition was cased and without a jacket.

4 & 5   Inside the two editions, showing the different column widths, and the British edition's wired binding under strain.

lows: in 1957 Harvill was taken over by the long-established Scottish family firm of Collins, which was taken over by Granada in 1983, and then in 1989 bought by News Corporation (becoming Harper-Collins). But in April 1995, the Harvill management, with the help of a consortium of backers, bought themselves out of HarperCollins, and the imprint regained its independence.

Harvill is also interested in some degree of aesthetic surplus in their books. Nowadays their typesetting is done by the Libanus Press in Marlborough, Wiltshire. This had been a small 'private press' with metal type for handsetting and letterpress printing equipment: a part-time operation. The proprietor of the Libanus Press, when I met him in the 1980s, worked as a dentist. But now, certainly in the typesetting that the Libanus Press does for Harvill, the instrument is a computer.

In 1998, following the success of their edition of *Die Ausgewän-derten*, Harvill published an edition of *Die Ringe des Saturn*, as *The rings of Saturn*. A comparison between the original edition and the Harvill edition tells us something about present-day literary culture in the two countries, Germany and the UK. I also want to suggest that the form of the book in its original edition tells us something about Sebald's enterprise as a writer, and about this particular text: things that you miss if you have access only to the Harvill edition.

Looking at the books side by side (figures 2 to 5), it is clear that the German edition puts up some resistance to the market-place: to the book as a package. It has no jacket, only a removable cardboard 'pullover'. This is a feature introduced to the Andere Bibliothek since the take-over by Eichborn. The cover of the Harvill edition uses a well-worn recipe of instant culture: a detail of a painting. This is from a painting by James McNeill Whistler, of the beach at Trouville, 1865, in a museum in Boston, USA. The date is perhaps acceptable for Sebald's text, but nothing else is.

Things get worse inside the Harvill edition. The paperback edition has flapped covers that are, in this copy, ill-applied to the book-block. The lower flap recedes rather than projects. The sections of the book are not sewn, but rather cut and held together by a process that involves wire-fixing and glue. The grain of the paper runs across the page, at right angles to the spine, so that it tends to buckle, wanting to bend horizontally. The book opens badly. Further, the paper seems noticeably greasy, as if laminated, and after some months of free existence, it still smells noticeably.

By contrast, the German edition is exemplary in all these respects of materials and construction. One telling comparison is the weight of the two editions. Both books weigh 575 grammes: yet the UK edition is a paperback book of 296 pages, while the German book has 376 pages and is case-bound. This alone should tell us that there is something wrong with the UK edition.

Inside, the pages of the German book are elegant: the width of lines is relatively narrow. At the end, the sequence of what one might call postlims is notably considered: information on the author, contents list, information about the edition. The last page is empty. The endpapers give us two useful and different maps, showing some of the terrain covered in the book. By contrast, the UK edition has a very clumsy and unpleasant ending: text running on to the last page, facing the back flap.

Die Ringe des Saturn belongs to no simple category of literature. It is the report of a writer in the world, and in that part of England (Suffolk): what he sees, what he remembers, what he dreams about. It is informal, occasional, without much sequence apart from the journey described. In fact it is an unambitious and unremarkable journey. The subtitle of the German edition – 'eine englische Wallfahrt' ('an English journey' – or 'pilgrimage', one might even say) is dropped in the English edition.

The component of Sebald's work that has surprised its reviewers – both of *The rings of Saturn* and *The emigrants* – are the pictures dropped into the text. The presence of images is most notable in *The emigrants*, which one might otherwise have taken to be simple fiction. These images are of varying technical quality: some are obviously photocopies of printed images, others are rather fuzzy and bad snapshots. But this does not matter. It is like a collection of working images that a writer might gather as an aid; except that Sebald has decided to include them in his book, to intersperse them in his (by contrast) highly considered prose.

Here again, the two editions show a difference. In the German edition, the images tend to be placed exactly where the text demands that they fall, even if this means that just two or three lines run above or below. In the English book, there is a rather more conventional approach: an image will be put right at the top or right at the bottom of a page.[3] I feel that this tidying up is some betrayal of meaning, and of the innocence of the work that Sebald produced.

British reviewers of *The rings of Saturn* have rightly praised the quality of the translation into English, by Michael Hulse (the British poet, resident in Germany). And they have struggled to describe the strange, hard-to-pin-down quality of the whole work. The Harvill edition delivers us the elements of Sebald's book, but it does not embody them satisfactorily. I am inclined to think that it betrays the work.

Die Ringe des Saturn is a work of melancholy, through and through. It is not so much a journey, but rather a meander, with episodes of reverie, of déjà vu, of dislocation. The book dwells on life gone wrong, on damaged life (to use Adorno's phrase). Life is leaving the parts that Sebald travels through. He writes: 'A strikingly large number of our settlements are oriented to the west and, where circumstances permit, relocate in a westward direction. The east stands for lost causes.'[4] In counterpart to this local focus, there are recurring digressions into imperial themes: but again, lingering on the calamitous. There is a chapter on Joseph Conrad and Roger Casement in Africa, which ends by suggesting a connection between Casement's homosexuality and his sympathy for those oppressed by empire. This suggestion, I could add, reminds me of Hans Magnus Enzensberger's cast of mind.

To return to the question of genre: what category of literature could this book belong to? It aspires to be a book of the kind that Sir Thomas Browne wrote; and Sebald gives much attention to Browne, a Norwich man, both at the start and towards the end of *Die Ringe des Saturn*. It seems to want to be one of those occasional books, published outside the metropolitan circuit, written by the gentleman amateur. It does not seem to belong to late-twentieth-century

3. In the German edition there are 73 pictures; in the English, 72 pictures (one at the start of chapter 9 is lost). The changes incurred in making the English edition are as follows: moved from top/bottom to mid-placed, 10; moved from mid-placed to top/bottom, 29. So the overall number suffering change of status is 19 out of 72: just over a quarter of the total.

4. W. G. Sebald, *The rings of Saturn*, Harvill, 1998, p. 159.

European publishing. It does not sit easily with some of the other titles in the Harvill list, which exemplify the new category of 'Euro-literature' (for example, Peter Høeg's *Miss Smilla*).

But *Die Ringe des Saturn* does belong somewhere. It belongs to the Andere Bibliothek. This is the context that has helped Sebald to develop as a public writer, and whose range of titles helps us to make sense of this work. I do not think one can ascribe any simple programme to Enzensberger's list. But one can begin to character-ize it: various, sceptical, critical, anti-utilitarian, cosmopolitan, ec-centric, anarchic. (Enzensberger has always been on the Left in Ger-many, but on the non-party New Left. Greno is reported as having served as a Social-Democratic town councillor in Nördlingen.) 'We only print books that we ourselves would like to read', was the motto that Enzensberger and Greno used at the start of the venture: they meant in form and content, both. The books got rid of jackets; they hoped to put forward content without advertisement. Their material surplus was a defiance of narrow rationality, a championing of a lost cause. In retrieving Monotype setting and letterpress printing, Franz Greno was perverse, and not unlike the eccentric characters that Sebald encounters in Suffolk: for example, the farmer Thomas Abrams who has spent twenty years building a model of the Temple of Jerusalem.

All of this is lost in the English edition. Here, apart from the marvellous translation, we have appearance without substance: a book that wants to look like a book, but is not one.

There are qualifications to all this, which I will make by way of conclusion. One could say that the German edition and Sebald's work with it – his project, his 'Versuch' – simply cannot enjoy the innocence that my account is attributing to it. Sebald is not a gentle-man amateur, but a very conscious and thoroughly sophisticated writer and a long-time teacher of literature. One could say that it is not within late-twentieth-century European culture to allow such an innocence. One could argue that the Andere Bibliothek, especially since their crisis of 1989 (the date is perhaps not without significance), and Sebald's books with it, suffer a kind of archness. Even before then, when I first saw these books in the mid-1980s, in the house of a friend in Berlin who was a subscriber to the series, they seemed affected: especially the bindings. They were much bet-

6 The cover of the Dutch edition (200 x 125 mm) used an image that referred to one of the book's topics, but which was not taken from the book itself.

ter done than the sherry-party kitsch of the Folio Society's books; but still … And one could look at other editions of Sebald's book. For example, the Dutch edition provides a third term that unsettles the polarity I have been sketching. *De ringen van Saturnus: een Engelse pelgrimage* was published in 1996 by Van Gennep in Amsterdam (figure 6). It appeared in a paperback edition (only), which did not attempt to match the material qualities of the original, but neither did it attempt the weak 'European' pastiche of the Harvill edition. This Dutch book, designed by Jacques Janssen within a series style that he set for Van Gennep, feels normative and without any pretension in typography and materials. And one should add that the process has moved on: there have been further changes to the Andere Bibliothek since the publication of *Die Ringe des Saturn*. In the following year, 1996, after the series had reached 144 titles (12 years' worth), the books ceased to be printed letterpress. And now, in the wake of his success, W. G. Sebald has left the Andere Bibliothek's list. In 1998, with his book *Logis in einem Landschaft*, a set of essays on Swiss or 'Alemannic' writers, he joined the Hanser Verlag: a larger and more mainstream house. And in autumn 2001, Sebald's latest book, *Austerlitz*, was due for publication in English-language translation – not by Harvill, but by Hamish Hamilton, part of the Pearson conglomerate of publishing and other media interests.

The text of a talk given at the 'Ma(r)king the Text' conference, Trinity College, Cambridge, September 1998, and previously unpublished. For publication here, it has been lightly modified. During the days of the book fair at Frankfurt in October 1998, I had the chance to join a colleague, Søren Møller Christensen, in an interview with Franz Greno: a conversation that helped to confirm my suppositions. As the present book was in the last stages of its preparation, two further events took place. In December 2001, W. G. Sebald died in Norfolk while driving his car. In March 2002, Harvill was taken over by Random House, and thus joined the Bertelsmann empire.

The book of Norman: Otl Aicher and Foster's *Buildings and projects*

The architectural monograph, when the architect is still alive and producing, presents both a problem and an opportunity. Beyond the provision of simple information, the book becomes a continuation of the work – by other means. Not only is there the question of matching book design to architecture, but a much more difficult matter is raised: that of approach, of how the work has been tackled and how it is now discussed. Most such books are content to serve up the buildings cold, with visual documentation of the finished works or projects, some extended captions, and perhaps a critical or not-so-critical introductory essay. By the book shall they not reveal themselves.

The idea of a book about the work of Norman Foster and Foster Associates – something more substantial than the various exhibition catalogues that have appeared – has been around for some years. But the various schemes for it have never quite taken off. Now a series of incidents or accidents has provided the necessary elements, and what will become the major Foster book is published this autumn: or rather, the first two of at least four volumes.

The present project started to take shape in 1986, with the prospect of a major exhibition of Foster's work at the Museum of Modern Art in New York. The MOMA show was eventually abandoned, after Arthur Drexler's death, but by then (early 1987) the book had gained its own momentum. The practical problems of such a book turn around contradictory motives: the architect's wish for control over content and presentation; the publisher's more commercially constrained view, and the wish to fit the title into a list. Even if the architect subsidizes the book, these conflicts may not be resolved. Foster had had discussions with established firms, but eventually settled for a new publisher, Ian Lambot.

Lambot was trained as an architect but has gravitated towards graphics and presentation, with a photography and design studio in Hong Kong. When the Hongkong & Shanghai Bank job started up, Lambot was persuaded to join the Foster office, for whom he worked on presentations for two years both in Hong Kong and London. Then, as an independent venture, he photographed the building of the Bank, producing a remarkable sequence of images. Wanting to publish these and unable to get a satisfactory deal with an established firm, his portfolio of photographs of the Bank was issued as a self-published book in October 1986.

The Hongkong Bank also led to the discovery of the book's designer. Foster had been recommended to see Otl Aicher in the search for someone to do the signing for the building. Aicher can be described as the father of post-war German graphic design: a co-founder of and long-serving teacher at the Hochschule für Gestaltung Ulm, designer for the 1972 Olympic Games at Munich, he has been consultant to almost every immaculately turned-out company that comes to mind (Braun, Lufthansa, ERCO, Westdeutsche Landesbank, Bulthaup ...). Aicher turned the signing job down, reluctantly: '49 per cent for, and 51 per cent against'. The problems of the project were political, and also for Aicher those of distance and the wish for a calm life. But though he is 66 now, he doesn't look back much, or waste time with interviews. The prospect of collaboration on a book was manageable – and was enhanced by what seems to have been love at first sight between the principal protagonists.

For Aicher, Foster is clearly the present-day architect above all others: pursuing the task with the greatest commitment, the truest philosophical resonance, and the best results, which stand as a living rebuke to the trash that is thrown up by our society, some of it now dignified by the name of postmodernism. Conversely, Foster recognized the qualities of Aicher's work, and particularly the 'cell of good living' that Aicher and his wife, Inge Aicher-Scholl, have created in Rotis, in the far south of Germany.

Rotis is rather more than just a designer's home and studio. There are several studios, and there is an 'Institute for Analogical Studies', which publishes papers and holds discussions. The championing of the 'analogical' – against the 'digital' – is part of an effort to promote a concern with the concrete and the visual. They are for systems, but against empty patterns; for models and against mere theories. The community at Rotis thinks of itself as an autonomous republic; they generate their own electricity, clean their own water, and take vegetable growing seriously. The new buildings, designed by Aicher himself, exemplify these beliefs: a mix of low and high technology, of the local and the international; like all of Aicher's work, the attempt is for a modern vernacular, an everyday design that renounces self-indulgence and special effects.

Along with the mutual recognition between Aicher and Foster, and the same mentality of wanting to do a job properly, there is also a fruitful contrast of temperament. While Foster thinks always of alternatives, Aicher goes for hunches and sticks to them. At the first meeting with Foster and Lambot, it was Aicher who argued conclusively that one book would not be enough; rather, to do justice to the subject, there must be at least four volumes.

Aicher also arrived very quickly at a page format. (See figures 1 & 2.) It is A4 with 3 centimetres added to the width. The grid on which text and pictures lie has six columns of equal width; the main text is set over two columns, subsidiary text set over one column in a smaller size. Text hangs from a top line, and ends where it ends – to leave an unembarrassed white space. This has helped to meet a strategic problem of the book. Two volumes of 200-odd pages were to be produced in just over a year: a very tight schedule, which has in fact been overrun. Pages would have to be designed before the text was written. With this loose-fit system, text can be written

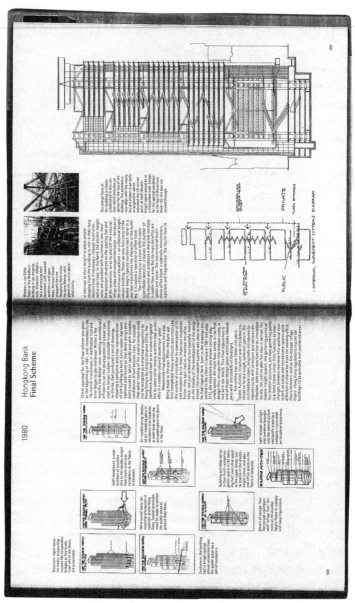

1980

Hongkong Bank
Final Scheme

189

INTERNAL MOVEMENT SYSTEMS DIAGRAM

PUBLIC   PRIVATE

188

2

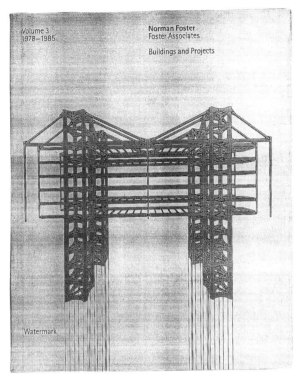

Volume 3
1978–1985

Norman Foster
Foster Associates

Buildings and Projects

Watermark

1 & 2 Typical spread and cover from Norman Foster / Foster Associates, *Buildings and projects* (Hong Kong: Watermark, 1989). The series ran to four volumes, each of which had on its jacket a drawing of one of the main subjects treated within. The pages (297 x 240 mm) carried the material on a flexible grid, in the manner of a magazine, rather than the traditional illustrated book.

with the allowance of a 30 per cent margin of deviation from a standard length. Pictures are all separately captioned with different and rather more technical information than is in the main text: so this provides a further way of using the book, another layer. There is also an upper area of the page which will be used as a 'side plate' for verbal and visual commentary on the matter below. The grid gives the strict rules that then give maximum freedom for the dialogue that goes on between the elements of the page. The result is, as

Aicher explains, 'not beautiful typography, but like a machine that works: art without art'. It is a democratic approach, of openness, interaction, equality. One sees the kinship with Foster's architecture.

Between the four volumes the material is divided by rough chronology and by a certain thematic grouping. Volume one has early work and traditional materials; then the leap into technology and specially-made components in volume two, which is examined more closely in volume three (the Bank and the Tecno furniture); and the growing preoccupation with context in volume four (the BBC, Nîmes). First to appear will be volumes two and three. The standardized looseness of the scheme allows the possibility of continuation, and one can imagine a thick sequence that will compare interestingly with the eight volume *Œuvre complète* of Le Corbusier. The Corb books are of course the unavoidable precedent, but one that has been resisted: both in respect of its physical format (floppy landscape-A4) and of the authorial presence of the architect. Norman Foster is no doubt the prime figure in Foster Associates, but the office's design process is emphatically one of collaborative teamwork. Foster's role in the book is rather distanced, partly through sheer busyness with the primary tasks of the office. He also seems to operate best in dialogue with proposals made by Lambot or Aicher. But all the key decisions have been made by the three chief participants in a number of intensive and very productive work sessions.

The aim of the book is to tell the story of the work and explain its processes, project by project. The first step for Ian Lambot, who is editor as well as publisher, was to gather the visual material. In addition to photographs and finished drawings he had access to the unique resource of Foster's sketchbooks, which have been kept up and filed away since the early days. Working with this image bank, Aicher and Lambot then set out to design the books, in sequences of pages. Aicher's first attempt was a hand-produced dummy: the images shown by sketches, the text by wavy lines. Then they adopted the reducing photocopier and have since stuck with that. Another vital tool has been the large pinboard, either at Aicher's studio (mapping pins on wood) or at Foster's in London and Wiltshire (magnets on metal panels). Sequences of pages can then be seen whole, up to twelve spreads to a row, from a distance. The job becomes one of composition in an almost musical sense: to command the reader's attention with a bold introduction, then into detailed exposition and variations, photographs punctuating drawings, then a proper conclusion. Within the rationality of the structure of a page, there is scope for a strong intuitive element, which Aicher brings from his vast experience of making such books. Sitting back at the end of a session, Aicher knows whether it is working: 'Yes, I have a good feeling about this.'

To anyone accustomed to habits of book design in Britain, this method is unusual. Traditionally, we would start with a text and then find illustrations. In this project, the priority of images is being taken to an extreme, to cater for the tight time-schedule and also for reasons of geography: the pictures are being proof-printed (in Hong Kong) before the text has been set (in Germany) or even wholly written (in London). The writers are teamworkers who will write to a brief and a length – though some of the layouts have been changed to meet their needs. The book has a collaborative spirit: a dialogue of views rather than a single opinion. In addition to the narrative body of text, there are key-setting introductions by professional critics. The 'side-plate' area at the head of pages will carry other ingredients, including quotations from Norman Foster (mainly culled from his lectures), from others in the office, and from clients. Aicher has contributed a text on 'Architecture and epistemology', which makes the case for the depth and seriousness of Foster's work.

If this method succeeds, it will be because both Lambot and Aicher know their subject from the inside: the images are not merely images, but are charged with meaning and narrative content. Thus the possible formalism of treating the text as just 'grey colour' will be avoided. In Aicher's strongly graphic practice of book design, the colour of the text – the 'Satzbild' – is of vital concern. (It is significant that there is no English word for this: we don't work like that.) For Aicher, the text should, at a first overall view, exhibit an even tone. This implies that there should be no perceptible space between the lines.

Another element enters the story here, to meet just this point, and it promises to make this book an even more special endeavour. Aicher has been designing a typeface, which will get its first extended application in these volumes. The motivation behind the typeface, to be called 'Rotis', is the attempt to resolve a dichotomy of form and readability. The classical seriffed forms may be readable, but do not provide adequate resources for contemporary requirements and are not 'of this age'; with sanserif, the reverse is the case. How to make a sanserif that can be read comfortably in a full-length book? Make it more flowing, like handwriting. The German sanserifs of the 1920s and 1930s, such as Futura, now seem too crudely geometric. Aicher wants an 'intelligent technics' – here is the Rotis philosophy – and, for comparison, gives the example of a pair of scissors moulded asymmetrically to the shape of the hands. The grips of unintelligent (postmodern?) scissors would be two semi-circles, rather like back-to-back Futura 'P's. So the 'Rotis Semi-Grotesk' has some awkward, ungeometrical characters, notably the lowercase 'c' and 'e'. While the overall stress of the letters is vertical, achieving the desired 'colour' of text, there is also, through these characters, a sense of flow. The unusual forms are like beer, Aicher suggests: at first you don't like it, but then it comes to seem natural. As a partner to this essentially sanserif typeface, there will be a seriffed version: a 'Semi-Antiqua'. The results were too sour for this beer-lover, at the early stage at which he inspected them, but the problem is an interesting one, and it is being tackled under Aicher's guidance by a skilled draughtswoman with the best computer aid.

The Foster *Buildings and projects* is thus an unusual venture in every respect: the first full discussion of some remarkable architecture; the first extended English-language work by a unique designer; the start of what should be an interesting publisher's list. The elements will combine to make a powerful assertion of a particular approach, splendidly indifferent to the reactionary mood of the times.

Blueprint, no. 51, October 1988

Adieu aesthetica

Adieu aesthetica & mooie pagina's! J. van Krimpen en het 'schoone boek'. Letterontwerper & boekverzorger 1892–1958, with contributions by Sjoerd van Faassen, Koosje Sierman, Sjaak Hubregtse; Museum van Het Boek / De Buitenkant / Museum Enschedé, 1995

An exhibition surveying the work of Jan van Krimpen was shown last summer at the Museum van het Boek (Rijksmuseum Meermanno-Westreenianum) in The Hague, moving later in the year to the American Institute of Graphic Arts in New York. The show, selected by Mathieu Lommen, included many things of great interest. As well as the expected display of printed products – including (less expectedly) a final section on the legacy of the subject – a full gathering of drawings and documents from the archives helped to ensure that the processes of Van Krimpen's work were well represented. This enquiring spirit also animates the book that was published on the occasion of the exhibition.

Adieu aesthetica contains a short essay on the formative years of the subject (by Sjoerd van Faassen), a year-by-year biographical account (by Sjaak Hubregtse), and an essay (by Koosje Sierman) on the dominating part of Van Krimpen's career: the years in which he worked at the printing house of Joh. Enschedé & Zonen, from 1925 until 1958, the year of his death. At seventy pages, in a richly documented and illustrated discussion, Sierman's piece constitutes the book's major contribution. It is sad that her sparkling essay will remain unavailable to readers without any Dutch. For the US exhibition an English-language pamphlet with just the chronological outline biography was published. Neverthless, if only for its splendid illustrations, good bibliography and index, and as itself a nice piece of book-making, *Adieu aesthetica* is worth getting hold of.

The title of the book comes from a letter that Jan van Krimpen wrote to the publisher A. A. M. Stols in 1927, apropos the latter's small-press edition of William Blake's *The marriage of heaven and hell*. Van Krimpen says goodbye to the Arts & Crafts ethos in which he had grown up: 'Farewell to aesthetics and pretty pages! Farewell colours! Farewell title-pieces and initials! Farewell to the whole damn thing!' (My translation. One might remark on the fact that the title of the English-language pamphlet, *The aesthetic world of Jan van Krimpen*, gets the meaning exactly the wrong way round.) By this time he had chosen firmly for a typography of reserve and – a key word – discipline.

From at least the late 1920s, Jan van Krimpen's work has an air of perfection and refinement about it. The familiar contrast is with the rougher, more vulgar productions of S. H. de Roos: his slightly older rival, working for the less ancient and less prestigious Lettergieterij Amsterdam. This immaculate impression was certainly cultivated by the previous monograph on Van Krimpen's work (of 1952), written by John Dreyfus, with a foreword by Stanley Morison, and printed and published by the firm of Enschedé itself. Gradually some varnish was removed: by Van Krimpen's own quite frank writings (*On designing and devising type* of 1957, and especially the tortured reflections published posthumously in his *Letter to Philip Hofer*). Sebastian Carter's extensive publication of the correspondence between Van Krimpen and Stanley Morison, in *Matrix* (1988–91), added further reality to the picture.

Adieu aesthetica now situates Van Krimpen more clearly in his contexts, and brings him firmly down to earth. 'Goodbye to the aesthetic view of Van Krimpen', the title might be also saying. The image that introduces Sjoerd van Faassen's essay shows one of the perfect title pages, but now marked by a library stamp and other annotations. Sierman's caption reads: 'Van Krimpen now. Claimed, ear-marked and disposed of. But in the unprotected circuit of the second-hand book trade the "noblesse" of Enschedé can find new admirers.'

The criticism that Van Krimpen's typefaces were those of an artist and were hardly suitable for ordinary use – this is the conclusion that Walter Tracy came to in *Letters of credit* – is here given some material flesh. Sierman refers to the disappointing sales of Monotype matrices for the Van Krimpen typefaces, and, in a sidenote, to the 'unimpressive' royalties on the typefaces that Jan van Krimpen's son and heir, Huib, now receives: rarely more than a thousand guilders (£400) a year.

If sales figures were small, Van Krimpen's typefaces, Sierman writes, 'had an almost symbolic value for a small elite; they were ambassadors for Enschedé and Monotype'. Making full use of the correspondence which Van Krimpen himself deposited in the Universiteitsbibliotheek in Amsterdam, Koosje Sierman builds a picture of a culture and a cult, which was sustained not just by 'first principles of typography', but by Savile Row tailors, Rothman's cigarettes, Gillot pens, and Cumberland pencils. Van Krimpen's aura must have been intimidating. Thus this remark quoted from a letter to him of 1956, from a now senior English typographer: 'Please excuse the typewriter but I have lost my pen'.

Van Krimpen was working for a firm that had quasi-official status. Enschedé was the printer of the nation's banknotes, stamps and Bibles, as well as being a main keeper of its typographic heritage. One could see this situation as being merely a rich cushion for his elitism (though, to his chagrin, he was never made a director of Enschedé). Yet it also offered the chance of some connection to mass-production and mass-circulation. Here the firm seems to have failed to use him fully. Certainly much of his endeavours of this kind were for other commissioners. The prime instance of this is the series of standard stamps that he designed (from 1946) for the PTT. One could mention also the basic design that he provided for the ENSIE ('first Dutch systematically ordered encyclopedia'), the Bible typeface Sheldon designed for Oxford University Press, as well as the alphabets that he drew as models for the Dutch Standards Institute, published in the standard NEN 3225. These latter comprised a characteristically refined roman, and a sanserif that is still in use as the basis for Dutch street signs. Sierman suggests that with this roman, Van Krimpen wanted to make his own taste into a general norm. But a full historical discussion of Van Krimpen could see him walking a line between limited editions and mass-production, between great refinement and the ordinary, the everyday.

Adieu aesthetica is, in the best sense, a work of revisionism: it brings a hero into more realistic, more social light (and without any sexual scandal, such as tempts British biographers). Although brief, hastily made to meet the exhibition deadline, and without any clear editorial direction, the book does offer a suggestion of how we might write about these heroes, as they recede into history, out of the warm embrace of their friends, families and admirers.

The illustrations, edited by Koosje Sierman and the book's designer, Martin Majoor, play an essential role here. Freshly made and very sharply reproduced, they are at one with the fine grain of the text.

Both book and the exhibition are products of a newly flourishing Dutch typographic culture. *Adieu aesthetica* is set in Van Krimpen's Romanée, recently digitized by two original typeface designers, Peter Matthias Noordzij and Fred Smeijers, and to be issued by the former's Enschedé Font Foundry. The typeface, though certainly affected, now looks more workable and resilient than in its metal embodiment. We are allowed to make this comparison within the book itself, each copy of which contains a bound-in page from the Limited Editions Club *Odyssey*, set in the metal Romanée. This interpretation of an old design suggests, as Koosje Sierman also speculates in her closing paragraph, that Van Krimpen's typefaces may be about to enjoy a more successful phase of existence: released from the difficulties of lead and the miseries of photocomposition, they can be put into the digital realm, where flexibility and subtlety of form are more possible. The design of the book by Martin Majoor (himself another assured type designer) manages to be respectful to Van-Krimpen-classical discipline, makes full use of the italic for captions and notes, while using the untraditionalist method of integrating illustrations with text. The book's printer and co-publisher, Jan de Jong, should be mentioned too, as another regular contributor to the Dutch typographic culture.

Further evidence of this culture came in the public discussion held to launch the exhibition in The Hague, with almost all of the many Dutch type designers present. A panel of them, convened and chaired by Mathieu Lommen, debated the issues arising from Van Krimpen's work. Just as he had worried about the problems of reviving old typeface designs – most famously, in dialogue with Stanley Morison – so these living designers debated the issues of reviving Van Krimpen, and much else. Sem Hartz, one of the last surviving colleagues of the subject – though, as it turned out, shortly before his death – spoke up from the floor to reproach the younger generations. But they are already well on their way in critical assimilation of the lessons of this master.

Printing Historical Society Bulletin, no. 41, 1996

Best books

National 'best books of the year' competitions began to appear first in the 1920s and 1930s, initiated by people in the 'new traditional' typographic and bibliophile circles of Western Europe and the USA. Certainly this was the case in the Netherlands and the United Kingdom, whose national 'best books' events date respectively from 1925 and 1929. A not wholly untrue picture of their juries would find gentlemen in three-piece suits gathered around a polished table, enjoying vintage wines and arguing over the question of which typeface was a suitable match for the drawings of a certain illustrator. Though they saw printing as in need of reform, those years between the two world wars may seem to us now as a golden age, in which good printers hardly needed to be instructed. Someone in a publishing house sent a typescript (even a manuscript) to a printer, with a note asking for 'the usual'. Back came a solid book, intelligently typeset, decently printed, nicely sewn and bound in real cloth. Indeed, those books were often dressed as well as the gentlemen sitting round the polished table.

After 1945, the situation was different. As the publishing and printing trades began to recover from the destruction and overall standstill of the war years, new realities emerged. Labour was no longer cheap; good workmanship was less certain; good materials had to be searched for by ingenious production managers; and people called 'book designers' began to emerge. In these years one began to see their names in the colophons of books, and in the indexes of the 'best books' catalogues.

In the UK, the 'best book' exhibition was revived in 1945, now under the auspices of the National Book League: a sort of pressure group for the British book, very much like the Stichting Collectieve Propaganda van het Nederlandse Boek (the CPNB), which has been the main body behind the Best Verzorgde Boeken event (literally: 'the best cared-for books'). It is interesting to trace the shifts in the British event. For as long as the NBL was in sole charge, it was amiable and harmless. Held in the organization's eighteenth-century house in Mayfair (London W1), it was the sort of place where one might meet one's aunt, when she was up from the country for a day in London. From 1960, the NBL joined as one of a triumvirate with the British Federation of Master Printers and the Publishers Association, and then the sectional interests of the trades began to show. In the 1980s the printers even broke away to hold their own show. One year their catalogue carried an article with the title 'Why British produced books are best'. By 1987 the NBL had metamorphosed into the Book Trust, with offices in South London – not such a good venue for country aunts – and within a few years the British Book Design & Production exhibition had disappeared. So today there is no exhibition or competition to represent British books: neither to the British themselves, nor to the world book-trade people who inspect the collected national exhibitions on display every October at the Frankfurt Book Fair.

Meanwhile the Best Verzorgde Boeken has turned into a star among the national book competitions. The only doubts one has are that it burns too brightly. In recent years, too many of the books have seemed too intensively designed. Designers, fresh out of art school and eager to amaze their colleagues, torture printers and binders into producing perverse delights: heavily coated paper carrying lines of inhuman length, set in Eurostile or some such newly modish typeface, out-of-focus images, gold-smeared book-blocks, velvet cases. It is a fetishist's paradise. Where is the content of such books? Where can you keep them? In a sealed bag? In a cupboard? I exaggerate, of course. Even in the recent BVB shows, where such designer-items have been featured, there have also been a few noble books: works of real content, painstakingly edited, and designed and produced to standards that even those sober-suited gentlemen might have approved of.

The Best Verzorgde Boeken exhibition and catalogue have certainly been a good advertisement for the Dutch printing industry. Even if the designers have strange desires, one can see that the skills of production are still alive. Usually enough books of interest can be found, with just a handful needing to be placed in the 'hors concours' section: because they have been produced partly or wholly outside the Netherlands, even if published within the Dutch national borders; or, more rarely, published outside, produced within. Publishing books for a narrowly confined linguistic community – as, despite the pressures of English, is still the case in the Netherlands – does have some advantages. It means that there is in Dutch publishing some inherent resistance to the savage rationalizations of transnational, but predominantly English-language corporate publishing culture. One of the troubles of the British book is that it becomes increasingly hard to know what that term really means. Printed in Italy or Hong Kong, from digital files generated in the USA or Germany, with just part of the edition given a UK imprint? Such homeless items are almost certain to lack character or interest. Much of British publishing has gone this way.

The attempt to restart a best book competition in the UK may have to emulate Jan Tschichold's situation in Switzerland, when in 1943, with an article in *Der Schweizer Buchhandel*, he started a one-person campaign for an annual choice of the 'Schönste Schweizer Bücher': just ten books, he suggested. His proposal was eventually accepted, to grow into what is now one of the more solid and worthwhile of the national exhibitions. The British situation seems to require the same mixture of arrogance and humility that Tschichold displayed. Certainly we will be lucky to find ten decent books each year. But starting fresh would give us a chance for a fresh set of principles of selection. We should certainly get rid of the idea of 'made in the UK'. 'Conceived in the UK' is more appropriate. Britain has a predominantly literary culture, and there are still many good editors quietly at work in publishing here. Within the best book competition, we need an award for good editing. And it would be interesting to test the thesis that good design is only possible with books of substance, their material intelligently sorted out. The only fetishistic books chosen would then be books that are actually about fetishism.

Pts, no. 2, 2000

This was written for a small magazine edited and published by Bas Jacobs and Edwin Smets, just out of art school at Maastricht. In 2001 the British Book Design and Production Awards was restarted, under the auspices of Oxford Brookes University, but to minimal effect. Meanwhile, the sober Swiss competition has begun to go the way of the Dutch event, being given a layer of up-to-the-moment design glitz.

The Oxford dictionary for writers and editors

Oxford English Dictionary Department (compiler), *The Oxford dictionary for writers and editors*, Clarendon Press, 1981

The first edition of the *Authors' and printers' dictionary* compiled by F. Howard Collins was published by Oxford University Press in 1905; the eleventh and last edition appeared in 1973. Collins, as it was known, was a dictionary of printed British-English. It recorded and codified the forms in which the language of texts published by Oxford University Press was set – and multiplied, and distributed all over the world. Through Collins, and its sister publication *Hart's rules for compositors and readers*, Oxford printed English became the standard and most authoritative variety.

Collins was not concerned to explain the meaning of words or to give guidance on pronunciation. Rather, it attempted to list words and other items that might cause difficulty in printed form, and to give an authoritative version of that form (with warnings of possible common errors). Any indication of meaning or pronunciation was provided merely in the service of identification. Thus the book was concerned with matters of capitalization, italicization, hyphenation, as well as with spelling: it tackled the ways in which language is 'dressed' on its momentous journey from copy to print. Proper names, abbreviations, contractions, foreign-language words in English use, were staple material. There were also lengthier entries on such matters as punctuation, proof correction, decimal currency (in the last edition), astronomical signs. It was very much a compositor's book: a slightly miscellaneous compilation of difficult words that had arisen on the job. It was at home in printing offices, its pages steadily accumulating the grime of printing ink and lead.

The *Oxford dictionary for writers and editors* now replaces Collins. Its content is of the same essential character as that of the earlier book, though the material has been revised and updated. The often very small modifications to old entries suggest that much consideration has gone into the revision: one imagines that every entry was queried, even if the majority remain unchanged. However, something more than a simple revised edition has been attempted, and this is signalled in the new title. From 'authors and printers' to 'writers and editors', from composing room to publisher's office, from metal to film and the VDU: the shift is the same as that in the recently overhauled Cambridge University Press 'guides' (previously for 'authors and printers', but now for 'authors and publishers'). The latest revision of *Hart's rules* (thirty-eighth edition, 1978) also makes some accommodation for these changes in practice, notably with its ground-breaking attempt to provide rules for page make-up (previously the unarticulated secret of the printer). The metamorphosis of the *Authors' and printers' dictionary* is just one more reflection of this change in the processes of the production of print.

If the essential matter of the book has not changed, the new title is still fully justified. The book was always aimed at people concerned with details of copy: their concerns remain unaltered, but now they are more likely to be designated 'editors' rather than 'printers'. The book seems not to have had a wide circulation among authors – the people who have most to learn from it – and its new status as an Oxford dictionary ought to do something to remedy this. With the disappearance of the perhaps slightly forbidding label of 'printers', writers of every kind can have no excuse for not using the book.

In view of the change of title, one must question the retention of a surprisingly large number of specialist printing terms (for example, 'pick', 'set-off', 'pie'). Even during its life as a 'printers' dictionary', the inclusion of such terms was justified only by the confusion between 'words that printers need guidance on, when setting copy' and 'special words of printing technology'. Collins set out to cover both areas – though dealt with the second, only patchily and unsatisfactorily. The new book states its intention of discarding the purely specialist printing terms, but yet on the jacket there is the boast that 'important terms in computer typesetting' are included. This is a claim that has been made (with varying degrees of truth) for several recent books in the field – as if the inclusion of these terms were an index of tough effectiveness. Two observations can be made: there are in fact not very many computer typesetting terms in the book (an intensive search revealed three); and, why should they be included anyway? New words from computer technology are obvious candidates for inclusion ('program' or 'programme', 'BASIC' or 'Basic'?), but why should writers and editors need to know typesetting terms in particular?

Among the shifts in printed language that it records, the new dictionary is notable for one important change of attitude. As in the most recent *Hart's rules*, Oxford practice is now to set groups of initial letters (except in personal names) and other abbreviations without points: thus 'TUC' and not 'T.U.C.', 'Mr' not 'Mr.'. (And 'Ms' is now given official Oxford recognition.) Other signs of advance in this revision include: the recognition that 'scientific and technical bibliographies often capitalize first word and proper names only'; guidance on the Harvard system of citing authorities; an honest report on the state of proof-correction practice in Britain ('two systems are in current use ... BS 1219 and 5261 part 2. One or other must be used consistently ... '); directions on the setting of British post-codes. All this information comes in the small number of slightly extended entries. Elsewhere, in the one- or two-line entries that make up the bulk of the book, one can observe the small changes of form that are indexes of the movement of printed language. For example 'anti-freeze' in the last Collins becomes 'antifreeze', 'on-coming' becomes 'oncoming'. And the new entries: 'ongoing', 'down-market', 'Lévi-Strauss', 'gnocchi', 'skinhead', 'high-rise' (though not yet 'high-tech'), and so on: the new material of this kind is considerable.

A new and welcome feature of the book is a three-page explanation of 'conventions used in the dictionary'. The typographic codes devised to present the book's information are here explained with meticulous clarity. Some features that may have more general application are as follows. Full points are no longer used at the end of an entry, as they were in Collins. This means that when an entry closes with a point of abbreviation or contraction (as quite often happens) then this can be seen. Conversely, entries are only given initial capitals if they would normally, as proper names, be capitalized. Some dictionaries and indexes still avoid this problem by capitalizing the first letter of all entries.

Another convention of wider interest seems to be an invention of this book: it concerns normally hyphenated words that have to be broken at their point of hyphenation. In such cases a hyphen is shown both at the end of the first part and (on the new line) before the second part. Words that have to be hyphenated merely in the course of setting over two lines are treated in the conventional way. This innovation is one that could find uses outside lexicography – in the preparation of any manuscript for printing. (Though here the best practice would still be never to break words at all.)

The new book follows the physical and typographic format of the last edition of Collins – except that its text is now photocomposed. Those who savour the physical and optical pleasure of metal-and-letterpress may regret this, but must by now be hardened to the change. At least the new book is more stoutly bound (in an 'Oxford hollow') than the last Collins.

The only substantial losses of content are the preface to the first edition of 1905, by Collins himself, and the essay 'Author and printer' by R. W. Chapman that first appeared in the fifth edition of 1921. One can understand that these may have seemed out of place in the new book – with its more lexicographic, less personal character. But it is sad to see the disappearance of 'Author and printer', in particular; it is quite out of date technically, but full of marvellous apophthegms: 'sentences will bear printing if they will bear reading aloud', 'words do not arrange themselves', 'you cannot make books cheap by making them nasty'. R. W. Chapman was Secretary to the Delegates of Oxford University Press, and an editor of Jane Austen and Samuel Johnson; this text should be kept in print somewhere.

Information Design Journal, vol. 2, no. 2, 1981

In 2000, Oxford University Press issued the *Dictionary for writers and editors* in a second edition, in a larger format and with a coarse typography that lost all of the charms that the first edition had possessed. In 2002, *Hart's rules* was transformed into the *Oxford guide to style*, and given a format that matched the *Dictionary*.

In contrast to the continuous text matter of the body of a book, the index has certain special features that make it a subject of interest to the typographer. The material of indexes is non-continuous and takes the form of a list. One reads both vertically and (within entries) horizontally. The language of indexes is compressed, and abbreviations are much employed. These things give the text matter of indexes their characteristic complexity. And one may see this complexity of content as placing demands, to which the editorial and typographic form of the index must correspond.

Another kind of demand is made by the reader of the book. The nature of this demand will be indicated when one says that most indexes are not read but used – flipped through and scanned. The time spent by the reader in thus using the index becomes a factor for consideration – as it is not in the usual reading process. Again, the typographic and editorial form of the index must be adequate to these demands, in doing what can be done to assist – or, at least, not to impede – the reader.

In addition to meeting the requirements and constraints of the production process (which will be touched on at the end of this article), the index may therefore be seen as having to satisfy two sets of demands: those made by its content and those made by its readers. But this distinction is hard to maintain in consideration of any specific example. Thus, one may ask 'is this system of alphabetization appropriate?', or 'should the subheadings have been broken off rather than run on?' But these questions can only be answered by a reader (or by the reader imagined by those making the index), and will therefore be decided in readers' terms, rather than in the illusory terms of 'what the content demands'.

Here one should mention another set of demands on an index – those made by the publisher. The limits on the space allowed to the index, and on the time and money allowed to the indexer, will have their effect on the final product. Such constraints need not be disadvantageous to the quality of the product. But whatever the outcome of these external pressures, in that they are unrelated to

MALMAISON. *See* Napoleon.
MALMESBURY, Lord, xiii. 317.
MALONE, Edmond, Chatterton (*q.v.*);
   Life of Reynolds, xvi. 182; also ref. to,
   iii. 184; xi. 220, [358].
MALTA, English occupation of, i. 99;
   xiv. 163, 189, 190, .194, 196, 198;
   importance denied, i. 101; Knights
   Hospitallers (*q.v.*); Napoleon (*q.v.*);
   also ref. to, iii. 173, 175.
MALTHUS, Thomas Robert :
   American tribes, on the, i. 298.
   ' amorous complexion,' i. 242.
   answer to, vii. 221.
   argument summarized, i. 205.
   authors studied by, i. 189.
   character of (*The Sp. of the Age*), xi.
      103–14.
   Cobbett's apostrophe to, vii. 351.
   ' cockney,' a, i. 288.
   Condorcet (*q.v.*).
   corn, on the monopoly of, i. 363.
   cultivation, on (quoted), i. 213.
   doctrines examined, vii. 332–7.
   Edinburgh Review, encouraged by, xi.
      129.
   equality of man, argument against
      (quoted), i. 208.
   errors, two capital, i. 219.

1   The 'General index', compiled by James Thornton, to *The complete works of William Hazlitt*, Dent, 1934.

the essential issues of the typography of indexes, they need not be considered further here. One can simply notice that the publisher's typical demands on the index serve to add further complications to the process of making this most complex part of the book.

These special demands may lead to the suggestion that typographic form may make some difference to the ease with which a reader is able to use an index. The complexity of the material, and the reader's demands of speed and ease of discovery, suggest that appearance and configuration of material might be factors of significant importance to the process of use – as they do not seem to be in the case of simple continuous text matter. The question of what typography could do for an index will not however be addressed directly here. Rather, what will be considered are these necessary prior questions: is it possible to consider the typography of an index separately from its contents (that is, what the indexer generates)? what happens if these two things, typographic form and the content, are considered separately? if – as will be suggested – the form and content of an index are inseparable, then what part could a typographer play in the making of an index?

Figure 1 indicates the impossibility of treating as separate the content and the typographic form of an index. The details of typography – the system of punctuation and of capitalization, the use of italics, for example – are coincidental with, and follow from, the generation of the matter of the index. That subheadings in important entries are broken off rather than run on, for example, can only be described as a decision of editorial-design policy.

This index was produced before the specialized 'typographic designer' had begun to play much part in book production. And such a typographer might now question the decision to justify the lines (that is, where possible, to set lines of equal length), or the use of full points at the end of entries. But such reservations do not affect our judgement of this index as exemplary in its typography. And this high quality seems to stem largely from the standard of the editorial and indexing work. This is just one example of a body of model indexes that are well-designed in the widest sense – products of a particular (British) tradition of serious publishing.

Another example may help to show the soundness of conventional index typography. Looking at the index to *Hart's rules* (figure 2) one sees nothing remarkable. But consider this in relation to the contents pages list in the same book (figure 3). The contents pages functions as a preliminary index, giving the user an outline of the matter of the book. The typography of these pages, whereby page references are pushed to the right of the page, certainly discourages the reader from connecting heading and page number. Though, one might argue that this arrangement gives the page numbers an emphasis that they do not enjoy in the index. Both this emphasis and an easier horizontal connection could however be obtained by setting page numbers to the left of headings. But this would destroy the symmetry of the page. And this aim of symmetry and balance is, one suspects, the main consideration behind the convention adopted. When nowadays type is not set by hand in rectangular 'chases' (frames), the argument that this arrangement arises naturally in production no longer applies.

ʃ and ɓ, use of, 102
Scientific work generally, 52 ff.
  abbreviations for units, 53
  abbreviations in metric system, 5–6
  chemical names, 55
  degrees of temperature, 4
  displayed formulae, 54, 55
  italic for theorems, 23
  italic or roman for symbols, 53
  numbers above 9999 to be spaced, 55
  omit rule from square-root sign, 54
  preparation of copy, 52–3
  punctuation of formulae and equations, 55
  reduction of handwork, 53–5
  references to footnotes, 18
  symbols easily confused, 52–3
  text references to symbols in plates, 12
  titles of papers, how to print, 49
Scripture references, 6–7, 50
Semicolon, 38–9
Shakespeare's plays, references to, 50
Signs for reference indices, 18
  special, 57
Singular forms with plural numbers, 67
Slang terms, quotation marks for, 42
Slavonic languages, *see under* Russian language
Small capitals, accented in French, 85
  when to use, 12
Spacing generally, 56
  in abbreviated titles of books, 56
  in abbreviations of honours, etc., 56
  in French, 92, 95–6
  in Greek and Latin, 107
  in Italian, 108–9.
  letter-spacing in Russian, 112, 113, 117, 118–19, 121
  of German words for emphasis, 101
  of Greek words for emphasis, 107
  of last line of paragraph, 56
  of poetry, 56
  of references, 56
Spanish language, works in the, 122–4
  accent, 122–3

2 *Hart's rules for compositors for compositors and readers*, 37th edn,
   Oxford University Press, 1967.

Punctuation marks and references to footnotes 47
Points in title-pages, headlines, etc. 47
Quotations 47
References to Printed and Manuscript Sources 48
Printed works 48
MS. and unpublished sources 52
Government and official papers 52
Scientific Work 52
Spacing 56
Special Signs and Symbols 57
Thorn, Eth, Wyn, Yogh 57
Vowel-Ligatures (Æ and Œ) 58

SPELLINGS

Alternative and Difficult Spellings 59
Doubling Consonants with Suffixes 63
Fifteenth- to Seventeenth-Century Works 65
Formation of Plurals in English 65
Words ending in -e and -y 65
Words ending in -o 66
Compounds 66
Formation of Plurals in Words of Foreign Origin 67
Hyphened and Non-Hyphened Words 70
Words ending in -able 75
Words ending in -ible 78
Words ending in -ize, -ise, and -yse 78
Words ending in -ment 79
DECIMAL CURRENCY 80

RULES FOR SETTING
FOREIGN LANGUAGES

French 81
Abbreviations 82
Accented capitals 84
Awkward divisions: abbreviated words and large
numbers expressed in figures 85
Capital and lower case 85
Division of words 89
Grave and acute accents 90
Hyphens 91
Italic and roman type 91
Metal-rules 92
Numerals 92
Punctuation 93
Quotation marks 93
Reference figures 95
Spacing 95

3 *Hart's rules for compositors for compositors and readers*, 37th edn,
Oxford University Press, 1967.

Curried meat balls   53
Custard sauce   76

Dab: Fish fillets in cheese sauce   51
Dandelion salad   214
Desserts: *see* Puddings and desserts
Devilled chicken legs   144
Dried fruits   19
Dumplings: Boiled potato dumplings
        73
    Claudia's dumplings   115

Egg: Bacon and egg flan   45
    Baked eggs   207
    Chinese egg drop soup   121
    Eggs baked in potatoes   132

Fried sprats   128
Fritters: Bacon fritters   160
    Brain fritters   55
    Fritter batter   55
    Ham fritters   160
    Normandy apple fritters   110
    Split pea fritters   99
Fudge, chocolate   226

Gammon   18; Baked gammon   183
    Stuffed gammon rolls   129
Garbure   158
Garlic soup   120
Gazpacho   165
Gingerbread men   224
Gingerbread, Orkney oatmeal   224

4   Jocasta Innes, *The pauper's cookbook*, Harmondsworth:
     Penguin Books, 1971.

The different typographic treatment of the essentially similar material of index and contents page suggests that indexes have been comparatively free from the purely formal considerations of symmetry and balance – the 'display' values usually unrelated to use or to meaning. This may, it is suggested, be connected with the peculiar characteristics of indexes noted at the start of this article – their unusual clarity of function. This is something that is harder to attribute to a contents page list or, say, a list of illustrations. Such parts of a book simply do not have to meet the kind of demands made on an index. And one might go on to wonder whether indexers (and editors), having been left to get on with their work without much interference from book designers, have not thus been at an advantage, in being able quietly and unselfconsciously to develop conventions firmly based on the reader's needs.

It is suggested then that it has been characteristic of index typography (more so than the typography of other parts of a book) to employ conventions that best suit the reader – rather than, say, the designer or the printer. The effect that certain typographic practices, outside the indexer's sphere of influence, can have on an index is shown in figure 4. In this index to a cookery book the majority of entries relate to only one page reference – recipes being the only

pica – about 12-point: as 12-point, used as a
    unit of typographical measurement – 34
Pickering, William 90 100
pitch-line – line across bed of press to show
    how far printing-surface can extend without
    fouling grippers – 235–6
planographic – see *surface processes*
Plantin, Christophe 84: *Plantin* (type)
    84–5 401–7, x-height of 73, & paper 74, &
    Times 106, proportions of 110, & verse
    124, examples 132 136–7 154
plastic stereos 220
plate – illustration printed separately from
    text – 321–3, numbering of 143 282, &
    list of illustrations 194, & colophon 203,
    & paper 300 304 310 365, & imposition
    318, folding 323, & estimating 367, &
    proofs 374–5, & tenacity 375: *plate-glazing*
    – method of smoothing paper surface –
    298–9 302: see also *albumen plate, duplicate
    plate*
platen press – press which brings paper and
    printing-surface together as plane surfaces
    – 233 236
plays 109 124 128 255
pochoir – stencil process – 252
poetry – see *verse*

5   Hugh Williamson, *Methods of book design*, 2nd edn,
Oxford University Press, 1965.
6   Marjorie Plant, *The English book trade*, 2nd edn,
Allen and Unwin, 1965.

items indexed. This fact perhaps encouraged the decision to set an
em space between heading and page reference, rather than the conventional comma and word space. However, the printer's decision
to justify has meant that – while this em space is consistently maintained – the spaces elsewhere will not be of fixed dimensions. To
squeeze 'Gammon 18; Baked gammon 183' into a line, the compositor had to set '18;Baked' without intervening space. And thus the
dislocation occurs, whereby one groups page reference ('18') and
entry ('Baked gammon') wrongly. This unfortunate incident illustrates the fundamental objection to justification of lines: the variation of word space entailed introduces an arbitrary element into

6   *Seasons, The*, copyright, 119–20, 420

Secondary occupations, 95–7

Senefelder, invention of lithography, 306

Seres, patents, 101, 103

Series, publishers', 432

Service books, early editions, 24–5
      patent for, 101, 106–7
      prices, 240

Sewing, 345
    machine, 350

Shares in books, 110, 225–6, 429–30

Sheepskin, 213, 342, 354
    cost, 212, 243
    fines for using, 207
    See also Parchment

Size, of books, 95, 418
  of the edition, 92–5, 300, 331, 404, 412, 414, 416
  of the firm, 86–8, 356–9
  of binderies, 348
  of the industry, 80–86, 449

Skiver, patent for, 213

Soap, ingredient of ink, 323

Social conditions, 150–3, 367–72

Socialism among printers, 381–2

Society for the Encouragement of Learning, 223–4

Solaces, 146, 158–9

Sörensen's composing machine, 283

Specialisation, by apprentices, 367
    in manuscript production, 24
    of demand, 448
    of production and distribution, 59–79
        due to shortage of type, 175
        effect on costs, 407
        encouraged by patents, 109

Spilman, 192–4

Stalls, 82, 254, 415, 432

Stanhope, press, 271–2, 287
    stereotype process, 301

Star Chamber decrees regarding bookselling, 255–6
      importation of books, 261
      licensing, 31, 33
      number of apprentices, 133–4
      number of presses, 86–7, 171
      number of printers, 83
      provincial printing, 81
      type-founding, 62
      unemployment, 154

the system of words and space that constitutes text matter.[1] In normal continuous text matter this may not be of great concern. But in the more complex configurations of an index, where horizontal space carries more precise meanings, justification begins to become a significant factor and, one would suggest, an unhelpful one. The conventional narrowness of width of the lines of an index contributes to the problems attendant on justification. The mistake of figure 4 could have been avoided by setting equal spaces between words and by carrying whole items over on to new lines. But in any case, whether justified or not, the more conventional, watertight system of punctuation and normal word space would prevent such misreading.

Objections, similar to those made against the example of figure 4, could be applied to the index shown in figure 5, where lines are justified and an unconventional system of space and punctuation is employed. But, though the risk of confusion is there, in practice the composition avoids the dislocations of figure 4. This index is an interesting example of the kind of typographic innovations that are possible in indexes – given the particular needs of a particular index. That such innovations were carried out in this case, and that this index seems to be good and useful, may follow from the fact that author, indexer and typographer were one man. The inclusion here of definitions of terms (between en dashes) is an example of an author's involvement with the index. Some of the practices adopted seem uncomfortable: for example, the use of a colon to mark a conclusion, where one is used rather to connect items on either side of this mark. But, taken as a whole, this index is a good instance of the unity of typography and indexing, and it is a good argument for indexing done with full awareness of typographic possibilities.

That indexes are a peculiar and distinct part of a book is again suggested by the next example (figure 6). The width of indentation of the vertically aligned sub-headings is determined by the natural length of words in the main heading. In this feature, therefore, the content of the heading and subheading (before the point of indentation) determines its visual or typographic form. This is

1. James Hartley & Peter Burnhill, 'Experiments with unjustified text', *Visible Language*, vol. 5, no. 3, 1971, pp. 265–78.

something that has often been the aim of self-consciously radical typographers, but it is achieved here (unselfconsciously, one supposes) in a book that is elsewhere traditional in appearance. This system does of course use more space than the traditional narrow column setting; on the other hand, the reader may find a readier access through it. However one judges this, the point that may be made here is that this typographic innovation derives (one supposes) from the author-indexer considering the nature of her material – and not from any considerations of the designers or producers of the book; for elsewhere in the book the typographic configurations are imposed on, rather than derived from, the content.

One should make clear however that the 'content' here referred to is the apparent or surface content of the words, as against the deeper content of the meaning of the material – its hierarchies and system of internal relationship. The visual patterns which the surface content produces depend merely on how much space the words occupy, and, in that words have no intrinsic relationship with the things that they denote, the visual patterns of words are arbitrary. In order to carry the deeper content of the material, a non-arbitrary visual system (of indentation, word-space, line space, punctuation, capitalization, and so on) must be devised – one that provides a suitable coding system for the material, rather than an attempt at literal representation of it. But this non-arbitrary system of visual coding is, couched in theoretical language, no more than the aim of any serious index.

Examples such as those of figure 5 and (perhaps) figure 6 would seem to confirm the suggestion that the peculiar demands of content of an index encourage clear (and fresh) thinking about typographic form. For, as well as exhibiting a body of sound typographic convention, indexes also show a capacity to innovate and experiment in response to the needs of the occasion. Figure 7 is included here as a warning against the acceptance of such a suggestion without qualification. It is taken from an index with which almost everything is wrong, in its construction and in its typography. One may mention the lack of system and indentation, punctuation, capitalization, and the separation of headings and page references that necessitates the use of 'leaders'. Such an example summarizes all the possible sins of making indexes. But, though a counter example,

Liberty of the Press . . .	180	— by airship	244
Libel, What is? . . .	181	— agencies, various . .	115
Libelling the dead . . .	182	— — and Press photographers	115
Libelling a thing . . .	181	— pictures, How to find .	170
Libel, Criminal	191	— — must tell a story .	170
Libel insurance . . .	216	— service, Building up the .	132
Library, Journalist's reference .	32	— story, Reporting a great .	132
Lifting forme, Meaning of the term	56	N-E-W-S	138
Line block, How to make a .	173	Newseditor and news organisation	130
"Live" copy, How to produce .	61	— — scope of his activity .	130
Local touch, Some dangers of .	152	— — backbone of a paper .	131
— personalities, News value of .	66	— — Cool direction essential in .	132
— journalism, Personal element in	119	Newspaper, What is a? . .	180
— journal a link with home .	120	— technique, Acquiring a know-	
— — Politics on the . .	120	ledge of	34
— M.P.'s speeches in Parliament.	121	— work, Absorbing nature of .	63
— Bills in Parliament . .	121	— a reflex of life . . .	61
— Government enquiries . .	121	— types most generally used .	37, 53
— news, subbing . . .	121	— What makes a great? . .	139
Locking up, Meaning of the term	55	— works organisation . .	217
Lofty ideals . . . 141,	148	Newspaper, Legal definition of a .	180
London and Provincial Journalism,		— illustrations, Proper handling of	173
The difference between . .	150	Newspaper manager, The . .	212
London sets the pace, How .	150	— — Duties of . . .	212
— the centre of the British Press	150	— — Office and staff control .	213
— representation . . .	225	— — Accounts . . .	215

7 Low Warren, *Journalism from A to Z*, 3rd edn, Herbert Joseph, 1935.

it does serve to support a thesis of this article – that the content of an index and its typographic form are related intimately and organically. Typographic disorder inevitably follows from disorder in construction; and, equally, typography by itself (if it could be 'by itself') cannot be effective with bad copy.

These examples may suggest the diversity and the particularity of each index. As every indexer knows, there are limits to the application of rules and conventions – there will always be awkward decisions to be made. For this reason one may be suspicious of the prospects of empirical research supplying useful advice on making indexes. The attempt to apply such research seems to rest on the fallacy that one can draw general conclusions from particular (and often rather strange) instances. And, given the typical complexity of an index, it seems unlikely that much can be learned from the necessarily simplified indexes that supply the test pieces for experiments.

Also, empirical research isolates factors for evaluation, hoping to report on the effectiveness of certain conventions. This isolation of features denies the essential unity of form and content in an index. One cannot discuss, or test, the effectiveness of, say, letter-by-letter alphabetization or bold type without considering the function of such conventions in a particular case. And this consideration will bring in all the issues that relate to the decision about alphabetization or bold type.

This brief investigation of the typography of indexes has suggested that the content of an index and its typographic form are organically related. The stress laid on this may have implied that a typographer can contribute nothing to index making. Such a suggestion would be misleading. For although much of the typographic form will be generated by the indexer and editor, decisions that they take in this work of generation could, and should, be significantly affected by advice from someone with specialist typographic knowledge. Coding conventions such as the use of bold or italic or small capitals, or the use of special signs, depend on the facilities offered by the system of composition used. A thorough understanding of typographic possibilities may, as the case of figure 5 indicated, help to meet the special demands of a particular index.

This function for the typographer of supplying advice concerning composition becomes especially important with the demise of hot-metal composition. Such systems (Monotype, Linotype and Intertype) have been the traditional means for setting books; Monotype, as the most complex composition system, has been able to provide rich possibilities for typographic coding. The use of much less sophisticated systems in book production introduces different sets of typographic conventions. Indexes to be set on a machine that cannot supply italic, say, need to be designed to allow for this – designed, that is, from the point when the indexer starts work. And with the growing practice of printing books set on the typist's (or author's, or indexer's) own typewriter, this need to incorporate design considerations at an early stage becomes even more acute.

One might suggest then that indexers would benefit from an education in typography. Equally, it will be clear that typographers must understand the procedures of indexing – for even the more purely typographic decisions, such as the determination of line length or space between lines, will proceed from an appreciation of the nature of the copy. The work of indexing and of typography forms a unity that is ideally taken on by one person. It would not be realistic, however, to see the indexer-typographer as more than the rare exception. But one may say that the indexer and the typographer should certainly get to know each other better.

The Indexer, vol. 4, no. 4, 1977

Deriving from an informal and extra-curricular talk given in the Department of Typography at the University of Reading, the text bears the marks of this origin: spoken delivery, with the discussion focusing on a succession of examples, shown originally as slides. The Society of Indexers, in whose journal this piece was published, provided a forum of some interest to me at that time: they were concerned with editorial procedures and with meaning. Thanks again to L. M. Harrod, the editor who accepted this piece.

Stages of the modern

Universal faces, ideal characters

A typeface that meets all needs: of composing and printing techniques, of legibility, of aesthetics, of phonetic and semantic representation. At one stroke – or with a series of rationalized strokes – all special requirements would be solved. We could stop the endless, uneconomic devising of new forms, and could get rid of the dross piled up by centuries of fiddling invention, settling happily for a world of purified communication, of meaning unencumbered by the obstacles of form.

Stern pragmatists will always dismiss this as a crazy and unreal vision. But it is one that has cropped up repeatedly, encouraged by the standardization that is inherent in printing. And, like all dreams – especially recurring ones – it seems to say a good deal about the dreamer.

Precursors
Although attempts at a universal typeface are a phenomenon of the twentieth century, proposals for an ideal system of orthography go back much further – at least to the sixteenth century in Europe. A language is a haphazard affair, in both its spoken and written forms, and the mismatches between the two systems (phonetic values and the marks representing them) have been an irritation to the logically-minded. But reformers such as John Wilkins (in seventeenth-century England), Isaac Pitman, and – in the twentieth century – Robert Bridges and George Bernard Shaw, were literary people, concerned with ideal character sets rather than with ideal visual forms. It was only with the coming of the self-conscious typographic designer that the project of a universal typeface came to be formulated. As background to the twentieth-century experiments, one should mention the Renaissance theorists of correct proportion in letters and, in particular, one very concerted attempt at a theorized and rational typeface.

In France towards the end of the seventeenth century, a committee was set up to investigate the design of letterforms, and to produce a typeface for use in printing a book: the *Médailles de*

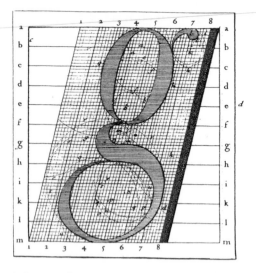

1 A character from the 'romain du roi', perhaps the first attempt at an ideal typeface. It existed as a series of engraved plates (made between 1695 and 1718), from which a set of types was derived. Characters were arrived at with the aid of an underlying grid: thus the cursive form could be simply a 'sloped roman'.

Louis XIV. The resulting letterform – known as the 'romain du roi' – in its various engraved versions and in its form as cut, can be seen as an attempt at an ideal solution (figure 1). Though it was entirely restricted to use at the Imprimerie Royale, it did, with its royal authority, constitute an important style model, and the 'romain du roi' lies at the start of the development of the 'modern' letterform. One can use 'modern' here both in its special typographic sense (as against 'old style') and in the sense that this project of the early Enlightenment in France looks forward to the modern movement of the 1920s and 1930s in continental Europe.

The German context
The new typography – and with it the search for a universal typeface – had its strongest base in Germany. The peculiar legacy of German typography was frequently cited in arguments for reform. The two main irritants were the convention that all nouns should start with a capital letter, and the use of blackletter (Schwabacher, Fraktur) as the standard printed letterform.

Reaction against conventional German orthography can be traced back at least to the Brothers Grimm, early advocates of 'Kleinschreibung' (capitals only at the start of sentences). The poet Stefan George made orthographic experiments – 'Kleinschreibung' and a simplified system of punctuation and went so far as to have a typeface specially augmented (in use by the early 1900s): it was a sanserif.

For George, as for the modernist designers soon to arrive on the scene, sanserif was an appropriate vehicle for a new vision of life: simple and beautiful in its purity. Though to this vision the modernists were to add another dimension: sanserif was the letterform of the machine age. It had visual associations with 'the machine' (gleaming, streamlined, without fussy excrescences), and was also somehow more appropriate than seriffed letterforms were for machine production. Though whether this meant design with the aid of a machine-tool (the Benton punchcutting machine) or machine composition (Linotype, Monotype) or electrically powered presses (after all, Gutenberg had used a machine), the advocates of modernism tended not to discuss.

In the chaos and economic deprivation of post-1918 Germany a political revolution was aborted and utopian schemes were hatched on many drawing boards. This was the moment of Expressionism, in which the Bauhaus was born at Weimar in a frenzy of Arts & Crafts rhetoric, strongly laced with visionary socialism. But the social dialectic that included this strain of Teutonic romanticism encompassed also Prussian good order, and these years saw the introduction of the Deutsche Industrie-Normen: standards for the regulation of industrial and commercial activity. The DIN paper sizes – now adopted throughout the non-American world – derive from this time. In conditions of scarcity the economic rationale for standardization was compelling. And it was in this mood of shedding all unnecessary baggage, returning to the zero point, and proceeding rationally, that the idea of a universal typeface received its fullest exploration.

Attempts at the ideal: formal and phonetic
The project drew a good deal of its intellectual energy from a book published in Berlin in 1920: *Sprache und Schrift* by Walter Porst-

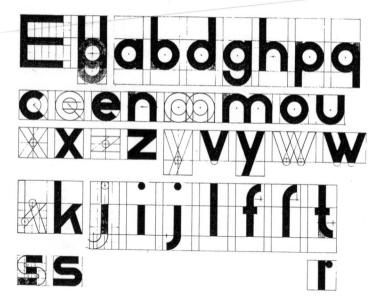

2   Joost Schmidt's alphabet composed of limited geometric elements, from his 'Vorkurs' teaching at the Bauhaus, and dated 1925. (From: *Joost Schmidt: Lehre und Arbeit am Bauhaus 1919–32*, Düsseldorf: Marzona, 1984.)

mann. He was an engineer associated with the DIN committee, for which he wrote an exposition of the new paper sizes. Porstmann went beyond the previous advocates of 'Kleinschreibung' to propose that capital letters be abolished: one alphabet only (thus making savings of materials, labour, time, money) and an alphabet modified so that it provided consistent and rational representation of sounds. As the new typographers were glad to point out, this suggestion came not from some eccentric poet, but from a 'level-headed' engineer (and *Sprache und Schrift* had been published by the Verlag des Vereins Deutscher Ingenieure). What could better exemplify the dictum of Le Corbusier: 'The Engineer, inspired by the law of Economy and governed by mathematical calculation, puts us in accord with universal law. He achieves harmony.' (*Vers une architecture*, 1923.)

There are implicit anticipations of the universal alphabet idea in the work of the Stijl designers in the Netherlands. But the elaborated suggestion of a universal typeface came from among the Ger-

abcdefghi jklmnopqr stuvwxyz

sturm blond

Abb. 2. Anwendung

3 The alphabet designed by Herbert Bayer for which the claim 'universal'
was made, shown here in its first published state. (From: *Offset*, no. 7,
1926.)

man modernists. On the evidence of his writings of the times László
Moholy-Nagy was perhaps the first to recognize the idea. (Moholy-
Nagy was the boiler-suited engineer-artist who replaced the eccentric and anti-rational Johannes Itten at the Bauhaus in 1923.) The
idea would then have been picked up and developed by others at the
Bauhaus, notably by two students, Herbert Bayer and Joost Schmidt,
who joined the teaching staff of the school in 1925. This was the
time of the transfer from Weimar to Dessau; a move that completed
the transition to the school's fully modernist phase. In October 1925
capital letters were abolished within the Bauhaus. Joost Schmidt's
first exercises in the construction of basic alphabets seem to date
from this year (figure 2). In the next year Bayer's new letterform
was published in a special Bauhaus issue of the magazine *Offset* (figure 3). Though not at this point designated 'universal', it became the
first alphabet for which the claim was made. And while the alphabets of Schmidt and also of Josef Albers remained essentially pedagogic exercises, Bayer's letterforms did find application in posters
and other display typography. But it was never cut as a type. Only in

4   The 'Systemschrift' of Kurt Schwitters (first published 1927) was a
    single alphabet, constructed from a limited stock of elements, but –
    defying notions of unity and balance – related shapes were assigned
    to related sounds. This example is one of two posters designed by
    Schwitters and using the letterforms in more conservative versions.
    875 x 660 mm. (From: Kurt Schwitters: *Typographie und Werbegestal-
    tung*, Wiesbaden: Landesmuseum Wiesbaden, 1990.)

recent years has it surfaced again, in close copies, as a typeface for photocomposition or dry-transfer application.

Bayer's alphabet was a very pure expression of modernist ideology: an attempt to construct – this word carried a heavy charge – a set of forms out of simple geometrical elements. It thus broke with the tradition of calligraphically derived typefaces (if one accepts that free forms and thinning and thickening of strokes betray the underlying influence of the pen). With unswerving self-assurance, Bayer settled the matter thus: 'to print a hand-produced letterform on a machine is false romanticism'.

But the revolution, as conceived by the most experimental of the new typographers, was not to stop at mere form. Following the suggestions of Porstmann, various attempts at phonetically correct alphabets were devised. Kurt Schwitters published his suggestions for a 'Systemschrift' in 1927: related sounds were to be represented by related visual elements (figure 4). In its most radical version the result was an almost complete break with the Latin alphabet. Jan Tschichold's experimental work towards a new alphabet was published in 1930: a typically elegant set of forms (figure 5). And, rather as an afterthought, Bayer developed his 'universal' into a 'basic alfabet' in the late 1950s: phonetically more correct and with a nod towards the computer.

If these alphabets remained as drawing-board schemes, published only in magazine articles, at least one lasting and very practical typeface did emerge from this time of experiment in Germany. This was Futura, the typeface that best represented the ideal of geometrical construction, but with the refinements and modifications that make a typeface actually work when set as text (as opposed to seeing the characters in splendid isolation). The designer, Paul Renner, seems to have started work on the job in 1925 (figure 6), and the typeface was first issued commercially in 1927. With the appearance of Futura, and especially as further weights and variants were added, the new typographers acquired a typeface that could go a good deal of the way towards fulfilling the claims made for sanserif as the letterform of the modern age.

It is one of the ironies of typographic history that the political force that finally put paid to blackletter as the German standard letterform was not international Marxism, nor Weimar social-a b d E f g k h i j l m n o o

a   b   e = TS   d   é (in meer)   kurz-ä (in selbst)   f   g   k für k und q   h   i   j   l   m   n   o   o   u

x = KS   y = 1 oder u

T u ü

p   q = K   r   s,ss   t   u   ü   deutsches v = f   w

unfertig

unterscheidet sich zu wenig von r und ist jetzt nur im zusammenhang der zeile erkennbar

soh (in schon)

z = TS   oh (in ioh)   ng (in lunge)   oh (in ach)

punkt   komma   anführungszeichen

lange vokale werden mit dem dehnzeichen versehen,
jedoch nur in zweifelsfällen, in fremdwörtern
und in eigennamen, und nur wenn notwendig:

ah   äh   ih   oh   üh   uh

é (ohne dehnzeichen, da stets lang)

kurze der vokale kann mit einem punkt bezeichnet werden:

a (immer kurz)   o   i   ö   u   u

democracy, but rather National-Socialism. Having killed off modernism and with it the belief in sanserif as the neutral, international machine-age letter, the Nazi cultural ideology flirted for some time with good old Teutonic letterforms, but finally – in a decree of 1941 – declared that Roman letterforms were to replace the 'Jewish' Schwabacher as the standard in printing and for all other uses. The words of the thousand-year Reich were to be given unimpeachable Roman authority.

After 1933, modernism – where not extinguished – went into hibernation, or emigration. Notions of a universal alphabet would have been a bad joke in the conditions of world war. But during the 1950s the idea emerged again, suitably mutated in the new context of post-war recovery and technological and social optimism.

Universal Univers

It is doubtful that anyone, not even the most wishful publicity officer, seriously thought of Univers as a universal typeface, though it did have more realistic claims to this title than those of the between-the-wars experiments. It was, first of all, a highly refined set of forms: dogmatic adherence to geometry was no longer tenable by the time that Adrian Frutiger started work on the commission in 1954. When it was new, Univers was seen as a break with the clumsy nineteenth-century 'grotesques' (its contemporary Helvetica, though a 'new grotesque', still suffered from this legacy), but its refinement had further dimensions. Designed from the outset as a family of related weights and variants (figure 7), it seemed to provide answers to all problems. Different languages set in the typeface would give the same visual impression (thanks to the slight adjusting decrease in the size of its capital letters). And in due course non-Latin versions (including Cyrillic and Japanese) appeared. It thus seemed to be the typeface of that moment, when international agencies and multinational companies were still bathed in a glow of optimism. Univers was nowhere more at home than in the trilingual square-format, persil-white publications that emanated from Switzerland in the 1960s.

5 Opposite: Jan Tschichold's new alphabet assumed a revolutionary orthography, following Walter Porstmann: no capitals and a consistent representation of sounds. (From: *A bis Z*, no. 7, 1930.)

EINLADUNG zum Vortrag
des Herrn Paul Renner aus München:
TOTE ODER LEBENDE SCHRIFT?
am Freitag, den 3. Juli abends 8 Uhr
im großen Saale des Löwenbräu
Große Gallusstraße 17
Bildungsverband der deutschen
Buchdrucker Ortsgruppe Frankfurt

6   An invitation card set in an early version of Futura (1925), showing the
experimental characters that were later dropped. 119 x 151 mm. (From:
Philipp Luidl [ed.], *Paul Renner*, Munich: Typographische Gesellschaft
München, 1978.)

Univers was designed initially for photocomposition, but made
its mark first as a hot-metal typeface, in the dying years of that technique. But with the coming of non-metal and then non-film composition processes and with the advent of machine reading, the
'universal' idea has reasserted itself.

The advance of the machines
Where cultural propaganda had failed (in the period of heroic modernism), 'the machine', in the form of optical character reading,
and economic interest, now forced the issue of a standard typeface.
First OCR-A (a US Standard was conferred on it in 1966) and then,
with advances in the technology, OCR-B. This latter typeface was
designed along Univers lines – though with inevitable deviations –
by Adrian Frutiger for the European Computer Manufacturers Association, and has been recognized as an International Standard since
1973. So, without many fanfares, the modernist dream of a stand-

7 Adrian Frutiger's Univers (in use from the early 1960s) broke with nineteenth-century grotesques and with the geometric letterforms of heroic modernism. Among its 'universal' qualities were its co-ordinated weights and variants, and the 'non-Latin' emulations that were made.

ard, neutral, machine-determined typeface has come true. Though one may guess that Kurt Schwitters or Theo van Doesburg would have felt more at home with another machine-readable letterform of this time: the minimal rectangular typeface developed at the National Physical Laboratory by Timothy Epps and Christopher Evans (figure 8). This example was designed on a five-unit square grid, and may serve here as an acknowledgement of dot-matrix alphabets: perhaps – on one view – 'universal' in their further reduction of elements.

The special conditions of cathode-ray generation of characters encouraged the 'new alphabet' by Wim Crouwel, published first in 1967 (figure 9). This experiment came with a good deal of ideological trumpeting. True to his native modernist heritage, Crouwel's explanation was saturated with echoes of the new typography: 'the manufacture of type has not changed since the moulded type [sic] was first introduced ... the machine age has to be accepted as essential if we are to cope with the demands of our age'. This new alphabet – in the best modernist tradition – was 'intended merely

⌐⌐⊐⌐⊐⌐⊏ ⊔⊐⌐⊐

8 A typeface for machine reading designed at the National Physical Laboratory (England) by Timothy Epps and Christopher Evans (1969). (From: Spencer, *The visible word*.)

9 The starting point for the forms of Wim Crouwel's 'new alphabet' (1967) was the movement of the light-beam in a cathode-ray tube. (From: Spencer, *The visible word*.)

as an initial step … for further research', but no further work was done on it. Now it seems to belong with the minimal art of its time: possessing a certain rather barren beauty, but pandering to 'the machine' at the expense of readability.

In a riposte to Crouwel, Gerard Unger made this point. But he also refused a simple imitation, and inevitable distortion, of old forms: for example, as in the now countless 'Garamonds', which imitate imitations of imitations. Instead, Unger's suggestion was that machines should be adapted to forms that human beings find easily perceivable, and that received style models should be reconsidered in the light of new technology.

'Light' does seem to be the operative word in describing the latest phase of this search. At the Bauhaus there was a dream that chairs were turning from wood into tubular steel and finally, at some time in this century, into 'resilient air columns'. Now that type has dematerialized from metal into rays of light and electrical pulses, a technological optimist might be encouraged to believe that finally we have the conditions for the ideal, the universal typeface; that without these old, constraints anything may be possible. Material, political realities – no less than the realities of language and of human perception – suggest otherwise.

244

Bibliography

Statements by designers

Herbert Bayer, 'Versuch einer neuen Schrift', *Offset*, no. 7, 1926

Kurt Schwitters, 'Anregungen zur Erlangung einer Systemschrift', *I10*, no. 8/9 (1927)

Joost Schmidt, 'Schrift?', *Bauhaus*, no. 2/3, 1928

Jan Tschichold, 'Noch eine neue Schrift', *Typographische Mitteilungen*, March 1930

Adrian Frutiger, 'Der Werdegang der Univers', *Typographische Monatsblätter*, January 1961

Wim Crouwel, *New alphabet*, Hilversum: De Jong, 1967

Gerard Unger, *A counter-proposal*, Hilversum: De Jong, n.d.

Adrian Frutiger, 'OCR-B: a standardized character for optical recognition', *Typographische Monatsblätter*, January 1967

Timothy Epps & Christopher Evans, *Alphabet*, Hilversum: De Jong, 1970

Historical discussions

Gerd Fleischmann, *Bauhaus: Drucksachen, Typografie, Reklame*, Düsseldorf: Marzona, 1984

André Jammes, 'Académisme et typographie: the making of the romain du roi', *Journal of the Printing Historical Society*, no. 1, 1965

Herbert Spencer, *The visible word*, Lund Humphries, 1969

Baseline, no. 6, 1985

This was the first of the two articles that I wrote for *Baseline* in its days as the magazine of the Esselte Letraset company. (The second article, 'What is a typeface?', is at pp. 113–30 above.) The theme of this issue was 'typefaces for special needs'.

The Bauhaus again: in the constellation of typographic modernism

'Bauhaus typography'
'... what is called "Bauhaus Typography" – sanserif type and over-size numerals, and horizontal and vertical "bars" (whose function is sometimes to emphasize, to help organize the information, but sometimes ... to decorate).'[1] This description, from a recent history of graphic design, suggests that the phrase 'Bauhaus typography' is indeed a recognized term. To the meanings given here, one could add: words set in lowercase only; red used as a second colour to black; the use of circles, squares and arrows, as well as these 'bars'.

Looking at the corpus of work produced at and for the Bauhaus, it is clear that 'Bauhaus typography' emerged clearly only in 1923. The key figure in the change was László Moholy-Nagy, who took up his appointment at the school in the spring of that year. Before this time, we see graphic work drawn by artists (notably Oskar Schlemmer and Johannes Itten) in their personal styles. And where typesetting was used, then the key person in the design process seems to have been the printer. But in items from 1923 and 1924, such as the Bauhausverlag letterheading [Fl. 78] and the Bauhausbuch prospectus [Fl. 147–8], both credited to Moholy-Nagy, some of the typical components are there.[2] In the letterheading (figure 1), the primary forms of circle, square and triangle, are combined to make the school's emblem (we might now call it a 'logo'). As well as 'ele-

1. Richard Hollis, *Graphic design: a concise history*, Thames & Hudson, 1994, p. 19.
2. [Fl. 78] indicates that the item referred to can be seen reproduced on page 78 of the book edited by Gerd Fleischmann: *Bauhaus: Druck-sachen, Typografie, Reklame* (Düsseldorf: Marzona, 1984). The book in which this essay originally appeared was well illustrated with examples, and much of what I refer to here can be seen there in good reproduc-tions: Ute Brüning (ed.), *Das A und O des Bauhauses*, Berlin: Bauhaus-Archiv, 1995. Reference can also be made to the reproductions else-where in the present book, especially: 'Large and small letters: author-ity and democracy' (pp. 131–42); 'Universal faces, ideal characters' (pp. 233–45).

246

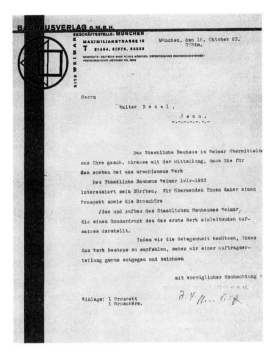

1 Letterheading of the Bauhausverlag (1923), black and red,
   285 x 225 mm.

mentariness', this emblem also suggests an arrow-form, which we
can understand as suggesting 'to-the-point-ness', urgency, movement, perhaps progress. One can note that the words here are set
entirely in capital letters, in a bold sanserif typeface.

The 'Katalog der Muster' [Fl. 203–4], printed in November 1925
and designed by Herbert Bayer, is one of the first pieces produced
after the move to Dessau. It is a four-page A4-format leaflet, within
which loose single sheets describing Bauhaus products would have
been placed. Here we can see a more refined synthesis of the typical
elements. Where in earlier pieces almost everything is stretched or
squeezed into rectangular shapes, here there is a sense of greater
freedom and space. The cover and inside pages (figures 2 & 3) have a
clear axis, from which elements range to the right. Nevertheless, in
details such as the constant width given to the words 'Vertrieb durch

2   The front of the four-page leaflet outlining the prototype-products
    of the Bauhaus (1925), black and orange, 297 x 210 mm.

die Bauhaus GmbH' on the cover, one finds the 'block-mentality'
still at work.[3] This will-to-tidiness becomes very clear on the inside
pages where the five departments are equated visually with the five
conditions on the facing page. But this visual equation is without
meaning: the conditions apply to all departments equally. And here
we see the 'oversize numerals'. Large enough to be read from several
metres distance, they suggest an urgency of action that might be
more appropriate for instructions in case of fire. So here 'function'
is exaggerated – to become decoration.

This then is the phenomenon of 'Bauhaus typography'. Among
the large questions that a historian might want to put are the follow-

3. The principle of the 'block-layout' was part of a long vernacular
tradition in printing. Moholy-Nagy warned against it in 1923: 'Die
Buchstabentypen dürfen nie in eine vorbestimmte Form, z.B. Quadrat
gezwängt werden' ('Letters may never be forced into a predetermined
form, for example a square'). ('Die neue Typographie', published in the
book of the Weimar Bauhaus exhibition; reproduced and reprinted in:
Fleischmann, *Bauhaus: Drucksachen, Typografie, Reklame*, p. 15). But
such a deep mental structure could not be abolished overnight.

248

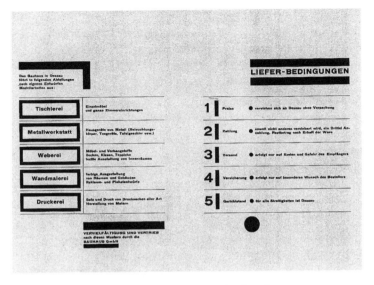

3   Inside spread of the prototype-products leaflet of 1925.

ing. Where did it come from? How did it develop? How much did
it spread beyond the Bauhaus? Is 'Bauhaus typography' the same
as 'modernist typography'? And, if not, who and what else played
a part in forming modernist typography? And how did these other
contributions affect the development of Bauhaus typography? The
very formulation of these questions suggests that the picture is complex and hard to pin down.

A further observation should be made here. Discussions of Bauhaus typography – and this essay is no exception – take as their
subject the school's own printed matter and the design work of the
teachers. Sometimes one may consider the work done by students
after leaving the school. In other words, we are largely dealing with
the public face of the school: what it wanted the world to see. And
even the design work done by teachers, cushioned by their (perhaps
not large) salaries, may have some quality of being done for demonstration rather than for need. What went on in the classrooms
is another matter, and very much harder to assess. Teaching and
learning may well have no simple visible outcome.

Discussions of sources and influences often tend towards pathology. We hear about styles (symptoms) passed on through personal contact (was there a handshake?) or perhaps just through visual means of transmission (did X see the work of Y?). The two celebrated principal sources for Bauhaus typography are Russian constructivism and the Dutch Stijl movement. By 1923, both were significant presences in the international artistic avant-garde. And one can trace their personal impact on the Bauhaus, via Moholy-Nagy's contact with Lissitzky (from 1921), and Theo van Doesburg's visits to Weimar (1922). However, there is more to say.

First, and so obvious that one sometimes neglects to mention it: the materials of printing played a part. Red has been the traditional second colour of printing since Gutenberg, who followed the scribal practice of 'rubrication'. In the context of socialist revolution, it could take on new meanings. Similarly, 'bars' had been familiar to printers since at least the early nineteenth century. Now they were seen freshly, through constructivist spectacles, as elemental forms. Much of the energy of Bauhaus and modernist typography comes from this process of old or already available materials being seen in a new light.

The propaganda for sanserif letterforms has the same character. Something that had its origins and development in the nineteenth century is now, in the 1920s, seen as 'the letter of our age' or of the future. One could trace the perception of sanserif as a bearer of cultural significance right back to its rediscovery by neoclassical artists and architects around 1800.[4] At that moment a complex of meanings was in play: the culture of antiquity was being recovered, but for modern effects. Relevant later instances would include its use in the 1900s in avant-garde literary and artistic publications. Here sanserif letterforms clearly signify a modern attitude: of simplicity and purification. This spirit is evident in Stefan George's adoption of sanserif for his books; and in the magazine *Ring* (1908–9), published in Düsseldorf and edited by the Dutch architect

4. See: James Mosley, 'The nymph and the grot: the revival of the sanserif letter', *Typographica* (new series), no. 12, 1965, pp. 2–19. This essay has since been published, updated and expanded, in a book of the same title (Friends of the St Bride Printing Library, 1999).

J.L.M.Lauweriks. This usage continued in *Wendingen* (1918–31), edited by the architect H.Th.Wijdeveld (with Lauweriks among the associate editors) and published from Amsterdam.

The single alphabet or lowercase-only principle that was adopted at the Bauhaus in 1925 has a similar lineage.[5] Among the ancestors here are the orthographic reforms proposed by Jakob Grimm in the nineteenth century, and – again – Stefan George's work. Grimm wanted to reform the convention of capitalizing every noun, in a more rational deployment of two alphabets. But the demand at the Bauhaus was for just one alphabet. At first, as we see in the work of 1923 and elsewhere in modernist work of the time, this was all-capital typography. The idea of singleness, and the greater urgency and authority that words set in capitals possess, here took precedence over qualities that lowercase letters might bring. Even as late as 1928, on the title-page of Jan Tschichold's *Die neue Typographie*, there are only capital letters.

In the shift to all-lowercase and to experiments with phonetic alphabets, the key source of ideas was Walter Porstmann's book, *Sprache und Schrift* (1920). This work is fired by the zeal of rationalism: linguistic and orthographic reform will save time, materials and money. Porstmann was working from within the business-efficiency and standardization movements. He became a principal figure in the work of the Deutscher Normenausschuß, particularly in the formulation and propagation of the DIN paper sizes that were another constituent part of modernist typography.

As a glance at *Sprache und Schrift* or at any of the DIN publications shows, these ideas, at their source, were innocent of any aesthetic dimension.[6] It was this that the artist-designers, at the Bauhaus and elsewhere, supplied. There is no mention of the idea of the single alphabet in Moholy-Nagy's programmatic text 'Die neue Typographie', published in the catalogue of the 1923 exhibition at Wei-

5. For a brief survey see my article 'Large and small letters: authority and democracy', *Octavo*, no. 5, 1988 (pp. 131–42 above).
6. 'Typographisch ist es freilich von erstaunlich geringer Qualität ...' ('Typographically however it is of astonishingly low quality ...'). Thus Jan Tschichold on a DIN publication, in his book *Die neue Typographie*, Berlin: Bildungsverband der Deutschen Buchdrucker, 1928, p. 116, footnote.

mar. But in an article of 1925, 'Bauhaus und Typographie', Moholy-Nagy refers to the lineage described above (and mentions Adolf Loos's views too) before summarizing Porstmann's argument: 'daß unsere schrift durch die kleinschreibung nichts verliere, aber leicht lesbar, leichter lernbar, wesentlich wirtschaftlicher würde, daß es unnötig sei, für einen laut ... die doppelte menge zeichen zu benutzen, wenn die hälfte dasselbe erreicht.' ('that our script loses nothing by being written small, but becomes easy to read, easier to learn, essentially more economic, and that it is unnecessary to use a double quantity of signs to represent a sound: half this number of signs is sufficent.')[7]

If Moholy-Nagy can be seen as the vehicle carrying the idea to Dessau, then it was his students Herbert Bayer, Joost Schmidt and Josef Albers who were prominent in taking it up and playing with it. All became teachers at the Bauhaus in 1925. In July 1926, the special Bauhaus issue of the printing journal *Offset* included the publication of Bayer's 'Universal' alphabet as well as Albers's 'Schablonenschrift' (stencil script).[8] Schmidt's teaching work of 1925 and 1926, along the same lines of an entirely geometrical set of forms, has now been published.[9]

Bauhaus typography in its contexts

In October 1925, just at the time of the reopening at Dessau, the first substantial anthology of the new typography was published. This was 'Elementare Typographie', a special issue of the magazine *Typographische Mitteilungen*. The editor was the then twenty-three-year-old Jan Tschichold: a typographer raised in the traditional culture of printing and lettering at Leipzig, but whose head had been turned towards modernism by the experience of seeing the

7. 'Bauhaus und Typographie', *Anhaltische Rundschau*, 14 September 1925. (Available in English translation in: H. M. Wingler, *Bauhaus*, Cambridge, Massachusetts: MIT Press, 1969, pp. 114–15.)
8. The articles by Albers and Bayer are, respectively: 'Zür Ökonomie der Schriftform' and 'Versuch einer neuen Schrift', *Offset*, no. 7, 1926, pp. 395–7, 398–404. (Reprinted in: Fleischmann, *Bauhaus: Drucksachen, Typografie, Reklame*, pp. 23–4, 25–7.)
9. *Joost Schmidt: Lehre und Arbeit am Bauhaus 1919–32*, Düsseldorf: Marzona, 1984.

1923 Weimar exhibition.[10] Tschichold went on to become a tireless, prolific and lucid advocate of modernist typography.

The design of 'Elementare Typographie' certainly shows the characteristics of 'Bauhaus typography', and the school is well represented in the work reproduced there and through a written contribution by Moholy-Nagy. This publication does, however, represent a line of thought and action that stood apart from the Bauhaus. *Typographische Mitteilungen* was a printing-trade magazine, published by the Bildungsverband der Deutschen Buchdrucker. It was thus an attempt to bring the ideas of the artistic avant-garde into the heart of trade practice. 'Elementare Typographie' initiated considerable debate among articulate printers both in the following issues of *Typographische Mitteilungen*, and elsewhere.[11]

The most striking contribution to 'Elementare Typographie' was Tschichold's ten-point manifesto of the same title. It is a synthesis of the leading ideas of modernist typography, but then given a practical dimension. Thus, calling for lowercase typography and orthographic reform, Tschichold refers to Porstmann's book – and gives us the price and publisher's address. The same information is supplied for the DIN paper formats, for which he would become the most eloquent champion. This marriage of theory and directly useful advice became Tschichold's characteristic method in the many articles and books that he went on to write. The major work was, of course, *Die neue Typographie*, published by the Bildungsverband in June 1928, which enlarged and greatly extended the concept of 'Elementare Typographie'. As its subtitle suggests – 'ein Handbuch für Zeitgemäß Schaffende' (literally translated as 'a handbook for contemporary creating') – it is at once a history, an anthology and survey, and a directly useful manual. Its primary readership would have been printers.

10. 'Er reiste zum Besuch dieser Ausstellung nach Weimar und kam aufgewühlt züruck.' ('He went to see the exhibition in Weimar and came back all churned up.') Thus Tschichold writing about himself in the book *Leben und Werk des Typographen Jan Tschichold*, Dresden: VEB Verlag der Kunst, 1977, p. 17.
11. See Friedrich Friedl's 'Echo und Reaktionen auf das Sonderheft "Elementare Typographie"', in the facsimile reprint: Iwan Tschichold, *Elementare Typographie*, Mainz: Verlag H. Schmidt, 1986, pp. 8–12.

If one looks for Bauhaus interventions into the printing trade, one could mention the special issue (July 1926) of *Offset* – 'das Blatt für Drucker, Werbefachleute und Verleger' ('journal for printing, publicity and publishing trades') – which, as already mentioned, published the articles on new alphabets by Albers and Bayer, as well as Moholy-Nagy on 'Zeitgemäße Typografie'. But though the articles in *Offset* certainly present ideas that can stand on their own, the effect of the whole issue is that of an advertisement for the Bauhaus, rather than an ordinary contribution to a journal. We are given an outline of the school's curriculum and a statement by Walter Gropius, as well as overviews of other areas of the school's work (by Gunta Stölzl and Oskar Schlemmer). Designed specially in 'Bauhaus typography' manner, as a separate supplement within the ordinary pages of the journal, the section stands out: like a piece by Arnold Schoenberg in a concert of music by Johann Strauss.[12]

In the summer of 1926, Jan Tschichold moved to Munich, to take up a teaching post at the Meisterschule für Deutschlands Buchdrucker, then being established under the direction of Paul Renner. He also taught lower-level students at the existing Graphische Berufsschule in Munich. This teaching work became another means of establishing the practices of the new typography within the ordinary printing trade. Evidence for this can be seen in the examples of student's work published by the Meisterschule in its journal, *Grafische Berufsschule*.[13] If it is clear that these students have been taught by particular designers – Tschichold and also Georg Trump – it is also true that these teachers passed on to their students an approach that was thoughtful, restrained, and widely applicable in everyday work. Here are the beginnings of a widely available 'language' of new typography, equivalent to the centuries-old 'language' of classical typography.

12. It is true that 'Elementare Typographie' was also a specially designed supplement within *Typographische Mitteilungen*, but the differences are not so striking as in the case of *Offset*. And *Typographische Mitteilungen* soon began to integrate the ideas of the new typography into its own design.
13. See for example the display advertisement project-work in an inserted section in *Grafische Berufsschule* no. 3/4, 1930/1.

A major contribution to the practice of modernist typography came in these years from Paul Renner: the typeface Futura.[14] Work on the project began in 1924. Early versions, used in trial printed pieces in 1925, show some eccentric characters that share in the same spirit as Albers's 'Schablonenschrift', Bayer's 'Universal', and other experiments of that moment. Here geometry and a certain dogmatic rationality prevail over accustomed forms. But, when Futura was finally released onto the market by the Bauer typefoundry in 1927, simplistic geometry had been tempered. Although the characters seem to be constructed of circles and straight lines, in fact their forms are subtly modulated. This resulted in a very usable typeface, unlike the experimental alphabets. Even the most realistic of these, Bayer's 'Universal', was never produced as a typeface. It remained as a theoretical hope, which was implemented only in drawn versions: for example in the masthead of the journal *Die neue Linie*, in the 1930s.[15] Herbert Bayer's later and more realistic Bayer-type was developed into a typeface – released by Berthold in the mid-1930s – but found little use. Its perilously delicate thin strokes would have presented mechanical problems to letterpress printers.

The pattern here seems to be that ideas about letterforms were picked up and developed in rather crude, didactic projects at the school around 1925; but that the translation of these ideas into usable and commercial form came from elsewhere. The case of Futura suggests this clearly. And there is no evidence of any special Bauhaus influence on the design of that typeface: these ideas were by then spread quite widely in avant-garde circles.

One may find the same sort of pattern in the case of the principle of 'typo-photo'. The conjunction of type and the photographic image was the enduring discovery of graphic modernism in this period: it gave birth to what in the years after 1945 began to flourish as 'graphic design'.

14. My remarks here are confirmed by the thorough research conducted by Christopher Burke, now published in his *Paul Renner: the art of typography*, Hyphen Press, 1998.
15. Much later, the Universal alphabet was adapted and released in versions for photocompostion and digital typesetting. An example is the typeface called Bauhaus, designed in the 1970s for the American company ITC.

The chief formulator of the idea of 'typo-photo' was Moholy-Nagy. As evidence for this, we have his Bauhausbuch *Malerei, Fotografie, Film*, published in 1925, and magazine articles of around this time. Thus his theoretical contribution to Tschichold's 'Elementare Typographie' had just this title: 'Typo-Photo'. But evidence that the practice of combining text and images was actually taught at the school, in any depth, is lacking. Certainly we find 'typo-photo' in practice in the design work done by Moholy-Nagy and also Herbert Bayer: especially after 1928, when they had left the school. But by this time the principle was becoming part of the repertoire of designers such as Max Burchartz, Tschichold, Paul Schuitema and Piet Zwart. One might speculate that this nascent principle of graphic design was something that had to be worked out in practice, in the commercial sphere, before it could be understood well enough to be taught in schools of art and design: at the Bauhaus or anywhere else. Or perhaps it was too commercial to be taught at the Bauhaus – or perhaps too commercial to be taught at the school that began to develop during the directorship of Hannes Meyer?

The Bauhaus and other groupings

The movement of modernist graphic design found concerted expression and embodiment in the Ring 'Neue Werbegestalter', which came into existence at the end of 1927, and became publicly evident during 1928. This was the nearest thing at this time to an international association of these designers, working as a pressure group to exhibit, publish and disseminate the principles of the movement. In its brief existence (which effectively came to an end in 1931), much of the energy that fuelled the group came from its co-ordinator Kurt Schwitters.

Here we can briefly note that the Ring existed outside and at some distance from the Bauhaus. It had no Bauhaus people as members. But among the 'guests' invited to participate in some of the Ring's exhibitions were Moholy-Nagy, Bayer, and Max Bill. Evidence that this attitude of reserve was a matter of discussion and policy is to be found in the typewritten 'Mitteilungen' that Schwitters circulated to Ring members.[16] Thus, in the 'Mitteilung 19', summer

1928, Schwitters reports on two related issues: whether to invite Joost Schmidt (then in charge of the 'Reklame-Abteilung' [publicity-graphics department] at the Bauhaus) to apply for membership of the Ring; and the matter of how their organization should define its relations with the Bauhaus. Schwitters's (unattributed) extracts from letters written to him on these matters by Ring members throw interesting light on the reputation of the Bauhaus at that moment, when Hannes Meyer had taken over as director, and the school was under attack from politically conservative critics. Some members felt that this was a bad time to make links with the Bauhaus. But there was a more general resistance to the school, conveyed in this view: '... das Gute am Ring war bisher sein Auskommen ohne Bauhaus ... bei jeder Bindung mit dem Bauhaus hat nur das Bauhaus profitiert ... rate zur Unabhängigkeit in jeder Weise ... jeder, der am Bauhaus ist und modern von innen heraus gestaltet, unser Mitglied sein, aber wir dürfen dem Bauhaus gegenüber keine Verpflichtungen übernehmen.' ('... the good thing about the Ring so far has been that it has managed to get along without the Bauhaus ... in every connection to the Bauhaus, only the Bauhaus has profited ... suggest independence in every respect ... anyone who is at the Bauhaus and does modern design, starting from the inside and working out from that, can belong to us, but we may be permitted to have no obligations with respect to the Bauhaus.')[17]

In this anonymous voice we hear a resistance to the Bauhaus from within the modern movement: from a small group seeking an autonomous existence, outside the sphere of that famous institution. After the discussion reported here by Schwitters, the question of the Bauhaus largely disappeared from the 'Mitteilungen'. Joost Schmidt did not become a member, and no special links were made

16. Those sent to Piet Zwart are now in the Special Collection of the Getty Center for the History of Art and the Humanities, Los Angeles (USA). Their texts can also be found in this catalogue: *Ring 'neue werbegestalter': Amsterdamer Ausstellung von 1931*, Wiesbaden: Landesmuseum Wiesbaden, 1990.
17. *Ring 'neue werbegestalter': Amsterdamer Ausstellung von 1931*, Wiesbaden: Landesmuseum Wiesbaden, 1990, p. 116.

between the Ring and the Bauhaus. There had been a suggestion that the Ring could collaborate with the Bauhaus journal. But the publication with which the Ring did establish some co-operation was *Das neue Frankfurt*.[18] This journal, and the municipal housing programme at Frankfurt (under the architectural direction of Ernst May) that formed its main focus and its basis, was another star in the constellation of modernism in those years.

We can extend this idea of a modernist constellation over Central Europe with a reference to an institution that was in these years working out principles for the graphic presentation of information: the Gesellschafts- und Wirtschaftsmuseum in Wien ('social and economic museum of Vienna').[19] Growing initially out of the 'Siedlungsbewegung' (estate-housing movement) in Vienna, this body was established by Otto Neurath in 1925. Its typical product was a chart for public display that represented social information in graphic form: symbols were drawn to represent a certain quantity of things and then they were repeated – not enlarged – to represent a greater quantity. By the late 1920s, the work of this Museum, which became known later as 'Isotype', showed considerable sophistication in its configuration of material and in its graphic and typographic design. A quite strict system of arrangement was in development, including standardized symbols and colours. The typeface used was Futura, asymmetrically deployed. This was team-work, whose leading contributors, apart from Neurath himself, were Marie Reidemeister (who 'transformed' the raw information into visual form) and the artist Gerd Arntz. As well as charts for display in Vienna, the Museum began to show its work inter-

18. *Das neue Frankfurt*, April 1928, carries a report of the establishment of the Ring. Thereafter, occasional contributions concerning Ring exhibitions or members' work were published. In his Mitteilung dated 16.6.28, Schwitters refers to *Das neue Frankfurt* as 'unser sagen wir "amtliches Organ"' ('our – as we say – "official organ"').

19. The source for this information is the Isotype archive at the Department of Typography, University of Reading (England), which formed the basis for an MPhil thesis on the topic, which I wrote there (1979). The term 'Isotype', although devised by the Neurath group only in the 1930s, after they had moved to the Netherlands, is the best descriptor for this work.

nationally, and to make printed publications. Its reputation grew, especially within progressive and visually conscious circles.

Relations between the Bauhaus and the Gesellschafts- und Wirtschaftsmuseum in Wien were established. Otto Neurath was among those who attended the opening of the school at Dessau in December 1926, after which he wrote a sympathetic yet not uncritical commentary on the Bauhaus project.[20] Later, in 1929, Neurath was among the members of the Vienna Circle who gave lectures at the school: his subject was 'Bildstatistik und Gegenwart' ('pictorial statistics and the present').[21]

Social information presented graphically in strikingly modernist forms by a museum of public education: there is no surprise that this should have been a topic of interest in a left-turning Bauhaus. Here we can observe that this is a case of the Bauhaus looking outside itself for sustenance, to work being done elsewhere. That this should happen is obvious enough. But it has a place in the suggestion of this article: that the 'Bauhaus typography' of around 1925 was a limited phenomenon that did not have the power to develop further, without learning from other practices.

Late Bauhaus typography

'Bauhaus typography' has a clear meaning and refers to the work of 1923–6. But what then of the work of the later 1920s, and up to the closure in 1933? The last letterheadings of the school [Fl. 254, 255], in use at Berlin in 1933, are frankly Tschicholdian: in their small type, one size only of a Grotesk, with the school's name set in a contrasting seriffed type, slightly larger in size (figure 4). The DIN guidelines are strictly observed. As if in confirmation of this, there is documentary evidence to show that right at the end of the life of

20. Otto Neurath, 'Das neue Bauhaus in Dessau', *Der Aufbau*, vol. 1, no. 11/12, 1926, pp. 209–11.
21. See the notice in *Bauhaus*, vol. 3, no. 3, p. 28. In the mimeographed publication also titled *Bauhaus* ('Organ der kommunistischen Studierenden am Bauhaus'), vol. 1, no. 2, June 1930, there is an unsigned critique of 'Der Austromarxisumus und Neurath'. The editor in charge of this issue was Heinz Walter Allner, who in around 1929, with Lotte Beese, worked briefly at the Gesellschafts- und Wirtschaftsmuseum in Wien.

4   Letterheading of the Bauhaus (1932?), black and red, 297 x 210 mm.

the school, mutual approaches were made between its director Mies van der Rohe and Jan Tschichold.[22]

In 1928, with the change of the school's directorship, from Gropius to Meyer, its two principle 'stars' of graphic design, Moholy-Nagy and Bayer, had left. Bayer, in particular, then began to pursue a different and more commercial approach to design, which we might call the 'Dorland' style, after the advertising agency that he

22. See the letter from Mies to Paul Renner of 16 May 1933, quoted in: Christoph Stölzl (ed.), *Die Zwanziger Jahre in München*, Munich: Münchner Stadtmuseum, 1979, pp. 205–6. Tschichold (who in March-April 1933 was held in protective custody by the new authorities in Munich) had 'vor einiger Zeit' ('some time ago') expressed interest in a teaching post at the Bauhaus. Mies, then trying to revive the Bauhaus, wrote to Tschichold's former employer, Paul Renner, to ask about Tschichold's financial expectations.

then directed.[23] Constructivist roots are left behind, and the work relies quite heavily on drawn illustration as well as photography; the choice of typefaces is catholic; and, where possible, colour is freely used. Something of this new style can be seen fed back into a piece designed by Joost Schmidt, who stayed on to lead the new Reklame-Abteilung, until the closure at Dessau in 1932.

The publicity booklet for the Verkehrsbüro der Stadt Dessau ('Tourist office of the city of Dessau') [Fl. 316–8] is dated at 1931.[24] Its style is certainly 'later' than the booklets and prospectuses produced for the school itself two or three years before. But these differences may also be due to the fact that this booklet was designed not for the school, but for an outside client. The back cover shows the new illustrational approach clearly. The feeling is surreal, but to some purpose. The juxtapositions convey the dual character of the city: both old (the classical column) and new (the gleaming machine part). The map-diagram on the front cover is a piece of information graphics with a 'Wiener' or Isotype flavour (figure 5). Even more clearly in that spirit are some pictorial statistics on the inside of the back cover. Inside (first page), the headline text shows the principle of 'Schriftmischung' (type mixture) that Tschichold was then just beginning to develop in display typography. And the script typeface was something that Tschichold would redeem from the sphere of kitsch: see the title page of his book of 1935, *Typographische Gestaltung*. In sum, if this booklet is Bauhaus typography, it is not like the work we know by that term. It is more worldly, more a synthesis of approaches and ideas that had arisen since 'Bauhaus typography'.

23. Bayer himself reflected on this change in his article 'Typografie und Werbesachengestaltung', *Bauhaus*, vol. 2, no. 1, 1928, p. 10. (Available in English translation in: Wingler, *Bauhaus*, p. 135.)
24. This text was written before I saw the reproductions in *Das A und O des Bauhauses*, where what had been confusing in previous reproductions becomes clear. There were two items: a 24-page booklet (pictures 216 and 217 in that book), and a folded sheet with map on one side, text and photographs on the other side (pictures 218–220). Seeing these pieces reproduced more fully, I realized that I was imagining one item where in fact there are two. The points I make are not affected by this.

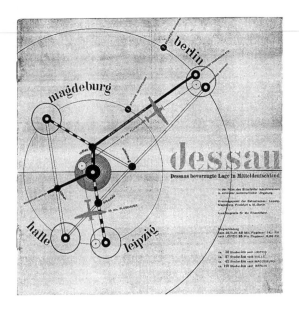

5   Front cover of the publicity booklet for the city of Dessau (1931), black
and red, 230 x 230 mm. The 24-page booklet is stapled at one side and
can be folded down the centre.

In conclusion

We can say that 'Bauhaus typography' was a phenomenon of a particular time: around 1923–6. As deployed in stationery, prospectuses
and books it served the interests of the school well, particularly as
it established itself in Dessau. 'Bauhaus typography' was first and
foremost a means of projecting a coherent and progressive image of
the school to the world. But developments elsewhere, from around
1925, showed the limitations of the general application of 'Bauhaus
typography'. It had little connection with the printing trade: with
the people who, before the rise of the graphic designer, were
largely responsible for the design of so much printed matter. The
school's work with script and typeface design had none of the formal subtlety and the willingness to modify, in dialogue with industrial craft-workers, which make possible the production of typefaces. Bauhaus typography, even at its most 'industrial', remains
haunted by the hand of the artist. Principles of layout were not
articulated in writing at the Bauhaus. It was Jan Tschichold who

could find the words to describe, in detail, how the new typography really worked.

In 1928, with the change of directorship and of direction, there was a chance to reassess. The new mood was against mere publicity, in favour of serious research. There are signs that developments in typography and design outside the school began to have some impact. But the heightened political criticism that came with the new direction under Meyer, as well as the growing larger economic and political crisis in Germany, worked to destabilize the climate of the school. Among the uncertain new directions was the commercially more realistic 'Reklame-Abteilung' led by Joost Schmidt. But these developments remained as hints and suggestions. Dominating them now in our perception of 'Bauhaus typography' is the touching, utopian fantasy – disguised as functionalism – of the work of 1923–6.

'Das Bauhaus im Kontext der neuen Typographie', in: Ute Brüning (ed.), *Das A und O des Bauhauses*, Berlin: Bauhaus-Archiv, 1995.

Written for a book accompanying an exhibition of graphic design at the Bauhaus, which was shown at the Bauhaus-Archiv (Berlin) and elsewhere in Germany in 1995–6. This text has not been published in English before.

The term 'new typography' refers to typographic work done in the spirit of the modern movement. And this paper has been written with the present, larger debate over the modern movement very much in mind. It is intended that some connections and wider implications will become apparent from this consideration of what may be one of the more specialized and enclosed fields of design.

An ordering approach

New typography will be taken here at its own best intentions: not so much concerned with style, as with an approach to work. Style is then formulated as a by-product of the work, rather than a main concern. To single out a defining quality of this approach: it was – and is – an organizing, ordering approach. This attempt at order exists on two layers. On the outer layer, there is the typographic designer working in the world to co-ordinate and bring order to all the processes by which texts get produced and multiplied: this is the designer going to meetings; making telephone calls; writing memos, reports, letters, specifications. The inner layer is one of ordering all the elements that constitute the text: this is the designer working at the typewriter and the drawing board.

The idea of an ordering approach will serve as a working hypothesis, for the purposes of this paper. But one would want to test how far it really serves to define new typography against other approaches, through a more extensive historical exploration than is possible here. The concept of 'order' is, meanwhile, adopted against (and in criticism of) the common assumption that 'asymmetry' is sufficient as a defining feature of new typography. Asymmetry is no doubt one of the more visible principles of new typography – and of the whole modern movement in design. An examination of comparable work in architecture and other fields of design could help to reveal other informing principles of new typography.[1]

1. For an attempt to articulate principles of the modern movement as a whole, see: Norman Potter, *What is a designer*, Reading: Hyphen Press, 1980, part 5.

Tschichold and the pre-war years in Britain

New typography is largely – though certainly not wholly identifiable with the work of its leading practitioner and theorist, Jan Tschichold.[2] In his book *Die neue Typographie* (1928) Tschichold provided the first substantial summary of the movement, and demonstrated, through the conspectus of work illustrated (his own and that of others), that it was a real movement. At the time of this book's publication, Tschichold's new typography was maturing rapidly, and in his work over the next few years (up to and immediately after the political and personal watershed of 1933) he begins to show an unrivalled sense of the right placing of visual elements. In this, and in knowing how to get printers to do exactly what he wanted, Tschichold stands out from the other 'pioneers of modern typography' – for example, Lissitzky, Schwitters, Moholy-Nagy, and also Herbert Bayer – whose typographic work remained, by comparison, crude. (The more purely graphic work of these first three is another matter.) Tschichold understood the processes of composition and printing, and knew how to specify for them; the 'artist typographers' were, to varying degrees, hazy about such matters. This distinction goes some way towards explaining Tschichold's power as an influence. His practice was in itself articulate and could be learned from; and, above this, he was an extremely clear theorist of his practice, and apparently quite tireless in his publicizing activities.

By the mid-1930s Tschichold's influence began to be felt in Britain. There had been some articles published in *Commercial Art*; then a visit to Britain and an exhibition at Lund Humphries in 1935. In 1937 the book *Circle* was published, with Tschichold's contribution 'New typography'. This article provides a convenient starting point for a consideration of new typography in Britain (figure 1). For here Tschichold contended with what he called the 'new traditionalism'. The term did not catch on, though it is convenient and will be used in this paper.

2. The best source of information on Tschichold is the book whose content and design were planned by its subject: *Jan Tschichold: Leben und Werk des Typographen*, Dresden: VEB Verlag der Kunst, 1977. But neither this book nor Ruari McLean's *Jan Tschichold: typographer* (Lund Humphries, 1975) begins to provide the critical discussion that is needed.

TABLE

NEW TRADITIONALISM	NEW TYPOGRAPHY
Common to both	
Disappearance of ornament Attention to careful setting Attempt at good proportional relations	
Differences	
Use of harmonious types only, where possible the same	Contrasts by the use of various types
The same thickness of type, bolder type prohibited	Contrasts by the use of bolder type
Related sizes of type	Frequent contrasts by the use of widely differentiated types
Organization from a middle point (symmetry)	Organization without a middle-point (asymmetry)
Tendency towards concentration of all groups	Tendency towards arrangement in isolated groups
Predominant tendency towards a pleasing appearance	Predominant tendency towards lucidity and functionalism
Preference for woodcuts and drawings	Preference for photographs
Tendency towards hand-setting	Tendency towards machine-setting

1 Jan Tschichold's tabulation of contemporary typography, from his article 'New typography' in: J. L. Martin, Ben Nicholson & Naum Gabo (ed.), *Circle*, Faber & Faber, 1937, p. 251.

The new traditionalism was a peculiarly British phenomenon: the reforming movement in printing and typography that is associated with the names of Stanley Morison, Francis Meynell, Oliver Simon, and others. And the new traditionalism should be borne in mind as the reigning enlightened orthodoxy, against which new typography began to be adopted in Britain in the 1940s and 1950s.

Tschichold's text in *Circle*, and the set of features given in the table that accompanies it remains largely on the level of style and appearance. So already, in attributing a deeper kind of feature to new typography, one goes beyond anything that Tschichold himself articulated: though there are hints and suggestions here and elsewhere in his writings, and there is the evidence of his practice.

There were other seeds of new typography sown in Britain before the War. One could mention the interest of the London advertising world in Continental developments (though mainly those in Paris, rather than Berlin): initially concentrated in posters and largely graphic work, but moving on to the design of text. And by the end of the 1930s one or two quite convincing specimens of native British new typography had been produced. (But perhaps only one: the catalogue for the MARS exhibition, 1938, designed by Ashley Havinden.) There was also the phenomenon of 'left-wing layout': covers and other display typography for the publications of Lawrence & Wishart and other socialist publishers.[3] The same issue of the magazine in which this phenomenon was noticed – *Typography* (edited by Robert Harling for the Shenval Press) – also published an article by Tschichold on type mixtures.[4]

In retrospect it seems natural that this least essential aspect of the new typography should have been picked up by the eclectic, relentlessly bright and light-hearted *Typography*. Tschichold's practice of mixing contrasting text and display typefaces clearly appealed to those (such as Robert Harling) who might have felt weighed down by the most forbidding exponent of the new traditionalism (Stanley Morison) and by new traditionalist injunctions to use one typeface only for any one job (even a mixture of weights was suspect).[5] But, on the other hand, type mixture could be detached from the otherwise austere set of features of new typography. And the idea of mixing types chimed in exactly with the contemporary rediscovery of Victoriana, which in the typographic world found its fullest expression in Nicolete Gray's book *Nineteenth century ornamented types and title pages* (1938). It was this book that provided authority and sources for the cult of Victorian display typefaces that came to its peak after the War – in the *Architectural Review*, on the South Bank, at the Royal College of Art, and elsewhere.

The war interlude and its aftermath

The major phenomenon of the war years in graphic and typographic design seems now to be the work done under the auspices of the Ministry of Information.[6] One factor in an explanation of the liberating effect of work for the MOI is that it introduced graphic de-

---

3. See: Howard Wadman, 'Left-wing layout', *Typography*, no. 3, 1937, pp. 24–8.
4. See: Jan Tschichold, 'Type mixtures', *Typography*, no. 3, 1937, pp. 2–7.
5. This observation derives from a reading of *Typography*, and was given some support by Robert Harling in a letter to me (8 September 1981).
6. The history of designing for the MOI remains to be written, though a solid piece of research on its work at policy-making level has been published: Ian McLaine, *Ministry of morale*, Allen & Unwin, 1979.

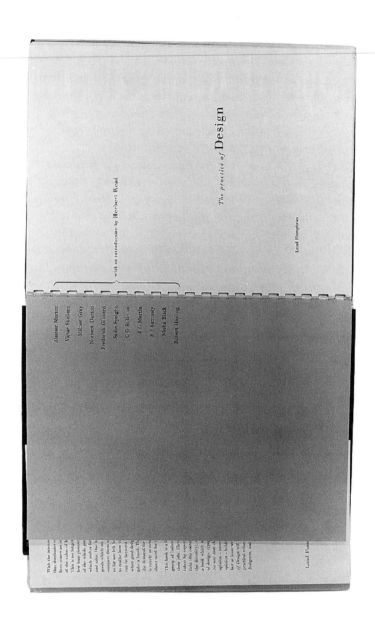

The practice of Design

with an introduction by Herbert Read

Alastair Morton
Vicar Stalker
Milner Gray
Norbert Dutton
Frederick Gibberd
Sadie Speight
C G Stillman
J L Martin
F J Samuely
Misha Black
Robert Harling

Lund Humphries

2   Title-page spread: Herbert Read (ed.), *The practice of design*, Lund Humphries, 1946. Page size 245 x 184 mm. Designed by Hans Schleger.

3   Title-page spread: Peter Ray (ed.), *Designers in Britain*, no. 1, Allan Wingate, 1947. Page size 306 x 238 mm. Designed by Peter Ray.

signers to jobs outside the field of books and publications. New traditionalists were rooted in (and limited to) book design – and essentially books consisting purely of continuous text. They claimed, in effect, that theirs was really the only way in which a book could be designed (this is the burden of Morison's *First principles of typography*).[7] By contrast, the field of exhibition design, which typographers now entered (through the MOI), was wide open and without clear precedent. Different kinds of designer – including architects – were brought together in team work. The war period therefore entailed, for those working for the MOI, a kind of shake-up, preparing them for new directions.

The immediate design landmark following the war, the 'Britain Can Make It' exhibition (1946), was, it seems, largely a product of the MOI connection – recently established in civilian dress as Design Research Unit. One rather wayward typographic specimen of that year was the book *The practice of design*, the DRU symposium published and printed by Lund Humphries, and designed by Hans Schleger (figure 2). The book seems 'wayward' because it is a good deal more 'modern' than what was then the normal typographic dress for the promotion of design. The self-consciousness of its appearance – witness Schleger's note on his design decisions – and its air of knowing just what it wants (plastic binding, bled-off illustrations, headlines set in small letters only): all this marks it out as a distinctly non-British contribution.

And here one can do no more than mention the emigré presence. Hans Schleger, F. H. K. Henrion, Ernest Hoch: these may be among the better-known graphic designers who came to Britain from the Continent, but the phenomenon extended widely throughout the profession. It was certainly an important factor in the broadening of British assumptions. But emigrés are by definition exceptions in their country of adoption – and, however influential, marginal to the development of the native culture.[8]

7. Published first in *The Fleuron*, no. 7, 1930; and see also Morison's 'Postscript' added to the edition of 1967 (Cambridge University Press).
8. Perry Anderson's theory of the conservative character of the emigré contribution would seem to apply less certainly in the sphere of design; see his 'Components of the national culture', *New Left Review*, no. 50, 1968, pp. 3–57 (now reprinted in his *English questions*, Verso, 1992).

Peter Ray

A native British practice of new typography can be seen in the work of Peter Ray, whose career seems in some ways representative: starting in the 1930s as an apprentice signwriter, graduating to commercial artist, working eventually at the Metal Box Company (under Norbert Dutton), then art editor of *Shelf Appeal*, and, during the War, doing typography for MOI exhibition work (ending up as head of the Story Presentation Unit).

The MOI experience was a crucial one for Ray and (one may assume) for others in that group: particularly in forcing the need for meticulous, foolproof specification of a job. This, of course, is a commonplace for architects and industrial designers, but, certainly at that time, graphic designers were not used to controlling and coordinating a job sent out to different contractors. Dyeline layouts, carrying complete instructions, became a habit that Ray continued with in his subsequent freelance career. In this he exemplifies the larger organizing aspect of new typography. On the smaller scale he also applied an organizing approach – for example in his design of the early numbers of the *Architects' Year Book* (1946, 1947, 1948) – though he also worked (during the same period) in a visually traditional manner, when this seemed appropriate to the subject.

A concern with matters of organization overlaps with considerations of the professional practice of design: Peter Ray played a leading part in the re-formed Society of Industrial Artists, in the immediate post-war years and subsequently (particularly with respect to the SIA's entry into design education). His work for the SIA is now most visible in the editing and design of the first three volumes of *Designers in Britain* (1947, 1949, 1950; he was also responsible for number 7: 1971). These samplers of the upper and most conscious crust of design do provide some sense of the extent to which new typography began to impinge on the new traditionalism: at first evident in the work of only a few names – Peter Ray, Anthony Froshaug, Herbert Spencer – then, during the 1950s, becoming more widely adopted. The contrast of Ray's 1947 volume of *Designers in Britain* with Spencer's of 1954 may suggest also a process of refinement within the same broad approach of new typography (figures 3 & 4).

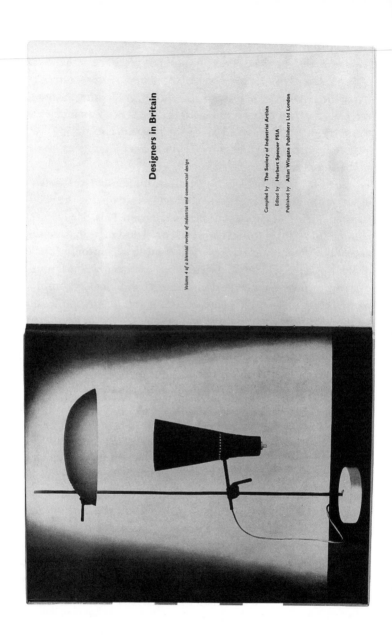

4 Title-page spread: Herbert Spencer (ed.), *Designers in Britain*, no. 4, Allan Wingate, 1954. Page size 306 x 238 mm. Designed by Herbert Spencer.

5   'Perpetua Titling gives dignity and ease to this HMSO restyling of a
    booklet cover.' Thus ran the caption to these 'before and after' images
    in the *Monotype Recorder*, vol. 39, no. 4, 1952, p. 15.

Herbert Spencer

Herbert Spencer derives from the MOI group at one remove, in that
he worked for two years (1946–8) with London Typographical Designers, a partnership of ex-MOI typographers set up in 1945.[9] LTD
claimed to break new ground in their mode of organization: they
worked directly with their clients, unmediated by salesmen or executives. But, certainly in the years under focus, they belonged firmly
to the new traditionalism in their approach to their material. The
Monotype Recorder of summer 1952 provides interesting evidence:
devoted to the theme of 'typographic transformations', it reported
on an exhibition of recent work by new traditionalists, including
LTD, and suggested by a series of 'before and after' comparisons

9. Information on Herbert Spencer's work is drawn from his autobiographical article 'Getting going', in *Designer*, January 1980, pp. 6–8. The
archives of London Typographical Designers are now at the Library of
the University of Reading.

6 'Nearly all the leading typographic designers of Great Britain attended the opening of the exhibition, as well as a number of younger designers of great promise. The screens in the background were devoted to typical "before and after" examples of the massive HMSO typographic restyling.' Thus the caption in this picture from the *Monotype Recorder*, vol. 39, no. 4, 1952. Among the figures here are Herbert Spencer (front row, far left) and next to him, Harry Carter; in the second row – Stanley Morison and Francis Meynell; in the third row on the right – Ruari McLean (leaning forward) and Allen Hutt (smoking).

how the degenerate and undesigned typography of printers could be cleaned up (figure 5). The accompanying article was written by Beatrice Warde, head of publicity at the Monotype Corporation and doyenne of the new traditionalists; her text contains a poignant discussion of the ethics of over-precise typographers leaving no freedom of decision to printers.

Herbert Spencer was among the typographers who gathered at the Monotype offices at the opening of the 'Typographic Restyling' exhibition in 1950 (figure 6). Though by this time he had become dissatisfied with the new traditionalism of LTD and had left in 1948 to work in private practice. And, fairly quickly, Spencer now became the principal popularizer of new typography in Britain, notably through his association with the printers Lund Humphries and in particular through his editorship of the magazine *Typographica* that this firm started to publish in 1949. Important steps in his work of helping to spread new typography were the exhibition of post-war Continental and British typography 'Purpose and Pleasure' (1952) held at Lund Humphries' Bedford Square offices, and his book *Design in Business Printing* (also 1952), commissioned by the printing firm of Tillotsons.

The assimilation of Tschichold

A comparison of *Design in business printing* with an indirect ancestor, Tschichold's *Typographische Gestaltung* (1935), is instructive (figures 7 & 8).[10] Tschichold's more ruthless and more stylized typography is translated and adapted, so that it may be accepted (even) by the British businessmen to whom the book hopes to speak. Where Tschichold tends to aesthetic and ideological argument, Spencer remains reassuringly practical and economic. The argument that new typography would save time and money, which had always been there as one theme in Tschichold's exposition, now becomes more prominent. It is most memorably presented in Spencer's experiments in setting tabular matter and a letterheading in traditional and new configurations. Examples set according to the

10. This follows a suggestion by Paul Stiff in his undergraduate dissertation: 'Critical typography: notes on the typography of complex texts in England, 1919–1966', Department of Typography & Graphic Communication, University of Reading, 1978.

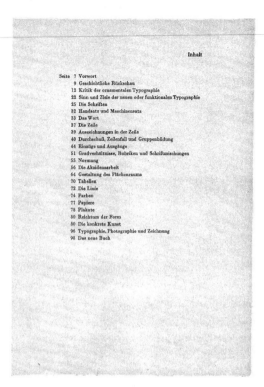

Inhalt

Seite 7 Vorwort
     9 Geschichtliche Rückschau
   12 Kritik der ornamentalen Typographie
   22 Sinn und Ziele der neuen oder funktionalen Typographie
   25 Die Schriften
   32 Handsatz und Maschinensatz
   33 Das Wort
   37 Die Zeile
   39 Auszeichnungen in der Zeile
   40 Durchschuß, Zeilenfall und Gruppenbildung
   44 Einzüge und Ausgänge
   51 Gradverhältnisse, Rubriken und Schriftmischungen
   55 Normung
   56 Die Akzidensarbeit
   64 Gestaltung des Flächenraums
   70 Tabellen
   72 Die Linie
   74 Farben
   77 Papiere
   78 Plakate
   80 Reichtum der Form
   80 Die konkrete Kunst
   96 Typographie, Photographie und Zeichnung
   98 Das neue Buch

7   Contents page: Jan Tschichold, *Typographische Gestaltung*,
     Basel: Schwabe, 1935. 210 x 148 mm.

principles of new typography took less time to compose. The comparison of these two books seems representative of the tendency of British designers to modify modern movement theory, to adapt it to local circumstances and assumptions. This, no doubt, is natural enough; the pressures are well known.

Fifteen years after *Design in business printing*, Tschichold himself was involved in another assimilation of *Typographische Gestaltung*, when he collaborated in an English-language version of the book. Danish (1937), Swedish (1937), and Dutch (1938) editions had followed the original German-language book, in spirit and in content, though Tschichold had begun to turn away from new typography in the late 1930s. His work of this later period (from the 1940s onwards) shows a break with the 'inner' organizing principles

Contents

Page 9   Acknowledgements
11   **Introduction**
15   **The development of business printing design**
    Illustrations:
    Cover design, Catalogue of the Great Exhibition, 1851
    American printer's leaflet, 1860
    Page from *Halling's Circular*, 1878
    Cover design of a booklet, 1885
    Printer's advertisement, 1885
    Advertisement from *Halling's Circular*
    Old-Style advertisement
    The Cheltenham series of types
    Futurist design, 1915
    Dadaist advertisement, 1923
    Type arrangement by Guillaume Apollinaire
    Bauhaus design of 1923, by Moholy-Nagy
    Letterheadings designed by Jan Tschichold
    Herbert Bayer's Universal type, 1925-8
    Post Office form, before and after restyling
37   **Business printing in practice**
38   The importance of detail
42   Type and paper
64   The word
66   Punctuation
69   Figures and dates
70   The line
77   The paragraph
80   Tabular matter
80   The page
84   Footnotes
85   The book
87   The spine
87   The economic factor
102   **Bibliography**
104   **Index**

8   Contents page: Herbert Spencer, *Design in business printing*, Sylvan Press, 1952. 248 x 182 mm.

of new typography; though one could argue that Tschichold still continued to practise an organizing approach in what is being called the 'outer layer', most notably in his 'reform' of design and production at Penguin Books (1947–9). In the light of the essential ('inner') change of approach, it is understandable that the 1967 edition of the book that had summarized his mature new typography should show signs of compromise and embarrassment (figure 9). There are changes in content: 'passages of value and interest for Swiss and German readers only' (as Tschichold wrote) are omitted – most

Contents

9 Translator's foreword
11 Introduction by W. E. Trevett
12 Author's note
15 Historical survey
20 Decorative typography
24 The meaning and aim
   of the new or functional typography
28 Types
36 Hand composition and machine composition
37 The word
40 The line
43 Emphasis in the line
44 Leading, length of lines and grouping
48 Indentation and line endings
50 Type sizes, headings and type mixtures
54 Jobbing work
58 The use of space
62 Tables
66 Rules
67 Colours
68 Paper
72 Posters
72 Richness of form
78 Abstract art
84 Typography, photography and drawings
87 The book today
94 Other books by the author in print

9   Contents page: Jan Tschichold, *Asymmetric typography*,
     Faber & Faber, 1967. 233 x 148 mm.

significantly, the chapter on standardization; disclaiming footnotes
by the older Tschichold are inserted; the beautiful epigraph from
Goethe is no longer included. And in its visual appearance, the 1967
edition loses the quality of the original book: for example, headings
and page numbers are uncertainly placed, and a subtle weakening
of conviction is evident in the typefaces now used, in text and headings. The change in meaning in the title is significant of the whole
enterprise: from *Typographische Gestaltung* – in other words, a complete approach to typographic designing – it becomes merely *Asymmetric typography* – just one partial and perhaps questionable way
of doing it. It is exactly the same movement of assimilation and

watering-down that has often been noticed in the translation of Le Corbusier's title *Vers une architecture* as *Towards a new architecture*. In the Tschichold of the mid-1930s, as in the work of other modern movement designers of that period, one senses the proposal that the newness of their work was not really the point, and that they felt themselves to be reinventing old values.

Anthony Froshaug

The work of Anthony Froshaug provides the most interesting and in some ways the most instructive case of British new typography. After some training at the Central School of Arts & Crafts, he began to work during the War as a freelance typographer – including jobs as production manager on the magazine *Scope* (successor to *Shelf Appeal*) and as art editor on *Our Time* (the Communist Party cultural monthly). By the end of the War, he could reproduce faithfully the visual manner of Tschichold. For by now he had absorbed the new typography neat and undiluted by any British interpreter – from such source books as *Die neue Typographie*, *Typografische Entwurfstechnik*, *Typographische Gestaltung*. Froshaug was part of a tiny group of dissenting designers and their friends; based in London, they were strictly international in their allegiances, and interested not only in the formal possibilities thrown up by the modern movement, but also in design as 'a visible form of social philosophy'.[11] The group eventually became influential in design teaching: the work of Froshaug, Norman Potter, Edward Wright, John Turner, may be mentioned here, and one of its most articulate members, Geoffrey Bocking, acted as chairman of the National Conference on Art & Design Education at the Round House in London (1968).

In Froshaug's work, the organizing principle of new typography – in both 'outer' and 'inner' layers – becomes very clear; and this is a reason for its considerable pedagogic value. For example, in a layout that survives from 1950, the final appearance of the job is drawn (down to the smallest detail) and, in the margin, visual elements are named and their position exactly stated. It was this kind of precision

11. The phrase is Norman Potter's, in a lecture entitled 'Box and fox', published in altered form as 'Enemies of design', *Twentieth Century*, no. 1039/40, 1968/9, pp. 77–83.

Reprinted here as a conspectus are specimens of jobbing
printing selected from the first two years' work of this press

Equipment is deliberately minimal and simple in mechanical
design; rather than behaviourist engines, it tends towards
workshop tools & machine-tools enjoying maximal degrees
of freedom, within which one individual may solve new
problems in configuration

Postulates of hand composition and hand & foot presswork
have bound output to 180 jobs each year – ranging from
visiting cards to 24-page catalogues, and printed for various
individuals & organisations – standards of typesetting are
therefore high, those of machining reasonable; resultant
prices are a mean between country and London rates

Reproduced in Swiss & English periodicals, work has also
been chosen for the printing section of the South Bank
Exhibition; the press is included in the 1951 Stock List

Though interested in general jobbing, the predilection is
for bookwork and other jobs whose required solution is in
terms of variation & counterpoint on a theme; orders for
work and/or requests for type sheets and other mailings are
welcomed from addressees, their friends & acquaintances

anthonyfroshaug

Better Books Limited
Design & Industries Association
St. George's Gallery Limited
Church Street Bookshop
Herbert Rieser Photography
William Campion
Clive Latimer MSIA
Gerik Schjelderup Esq
Triangle Film Productions Limited
Ian Gibson-Smith Photography
Editions Poetry London Limited
Norman Potter Constructions
Children & Youth Aliyah
Mill House (Penzance) Limited
New Europe Medical Foundation
Boltane School Limited

La Torrasse Coffee Garden
Toy Trumpet Workshops
Roger Wood Photography
Norwegian State Railways
Penwith Coiled Baskets
T H Verran & Son
Barbara Hepworth
Penwith Society of Arts in Cornwall
Taylor's Foreign Press
Jesse Collins FSIA
Michael Wickham Photography
London Opera Club
St. George's Gallery (Books)
Design & Research Centre
Gaberbocchus Press Limited
Whitehill Marsh Jackson & Co
Picture Post
Rupert Qualters Esq
Institute of Contemporary Arts
Delbanco Meyer & Company Limited

Lea Jaray
F H K Henrion FSIA
Festival of Britain
Joseph Rykwert Esq
Religious Drama Society
&c

10   The front of Anthony Froshaug's four-page first 'conspectus of work',
1951. Black and red printing, 281 x 215 mm.

of specification that disconcerted Beatrice Warde in her *Monotype Recorder* article.

This precision and determination on the part of the typographer were quite unusual at that time in Britain (or, one imagines, elsewhere). The special necessity for such procedures, in Froshaug's case, was that what he wanted to specify was a typography new and foreign to the compositors with whom he was dealing. While new traditionalism could, as Beatrice Warde argued, rely on the understanding and co-operation of compositors, new typography had to employ an ungentlemanly exactness of specification. The difficulty of getting layouts satisfactorily implemented is cited by Froshaug as a reason for his move in setting up a printing workshop at Ludgvan in Cornwall, which he ran and lived by from 1949 to 1952.[12]

The decision to work in direct production in Cornwall may seem unexpected and contradictory – given Froshaug's commitment to the modern movement, and given the modern movement's characteristic assumption of the urban designer specifying decisions to the factory by letter or telephone. Certainly one could never imagine Tschichold setting type or feeding a treadle press (to earn a living).

A statement of 1951, introducing a conspectus of Froshaug's printing, will help to explain the workshop enterprise (figure 10). The second paragraph reads: 'Equipment is deliberately minimal and simple in mechanical design; rather than behaviourist engines, it tends towards workshop tools & machine-tools enjoying maximal degrees of freedom, within which one individual may solve new problems in configuration'.

This, of course, recalls the argument for workshops that Lewis Mumford offered towards the end of *Technics and civilization* (1934).[13] No doubt Froshaug would have embarked on his workshop without the existence of Mumford's book – given his difficulties in getting what he wanted otherwise, and given an affinity for work on

12. See his statement in: Gerald Woods, Philip Thompson, John Williams, (ed.), *Art without boundaries 1950–70*, Thames & Hudson, 1972, pp. 206–7 (now reprinted in *Anthony Froshaug: Documents of a life*, Hyphen Press, 2000, p. 245).
13. Lewis Mumford, *Technics and civilization*, Routledge, 1934; see especially pp. 415–17.

a small and limited scale (and a love for printing as such) – but it was Mumford's book that helped to provide reassurance, a philosophy, and a set of supporting social implications for this experiment, and for another venture of the same period: the construction workshop of Norman Potter and George Philip. As Potter wrote later 'Mumford was our book of words'.[14] The Froshaug and Potter workshops should be clearly distinguished from the Arts & Crafts workshops of that (and perhaps any other) time. Besides inhabiting a different visual world, on the question of 'the machine' – or, more precisely, the machine-tool – the Froshaug/Potter attitude was one of unembarrassed delight. Yet, despite this inspiration drawn from the characteristics and constraints of particular machine-tools, their way of working could not be accepted by orthodox modernism of the Gropius or Jack Pritchard kind; it represented a deviation from the assumption of mass-production.

To return to purely typographic matters, a feature to notice in Froshaug's work is the use of 'unjustified' setting (in which the spaces between words are equal, and the right-hand edge of the text is consequently 'ragged'). This was a mode of setting that Tschichold had almost never employed, and rarely mentioned – though it seems to follow from the most essential postulate of new typography. For it is only when spaces between words are equal and specifiable that text is properly ordered. Spencer pointed towards this rationale for unjustified text in *Design in business printing*, and it was through its use by such post-Tschichold typographers as Max Bill (in Switzerland), Willem Sandberg (in the Netherlands), Froshaug, and Spencer, that unjustified setting began to be accepted as a possible and sensible way of treating text. Though one should also refer to an earlier advocate of unjustified text – Eric Gill, who had argued for this mode of setting in his *Essay on typography* (1931). (And one may note, in passing, that Froshaug's printing workshop does show some kinship of spirit with the press of René Hague and Eric Gill, untouched though they were by modernism.) Froshaug's work has been more influential than this account might so far have seemed to imply. Outside the workshop he taught at the Central School

14. In 'Box and fox' (note 11 above). Potter discussed the case for the 'designer as artisan' in his *What is a designer*.

(1948–9, 1952–3, within the period under discussion), and through this activity of teaching, his attitude to typography has become quite widely disseminated. Among his pupils figure several of the British typographers who came to prominence in the 1950s and 1960s. And one printing workshop followed in his path: that of Desmond Jeffery in London and Suffolk (from 1955 to 1971).

Max Bill has been mentioned as one of the post-Tschichold typographers (though only slightly younger than Tschichold). And Bill was one of the figures towards whom the British modernists looked – as someone working, apparently, in all fields of design, even including typography.[15] Froshaug had been in contact with Bill, and was invited to teach at the Hochschule für Gestaltung (Ulm), which opened officially in 1955 (under Bill). Eventually in 1957, after a re-invitation from Tomás Maldonado, Froshaug joined the school, teaching for four years on the foundation and visual communication courses.[16]

The most obvious permanent record of Froshaug's work at Ulm is the design of the first five numbers of the school's journal, and his contribution on 'Visual methodology' that constitutes the fourth number. In this article, the organizing or ordering preoccupation – new typography's deeper concern – is worked out at a fairly high academic level: the aim being to test the hypothesis that 'decrease in redundance … increases the clarity with which an object can be seen and understood'. It would be straying beyond the bounds of the subject to dwell further on Ulm or on the wider Ulmisch concerns and theses. But, in their depth of penetration, the arguments developed in the pages of the school's journal make an important contribution to the progress of the modern movement, and provide support for the conclusion that follows.[17]

15. Bill's major statement on the subject is his article 'Über Typografie' in *Schweizer Graphische Mitteilungen*, April 1946, pp. 193–200, which includes an ostentatiously veiled attack on Tschichold. (Now available in English translation in *Typography Papers*, no. 4, 2000.)

16. See now the documents reprinted in *Anthony Froshaug*, Hyphen Press, 2000.

17. See particularly: Abram Moles, 'Functionalism in crisis', *Ulm*, no. 19/20, 1967, pp. 24–25.

Conclusion

The dominant typography in Britain up to and for some time after 1945 was the new traditionalism. New typography – the modern movement in typography – only became current in Britain gradually after 1945, through the work of a few people: some emigrés from central Europe, some native practitioners such as Peter Ray (particularly through the channels of the SIA), Herbert Spencer (enjoying the enlightened patronage of Lund Humphries), Anthony Froshaug. This latter, most rigorous attempt at a new typography had to move to the workshop – to get in touch with its material, and perhaps to find itself fully. And here the larger implications of the approach become clearer. To put it rather baldly, new typography's search for order, its maximal use of minimal means, its attempt at 'a decrease in redundance' – this approach to design is predicated on the assumption of a society that deploys its material rationally, that has reached some state of 'dynamic equilibrium' (Mumford's phrase). New typography would then provide, in miniature, a model reflection of its surrounding context. The consumer society of Britain in the 1950s and 1960s moved in the opposite direction: towards irrational modes of production, distribution, consumption. Paradoxically it was in these years that the manner of new typography became fairly widely diffused in Britain – spreading from the work of these few forerunners. The influence of Swiss typographers of the generation following Max Bill provided a fresh current of influence.[18] But in the condition of Britain in these years, new typography could be no more than a fashionable garb. It is possible, and plausible, to see an irrational society aspiring to a veneer of rationality through the adoption of this logical, rational, functional style of dress and discarding the deeper aspirations that give life to the modern movement.

Nicola Hamilton (ed.), *From Spitfire to microchip*, Design Council, 1985, pp. 45–9.

18. For a document of this interest in Swiss (and also North American) typography, see: Ken Garland, 'Substance and structure', *Penrose Annual*, vol. 54, 1969, pp. 1–10.

This text derives from a lecture given at the Design History Society Conference at City of London Polytechnic, 1981, and was written with that audience in mind. It was published after much delay and muddle in a book of the conference papers: some notes were missing, illustrations crazily sized or omitted, and one crucial word left out. A note of acknowledgement was however accurately given: 'In preparing this paper I have drawn information and encouragement from conversations with Anthony Froshaug, Norman Potter and Peter Ray; they have also read and commented on a draft of my text. Some of the ideas here were first presented formally in an undergraduate dissertation written for the Department of Typography & Graphic Communication at the University of Reading, and were developed during a subsequent period of teaching there; among colleagues at Reading, I am particularly grateful to Paul Stiff.'

I have not tried to update the text for this present publication. But the two essays that follow here expand and elaborate on some of its themes. My book *Anthony Froshaug* (2000) added much documentation on the work of this key protagonist.

This text is composed in the conditional: this is what I would write, if there was time and space for something more. It is about something very big and general: a principle of design, in fact a more or less eternal problem that presents itself every time you set down or make manifest more than a few words. At the same time, I am interested in some small and marginal specific happenings: a few odd people, struggling with the circumstances in which they found themselves. The context is the 'Stunde Null' of around 1945: the 'zero hour' of much of continental Europe in ruins. [1]

Both that long essay and this short one must start with this quotation from a German writing in Los Angeles, California, in 1944.

Pro domo nostra. When during the last war – which like all others, seems peaceful in comparison to its successor – the symphony orchestras of many countries had their vociferous mouths stopped, Stravinsky wrote the *Histoire du Soldat* for a sparse, shock-maimed chamber ensemble. It turned out to be his best score, the only convincing surrealist manifesto, its con-

1. The fact that we have to use the German term is significant: the British managed to avoid it. Some weeks after this lecture was given, the sense of the 'Stunde Null' in 1945 was very well explained by Neal Ascherson in his *Independent on Sunday* column (13 February 1994):

'The cities stood in ruins or were burning. The roads were jammed with lost human beings, men in every imaginable uniform and families in rags, pressing this way and that as the Allied aircraft plunged down on them with rockets and cannon. Abandoned trains stood in rainy fields, their locomotives still smoking, corpses humped across rails already turning crimson with rust. No newspapers or radio remained to give news or instructions. The roofless factories were silent; the shops gutted. Bandit gangs, some of them still in concentration-camp clothes, ranged the land murdering and plundering. The Seven Seals had been opened.

This condition, which spread far beyond Germany, is called by the Germans "Stunde Null". That means much more than "zero hour". It means the moment at which the world has ended – but also the moment at which the next world is conceived.'

vulsive, dreamlike compulsion imparting to music an inkling of negative truth. The pre-condition of the piece was poverty: it dismantled official culture so drastically because, denied access to the latter's material goods, it also escaped the ostentation that is inimical to culture. There is here a pointer for intellectual production after the war, which has left behind in Europe a measure of destruction undreamed of even by the voids in that music. Progress and barbarism are today so matted together in mass culture that only barbaric asceticism towards the latter, and towards progress in technical means, could restore an un-barbaric condition. No work of art, no thought, has a chance of survival, unless it bear within it repudiation of false riches and high-class production, of colour films and television, million-aire's magazines and Toscanini. The older media, not designed for mass-production, take on a new timeliness: that of exemp-tion and of improvisation. They alone could outflank the united front of trusts and technology. In a world where books have long lost all likeness to books, the real book can no longer be one. If the invention of the printing press inaugurated the bour-geois era, the time is at hand for its repeal by the mimeograph, the only fitting, the unobtrusive means of dissemination.

This comes from Theodor Adorno's most brilliant, most depressed book, *Minima moralia: reflections from damaged life*, in Edmund Jephcott's phenomenal translation.[2]

The shocking closing thought about 'printing being replaced by the mimeograph' was, I am sure, inspired by the mode of publica-tion that the Institut für Sozialforschung – the 'Frankfurt School' of social-critical thought, then exiled in North America – had begun to adopt, out of necessity. For example, Walter Benjamin's last piece, written in 1940 in France, the theses 'Über den Begriff der Geschich-te' ('on the meaning/concept of history'), was first published in 1942, after Benjamin's death, by the Institut in Los Angeles. By the

---

2. Theodor Adorno, *Minima moralia: reflections from damaged lif*e, New Left Books, pp. 50–1. [Original publication: Frankfurt a.M: Suhrkamp, 1951.] *Minima morali*a is a sequence of short, aphoristic meditations, divided into three parts. This passage, section 30, comes from the first part, dated 1944.

Pro domo nostra. When during the last war — which like all others, seems peaceful in comparison to its successor — the symphony orchestras of many countries had their vociferous mouths stopped, Stravinsky wrote the Histoire du Soldat for a sparse, shock-maimed chamber ensemble. It turned out to be his best score, the only convincing surrealist manifesto, its convulsive, dreamlike compulsion imparting to music an inkling of negative truth. The pre-condition of the piece was poverty: it dismantled official culture so drastically because, denied access to the latter's material goods, it also escaped the ostentation that is inimical to culture. There is here a pointer for intellectual production after the present war, which has left behind in Europe a measure of destruction undreamed of even by the voids in that music. Progress and barbarism are today so matted together in mass culture that only barbaric asceticism towards the latter, and towards progress in technical means, could restore an unbarbaric condition. No work of art, no thought, has a chance of survival, unless it bear within it repudiation of false riches and high-class production, of colour films and television, millionaire's

Pro domo nostra. When during the last war — which like all others, seems peaceful in comparison to its successor — the symphony orchestras of many countries had their vociferous mouths stopped, Stravinsky wrote the Histoire du Soldat for a sparse, shock-maimed chamber ensemble. It turned out to be his best score, the only convincing surrealist manifesto, its convulsive, dreamlike compulsion imparting to music an inkling of negative truth. The pre-condition of the piece was poverty: it dismantled official culture so drastically because, denied access to the latter's material goods, it also escaped the ostentation that is inimical to culture. There is here a pointer for intellectual production after the present war, which has left behind in Europe a measure of destruction undreamed of even by the voids in that music. Progress and barbarism are today so matted together in mass culture that only barbaric asceticism towards the latter, and towards progress in technical means, could restore an unbarbaric condition. No work of art, no thought, has a chance of survival, unless it bear within it repudiation of false riches and high-class production, of colour films and television, millionaire's

Pro domo nostra. When during the last war – which like all others, seems peaceful in comparison to its successors – the symphony orchestras of many countries had their vociferous mouths stopped, Stravinsky wrote the *Histoire du Soldat* for a sparse, shock-maimed chamber ensemble. It turned out to be his best score, the only convincing surrealist manifesto, its convulsive, dreamlike compulsion imparting to music an inkling of negative truth. The pre-condition of the piece was poverty: it dismantled official culture so drastically because, denied access to the latter's material goods, it also escaped the ostentation that is inimical to culture. There is here a pointer for intellectual production after the present war, which has left behind in Europe a measure of destruction undreamed of even by the voids in that music. Progress and barbarism are today so matted together in mass culture that only barbaric asceticism towards the latter, and towards progress in technical means, could restore an unbarbaric condition. No work of art, no thought, has a chance of survival, unless it bear within it repudiation of false riches and high-class production, of colour films and television, millionaire's magazines and Toscanini. The older media, not designed for

Pro domo nostra. When during the last war – which like all others, seems peaceful in comparison to its succcessor – the symphony orchestras of many countries had their vociferous mouths stopped, Stravinsky wrote the *Histoire du Soldat* for a sparse, shock-maimed chamber ensemble. It turned out to be his best score, the only convincing surrealist manifesto, its convulsive, dreamlike compulsion imparting to music an inkling of negative truth. The pre-condition of the piece was poverty: it dismantled official culture so drastically because, denied access to the latter's material goods, it also escaped the ostentation that is inimical to culture. There is here a pointer for intellectual production after the present war, which has left behind in Europe a measure of destruction undreamed of even by the voids in that music. Progress and barbarism are today so matted together in mass culture that only barbaric asceticism towards the latter, and towards progress in technical means, could restore an unbarbaric condition. No work of art, no thought, has a chance of survival, unless it bear within it repudiation of false riches and high-class production, of colour films and television, millionaire's magazines and Toscanini. The older media, not designed for

1 & 2 Top: unjustified and justified setting of text, in monowidth characters. Set without word breaks and without 'tracking'. Bottom: unjustified and justified setting of text, in proportional width characters. Set without word breaks; the justified setting uses 'tracking'.

way, Benjamin's famous statement that 'there is no document of civilization which is not at the same time a document of barbarism' – the idea that Adorno picks up in this passage – occurs in those theses. To publish such a text in Los Angeles in 1942 one had to do it in samizdat: with the informal techniques of office-printing. So the words of Benjamin – the 'last European', for whom American exile was inconceivable – were typewritten onto stencils and spirit-duplicated. I have never seen this book or booklet, but I would bet that the right-hand edge of the text will have been ragged. The characters of the old manual typewriter were of a single width, and word-spaces had this same constant width. So the text had to be set without justification.[3]

Figure 1 shows the simple difference between justified and un-justified in single-width character setting. The folly of justification here should be evident. These examples were made on a computer with a DTP program, in which justification is as easy as unjustified setting. But that is a recent luxury. In figure 2, the same difference is shown with fully typographic, proportional-width characters. But even here, you see what may happen with justification, if you are not careful. You have to put the space somewhere: between words, even between letters. And that can make for an unwanted emphasis to words: a drawing-of-attention where you do not want it.

The English word 'justify' has legal and theological senses, before its specialized typographic one, and it is the same in other European languages: to prove, to vindicate, to absolve. Justified text has been the norm ever since 1450, when Europe was first blessed with the procustean tools of the setting stick and the printing 'forme' or frame. It is text made exact and formal. With unjustified or ragged or what is even sometimes called 'free' setting, the spaces between words are equal, so the right edge has to be ragged, lines find their own length. Free, informal, self-determining: the social overtones are clear.

It is a good surmise to say that the increasing acceptance of

3. The term 'unjustified' is used here as the one most widely understood by lay people. Among several alternatives, 'fixed word space setting' is a more exact description. The topic has been thoroughly discussed by Paul Stiff in 'The end of the line: a survey of unjustified typography' (*Information Design Journal*, vol. 8, no. 2, 1996, pp. 125–52).

3 Max Bill, 'Über Typografie', *Schweizer Graphische Mitteilunge*n, no. 4, 1946. Page size of the magazine is 297 x 210 mm. This reproduction is made from the uncut pages of an offprint.

SICILIANA *Aus griechisch-römischer Zeit / Von Ferdinand Mainzer*

114 Seiten mit 20 Abbildungen auf Tafeln. 8°. Kartoniert RM 5.50, Ganzleinen RM 6.50. Einband und Umschlag nach Entwurf von *Georg Salter*

Das Deutsche Buch:

Ferdinand Mainzers Werk „Siciliana" ist kein Reisebuch im üblichen Sinne, sondern ein Buch für Feinschmecker, aber nicht für Snobs. Dafür ist Ferdinand Mainzer zu menschlich und zu liebevoll mit der Welt verbunden, die ihn zur Feder zwang. Man liest alles mit der seltenen Wonne, plötzlich eine liebenswürdige Auferstehung seiner Pennälerschrecken zu erleben. So ist uns die Antike noch nicht serviert worden. In diesem Buch wird die sagenhafte Landschaft des Odysseus mit ihren Vorstellungen wieder lebendig. Diese Siciliana ist aber überdies eine vornehme Art der Geschichtsschreibung. Schon dieser Einblicke wegen, die in ihrer historischen Distanz nicht nur das geschickte, objektive Forschertum des Verfassers bestätigen, sondern auch manche zeitgeschichtliche Parallele herausfordern, ist das Werk lesenswert. *Wandrer, kommst du nach „Sikelia" — so lies dieses Buch. Kommst du nicht hin, so lies es auch. Du wirst hinkommen.*

Klinkhardt & Biermann Verlag, Berlin W 10

4   Advertisement from: Franz Roh (ed.), *L. Moholy-Nagy: 60 Fotos*, Berlin: Klinkhardt & Biermann, 1930. The text-setting, in which the descriptive text is justified, would almost certainly have been specified by Jan Tschichold.

unjustified text through this century followed from the fact that people became used to seeing it in typewritten text, in mimeography, and then in the small-offset printing that became widespread in Europe after 1945. Here I would want to find out more about this unglamorous and so far unwritten chapter of printing history: the development of office printing. One would have to look at typewriters. For example in 1941, as if in response to a growing need, IBM first put their successful Executive typewriter onto the market. This had characters of various widths. Justification was possible, although it took twice as long as unjustified.

In the *Schweizer Graphische Mitteilungen* of April 1946, the artist and designer Max Bill published an article entitled 'Über Typografie' ('on typography'). Bill determined the typography of the article (figure 3). It is very cool: lowercase only, 8 point sanserif type printed in grey, unjustified setting without word-breaks, and illustrated by Bill's own work. But Bill's words are not so cool. His starting point was a lecture by the typographer Jan Tschichold, given in Zurich in December 1945. In that lecture Tschichold had for the first time explained his turn away from modernism, of around 1937, towards a kind of enlightened traditional typography. Tschichold then replied

291

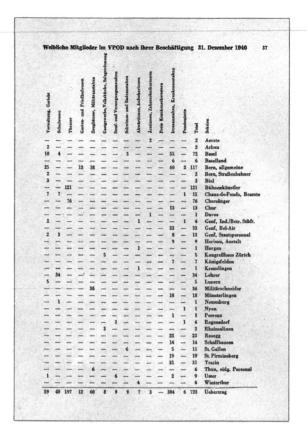

5 An example of Max Bill's typography, shown in his 'Über Typografie'. Bill notes in his caption: 'machine-setting without rules, clearly arranged, avoidance of unnecessary gaps between word and number'. Page size of original item: 230 x 155 mm.

to Bill in the June issue of the SGM, in an article with the Goethe-like title of 'Glaube und Wirklichkeit' ('belief and reality').[4]

This is one of the really fascinating debates in typography. It is of interest here because unjustified text appears in it as one of the markers dividing pre-war and post-war modernism. In the typography of heroic modernism – let us call it that – up to the

4. These articles by Max Bill and Jan Tschichold have now been published in English in *Typography Papers*, no. 4, 2000.

mid-1930s, although the overall configuration may be asymmetric, columns of text are not set unjustified. It never happened at the Bauhaus, never in Tschichold's work either. Figure 4 shows a modest sample of Tschichold's design work from his mature 'new typography' of the early 1930s: a publisher's advertisement for a book. The point to make here is that one might have expected the paragraph of text to be set unjustified. But Tschichold did not take his asymmetry as far as that.

In his article, Bill makes some play with the need to accept machine typesetting. He mentions in some of the captions to the reproduced examples of his work that the type was machine-set. Although Tschichold suggests that this is a glorification of something banal (machine production), in fact it is of interest if the whole of some of these pieces were set on a machine: because that would have required rather careful and clear instructions from the designer. Tschichold referred to Bill disparagingly as 'an artist', but if he could specify such things, then he was more than just an artist (figure 5).

Bill does not say this, but the implication of his article is that unjustified setting goes together with machine setting. In fact it doesn't. In the technology of that time – Monotype and Linotype – justified was as easy to produce as unjustified. Unjustified was easier in hand setting, as Tschichold pointed out.

This exchange of 1946 is full of very heavy accusations. Both participants had good reasons to feel that an awful lot was at stake in such apparently simple a thing as how you set text. Tschichold had been taken into custody in Munich in 1933, as a 'cultural bolshevik', and had then emigrated to Switzerland. Meanwhile Bill had been and remained a utopian socialist and a strong anti-fascist. Their argument was unresolved. But Max Bill's text and his design work stood at the start of what was to become known as 'Swiss typography', over which he presided as one of the godfathers. From the late 1950s to the late 1960s, Swiss typography was really the hegemonic typography of design-conscious, modernizing Europe.

In March 1946, Max Bill received a letter from a typographer in London: Anthony Froshaug, then twenty-five years old, who had resisted call-up in the war. Froshaug's mother was English, but his father was Norwegian. I suppose this was one factor in his feeling

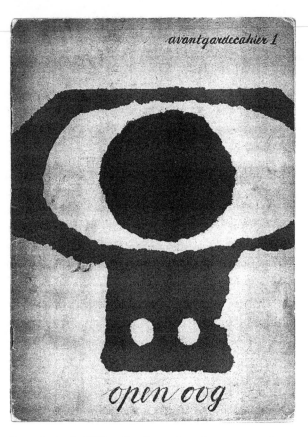

6   Cover design by Willem Sandberg. *Open Oog*, no.1, 1946.
    Grey and red printing, 258 x 190 mm.

of not fitting well into English society; at least not well enough
to join up in its army, not even to fight in a war against fascism.
Nevertheless, he was inspired by a kind of utopian-anarchist-mod-
ernist hope. Froshaug was then running a cross-disciplinary small-
publishing venture, Isomorph Ltd, and he hoped to entice Bill onto
the list. The letter is quite smarmy: 'I have been very pleased and
interested to see some of your typographical and exhibition work
reproduced in various magazines over the last few years – not for-
getting the Roth book. I see from the Swiss lists that we may one
day hope to see copies of your book on Maillart, and other produc-

Het tijdperk 1914–1918 was de inleiding tot de scheppingsroes der volgende jaren.

In Parijs schilderen Picasso en zijn genoten meesterwerken.

In Berlijn woedt „der Sturm".

In Leiden ontstaat „de Stijl".

De schilders fabriceren niet langer geportretteerde natuur, maar experimenteren met vorm en kleur (Picasso, Mondriaan), of gaan uit op onderzoek naar de psychologische betekenis van een lijn, een structuur (Klee).

Een schilderij van Mondriaan is geen wandversiering, maar is een oproep tot levensvernieuwing.

Hangen wij het op in onze kamer, dan schept het dat nieuwe ruimtewereld en alles wat willekeurig is, elk meubel, dat niet simpel en alleen zichzelf is, maar meer wil schijnen door versiering, mistaat en moet het veld ruimen.

Picasso, Klee en vooral Mondriaan openen ons de ogen voor zuiverder ruimtevormen, hun werken stellen eisen.

Deze eisen kunnen we afwijzen en wij kunnen ze aanvaarden, maar wij kunnen er niet aan voorbijgaan.

Vreemd: een doek met enkele kleurvlakken, rood en geel met enkele lijnen beheerst niet alleen een wand, maar heel een ruimte — al wat onzuiver is, wat niet eerlijk is en klaar, moet verdwijnen.

We gaan nadenken over het wezen van de tafel en de stoel, het overbodige gaat ons hinderen, we gaan ons bezinnen op de functie der dingen.

De functie van de stoel in de ruimte.

De functie van de stoel als zinmeubel.

Een nieuwe bouwkunst ontstaat,

Een functionele architectuur, los van het conventionele.

la maison est un outil à demeurer, zegt le Corbusier.

Nieuwe vormen voor nieuwe mensen.

De gebonden kunsten ondergaan alle de invloed van de vrije kunsten,

van het abstracte schilderij in het bijzonder.

De typografie verlaat de symmetrische ordening en krijgt richting, beweging — tracht het oog te leiden over de pagina (symmetrie is evenwicht, is stilstand).

De gebruiksvoorwerpen worden geheel op het gebruik ingesteld.

Er komt een groote voorkeur voor doorzichtig materiaal, voor rasterwerk, voor glas, omdat het de ruimte niet deelt, maar ruimten verenigt.

Groote glazen wanden stellen de huizen open voor de natuur.

In Duitsland ontstaat het Bauhaus.

In Frankrijk werkt le Corbusier.

In Nederland groeperen zich jonge architecten rondom „het nieuwe bouwen".

Maar dan, na 1930, '35, blijkt dat deze vernieuwing voor velen slechts uiterlijk was, iets wat men weer afleggen kan, een mode.

De reactie komt, men wordt onzeker en zij, voor wie de vernieuwing slechts mode was, beginnen te aarzelen, grijpen terug naar oude vormen : classicisme, rococo, barok, gothiek,

de vlucht in het verleden

de klemtoon valt op de verdeeldheid, „het streekeigene".

Dan steekt de orkaan op en blaast veel wat voos was onver.

1945.

de storm trekt voorbij

Hitler sterft, maar flarden van zijn wereldbeeld leiden een schichtig bestaan in de hoofden van velen.

Zeldzaam, zijn de mensen, die geheel in het heden staan, die de consequenties van deze makke, vurige, grootse tijd aanvaarden.

Zal de oorlog 1939–1945 een nieuw tijdperk inleiden ?

Wij staan met open oog op de uitkijk.

redactie

7   Editorial statement from *Open Oog*, no.1.

tions. I have also been informed by the Director of the Amsterdam Museum of Modern Art that you are starting the publication of a review in collaboration with Le Corbusier and others.'[5]

I could go on to describe the sporadic contact that developed between these two men. It led to an invitation to Froshaug to teach typography at the experiment in reconstruction that Max Bill became involved with: the Hochschule für Gestaltung Ulm. But I want to break off and explain this last reference in Froshaug's letter. It is to Willem Sandberg, the director of the Stedelijk Museum in Amsterdam, who was just then collaborating on a new magazine with the title *Open Oog*: 'open eye'. The first of only two numbers is dated September 1946. Its cover (figure 6) is a very typical example of Sandberg's graphic work. The editorial group consisted of the designer Wim Brusse (who may have had some hand in the magazine's design), the art historian H. L. C. Jaffé, the architects J. P. Kloos, Gerrit Rietveld, and Mart Stam, and the designer and curator Willem Sandberg. The outer ring of associates did indeed include Max Bill and Le Corbusier.

Open Oog is a document of the pre-war avant-garde in Europe at that post-war moment: trying to regroup, to face the conditions of desolation, of zero, and see what they could do. Figure 7 shows the facing pages of the editorial statement. It is set unjustified, and in fact with lines broken according to sense, where possible. This statement recalls the 'period of creative intoxication' before the war: 'New forms for new men and women ... Typography abandons symmetric layout and assumes direction and movement; tries to guide the eye across the page. (Symmetry is equilibrium, stagnation.) Articles of use are produced exclusively with a view to their being used.' The statement ends as follows: '1945. Now the storm is passing. Hitler is dead; but the tatters of his world image still conceal themselves in the thoughts of the misguided. Rare indeed are those who, standing wholly in the present, can assume the responsibilities and implications and face the naked truth of this grand and fiery epoch. Shall the War of 1939–1945 herald a new age? We pause, and scan the horizon of time – with open eye.'

5. Letter dated 9.3.1946, now published in full in: *Anthony Froshaug: Documents of a life*, Hyphen Press, 2000, p. 143.

Willem Sandberg was active in the Dutch resistance movement during the war, helping with sabotage activities and with illegal printing. He spent the last two years of the war in hiding. Some experimental typography from that time showed him trying out unjustified text: the way of setting that then became habitual with him. It is in Sandberg's typography, I think more than any other designer's, that one sees the social meanings that can be found in unjustified setting. Sandberg's is a typography of openness, of imperfection, of informality, of equality, and so of dialogue. I still find it very moving. Although, having said that, one could make a whole series of typographer's qualifications: about word-breaks, hyphenation zones, and multi-column setting.

Sandberg did write a short defence of unjustified setting, published in 1952 in the English magazine *Typographica*, edited by Herbert Spencer.[6] And in that year Spencer published his book *Design in business printing*, which includes arguments for unjustified, on purely pragmatic grounds. Here, with more time and space, one could make a detour into the English-British situation.

But I want to go back to Anthony Froshaug and to another person perching just then in the margins of English life. This was Stefan Themerson, a Polish writer, whose itinerary of exile from Warsaw had been Paris (1937) and then London in 1942. Themerson and Froshaug met in 1944, and began quite an intense dialogue over the next five years or so. A book by Themerson on experimental film was one of the many never-to-appear titles announced by Froshaug's publishing imprint. Themerson and his wife, the painter Franciszka Themerson, went on to start their own publishing venture, the Gaberbocchus Press: in Chelsea, then Maida Vale, but absolutely outside the English literary scene. The strand of the Froshaug–Themerson dialogue and collaboration I want to touch on here is their work on what Themerson named 'semantic poetry'. One of the examples in Themerson's novel *Bayamus* shows this idea at work (figure 8). The 'Semantic sonata', a long poem by Themerson to be printed by Froshaug, would have been the most concentrated expression of their collaboration. But it never appeared in this form. A prospectus was published in 1950.

6. W. J. H. B. Sandberg, 'Must line-length be uniform?', *Typographica* (first series), no. 5, [1952], pp. 30–1.

(To end I recited the S.P. Translation of a Nursery Rhyme, sung by English mothers to their children. 'For us, adults,' I said, 'the words have lost their meaning, they are merely conventional signs of a somehow nonpersonal reality. What if the child's mind apprehends them as in this S.P. Translation?')

TAFFY WAS A WELSHMAN.

Taffy was a male native of Wales
Taffy was a person who practised seizing property of another un-
                                    [lawfully
        and appropriated it to his own use and purpose
Taffy came to the structure of various materials
                    having walls
                        roof
                        door
                        and windows to give light and air
    he came to that structure which was a dwelling for me
And there he appropriated to his own use
                        one of the limbs of the dead body of
                        an ox
                        prepared and sold by butcher

I went to the structure of various materials
                    having walls
                        roof
                        door
                        and windows to give light and air
I went to that structure which was a dwelling for Taffy
Taffy was not there
Taffy came to the structure of various materials
                    having walls
                        roof
                        door
                        and windows to give light and air
Taffy came to that structure which was a dwelling for me

8   Stefan Themerson, *Bayamus*, Editions Poetry London, 1949.
216 x 135 mm.

Semantic poetry was an attempt to strip language down, and at the same time to embody – or body forth – meaning: typographically. Lines had to be ragged, of course, but they were broken according to sense, and, further, internal vertical alignments were used. Max Bill sometimes used this principle too. In one of the pieces shown in his 1946 article, you can see elements configured around a central axis, but not symmetrically (figure 9). The placing of title lines, in the three language variants, is determined by the word 'Architektur/architecture'. In such things one can see the attempt to get beyond the merely formal: to reach meaning.

For Themerson, who was learning English, and Froshaug, who was helping him, 'semantic' setting was partly just an outcome of the process of looking up words in several dictionaries (Polish,

French, and English): they would write alternatives directly above one another. Partly also it was a response to the conditions of that time. As Themerson remembered later: 'It was a refusal to be taken away from reality, a refusal to be taken for a ride, that made me "devise" (not to say "burst into") semantic poetry ... at a time when political demagogues of all sorts were using oratory devices stolen from poets...'[7]

Themerson is an unclassifiable writer. He sometimes fell in with English positivism, though he was too funny and also too serious to be trapped by it. Certainly that attitude of stripping away the metaphysical rubbish is of that moment: one sees it also, for example, in Susan Stebbing's two war-time Pelican books, *Thinking to some purpose* and *Philosophy and the physicists*, in which she used the weapons of analytical philosophy to see off contemporary political and scientific rhetoric.[8]

The reference to Anthony Froshaug can be rounded off by looking at the first page of a conspectus of his work as a printer, published in 1951 (see p. 280 above). It is set unjustified, of course. There is a brief statement of what he was up to: going back to pre-industrial conditions and to the margin, but with a sophisticated awareness: 'Equipment is deliberately minimal and simple in mechanical design: rather than behaviourist engines, it tends towards workshop tools & machine-tools enjoying maximal degrees of freedom, within which one individual may solve new problems in configuration.' Yes, it is as Adorno proposed: 'The older media, not design for mass-production, take on a new timeliness: that of exemption and improvisation.'

The anti-metaphysical attitude I have been describing, as well as the results it produced, makes a clear contrast with the typographic and poetic avant-garde of around 1914: Futurism in Russia and Italy, Vorticism, Dada. It is true that those earlier people did try to shape text in response to meaning. But the meaning, the spirit, was quite different. The work of 1945 is cool, quiet, exact, without illusions. The inconceivable worst had actually happened (the death

7. Stefan Themerson, *On semantic poetry*, Gaberbocchus, 1975, p. 16.
8. Susan Stebbing, *Thinking to some purpose*, and *Philosophy and the physicists*, Harmondsworth: Penguin Books, 1939 and 1945 respectively.

Moderne Schweizer Architektur

Architecture Moderne Suisse
Modern Swiss Architecture

Herausgeber / Les éditeurs / Editors :   Arch. Max **Bill** . Zürich
Paul **Budry** . Lausanne
Ing. Werner **Jegher** . Redaktor an der «Schweiz. Bauzeitung» . Zürich
Dr. Georg **Schmidt** . Konservator der Öffentlichen Kunstsammlung . Basel
Arch. Egidius **Streiff** . Generalsekretär des «Schweiz. Werkbund» . Zürich

Verlag Karl Werner . Basel

9   Cover of a folder designed by Max Bill, reproduced in his 'Über
     Typografie'. Size of original item: 297 x 210 mm.

camps, the atomic bomb). One could only pause, strip away, to find
out what really was there. Then there might be a chance of some
decent reconstruction.

I have tried to point to the strong political mix of that time:
despair and hope. There is even a grain of hope in the Adorno of
1944. I think we tend to forget this politics, especially in looking at

what happened to the movement of reconstruction twenty years or so on from 1945. For example, there is a common perception of the Hochschule für Gestaltung Ulm as a sort of dried-out technocratic laboratory. But it had its origins in the reconstruction movement, and it was specifically a memorial to the 'Weiße Rose' resistance group in Munich. Anthony Froshaug, who taught there, once described the HfG as an anarchist dream, and I think that description suggests a truth.

To sum up: I do think it is interesting and significant that it was just at that moment, around 1945, and not earlier, that the ancient principle of unjustified setting was rediscovered. This was done by a handful of quite marginal people, as well as by the pervasive presence of the typewriter. It would be interesting to trace how the experiments of 1945 got taken into the broad stream of reconstruction and then prosperity, over the twenty or so years that followed.

Information Design Journal, vol. 7, no. 3, 1994

This was a lecture given at the conference on 'Design & Reconstruction in Postwar Europe', held at the Victoria & Albert Museum, London, January 1994; the text was then published in IDJ, largely as spoken.

Emigré graphic designers:
their reception and contribution

A talk given at the 'Art in Exile' exhibition, Camden Arts Centre, London, 24 September 1986

I am glad of the chance to speak about the emigré graphic designers, because they are only marginally represented in the exhibition. (Though one is used to design occupying the margins: something that architects do when there aren't any other jobs, or that artists take on as a last disgraceful resort.) Yet I sense that the emigré contribution in this field has been a significant one, and perhaps more significant than that in the field of fine art. I will speak from the local, British point of view, and find it easiest to approach the topic by telling something of my own involvement with the after-effects of the emigration, as a way of suggesting the place of the phenomenon within graphic design in this country.

My first real encounter with it was as a student of typography at Reading. There were two emigrés in our department, out of (I think) six teachers: a lettercutter from Germany and a typographer from Austria. Living a few miles away there was one of the most distinguished of the emigré designers: a typographer from Germany, whom I got to know after graduating. In a summer vacation I worked in the studio of one of the designers whose work is on display here. Then in the final year I collaborated on an exhibition about Isotype: the work done in Vienna, The Hague, Oxford, London, under the direction of Otto Neurath in partnership, later, with Marie Neurath. I went on to do postgraduate research on this topic and spent days reading through correspondence from the 1940s, written in imperfect English by and often between Germans and Austrians; and I met more people who spoke with a German accent.

For me that accent has always exerted a pull: a promise of intelligence, seriousness, precision, and – as important – an absence of the need to apologize for these things. Why one should find these qualities to be 'German', what it is in the German culture that produces them, and what it is in the German culture that expels them as emigrés (I am aware that the sample who came here are a specially defined group) – these are enormous questions, about which I won't begin to speculate. But I feel that these qualities are rare in British life, and especially rare in design circles here. And I am tempted to put forward the presence of this accent or inflection as my thesis about the emigré contribution, because anything more ambitious runs into difficulties at every stage. Each case – each person – is an exception, as soon becomes clear if you sit and talk with someone about how and why they came and how they got on. And we are not dealing with very many people: about fifty commercial artists, graphic designers and typographers might be the number to think of. So large-scale generalizations are not going to have much foundation. And yet those of us who have come under the spell of some of these people have felt the emigré presence very directly – and also poignantly, now that one reads about them so often in obituaries – and then it is natural to think that there is something larger that needs to be explained. So I will try to get beyond these immediate impressions.

First it may be useful to establish some of the differences between design and the fine arts, so called. I am prompted to do this by the essay by Raya Kruk on the emigré graphic designers in the catalogue of the Berlin exhibition that was the basis of the present show.[1] This puzzles over why the designers got on better – in worldly terms – than the artists: why they became more assimilated. I think that the obvious explanation is simply that design is a social, collaborative process: something that fine art tends not to be. Doing design depends on assimilation and integration: with customers, printers and manufacturers, with office staff. Design cannot exist in the seclusion of an artist's studio. This assimilation is not just a matter of 'commercialization' as the Berlin writer seems to suggest. I wouldn't want to dismiss design so easily. Design has a tradition of social motivation and can realize this impulse even when 'commercial'. Outside the commercial, there is the public sphere; and, in the war and post-war years, this was an area for some notable emigré contributions: London Transport, government bodies, and especially the Ministry of Information.

1. Neue Gesellschaft für Bildende Kunst Berlin, *Kunst im Exil in Großbritannien 1933–1945*, Berlin: Frölich & Kaufmann, 1986.

This leads to the question of the label we use for the phenomenon: the word in the title of the exhibition and on almost every page of the catalogue. I know that in some cases, people have refused the term 'exile'. They were not sent, but decided to come; they immersed themselves in British life, and never considered going back after the war. That is true of all the designers I've talked with. In one case I heard about, even the term 'emigré' was refused, by someone who felt it made him out to be strange, and perhaps slightly shady (not the kind of person you ask to join a board of directors). But I think that 'emigré' has the right feeling: it conveys the difference of accent and mentality, but allows that they have a new passport, have bought a lease on a flat, and have begun – or decided – to like English food. 'Exile' seems much too dramatic for such assimilated people. I suspect that its currency is not so much due to its accuracy as a descriptor, but has more to do with the feelings of Germans and Austrians born later: a controlled rage with those of the generation of their parents who were silent witnesses to the horrors, and a dramatization of the people who got up and left. It is as if by highlighting the latter, you show up the people who stayed. The flourishing business of 'Exilforschung' seems to have gained a good deal of its momentum from these feelings.

If 'exile' misstates the situation of the graphic designers, I can think of one designer (or not quite a designer?) for whom it might be an appropriate term. That is John Heartfield, who came at the last moment, in December 1938, from Prague. The book covers by Heartfield that are on display here are very much in the pattern of the work he had been doing in Berlin and then Prague, but they are rather unlike the jobs he mostly did while in Britain. He found no really satisfactory outlets for the photomontage work here: *Picture Post* proved to be no replacement for the *Arbeiter Illustrierte Zeitung* (the collaboration did not last beyond one cover, I think). And, as two of the books circulating suggest, Lindsay Drummond, with whom he had a long-term association, was no substitute for the Malik Verlag. Heartfield had a rather narrow talent – I don't think he had much feeling for book design beyond the covers – and it was a talent that could not work properly in Britain: in the English language and applied to politics outside Germany. He was also seriously ill while he was here. And, unappreciated by the British, he returned to Germany (the GDR) in 1950. The non-assimilation of Heartfield is interesting, because it also tells us something about British culture, as well as about John Heartfield: it would, I think, have been inconceivable for him to have made a success in this country. His work was too full of strong content, and content that was specifically German. In this, as in its methods (as Stuart Hall has suggested), it could not fit in to the prevailing spirit of homely realism: the spirit of *Picture Post*.[2]

Now, to take another kind of graphic work that was also full of content – too much so for it to be 'graphic design' proper – but which did have a marked success here. This was the work of the Isotype Institute, directed by Otto and Marie Neurath. In some ways, coming to this country was a kind of fulfilment for Otto Neurath. He had always been English-minded and an admirer of the English liberal-empirical tradition. For example, he had been active in the 'Siedlungsbewegung' (estate-housing movement) in Vienna after 1918, and so become familiar with the Garden City movement here; also with the Guild Socialism of G.D.H.Cole; he was, of course, a reader of Bertrand Russell (the political writings as well as the philosophical). Although Isotype work was certainly alien to the English tradition of gentle illustration, it did find acceptance here: the Isotype Institute (set up in Oxford in 1942) was given active support by a number of progressive intellectuals, distinguished by their desire to break down the professional confinements of knowledge: people such as Susan Stebbing, Julian Huxley, Lancelot Hogben, the architect Basil Ward, John Trevelyan, Jane Abercrombie. There were two main sources of work at first: a very productive collaboration with the film director Paul Rotha; and the work with Adprint, the book-packaging company (one of the first) run by Wolfgang Foges with – before he went off to start Thames & Hudson – Walter Neurath (no relation to Otto). The two books circulating (*There's work for all*, *Landsmen and seafarers*) are quite typical of these Adprint books with Isotype contributions: around 30 were published between 1943 and 1950. *Landsmen and seafarers*, incidentally, has a jacket with Heartfield's signature.

2. Stuart Hall, 'The social eye of *Picture Post*', *Working Papers in Cultural Studies*, no. 2, 1972, pp. 71–120.

Isotype fitted well with the needs and aspirations of people in the 1940s in Britain: the need to spread information widely, as part of the democratic-socialist reconstruction of 1945 and onwards. The Rotha films with animated Isotype diagrams inserted, such as *World of plenty* (camerawork by Wolf Suschitzky) or *Land of promise*, are striking and moving documents of that time. (Incidentally, Rotha was born in London, and his real name was Paul Thompson: perhaps a case of someone who wanted to be thought of as Continental?)

Someone whose work is well represented in the exhibition is F. H. K. Henrion: and the posters here have something of the same forthrightness as the Isotype work. Unlike the Neuraths or Heartfield, Henrion was and is a graphic designer proper: one of the most notable in Britain. These posters were one of the 'major rediscoveries' of the show for the art critic of *The Guardian*, which says something about the familiarity of British art critics with design. He had evidently not heard of Henrion before, nor of HDA International and Henrion, Ludlow & Schmidt, and the work for KLM, BEA, BL, C&A, LEB, the GPO, and the many other jobs that have issued from this practice since Henrion stopped being a poster artist and started on the career of consultant designer. I quite often wish that Henrion had done more marvellous posters like 'Aid the wounded' and less KLM, BEA, BL, etcetera; but that is not fair or realistic. And, in fact, the argument I want to make depends for one of its trump cards on Henrion's later career.

One thesis about the emigration turns around the question of modernism. This was formulated by Perry Anderson, for spheres other than art and design.[3] To simplify: the thesis says that the most modern people went to the USA, while we got the conservatives and reactionaries. So Popper and Wittgenstein came here, while Adorno and Marcuse went to the USA; we got Isaiah Berlin, they got Bertolt Brecht. If you extend it to art and design, then you note that Gropius and Breuer could not get decent work here and went on to Harvard; and that Moholy-Nagy only did muddled jobs – like the posters in

---

3. Perry Anderson, 'Components of the national culture', *New Left Review*, no. 50, 1968, pp. 3–57 (now reprinted in his *English questions*, Verso, 1992).

this exhibition (two of the least exciting things he put his name to) – before going on to Chicago. I used to find this thesis quite persuasive, but now begin to doubt it. Anyone making a radical or socialist case, as Anderson was, has also to see what happened to modernism after the war, and the history of its intimate relations with corporate capitalism in America. And, of course, people such as Brecht, Bloch, Adorno, Horkheimer, went back to Germany without much delay.

But to get back to graphic design: in Britain, as elsewhere in Europe and in the USA, graphic design is essentially a phenomenon of the last thirty or forty years. It is only since 1945, or perhaps 1955 in Britain, that one begins to see people producing graphic imagery that is integrated and predominantly abstract or abstracted, rather than illustrational and decorative. This graphic design is the extension or development from the Continental modernist work of between the wars: the new typography, in which photography and symbolic forms rather than illustrational drawing became the means of producing images. To put it in a nutshell: the transition has been from Henrion the poster artist (who signs his work) to Henrion the man who goes to meet company directors and who presides over a team of people who design such things as airliner liveries, National Girobank leaflets, London Transport signing systems. This shift has depended on people with different skills and interests from those of the pre-war commercial artists. Hand skills are less important; more necessary are analytical abilities, skill in human dealings, as well as – with luck – graphic talent and a feeling for good form. You can perhaps see the connection I want to make with the German accent: sharpness, intelligence, getting to the point without shilly-shally.

One can point to quite a few emigrés who played important parts in effecting this passage from commercial art to graphic design. Henrion and Hans Schleger come to mind first, as leaders in the field. And one would think also of Lewis Woudhuysen – he was Dutch, but came at the time of the German invasion of the Netherlands in 1940. I think especially, and with great affection, of Ernest (Ernst) Hoch, whose behind the scenes work as designer, teacher, and committee member, exemplified the approach I am trying to describe. And if one widens the field to include anyone who wasn't wholly English and who was not burdened with the English or British cultural characteristics – which is what I am really talking about – then the case becomes stronger. Anthony Froshaug (a Norwegian father), Edward Wright (South American parents), Romek Marber (Polish), Germano Facetti (Italian): all made important contributions.

This emphasis on the formation of graphic design leaves out, among others, the people who found their way into the world of traditionalist typography in Britain: Berthold Wolpe and Hans Schmoller, above all. Though within the conventions of this kind of typography, Schmoller's distinctive contribution at Penguin Books was thoroughly 'German': precise and analytical, and inheriting the best traditions of German book production. In this he was a true continuer of the 'reform' of Penguin Books typography that had been effected by Jan Tschichold, the great modernist, who by the time he came to work here (in 1947) was a traditionalist, but with an unchanged impulse towards order and co-ordination, applied here to organizing the design and production of a large publisher's list.

A good instance of the phenomenon that I want to point out would be the introduction in this country of the standard, DIN-Format, paper sizes: A4 and so on. This system is a product of the years of scarcity, immediately after the First World War in Germany, when it was introduced by the German standards organization, the Deutscher Normenausschuß. In the 1920s and early 1930s it was a key element in the 'new [modern] typography'. With the DIN-Formate, the world of paper and printing was given essential order: the system made possible the modernist dream of efficiency and beauty-through-efficiency (and good proportion). After the Second World War the system became an international standard (with the ISO) and in the 1950s there began to be agitation for its adoption in this country. Notable among the advocates were the Royal Institute of British Architects and the Building Centre, for whom standardization of the format of technical literature was a pressing matter. The system was accepted in a British Standard published in 1959 and during the 1960s it became generally adopted here in design circles and with the trade following: being given a boost with the change to the metric system, on which the DIN-Formate properly depend.

My suggestion is that here in the adoption of the DIN paper sizes there was an emigration – not an exile! – of a far-reaching and fundamental kind, taking place as a kind of delayed transmission of events of thirty years before on the Continent. And, as one would expect, some of the best advocates of the new paper sizes were the emigrés and the not-English: Ernest Hoch, John Tomkins (Julius Teicher) at the Graphis Press. The SIA (as it then was: the Society of Industrial Artists) played some part too, and in that organization the not-English element was important. My final piece of evidence – and closing image, if I could show it to you – is a photograph of Henrion that accompanied an article he wrote for the 1964 *Penrose Annual*, with the title 'The rationalization of paper and inks'. It shows the author in his office, in front of a filing system that covers most of one wall, proudly demonstrating the beauties of storing information that has been printed or typed on A4 sheets. The Deutscher Normenausschuß comes to Pond Street.

This was one of a series of talks that accompanied the 'Art in Exile' exhibition at the Camden Arts Centre in 1986: the programme was devised by Monica Bohm-Duchen. The audience was a small one, and I could use the exhibition itself as illustration, supplemented by a few books that I brought along and circulated. The text, which I delivered as it stands here, became the basis of an article for the *Journal of Design History* (vol. 3, no. 1, 1990).

Signs and readers

Semiotics and designing

Semiotics has been present in design theory for a considerable time: twenty-five years, at least. It has had a ghostly presence, as a possibility or promise, but never quite pinned down; its identity and its place within design have remained uncertain. Two factors can be identified as explanations of this. First, the problems of the semiotic enterprise itself. Is it a discipline in its own right, or rather a mediating inter-discipline? An art or a science? What is its relation to linguistics? 'Semiotics' or 'semiology'? Peirce or Saussure? And, if Saussure, then in which edition? The semiotic literature is large in ground-clearing discussion of such issues, and not so large in contributions that put semiotic ideas into practice. The second factor in the frustrated relation of semiotics to design has been the difficulties of designers in constructing theories about their own activities. What is the nature of design? Is it sensible to think of one all-embracing activity of design, from engineering at one extreme to fashion design at another? If it is a job and a profession, can it be a discipline too? Can it have its own theories, or must it always borrow from other fields of theory? Given the intractability of these conundrums, it is no wonder that the theme of semiotics and design has proved so largely unrewarding.

The notion of a theory of design can be clarified by making the distinction between ideas or theories that bear on the practice of designing, and those that concern the criticism or appreciation of design work. Of course, this cannot be a sharp distinction. Designers are ordinary people too: we live in a common world. Historical knowledge, for example, spans the divisions of design practice and criticism of design; while it may be generated by non-practitioners, it feeds into the consciousness of those producing new artefacts. And, in general, it is a condition of the well-being of designing and design theory that they stay in touch with the common world: the world for which they work. Nevertheless, despite this recognition of shared ground, the very notion of designing, as a distinct and professionalized activity, carries with it the supposition that there could be a body of theory peculiar to it. So one can proceed on the assumption that there will be a need for theories that bear on the practice of design – the field of design method – and, as another matter (though a related one), for theories that illuminate design products.

Much of what is said of semiotics suggests that it belongs with those theories that help us to understand the products of design. Thus David Sless (1986) likens the semiotician to a fashion critic (not a designer). Semiotics is always described as being concerned with reading, with decoding, with interpreting. These are essential activities – and reading is certainly an activity and a construction of meaning. Nevertheless, to interpret something given is one thing; to determine and to oversee its material production is another. Again, the distinction is not an absolutely clear one, and should not be overstressed. For designing is not creation out of nothing (as in the idea of the genius-artist, conjuring unexplainable beauties from a void). Rather it is a matter of working, usually with given materials, constrained by many interconnected and often pressing factors.

Consider a graphic designer, hurrying to complete layouts for a catalogue by next Monday. Which photographs to choose? It may be a compromise between those that show best what needs to be shown, and those that show less but which would reproduce better. The designer acts as an interpreter of the meaning of images; and it is in such moments that theoretical understanding comes to play its part in practical design work. To stay with this example of choosing photographs, it may well be that recent developments of theory, in discussions of the meanings of images, are coming to influence the ways in which designers are deploying images. For example, the question of whether to crop an image, whether to show the edge of the frame, whether to bleed it off the page. These questions are absolutely practical (the stuff of everyday graphic design) and also entail matters of high theory, in their concern with the representation of the world: does the imposition of a frame deny the continuum of reality, or does it rather acknowledge that we must always employ such markers in perception?

Such an example suggests that theoretical reflection and practical action do best when they coincide and play off against each other. But theory and practice are different, even if they can be intertwined. In the case of the person examining photographs, the activity could be either theoretical or practical – it depends on how it is directed. The critic may look as intensely as the designer, and may even earn money with this looking (if it results in some article or review), but the difference becomes apparent when we consider the kind of demand placed on each viewer and the contexts in which the viewers are acting. If the critic works to formulate ideas, the designer works to get the images produced (or reproduced) in a thoroughly real, material sense. While both may work to deadlines and under pressure, the pressures on the designer – the responsibility for a job of production – are of a different kind from those on a critic. So the two worlds of theory and practice come to distinguish themselves: the library or the private study (usually a world of solitary activity), and the more social world of the design office – its shelves populated by trade catalogues, directories, files, and specimens of work. Theory becomes manifest in books and journals, in lecture and seminar rooms – and splits off from the practice of the design office or workshop.

The promise of semiotics

The large and simple attraction of semiotics to design theorists is that it offers a concern with the meaning of objects and images. Information theory, which had provided the set of ideas most borrowed from in conceptions of design activity, can postulate no more than signals: disturbances in a cycle, passing down a channel, from an unintelligent emitter to an unintelligent receiver. There is no semantic dimension here. Semiotics introduces the sign, and with it the whole domain of meaning and the human world; and thus might point a way out of the aridities of information theory.

Information theory may have had its day as a source of ideas and metaphors with which to think about designing (this reliance was at its peak in the 1950s, and lasted well into the 1960s), but we are still living under the spell of 'information' – with the spread and popularization of 'information technology'. In this now universal phrase, 'information' serves to suggest the component of intelligence or software that differentiates this new technology from the old. On the other hand, and in other contexts, 'information' suggests the communication of essential messages (as against the fripperies of press advertising, for example), whose effectiveness can be really evaluated and probably quantified. The name of this journal testifies to the hopes that reside in this notion of 'information', as do the courses in 'information design' or 'visual information' that now seem to be springing up – where previously there had been mere 'graphic design'. Manœuvres in the labelling of courses may not amount to much more than a change of head-gear (with no effect on what goes on underneath) – though, even as such, they suggest at least a wish to come to better grips with the subject. And though the current vogue for 'information' may be partly traceable to a theory that proved a dead end for designers, this cannot be used as a stick with which to beat present attempts to direct graphic design to matters of need.

In this context of information design, with its characteristic emphasis on users' requirements, an awareness of the semantic dimension becomes all the more apposite: as a continual reminder that understanding is more than just reception of messages, but entails a construction of meaning and that this 'meaning' is subject to influence from a very large set of factors. In the fundamental insight of Saussure, linguistic signs are arbitrary and 'unmotivated': there is no necessary connection between the meaning of any word and its phonological structure. But, in the realm of visual depiction too, the meaning of an image is never obvious. A photograph may bear the imprint of reality (light acting on film at the moment of exposure), but even – perhaps especially – the meaning of a photographic image is never obvious. It may show a tree, yes; but what kind of tree? Here it is the viewer who decides, according to learned categories. What season of the year? How old is the tree? When was the photograph taken? Was there a wind blowing? What is the importance of such considerations in understanding the image?

The presence of a semantic dimension is inevitable. It invades even those communications that intend to be purely functional: texts and images are always produced by particular people with particular purposes, and so bear the traces of human intention. For example, the character of the producing institution can be seen in the linguistic and visual qualities of government forms: both (as is well understood) in the traditional byzantine-bureaucratic productions, and (as may be less obvious) in the recent experiments in simplified and humanized forms. The latter lay claim to a new spirit of enlightenment, or efficiency through the language of sympathy.

Analysis of the meanings and motivations of seemingly banal artefacts has indeed been one of the contributions of the semiotic habit of thought, as David Sless suggests. The consideration of semantics can open up the dimensions of ideology and of politics. This semiotic contribution is in the first place to the criticism of products, and it has largely remained as criticism. Any effect on the designers of products has come indirectly, through processes of feedback and through slow infiltration into the common culture.

In considering the possible contribution of semiotics to graphic design, as in the example of a semiotically-inspired analysis of government communications, it is necessary to make an obvious but fundamental distinction within the 'dimension of meaning'. Any text has a level of simple or literal meaning, and a level of attributed meaning. A form that requires a woman to state whether she is married or not has that as part of its literal meaning. An analysis of this question on a deeper level would consider assumptions behind it: of how women and men in this society are expected to conduct their lives; what are normal arrangements; what is accepted or condoned or refused. Such factors seep into the verbal texture of government communications (the smallest details of sentence construction and vocabulary), and they will also, there seems little reason to doubt, mark the visual texture of these productions. Or, to return to the example of the photograph of the tree, the literal meaning of the image has already been disclosed – it is just that (a tree). The further, deeper analysis might consider such things as the way this tree stands against dark clouds: a suggestion of threat; or does the tree betoken shelter and safety from a coming storm? Isolated in this flattened landscape it seems to be a last protest against rapacious agriculture. And so the analysis would go on.

It may be doubted that this kind of analysis has anything especially 'semiotic' about it. Is this not what any pragmatic commentator, sensitive to meanings and implications, has always done? Insofar as one accepts that semiotics amounts to this kind of analysis, one then accepts that the hoped-for 'science of signs' has become just a style of thought, characterized by a concern to demythologize, to show up latent ideology, using a language marked by a stock of key words (code, discourse, text, denote, signify, etc). It seems that attempts to develop a strict, quasi-scientific semiotic analysis have been given up by the cultural critics who might contribute to design theory.

The language analogy and its perils

One of the attractions of the semiotic view is that it has offered the means of attributing meanings to otherwise mute objects. In one field of design in particular – architecture – semiotics was welcomed by some critics and by theoretically-minded architects as providing a way through the obstacles against which post-Second-World-War versions of modernism had foundered. Semiotics provided a legitimation for elements in a building for which justification on grounds of simple function was lacking: elements of decoration. The vogue for semiotics in architecture is passing, now that the reaction against modernism has gained enough confidence to follow its instincts without intellectual justification. Buildings can again have meanings – as has been their ancient right, until the intervention of certain versions of modernism.

The analogy with language proposed by semioticians has the attraction and the sense of reassurance that is brought by all such attributions of larger significance. Just as with Freudian theories, we are told that however confused and muddled the immediate reality seems to be, it is amenable to analysis, can be shown to have causes and reasons, and can even be construed as a system. So, if we are to believe the suggestion that communication of all kinds can be understood on the model of verbal language, then we should expect to find an ordering system of the same kind as that found in language.

The difficulties of transposing linguistic analysis to other areas of enquiry are by now clear. For example, in the field of pictorial imagery, if one speaks of the 'syntax' of an image, what then in the image corresponds to the 'adjective', what to the 'noun', what to the 'verb', and so on? And even if someone were to posit isolable units, analogous to linguistic ones, in a non-linguistic example, can the analogy be sustained across a large number of examples, as ideas of linguistic structure can? It seems that such analogies can be no more than vague ones, and that they collapse as soon as one tries to work them out in any detail.

A particular confusion is likely in the application of semiotics to graphic design. Semiotics – or rather semiology (the strand that derives not from Peirce but from Saussure, and which has been most influential among commentators on visual images) – has been largely developed by the application of ideas taken from linguistics. This borrowing is evident in the anthropology of Lévi-Strauss, in the cultural analysis of Barthes, the psychoanalysis of Lacan, and in the trains of thought and investigation that all this work has set up. Here the linguistic analogy is stretched beyond mere analogy, to constitute an enormous extension of language itself: the world becomes a 'text', to be read and decoded or (in the most recent twist of theory) deconstructed. There are considerable objections to this view.

An immediate and local objection from the point of view of graphic design is the confusion caused when the apparatus of semiotics is applied to material that is closely allied to the linguistic: the text matter which is so large a component of graphic design. The semiotic tools, when turned back from the non-linguistic towards the linguistically saturated object of enquiry, come to seem at best over-emphatic, at worst superfluous. The first, literal meanings of a text can be understood without the application of the special armoury of semiotics, designed to unpick the meanings of mute objects.

Terminological confusions – such as Roger Smith discusses (1986) – make clear the unwieldiness of applying semiotics to graphic design. Words such as 'sign' and 'symbol', which have acquired precise and specialized meanings in semiotics, are then fed back into the gross, material world of design – where 'sign' may mean 'a rectangular sheet of wood bearing painted letters'. While 'symbol' in semiotics is a fairly precise category of sign, in graphic design it tends to be used very loosely, to refer to any more or less abstracted image that stands in for some idea or human enterprise. These confusions are then compounded by the disagreements within semiotics over terminology. All of which would help to explain why semiotics has never really proved of much assistance in the designing of graphic symbols and systems of symbols – the field for which best hopes for it as a contribution to practice have been expressed. The apparently common terms of semiotic theory and graphic design seemed to raise in some graphic designers hopes of help from the elixir of the 'science of signs': ungrounded promise is a characteristic of elixirs; characteristic also is the disappointment that follows application.

The gravest objection to a large strand of semiotics follows from certain emphases of Saussure.[1] In making his celebrated distinctions between 'langue' and 'parole', and between synchronic and diachronic approaches to the study of language, Saussure was concerned to move linguistics in the directions indicated by the first terms of these pairs. His aim was a study of the system of language ('la langue') and its rules and structures, with correspondingly less interest in the idiosyncrasies of individual utterance ('la parole'). And linguistics should turn away from its nineteenth-century, exclusively historical (diachronic) concern with the evolution of forms of language – towards a (synchronic) study of the system as a functioning whole, at any one time. Saussure's position can be seen as a necessary and appropriate one, given the context in which he was working. But that provides no justification for the semiotic enterprise of taking over Saussurian linguistics and applying it to non-linguistic material. One objection here is the doubtfulness of the linguistic analogy, as already discussed. And this criticism becomes all the stronger when one considers the characteristic emphasis of Saussurian linguistics on 'structures', without history and removed from the ordinary world of discourse between people. An ahistorical approach may be reasonable in a discussion of language – a uniquely slow-changing and intricate human institution – but such an approach becomes misleading when transferred to material of a quite different character. This 'material' is just that: composed of physical matter, where, by contrast, language is non-material and abundant. Physical objects, whose meanings the semiotician lays claim to, have a substance and a presence that discussion limited to 'significance' and 'structure' (mental, abstract structure) cannot begin to touch.

The tendency of semiotics, particularly as it has been developed

1. This follows the line of argument suggested by Timpanaro (1970, pp. 135–219); and see also the criticisms advanced by Eagleton (1983, pp. 109–15) and Anderson (1983, pp. 40–55).

in the hot-houses of seminar rooms and academic journals, has been to ignore the material nature of objects and conditions of production and use (their history). Even in the discussion of literature, where a non-materialist approach might be plausible (if literature is seen as composed of non-material language and ideas), the abstract interests of semiotics have proved unrewarding. Thus, in the literary criticism inspired by the structural anthropology of Lévi-Strauss, the mechanism of a text is unpicked and laid out, usually as a series of binary oppositions; but always leaving the reader with a feeling of 'so what? what does such analysis explain?' The structuralists have not made any impression on the criticism of design, partly for reasons of the non-academic and mysteriously enclosed world of design. But it would be hard to see what success structuralism could have in dealing with an activity so embedded in the material world – a world of deadlines, invoices, machine constraints, and the properties of glue.

The distance of recent theory from the world of practice is very marked – ironically – in the work of those who have been among the loudest in professions of materialism and political commitment. In Britain, this may be seen in the field of cultural studies, for example in some of the articles published in the journal *Block*. The dominant influence here (it is now on the wane) has been the structuralist Marxism of Althusser, in which the business of refining and polishing the theoretical apparatus absorbs all the critic's interest and itself comes to be seen as 'practice'; any concern for the world of everyday, practical realities is lost, and, if raised, dismissed as 'empiricism'. History is denied in this synchronic view, and with this denial there disappears any prospect of an explanation of material objects and processes.

The growing body of work in cultural studies is of some importance to the criticism of design – in particular as this exists in the theoretical and historical components of design educational courses (what is called in Britain 'complementary studies', 'liberal studies', 'related studies', or some other suggestion of the rag-bag) – and in view of the possibility that those teaching on these courses will turn to a semiotically-influenced set of ideas as a source of theory. The result of this teaching on the education and practice of designers is not easy to imagine: it is hard to see how what is often remote theory could impinge on workshop and studio practice. But one source of difficulty in this relation is clear: cultural studies has been developed in application to popular culture and is in opposition not only to an exclusive, high culture but also to all distinctions of value within culture. It thus conflicts with the highminded, reforming and occasionally revolutionary tradition of designing (of William Morris – and company), which would certainly maintain distinctions of good and bad in the ways in which the material world is ordered: on such presuppositions must any confident design education be based.

The passing of structuralist semiotics

It is characteristic of graphic design education in Britain that it should be registering the presence of semiotics a decade or so after these ideas have passed from the centre of the world of high intellectual discussion. That is, if one identifies semiotics with the Parisian or in fact Barthesian structuralist semiology, rather than with the tradition of Peirce and Charles Morris. In his later writings, Barthes came to abandon the method-governed approach of his structuralist phase (1964a, 1964b) for an approach that absorbed elements of semiotics but which gave up pretensions to strict system (1975, p. 145; 1977).

It is not necessary here to investigate in any detail the transforming of structuralism into poststructuralism, and the implications of this mutation for the semiotic theory that had been a part of structuralism. Anderson and Eagleton (both 1983) have provided succinct analyses of this development. It is clear that the shift to poststructuralism promises no benefits for design theory. Its chief ideas and slogans – as they will be percolated into complementary studies courses, for example – offer no better purchase on the world of designing than did structuralism: less, insofar as the notion of language becomes further inflated to eradicate any idea of individual identity and responsibility. The emergence of poststructuralism does however diminish (through its sometimes convincing criticisms of its earlier self) the claims of semiotics to constitute a science or discipline. Semiotics may provide scattered insights, but those still looking for a ready-made theory on which to depend will not find it in the corpus of semiotic writing.

This returns us to the question of a theory of design. It seems clear that no single, self-contained theory will ever be adequate to an activity as complex, various, and as rooted in the material world as designing: and certainly no off-the-peg theory bought from the academic fashion-houses. Design theory needs to correspond to the informal and mixed nature of its object – the activity of designing – and will inevitably borrow ideas, but needs also to think for itself, from practice.

Post-amble: the suggestion of a visual/verbal rhetoric

This paper has considered relations between semiotics and design, and has assumed some acquaintance with the essential ideas of semiotics, as taken up from the writings of Peirce and Saussure. It may be helpful now to point to the few contributions to the semiotic literature that bear directly on designing. The most substantial work has been that emanating from the Hochschule für Gestaltung Ulm, under the guidance of Tomás Maldonado. David Sless refers to the papers published in *Uppercase* (Maldonado and Bonsiepe, separately and jointly, 1961). These are of considerable interest, though they suffer from a wooden translation that makes difficult ideas unnecessarily obscure. Work on semiotics by Maldonado (1959) and Bonsiepe (1965; 1968) also appeared, in rather good English versions, in the school's journal *Ulm*, which may be as inaccessible as *Uppercase* but is worth the effort of hunting down. The passage on semiotics and design in the book that Maldonado wrote after leaving Ulm (1972, pp. 119–23) is of interest as an epilogue to that phase of work, up to 1968 – the year that proved fatal for the HfG, as for other things. The Ulm contribution is still relevant for its strenuous investigation of theories that might bear on practice, and for a continuously critical attitude that enabled it to work through a phase of unreasonable devotion to scientific method and on towards a more socially engaged position.

The work of Maldonado and Bonsiepe (and one or two others associated with the HfG Ulm) may seem uncomfortably 'intellectual' by certain standards (those of British design journalism, for example), but it never quite loses contact with the ordinary world of designing. One of its contributions was the beginnings of a new visual/verbal rhetoric: conceived as a development from classical rhetoric, but modified by the inter-discipline of semiotics. A particular appeal of this is its possible function as a common ground for theoretical and practical work. This rhetoric would be a way of understanding the mechanisms of a visual/verbal product and also an aid that could inform (and improve) visual/verbal production. The call for rhetorical analysis has surfaced more recently in the work of some literary critics. Thus Terry Eagleton closes his bracing survey of theories of literature with a proposal for the revival of this ancient practice that 'saw speaking and writing not merely as textual objects, to be aesthetically contemplated or endlessly deconstructed, but as forms of activity inseparable from the wider social relations between writers and readers, orators and audiences, and as largely unintelligible outside the social purposes and conditions in which they were embedded' (1983, p. 206). This remark, with appropriate substitution of terms ('designing and producing' for 'speaking and writing', etc), applies just as well to graphic design.

So far, in the articles by Bonsiepe and in Barthes's venture into this field (1964b), visual rhetoric has treated only 'persuasive communication' of the most obvious kind – press advertisements. Bonsiepe (1965, p. 30) – writing clearly as a designer – was concerned to dispute the suggestion that persuasive (rhetorical) communication was limited to advertising: 'Informative assertions are interlarded with rhetoric to a greater or lesser degree. Information without rhetoric is a pipe-dream which ends up in the break-down of communication and total silence. "Pure" information exists for the designer only in arid abstraction. As soon as he begins to give it concrete shape, to bring it within the range of experience, the process of rhetorical infiltration begins.' However, three paragraphs further on, Bonsiepe retreats from this position, and concedes that a train time-table or a table of logarithms might be 'examples of information innocent of all taint of rhetoric'. One doubts this. The truth seems rather to lie in Bonsiepe's first and more absolute statement: that as soon as content takes 'concrete shape' it takes on associations and meanings that exist beyond the hypothetical domain of pure information. Believers in purity of visual/verbal information might seem to be on stronger ground with cases of text or image produced on screens or by highly constrained typewriters. The lesson from such examples might be that a certain degree of technical sophistication is necessary to enable recognizably different products to be constructed by the same means; and also that a period of time is necessary, while conventions of arrangement evolve.

In two recent papers (1984a; 1984b), Hanno Ehses has revived Bonsiepe's suggestion of a visual/verbal rhetoric.[2] Ehses's presentation is attractive: 'since all human communication is, in one way or another, infiltrated rhetorically, design for visual/verbal communication cannot be exempt from that fact' (1984b, p. 4). So, he suggests, to accept that all communication is concerned to persuade, is to accept the social and moral-political dimensions of all designing, and it is to accept that all our actions and artefacts must answer to moral-political arguments, and it is to reiterate that there is no sphere of pure technique or pure information.

The difficulties of some new rhetoric appear when one starts on the business of applying the concepts of classical rhetoric in specific instances. One has to get over the barriers of Latin and of the complex definitions of rhetorical figures. In the practical experiment on which he reports, Ehses (1984a) asked his students to design a poster for a performance of *Macbeth*; each student was to produce a poster that corresponded visually to one of the rhetorical figures (antithesis, irony, metaphor, personification, and so on). The approach seemed successful to Ehses and his students – as a simple aid to thinking and to producing ideas that might not have been promoted otherwise. One knows this as a feature of any design method concerned to generate alternative procedures – and the least virtue of a design method is that it suggests a starting point and a way of getting down to work. At this quite modest level, as a stimulus and a guide to overall concepts in design work, a visual/verbal rhetoric would seem promising – in teaching above

2. Another recent call for a 'visual rehetoric' has come from Michael Twyman (1979). Twyman's long project of the description and classification of a postulated visual language lies outside the scope of this paper: the linguistic science that he sees as a model for a theory of typography is unspecified, though presumably not of the Saussurian-semiotic variety (Twyman 1982). But in this project, as in semiotically-derived work, an informal analogy (visual things are a bit like language: they have meanings) is perilously inflated to a suggestion of elaborate system.

all. But whether this rhetoric can go beyond identification of broad concept ('antithesis', etc) to touch the details of text and image has yet to be shown. The dangers of rhetoric are fairly obvious and are evident in the history of the degeneration of classical verbal rhetoric: of a new academicism and formalism, in which guide-lines grow into a restrictive network of fences.

As regards the analysis and criticism of design, the promise of rhetoric is that it can open up communication between the worlds of theory and practice, by providing common terminology and procedures. If this were to prove itself, then rhetoric would have succeeded where semiotics, which has remained irredeemably in the world of theory, has failed. But it is not at all clear how this visual/verbal rhetoric could extend its concerns back from the artefact produced to the full range of factors that inform the production of the artefact, nor how it could interrogate the fine details of an object. Again, as with semiotics, there is so much that this theory cannot discuss.

References (key dates are those of first publication)

Anderson, P. 1983. *In the tracks of historical materialism*, Verso

Barthes, R. 1964a. *Elements of semiology*, Jonathan Cape, 1967

Barthes, R. 1964b. 'Rhetoric of the image', in: R. *Barthes, Image, music, text*, Glasgow: Fontana/Collins, 1977

Barthes, R. 1975. *Roland Barthes*, Macmillan, 1977

Barthes, R. 1977. 'Inaugural lecture, Collège de France' in: S. Sontag (ed.), *A Barthes reader*, Jonathan Cape, 1982

Bonsiepe, G. 1961. 'Persuasive communication: towards a visual rhetoric', *Uppercase*, no. 5, pp. 13–34

Bonsiepe, G. 1965. 'Visual/verbal rhetoric', *Ulm*, nos. 14/15/16, pp. 23–40

Bonsiepe, G. 1968. 'Semantic analysis', *Ulm*, no. 21, pp. 33–7

Eagleton, T. 1983. *Literary theory: an introduction*, Oxford: Basil Blackwell

Ehses, H. 1984a. 'Representing *Macbeth*: a case study in visual rhetoric', *Design Issues*, vol. 1, no. 1, pp. 53–63

Ehses, H. 1984b. 'Rhetoric and design', *Icographic*, vol. 2, no. 4, pp. 4–6

Maldonado, T. 1959. 'Communication and semiotics', *Ulm*, no. 5, pp. 69–78

Maldonado, T. 1961a. 'Notes on communication', *Uppercase*, no. 5, pp. 5–10

Maldonado, T. 1961b. 'Glossary of semiotics', *Uppercase*, no. 5, pp. 44–62

Maldonado, T. 1972. *Design, nature, and revolution: toward a critical ecology*, New York: Harper & Row

Maldonado, T. and G. Bonsiepe. 1961. 'Sign system design for operative communication', *Uppercase*, no. 5, pp. 11–18

Sless, D. 1986. 'Reading semiotics', *Information Design Journal*, vol. 4, no. 3, pp. 179–89

Smith, R. 1986. 'Terminological inexactitudes', *Information Design Journal*, vol. 4, no. 3, pp. 199–205

Timpanaro, S. 1970. *On materialism*, New Left Books, 1976

Twyman, M. 1979. 'Criteria for education in "Schrift und Leser"', *Typographic* [USA], vol. 11, no. 3

Twyman, M. 1982. 'The graphic presentation of language', *Information Design Journal*, vol. 3, no. 1, pp. 2–22

Information Design Journal, vol. 4, no. 3, 1986

This article was designed to complement two other pieces in that issue of IDJ: by David Sless and Roger Smith.

Notes after the text

In the months that passed between completing the essay 'Semiotics and designing' and its appearance in *Information Design Journal*, I read for the first time – shamefully late in the day – the book *Mythologies* by Roland Barthes. It seemed to be a case of 'books that everybody's read so it's as if you had read them too', which Italo Calvino includes in his beautiful anatomy of unread books in *If on a winter's night a traveller*. This feeling of already knowing the book conspired with the embarrassment of not having read it ten or so years ago, when the English translation had first appeared. But I did break this resistance: taking care to hide the cover from the eyes of fellow passengers on trains and buses, as we correlated each other's reading matter with our other perceptions of the person. Among the discoveries of at last reading *Mythologies*, and especially its concluding essay 'Myth today', I found that a distinction I had rather laboriously made between literal meaning and deeper or further meaning (p. 316) is one that is present in much of Barthes's analysis; even my instance of the meanings of a tree is one that Barthes takes. Perhaps the correct thing here, if I had known about it, would have been simply to refer to Barthes and his discussion of the first-order language of the woodcutter and the second-order or metalanguage of those with less direct relations with trees (Barthes 1957, p. 146).

Also in the time between writing and publication, an essay appeared that throws light on this particular point and on the theme of semiotics and design more generally. In 'The hell of connotation' (*Word & Image*, vol. 1, no. 2, 1985, pp. 164–75), Steve Baker – a more assiduous reader of Barthes than I – discusses intended or designed meanings and attributed, further meanings. The distinction is that between the notions of, respectively, denotation and connotation. While this opposition is suggested in 'Myth today', it was in the essay 'Rhetoric of the image' (1964) that, according to Baker, Barthes gave these two terms their first extensive application in the analysis of visual imagery. He thus opened a debate within semiotics that has centred on the possibility of fixed, denotated meanings. Steve

Baker argues that 'the concept of denotation serves no useful purpose in the analysis of visual imagery, since it does not and cannot happen'. Readers and viewers find their own meanings, in splendid disregard for the intentions of the designers of the communication. Thus the 'hell of connotation': shared meanings and purposeful communication are fictions; the designer can only generate 'designedness', which is just connotation in disguise.

One of the useful services of Baker's essay is its reproduction of the *Paris Match* cover that Roland Barthes had taken as one of his examples in 'Myth today'. As David Sless observed in his contribution to the semiotics issue of IDJ (vol. 4, no. 3, p. 186), this image has become the subject of endless discussion, but with little likelihood of the commentators ever having seen it. Now we can see that Barthes misrepresented one aspect of the image: it shows a young boy, hardly a soldier. But for Steve Baker, as for any good semiologist, this is no cause for reproach: there is no such thing as denotation and all readings are bound to be misreadings.

A chief means by which this conclusion is reached is by ignoring or levelling out distinctions of kind among the examples discussed. 'The hell of connotation' sets out to apply semiotic ideas to graphic design, and it is good to see this attempt being made, but its author shows no recognition that 'graphic design' covers communications quite different in intention, and not only in intention, but in context of production and use. Maps, propaganda posters, magazine covers, press advertisements are lumped together with no willingness to consider that – to take the clearest example – a map has a definite, shared and agreed meaning. Though we experience a good deal of 'hell' (which, in semiotics, seems to be not 'other people', but ourselves), human beings do also sometimes manage to share meanings, and the maps that we make and with which we learn to steer courses through the world are good examples of this. To reduce all communications to the level of advertisements for Silk Cut cigarettes – which truly are products of hell – seems quite mistaken.

My essay on semiotics suffered at least one error of transmission: the word 'ahistorical' appeared as 'historical' (p. 320 above). This is the most annoying kind of error: the sentence, read in isolation, has sense, but its sense is the opposite of what I intended.

1 & 2   Both photographs taken at Embankment Station, 12 May 1986,
by the author.

Some semiologists, such as Steve Baker, believe that all meanings are the creation of the reader and that there is no stable or common meaning: on this view, there can be no grounds for objecting to, or even for believing in, misprints and errors. The compositor and proof-reader joyfully read their own meaning into the text, and who can object to this? Certainly not the author, or rather the 'author', whom poststructuralist semiologists see as no more than a fiction, a mouthpiece of language. At this point some of us will call an end to the game, and simply refuse what is just solipsism. Texts are constituted by a definite set of words, they do have intended meanings, and interfering with the words changes the meanings and produces mistakes that should be corrected.

The journal *Word & Image* is now into its second volume and has published interesting issues on such themes as 'Painting as sign', 'Poems on pictures', 'Children's art and literature'. Its base is in the traditional humanities (the history and criticism of art and literature), but as enlarged by recent developments in theory. Thus it has discussed advertising and other non-respectable instances of the interaction of the visual and the verbal; an issue on maps is promised. The editorial approach is pre-eminently open, without the feeling of sectarianism that often emanates from journals of advanced enquiry. Nor does it always suffer from the disablement that comes with theory – such as I feel Steve Baker's article exhibits – which prevents the analyser from saying anything of consequence about the world. For examples of critical bite, see the contributions to the issue on advertising (vol. 1, no. 4). It is good to find that there are still writers on this topic who are not – as many of the media studies people seem to be – secretly half in love with it.

By way of conclusion to these thoughts around the subject of semiotics and designing, there has been an instance of the theme vividly available to travellers on the London Underground. Over the last few years, stations have been pulled to pieces to make way for new installations (figures 1 & 2). It has been deconstruction of the most material kind: surfaces ripped away, temporary frameworks constructed, and, for weeks on end, one has been able to enjoy astonishing, gradually changing assemblages of rough concrete, exposed wires and piping, and scrambled fragments of the posters of perhaps thirty years ago (once I saw a Beck Underground map).

The work is done at night; the deconstructors (the critics who have usurped their subservient function, to become artists) have only a few hours at a time and work intensely in this unreal, cut-off environment, hurriedly leaving before the trains restart. One feels that they are doing it for us, the public; and certainly their work provides an interest that is absent from the art galleries, in these days of 'new image' painting and postmodern decoration. Unfortunately they are also building new ('brighter') stations. The decorative panels and tiling schemes of the refitted stations lapse into large-scale illustration (the British disease) or devise abstract motifs by a process of puerile analogy (Leicester Square equals film equals sprocket holes). These are overlays on the world we have been allowed to glimpse. In a time of false fronts, the truer state may be one of disassembled, critical limbo. Beyond this negative position, one dreams of a proper approach to design. Sometimes, in other cities, one sees it too.

References
Barthes, R. 1957. *Mythologies*, Paladin, 1973
Word & Image: a journal of verbal/visual enquiry, Basingstoke: Taylor & Francis

Information Design Journal, vol. 5, no. 1, 1986

Reading this piece, Rob Waller, editor of IDJ, wondered if I had gone postmodern, but accepted it nevertheless. It fitted into the 'back half' of the journal, which carried reviews and an editor's column, titled 'Sorts'.

The feeling of self is only the feeling of the particular being affected. Under the exclusive domination of this feeling, every being is its own universe. The winds blow and the sun shines for it and it alone. It is not the feeling of self, but the idea of self that carries man out beyond his own individuality, and places him on a level with all other human beings. He is now invested with a new set of emotions and passions. From being selfish, he has become social.

James Frederick Ferrier, 1849/50[1]

1. From Ferrier's 'Criticism of Adam Smith's ethical system', the text of lectures given at St Andrews University in 1849/50, and first published in *Edinburgh Review*, no. 74, 1986, pp. 102–7 (quotation at p. 107). See also note 40 of this essay.

Fellow readers: notes on multiplied language

Free-for-all meaning

'It is the world of words that creates the world of things'.[2] Jacques Lacan's motto – extreme, absolute, unreal – sums up as clearly as can any single formulation the tendency of poststructuralist theorizing. Over the last twenty years the quite rarified ideas of a few thinkers in Paris have become common currency in intellectual discussion. And now, late in the day, and after they have been seriously questioned at their source, these ideas have turned up in the rude world of design. A web of associated assertions starting from poststructuralism has spread into architecture, then into other fields of design, including typography. Some typical instances of this theory applied to typography and graphic design are quoted and discussed in an appendix to this essay (page 367). But this tight, self-enclosed circuit of ideas might be adequately described in a summary such as the following. We know the world only through the medium of language. Meaning is arbitrary: without 'natural' foundation. Meaning is unstable and has to be made by the reader. Each reader will read differently. To impose a single text on readers is authoritarian and oppressive. Designers should make texts visually ambiguous and difficult to fathom, as a way to respect the rights of readers.

This mish-mash of the obvious and the absurd goes under different names: poststructuralism, deconstruction, deconstructivism,

2. Jacques Lacan, *Écrits*, Tavistock, 1977 [original French edition, 1966], p. 65. The remark is quoted by Raymond Tallis in his *Not Saussure: a critique of post-Saussurean literary theory* (Basingstoke: Macmillan, 1988, p. 58). The clarity, humour and vigorous argument of Tallis's book will provide welcome relief to those lost in the world of muddy theorizing. A good resumé and extension of the case against poststructuralism is made by Brian Vickers in *Appropriating Shakespeare* (Yale University Press, 1993). I read Vickers after completing this essay, with the feeling that the points I make in this first section are accepted wisdom in some quarters. Strong criticism of value-free deconstruction is made by Christopher Norris in *Uncritical theory: postmodernism, intellectuals and the Gulf War* (Lawrence & Wishart, 1992). This book is of special interest in showing a former protagonist changing his mind.

and – more generally and much more vaguely – postmodernism. One could have a theological discussion of these terms; but not here. This essay is a loose and informal tour round some of the issues raised by deconstruction in typography and graphic design. I will wander off the path at times, believing that the academic discussion of typography, and of design in general, is too often hermetic and unreal: in unholy partnership with the proud anti-intellectualism of many practising designers.

Let us go back to the main theoretical source at the root of these ideas about reading. This is the book known as *Cours de linguistique générale* by Ferdinand de Saussure: Course in general linguistics. Saussure was a professor of linguistics at the University of Geneva. He died in 1913, and this book was first published in 1916. Its text is a reconstruction of lectures, based on notes taken by students, and edited by some of his colleagues. This helps to explain why professional linguists – not to mention amateurs without any special competence in linguistics – have found it an enigmatic and difficult text, although commentaries and improved editions have cleared up some mysteries.[3]

Saussure dismisses the simple-minded notion that words correspond to real objects: that, for example the word 'tree' corresponds to the real thing that we know as a tree. Instead he introduces a more complex notion of what he calls 'la signe' (the sign). 'A linguistic sign is not a link between a thing and a name, but between a concept and a sound pattern'.[4] And Saussure goes on: 'The sound pattern is not actually a sound; for a sound is something physical. A sound pattern is the hearer's psychological impression of a sound, as given to him by the evidence of his senses.' Coming to the end of this discussion he proposes to substitute 'concept' ('concept' in this translation) and 'image acoustique' ('sound pattern') by the terms 'signifié' and 'signifiant', which, in the English translation followed

3. The English translation quoted from here is that of Roy Harris (Duckworth, 1983). This may supersede the translation by Wade Baskin (New York: Philosophical Library, 1959), which has provided the basis for most English-language commentary on Saussure. See also: Roy Harris, *Reading Saussure: a critical commentary on the 'Cours de linguistique générale'*, Duckworth, 1987.
4. Saussure, *Cours*, Part 1, chapter 1: Harris translation, p. 66 and following

here, are 'signification' and 'signal'. This pair in combination constitutes the sign.

Saussure then describes the two fundamental characteristics of a sign: that the link between signal and signification is arbitrary; and that the signal is linear in character (it occurs over time). The first of these characteristics is at the root of the debate over typography and the reader.

As one reads Saussure's remarks on arbitrariness, it is hard, I think, to disagree. He says that different languages have different words for the same concept: the animal which the French know as 'un boeuf', the Germans know as 'ein Ochs'. And this is enough to prove the arbitrariness of the linguistic sign.

Two paragraphs after this Saussure drops in a speculation about semiology, the science which, he predicts, will extend the principles of linguistics to the understanding of every aspect of human life. This is why Saussure has assumed so much importance outside his part in linguistics. A few cryptic remarks in this text became foundation stones for the semiology that was developed half a century later. Semiology became part of the larger project of structuralism, worked out most notably in the anthropology of Claude Lévi-Strauss. Then later – gradually – semiology and structuralism turned into poststructuralism. The development of Roland Barthes's writing – from the scientific pretensions of the early work, to his frankly poetic later prose – exhibits this transition most clearly. Poststructuralism renounces the notion of the heart, centre or essence; but if it had such a thing (and perhaps its centre lies in its wearying championing of the periphery?) then this concept of the arbitrariness of the sign lies there. Another two paragraphs further on, Saussure says the following:

> The word arbitrary also calls for comment. It must not be taken to imply that a signal depends on the free choice of the speaker. (We shall see later that the individual has no power to alter a sign in any respect once it has become established in a linguistic community.) The term implies simply that the signal is unmotivated: that is to say arbitrary in relation to its signification, with which it has no natural connexion in reality.[5]

5. Saussure, *Cours*, Part 1, chapter 1: Harris translation, pp. 68–9.

It seems that the deconstructionists never read this. Or if they did read it, they never made their disagreement clear. Language, Saussure reminds us, is created by a community, and we use it within the constraints of this larger, communal understanding. In this fundamental sense, signs are not arbitrary, and we would do better to use the term 'unmotivated' to describe the quality of fortuitousness in our pairing of signal to signification. So deconstructionism contradicts Saussure, without acknowledging it. Certainly in its degraded forms, as in the recent typography debate, this theory very simplemindedly asserts that there is no such thing as community, or society – as Margaret Thatcher notoriously formulated it, at around the same time.[6]

Saussure regards language as a collective, social endeavour. But typographers and other designers who share that view should nevertheless have a deep disagreement with Saussure. The language that he considered was almost exclusively spoken language. Saussure's idea of language is a very theoretical and intellectual one. It is less material even than human breath. He remarks that 'a sound is something physical'. Can one sense a tone of disdain here? Then he turns away from such crude materialism to concentrate on concepts and sound patterns. The diagram in the *Cours de linguistique générale* of how sounds are produced by the organs of speech is about as material as Saussure gets.[7]

In the *Cours de linguistique générale* there is not even much sense of human beings talking with or to one another. It is true

6. 'There is no such thing as "society", there is only individuals and their families.' This is the quotation as made by Stuart Hall, principal analyst of 'Thatcherism', in *Marxism Today*, December 1991, p. 10. Another version runs: 'There is no such thing as society. There are individual men and women, and their families.' The source of this has been given as an interview with Margaret Thatcher, published in *Woman's Own*, October 1987.

Russell A. Berman traces connections between deconstruction and Reaganism in his 'Troping to Pretoria: the rise and fall of deconstruction', *Telos*, no. 85, pp. 4–16. But in his nice remark that 'deconstruction is the restaurant where one can only order the menu ... Let them eat tropes!' (at p. 10), Berman seems to exaggerate deconstruction's purchase on the material world (of paper, in this case).

that Saussure's famous distinction between 'la langue' (the system of language) and 'la parole' (individual acts of speech) makes provision for this, in this second term. But then his emphasis falls so largely on the speaker. And if you look for the form of language that most interests typographers – the language that uses letters, characters, images, of ink on paper, of scans across television screens, of grids and bit-maps, of incisions in stone – there is a large gap. Early in the lectures, Saussure has some pages on writing, but only to put it in its place: 'A language and its written form constitute two separate systems of signs. The sole reason for the existence of the latter is to represent the former. The object of study in linguistics is not a combination of the written word and the spoken word. The spoken word alone constitutes that object.'[8] This may have been a revolutionary attitude to adopt then: linguistics had been shaped as a study of language in its written forms. But its legacy has not been helpful to any discussion of the material world of the making and exchange of artefacts: the world to which typography belongs. The wish of semiologists, to study and explain the social world, suffers from this crippling weakness: it has no material foundations. So, after his brief discussion of writing, Saussure confines himself to spoken language. Indeed he uses the word 'language' ('la langue') to mean just 'spoken language'.

7. Saussure, *Cours*, Introduction, appendix, chapter 1, Harris translation, p.42. The version shown below is taken from the original French edition:

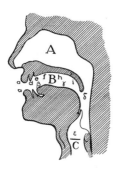

8. Saussure, *Cours*, Introduction, chapter 6: Harris translation, pp. 24–5.

Some attempts have been made to correct the blindness of linguistics to writing. From within linguistics itself, one could cite the work of Josef Vachek, and maybe others.[9] From a vantage point outside linguistics, the English anthropologist Jack Goody has produced a stream of books and essays on writing, understood in its full historical and material sense.[10] *The domestication of the savage mind* may be his most accessible and directly relevant book for typography. Goody here points forcefully to the distinctive properties of written language, as a system apart from and in mutual reciprocity with spoken language. His work also has the distinction of examining ways in which writing may be configured other than as continuous text: in tables, lists, formulae, and other related forms for which we hardly have an agreed descriptive terminology. These systems of configuration may be used almost unthinkingly, every working day, by typographers, editors, typesetters, and typists. And yet discussions about reading, legibility, print and the future of the book seem to know only continuous text (a page of a novel, most typically) as their object of reference. The real world of typography is far more diverse and awkward. If reflection on what is there before us is not enough to persuade semiologists about the reality and difference of written language, then a reading of Jack Goody should be persuasive. Afterwards it will be impossible to parrot Saussure on 'language'.

9. Josef Vachek, *Written language*, The Hague: Mouton, 1973. A helpful survey here is an unpublished PhD thesis by Robert Waller: 'The typographic contribution to language', University of Reading, 1987.
10. See: Jack Goody and Ian Watt, 'The consequences of literacy', in Jack Goody (ed.), *Literacy in traditional societies* (Cambridge: Cambridge University Press, 1968, pp. 27–68), and these books by Goody (also published by Cambridge University Press): *The domestication of the savage mind* (1977), *The logic of writing and the organization of society* (1986), *The interface between the written and the oral* (1987). Goody's work is illuminatingly scanned in the course of Perry Anderson's high-altitude essay 'A culture in contraflow' in his *English questions* (Verso, 1992, at pp. 231–8). I am grateful to Giovanni Lussu for reminding me about Jack Goody's work, in an article that bears on the themes of this essay: 'La grafica è scrittura', *Lineagrafica*, no. 256, 1991, pp. 14–19.

Shared copy

The recognition and analysis of written language is an essential correction to the Saussurian theory, but it needs to be developed further. There is writing and there is printing: two different phenomena. Writing exists in one copy; printing makes multiple copies of the same thing. Yes, you can duplicate writing: you can photocopy it, or photograph and make a printing plate from it. The more exact difference is between writing and typographic composition of text. But some such differentiation must be made: between the written and the typographic/printed; or, more widely (to include film, television, video, tape- and disc-stored information) between the single and the multiple.

Semiology, based on an abstract notion of language that does not recognize the independent life of writing, is of no help here. Theorists who do discuss 'writing', but just as some unified, undifferentiated sphere of visible language may have a tool of analysis. However, it is a blunt one, which cannot deal with multiplied language. Although here one should remember that this discussion is being conducted in English, and in this language a rather clear distinction is made between 'writing' and 'printing'. But, for example, German has 'Schrift' as a common term between writing (by hand) and printing (with a machine). Where in English one speaks of 'writing' and of 'type' (i.e. words with quite different roots), in German, one speaks just of 'Schrift', or perhaps of 'Handschrift' and 'Druckschrift'. As if to confirm the distinction that English makes, one can judge typographic innocence in an English-speaker by the extent to which they muddle 'writing' and 'printing'. Thus: 'I like the writing [i.e. type] on that record cover'. Or: 'please print your name and address' (i.e. write in capital letters).

Theorists of spoken and written language cannot divorce their subject from its place and time. Thus Jack Goody's main field of interest has been in Africa and the Near East, and in ancient societies. When Goody touches on European or modern societies, he is alert to the differences introduced by printing; but for the most part he can properly concentrate on written – handwritten – language.

From within the world of typography, Gerrit Noordzij has been a productive and powerful theorist of writing: which he usually takes to include typographic composition of text: 'typography is writing with prefabricated letters'.[11] This definition is offered as an alternative way of thinking, within the context of a discussion of graphic design and typography as processes of specification and worldly intervention between texts, commissioners, printers, and producers. Noordzij's wish to subsume typography within writing is the purest piece of dogma: an essential item of mental equipment for a master scribe, lettercutter and engraver, whose main focus is on the minutest details of letters and their production. But here, in this essay, our focus is on the world that Gerrit Noordzij sees when he puts down his magnifying glass and picks up his telephone: the social world of producers and readers. In this domain, typography and writing are essentially different activities.

Typography deals with language duplicated, in multiple copies, on a material substrate. Here we can add in screen displays, and any other means of multiplying text. And to 'text', we can add 'images' too: the same point applies. The exact repetition of information is the defining feature of multiplied text, and it is what is missing from writing. The historical elaboration of this perception has been made most thoroughly by William M. Ivins in his *Prints and visual communication* and by Elizabeth Eisenstein in her *The printing press as an agent of change*.[12] If printing was not, as Eisenstein sometimes

11. Gerrit Noordzij, *De staart van de kat: de vorm van het boek in opstellen*, Leersum: Uitgeverij ICS Nederland, 1991, p.12. Noordzij could be read in his own idiosyncratic English in the occasional publication *Letterletter*, published 1984–91 by ATypI (Münchenstein), and 1993–6 by the Enschedé Font Foundry (Zaltbommel). Noordzij's work has been too little discussed in print: Paul Stiff once wrote a long unpublished article, whose content was partly resumed in his 'Spaces and difference in typography', *Typography Papers*, no. 4, 2000, pp. 124–30. I wrote a brief survey: 'Type as critique', *Typography Papers*, no. 2, 1997, pp. 77–88. Robert Bringhurst has made a selected edition of *Letterletter* (Vancouver: Hartley & Marks, 2001), which has Noordzij's words but lacks his spirit.

12. William M. Ivins, *Prints and visual communication*, Routledge & Kegan Paul, 1953; Elizabeth Eisenstein, *The printing press as an agent of change: communications and cultural transformations in early-modern Europe*, Cambridge: Cambridge University Press, 1979. The social dimension of printing is more evident in the book that opened up this field of history: Lucien Febvre and Henri-Jean Martin, *The coming of the book: the impact of printing 1450–1800*, New Left Books, 1976 [original French edition, 1958].

seems to suggest, the lever of change in the history of fifteenth- and sixteenth-century Europe, it was certainly a fundamental factor in the changes that took place then. Printing could, for the first time, provide the steady and reliable means for the spreading and sharing of knowledge. Science and technology could be developed, ideas could be disseminated and then questioned. With a stable and common text for discussion, a critical culture could grow. Argument had a firm basis on which to proceed.

The emphasis of historians of print culture, such as Eisenstein, has tended to be on books, partly perhaps for the mundane reason that these are the printed documents that survive most abundantly. It is certainly harder for a historian to investigate newspapers or street posters: harder to locate surviving copies, and to consider their effects. Indeed this branch of history has become known as 'the history of the book'. A book is, most characteristically, read by one person at a time, and often that person will be alone. One can counter this perception by recalling the practice – now declining – of reading aloud, in churches, in schools and other institutions, and in the home. Texts are also read alone-in-public: on buses, in parks, in libraries. So reading often has a visible and apparent social dimension. But its truer and perhaps more real social dimension lies in the reading that happens when one person picks up a printed sheet and turns its marks into meaning. The page – it could be a screen too – is then the common ground on which people can meet. They may be widely dispersed in space and time, unknown and unavailable to each other. Or they may know each other, and come together later to discuss their reading of the text. Then the social dimension of the text may become a group of people around a table, pointing to the text, quoting from it, arguing, considering.

A text is produced by writers, editors, and printers. With luck, if they keep their heads down, designers might find a role somewhere here too. The text is composed, proofed, corrected, perhaps read and corrected further. Then it is multiplied and distributed. Finally it is read alone but in common, for shared meanings. When one starts to think along these lines, the semiology of texts and images doesn't seem to help much. Yes, 'signification' can be identified as part of a larger process. And within this small part, what of the 'arbitrary link' between signification and signal? Saussure's too-little noticed suggestion that 'unmotivated' is a better term than 'arbitrary' helps: because 'arbitrary' is not what typography is about at all.

The juxtaposition that one finds happening in typography is easy to grasp. It is the link between a keyboard and a monitor; between manuscript copy and a laser-printed proof; between information on a disc and on sheets of text on film; and finally, and differently, between the page and the reader. The links between these pairs are, we try to ensure, anything but arbitrary. Correcting proofs, with its attempt to turn 'arbitrary' into 'intended', can stand as the clearest instance of this defining characteristic of typography.

The argument made here is that deconstruction and poststructuralist theory can't account for the material world. The only material it knows is air: and its foundations are built not even on air, but on the entirely abstract and intellectual.[13] Certainly, when it takes on typography, the huge mistake that poststructuralist theory makes is not to see the material nature of typographic language.[14] Here screen display, because it is indeed so fluid – materially so – probably should be considered separately. But certainly in printing, language becomes real and materially present: ink on paper. Here lies the responsibility of the designer of printed matter: to bring into existence texts that will never be changed, only – if one is lucky – revised and reprinted. The idea that design should act out the

13. This point was first made for me by Sebastiano Timpanaro in his essay 'Structuralism and its successors', *On materialism* (New Left Books, 1976 [original Italian edition, 1970], pp. 135–219). I tried to amplify it in two articles: 'Semiotics and designing', *Information Design Journal*, vol. 4, no. 3, 1986 (see pp. 313–27 above); 'Notes after the text', *Information Design Journal*, vol. 5, no. 1, 1986 (see pp. 328–33 above).
14. Among more recent essays in this field, see: Ellen Lupton and J. Abbott Miller, 'Type writing: structuralism and writing', *Emigre*, no. 15, 1990. In their theoretical preamble, Lupton and Miller misread Saussure's 'arbitrary' (see above, p. 337), and then apply poststructuralist theory to typeface design – as if this is what constitutes typography. In a later essay on 'structure' in typography, Miller does discuss whole passages of text and their configuration, but to less clear effect: in *Eye*, no. 10, 1993, pp. 58–65. The first essay and material from the second were republished, along with much else of relevance to these themes, in Lupton & Miller's *Design writing research* (New York: Princeton Architectural Press, 1996).

indeterminacy of reading is a folly. A printed sheet is not at all indeterminate, and all that the real reader is left with is a designer's muddle or vanity, frozen at the point at which the digital description was turned into material. Far from giving freedom of interpretation to the reader, deconstructionist design imposes the designer's reading of the text onto the rest of us.[15]

This argument against poststructuralism in typography is not directly about style, nor is it about tradition and breaks with tradition. It is a social argument. Saussure's formulation, already quoted, that 'the individual has no power to alter a sign in any respect once it has become established in a linguistic community' makes the point firmly. Too firmly, because it seems to leave out the creative aspect of language, of syntax especially, and of the ways in which every one of us mints these signs freshly, with new meanings, every day.

The theme of language as the possession of a community was developed by Benedict Anderson in the course of his book *Imagined communities*.[16] This book is one of the handful of general works on history and politics that should be dear to typographers, because it takes notice of printing; in fact printing is at the heart of Anderson's thesis. In one chapter Anderson weaves together the rise of capitalism, the spread of printing, the history of languages, and the 'origins of national consciousness'. Arbitrariness is acknowledged. He writes about alphabetic languages, as against ideographic: 'The very arbitrariness of any system of signs for sounds facilitated the assembling process.' But, unlike the poststructuralists, he does not stop there. 'Nothing served to "assemble" related vernaculars more than capitalism, which, within the limits imposed by grammars and syntaxes, created mechanically-reproduced print-languages, capable of dissemination through the market.' But this is not a reductive account of mere capitalist exploitation. Anderson continues:

15. Paul Stiff succinctly takes apart the 'designer-centred ideology' of deconstructionism in *Eye*, no. 11, 1993, pp. 4–5.
16. Benedict Anderson, *Imagined communities: reflections on the origins and spread of nationalism*, Verso, 1983. The quotations that follow are from p. 47.

These print-languages laid the base for national consciousness ... they created unified fields of exchange and communication below Latin and above the spoken vernaculars. Speakers of the huge variety of Frenches, Englishes, or Spanishes, who might find it difficult or even impossible to understand one another in conversation, became capable of comprehending one another via print and paper. In the process, they gradually became aware of the hundreds of thousands, even millions, of people in their particular language-field, and at the same time that only those hundreds of thousands, or millions, so belonged. These fellow-readers, to whom they were connected through print, formed, in their secular, particular, visible invisibility, the embryo of the nationally-imagined community.

This 'imagined community' may be difficult for some people to grasp: particularly if they live within the community of one of the dominant languages of the world. But even in the English-speaking metropolis where these words are being written, it can be understood and felt. Greek, Italian and Irish newspapers are sold at corner shops in this neighbourhood: serving their readers here as conductors or life-lines out into the larger sphere of their linguistic-cultural community. This may describe the case for some, probably older readers. For others from those communities, and for us too – the mother-tongue English-speakers – the local weekly newspaper is the place where we come together, where we read the neighbourhood. The activity of reading, as Benedict Anderson puts it, may take place 'in the lair of the skull', but it has this social extension.[17] We always read in common, with fellow readers.

Places and nets

Some qualifications need to be made to this argument. I have been stressing the 'in-common' element of reading, against the idea that this is a wilful, arbitrary process, without an intersubjective dimension. But as an extreme of 'in-common' reading, one thinks of conditions in totalitarian societies. In China at the time of the the Cultural Revolution, Mao Zedong's 'little red book' became – despite its

17. Anderson, *Imagined communities*, p. 39.

praise of contradiction and dialectics – the emblem of a society in which an attempt was made at coercion even into feeling in unison. The book was a badge, as well as a manual of 'correct thinking'. Like the trim, beautifully made jackets into whose breast pockets it slotted, the 'little red book' was a model of fitting, unobtrusive design and production: but this uniform became oppressive. The project of complete, totalitarian standardization is inhuman, impossible, and will always eventually collapse. After a while, people rebel.

To the list of the non-determinable tendencies in reading, we can add that texts age and travel: or their contexts change both in time and place. Each generation, as well as each person, will find different meanings in a text. Much that is fresh in writing and thinking comes through recovery of old texts, and through reading them against the grain of current orthodoxy in an attempt to discover the original habits of thought and language in which the work was written.[18]

Thus among the freshest of recent tendencies in music has been the uncovering of 'early music', by the attempt to understand and reattain its original conditions of production. But, against any idea of static and finally knowable pieces, it is clear that there can only be performances of their time and place. Take the example of J. S. Bach's Matthew Passion: 'authentic performances' in the 1990s differ markedly from those in 1970s. The most moving and convincing readings are those that – perhaps just through their concentration on 'the work itself' – speak more directly to us. This was certainly the case in the recent 'performed' version of the work.[19] This production discarded the conventions of the concert performance (white ties, tails, diva dresses, upright posture) – often then uneasily

18. Here I am thinking especially of the art historian Michael Baxandall in his books *Painting and experience in fifteenth-century Italy* (Oxford University Press, 1972) and *The limewood sculptors of Renaissance Germany* (Yale University Press, 1980). His book on method, *Patterns of intention* (Yale University Press, 1985), discusses these and related themes in ways that design theorists could learn much from.
19. First performances took place in London in February 1993. The production was the initiative of the promoter, Ron Gonsalves, with the support of the conductor Paul Goodwin and the director Jonathan Miller.

situated in a church – and joined the work instead to the sphere of the everyday reality of the audience (jeans and sweaters, gestures and perambulation). Somehow this helped set free the emotional power in the Passion story, especially for the non-believer, for whom the work may otherwise remain a long-distance and largely 'aesthetic' experience. The audience, grouped around the action in stacked scaffolded seating, entered the event more intimately than is usual. The acting-out was quite limited: a touch on the shoulder, a gesture of the head, and not much more. But just in this very constraint it gained in effect. One could point to some historical legitimation for this performance (the work was felt to be surprisingly theatrical and operatic by its first audiences in Leipzig in the 1730s), but this was at most a starting point rather than a complete programme to emulate or recreate.

The 'reading' that is given before an audience gathered under one roof – or even that is broadcast on television – is of course a different matter to the reading that is the concern of this essay. Though, by comparison and contrast, it may illuminate. The director of the performance, in collaboration with others, presents an interpretation, a reading. We the audience receive it and interpret that interpretation; and our attention interacts with and may affect this interpretation. Afterwards, with others who have been there, we consider, discuss, develop, modify, revise our interpretations. These have been different experiences; maybe quite wildly different, if members of an audience bring very different assumptions and beliefs to the event (say, people of different religious beliefs at the Matthew Passion). This may be why theatre can be so vivid an experience in small communities, where audience members have shared pasts and a sense of who each other is. And it may be why theatre in a large city – however technically assured – can be such a desolate experience. Whatever the composition of the audience, there is a common event by which to measure. And the sense of community that may be engendered at such a performance is, of course, what makes the difference between public performance and private reading. But joint reflection over something that has been shared can happen with both these experiences, of watching and of reading. Both have 'public' and 'private' dimensions, if in different measures.

'The truth lies somewhere in between' may be a truism, but one that is also true in this case, or in these infinite particular cases of people reading texts. One only has to think of any reader turning the pages, misunderstanding, turning back to see what was said before, sneaking a look at the last chapter, being distracted by a phone call or the demands of a child, perhaps falling asleep and dreaming around the text, and then returning to this business of turning marks into meaning. The process is individual and unpredictable. As if we needed a designer to make this so! And yet the text is there as an irresistible and multiple fact: a common ground. For any writer, the intersubjective dimension of reading comes vividly to life when one hears from a friend that they have been reading something you wrote. Then you may reach for your copy of the text and read it again, but this time in the voice of that other reader, turning the words over, wondering what she or he made of them.

Computer-based means of transmitting texts are no doubt introducing fundamental changes to the model that is here taken as characteristic of reading. Text and images organized as nodes on a network, as in hypertext, or intercut and layered with other information and other kinds of media (animated images, sound) – this provides a different experience from that of reading a printed page. And here the deconstructionist rhetoric about the active reader may have more truth in its descriptions. At least here there really is fluidity and the possibility of change, as there hardly is in printed deconstruction.

Debates over the coming of the 'electronic book', at the expense of the printed one, have always seemed a little futile.[20] Futurist visionaries tend to underestimate the dimensions of bodily comfort and cost. Reading cheap small books in bed can still be a great pleasure. The dead duck of 'legibility' is hardly the issue here. Much more critical – apart, of course, from content – is page size, weight, openability and flappiness, lighting, temperature of the room, and how many pillows you have. Sitting in an upright chair at a screen brings a more serious air to the processes of reading, and there

20. Among recent works in this genre, Jay David Bolter's *Writing space* (Hillsdale NJ: Lawrence Erlbaum, 1991) is of interest here in its deployment of poststructuralist theory to rationalize hypertext.

would be some sense of contradiction in reading a thriller that way. To read an intimate letter sent over the wires to your terminal may also feel a little odd. The present upsurge in this mode of communication must bring large changes. One already noticeable effect is that an informal, unedited style which goes with private communication is spreading into multiplied communication. Electronic mail is fine; but not if this becomes the model for all communication. The formality that multiplication and publication demands of text carries a social function. And the social necessity of 'in-common' reading, which was won for us by printing, remains – even if it is now carried by other ways of transmitting text. If this is lost, then we really will all be reduced to 'individuals and their families'.

Time and place of modernity

My book *Modern typography*, first published in 1992, is shaped by an idea about history. Its premise is that modern typography is a long and still unfinished story, with its roots in developments in England and France around 1700. It was then that consciousness about the activity of printing began to be evident. 'Typography' really dates only from then: before that time there was just 'printing'. If early printing was consciously done, that consciousness was not articulated and disseminated. So typography is printing made conscious: printing explaining its own secrets with its own means of multiplying texts and images. And so typography is part of the long haul of 'enlightenment': of making knowledge accessible and spreading it, of secularization, of social emancipation. No doubt this thesis is oversimplified and could be infinitely modified with further research. But sometimes it is necessary to 'think crudely': as a start, and to get a discussion going.[21]

The bulk of *Modern typography* was written rather quickly in 1985–6. Then there started what proved to be a long process of trying to get it published. Established publishers did not know quite what to make of it. The book seemed to fall between the category of

21. Support comes from Bertolt Brecht: 'The most important thing is to learn to think crudely'. And see the commentary on this by Walter Benjamin, in English translation: *Understanding Brecht*, New Left Books, 1973, at pp. 81–2.

academic history and that of popular exposition. It was a work that contained a good deal of factual information and yet was one that engaged in current debates. This spanning of categories was part of its point. I wanted to draw the attention of practising designers to the perspective of history, but to a history that was different from the received, often tired accounts. Equally, for academic historians, I hoped to shift their perceptions of history by opening the subject up to present issues of practice.

In the years between completing the bulk of the text and its eventual publication, I tried to keep up with current developments. For example, the spread of desktop publishing – although initially conceived of as a marketing device – seemed to confirm the thesis of 'modern typography'. (It was also the means by which I could eventually produce my book.) This was another step in the movement of typography out of specialism and into the ordinary world. The extent of the desktop-publishing revolution is such that it is becoming hard now to conceive of 'non-practitioners'. Certainly anyone with access to a computer and a laser printer is a practitioner: this means most people in the 'professions' of western society, including the academic historians mentioned in the preceding paragraph.

Around the time that *Modern typography* finally came out, an important piece of historical research was published, but too late for me to take account of it. In an article, James Mosley discussed and reproduced – some for the first time – illustrations made as part of the investigations of the Académie des Sciences in Paris, around 1700.[22] These images confirm the importance of the work of the Académie, not just in the design of letterforms (the 'romain du roi'), but also in the attempt at a larger systematization of typography. In particular, one of these illustrations outlines – if cryptically – a system of type body sizes that relates directly to the system of measurement of inches and feet in general use then in France. The Académie's system, which was implemented at the Imprimerie Roy-

22. James Mosley, 'Illustrations of typefounding engraved for the *Description des arts et métiers* of the Académie Royale des Sciences, Paris, 1694 to c. 1700', *Matrix*, no. 11, 1991, pp. 60–80. See also Mosley's later report: 'French academicians and modern typography: designing new types in the 1690s', *Typography Papers*, no. 2, 1997, pp. 5–29.

ale, predates the system formulated nearly a hundred years later by François-Ambroise Didot, which gave continental Europe the Didot point (still in use, though being driven out by the DTP point as well as by metric measurements). In the 1730s and 1740s, Pierre-Simon Fournier had formulated his system, and this has always been given credit as the first real system of measurement for typographic materials. It seems now that the Académie gave us more than Fournier ever acknowledged: indeed, he made fun of these unworldly theoreticians and their impractical ideas about letter design. And the Académie's engraved plates, in their juxtaposition of a general view of the work process and annotated technical drawings of tools, seem to have been the models for the celebrated plates of the *Encyclopédie* (to which Fournier contributed). Maybe one can risk a moral to this story. It would be that unworldly investigators can provide us with schemes that may, surprisingly, be of great practical value.

The writing of *Modern typography* was spurred on by my context of place and time: Britain in the mid-1980s. The book's thesis of the 'unfinished story' of the modern was given shape and confirmation by a lecture that Jürgen Habermas had given in 1980, about 'modernity' as an 'incomplete project'.[23] Habermas's text was also a document of its time: that moment when the simultaneous and not unconnected phenomena of radical-conservatism in politics and of postmodernism in art, architecture and design, were beginning to take effect in the western world.

The thesis that modernity is not yet finished still has close resonance with the special situation of Britain. Here, in the 1980s, the political-cultural revolution of the new conservatism was being vigorously enacted. The broad national consensus that had been established after 1945 began, with its institutions, to be dismantled. This made itself evident in the discarding and disparagement of the modern architecture and design that had accompanied reforms in the public sphere (housing, education, transport, the cultural sector). If it had not been clear before, it became evident then that the

23. An English translation was first published in *New German Critique*, no. 22, 1981, and reprinted as 'Modernity: an incomplete project', in: Hal Foster (ed.), *Postmodern culture*, Pluto Press, 1985, pp. 3–15.

structures of government, and of public life more widely, were, in Britain, still thoroughly determined by legacies from pre-democratic, pre-modern times.[24] We had avoided the sharper experience of our continental neighbours, and evolved an organic pattern, which, if it has some virtues of informality and flexibility, still has grave weaknesses. No proper, written constitution; an unreformed monarchy, and no popular sovereignty; none of the written codes that provide safeguards to citizens, especially against the state – the charges run on, to make a long list. And 'Britain' is itself a confused concept: is it the United Kingdom? Or just 'England', as it is often called by reflex. But where then are Scotland, Wales, and Ireland (and what is 'Ireland')? So here in 'Ukania', more than anywhere else, it seems daft to celebrate the junking of the modern: something we have never properly had, and whose lack we still suffer from.

By concentrating on the large and long historical condition of 'modernity', and distinguishing that from 'modernism', one jumps over the immediate, ephemeral debates over style of appearance. The long view is salutary, calming, and durable, in keeping the short-lived in perspective. A danger in this approach – not wholly or consistently avoided in my book – is that too great an emphasis is placed on the rather abstract, almost structural and invisible themes of modernity. Standardization and the creation, agreement and implementation of norms; explanation of the processes of typography; work on the classification of typographic elements, and on the vocabulary of their description: such matters – though they

24. These ideas were then being powerfully formulated in Neal Ascherson's journalism, reprinted in his *Games with shadows* (Radius, 1988). Earlier, in the 1960s and 1970s, essays in the *New Left Review* by Perry Anderson and Tom Nairn had (certainly for this reader) established the groundplan of this view of British history. Anderson's *English questions* (Verso, 1992) comments on and reprints some of his contributions. Tom Nairn's *The enchanted glass* (Radius, 1988) took his arguments further, in a sustained and acid critique of 'Britain and its monarchy'. And also in the tercentenary of the 'Glorious Revolution' of 1688, the pressure group Charter 88 was formed, to articulate demands for constitutional modernization. Its leading light, Anthony Barnett, had been a member of the *New Left Review* editorial board.

can raise passions in the participants who debate and try to imple-
ment them – are indeed often dry and secondary.

The particular artefact, with all its material and formal qualities, provides the focus of a designer's attention, often to the point
of distraction from other considerations. But it offers a point of
resistance to the dangers of abstraction. Here, always and inevitably
to one side of all theorizing, and not finally to be captured by those
means, is this thing. Deal with it!

Critical practices

The graphic designer Otl Aicher attempted to make some critical
response to the world of the postmodern. His perspective – his history – was that of someone who had become a modern designer in
the 1940s in Germany, with all the political resonance that this suggests. As well as a designer, Aicher was a kitchen-philosopher (and
a philosopher of cooking and kitchens too). His writings through
the 1980s, until his accidental death in 1991, usually appeared in
typographic formats of his own or his studio's design.[25] Their strong
polemics and dogmatics go together with a very clear approach to
design. Aicher stood out for and tried to embody much that is argued for here. Typography results in material products. These things
should be communications, not works of art or personal designer-
expressions. They circulate in our common world, and must be so
judged. Design is thus a completely social act: part of the social
texture.

Over the last years of his life, Aicher was thinking and working
around a particular set of themes. Modernist design had developed
on from how it had been earlier in the century, even into the 1950s
and 1960s. It needed to become more organic. Simple geometry and
simple grid-design weren't adequate. Yet there needn't and mustn't
be any relapse into irrationalism or neoclassicism. The latter, espe-

25. The work of most relevance here is his *Typographie* (Berlin: Ernst &
Sohn, 1988), but readers who know Aicher only through this book will
miss the larger frame of his ideas. To grasp that, one needs to see and
read his quite large corpus of later writings. Among them: *Die Welt als
Entwurf*, Berlin: Ernst & Sohn, 1991 [in English as *The world as design*,
1994]; *Schreiben und Wiedersprechen*, Berlin: Gerhard Wolf Janus-Press,
1993.

cially, should still be read as a sign of totalitarianism. Centrally arranged texts set in capital letters fail to show meaning clearly enough. But worse: they are authoritarian. Text set in lowercase letters and with fixed word-spaces (i.e. unjustified) embodies principles of equality and informality. Aicher wanted a republican typography. And, trying to live out these ideas fully, he began to think of the cluster of designers and other workers among whom he lived as belonging to an 'autonomous republic', with aspirations towards self-sufficiency, at Rotis, between the 'Länder' of Bayern and Baden-Württemberg in the south of Germany.[26] An 'Institute for Analogical Studies' was established there. Against the abstraction of digital, analogue was real, material, concrete. To take a familiar instance: the hands on a clock face give a physical analogy for time. We have a model to hang on to and work with. The merely numerical information of a digital device may be much more precise, but it is abstract, elusive, and so less easy to do anything with. It is significant that analogical language is so often bodily ('hand', 'face').

The products of Aicher's philosophy, both typographic and in other areas of design, had an often steely and sleek certainty. If his philosophy had a 'green' dimension, its characteristic colours were black, grey, silver, and dazzling white. Despite his embrace of the organic, he still wanted pages of text to present an even colour: neither between words nor between lines should there be excessive space. The typeface that he designed in the 1980s, called Rotis, was an attempt to exemplify these theories, and it has a rather theoretical and dogmatic air. Pages of text set in Rotis (in any of its variants) according to the doctrine of even colour do not, I think, invite the reader.

Otl Aicher's typography could be compared to the architecture of his friend Norman Foster.[27] Its final products sometimes seem to

---

26. A book, privately published in 1987, gave a picture of the community and its ideas: Hans Hermann Wetcke (ed.), *In Rotis*.

27. Aicher was the designer, with a strong editorial contribution, to a planned series of books (reaching four volumes, the fourth of which was made after his death): Norman Foster/Foster Associates, *Buildings & projects*, Hong Kong: Watermark, from 1989. I reported on the venture in 'The book of Norman', *Blueprint*, no. 51, 1988 (see pp. 199–206 above).

belie the good thoughts that apparently generated them. Immaculate surfaces – as in the forbiddingly white and smooth paper of Aicher's book *Typographie* – have an anti-democratic feeling: they repel dialogue. So too Foster's buildings have tried to embody principles of openness and dialogue (for example, a workplace designed without hierarchy in its plan), while including elements of the monumental (the huge staircase in Foster Associates' London office) or the impenetrable (reflective materials). Yet in a context of unprincipled shoddiness and inane pretentiousness, such quality of finish and clarity of thought have been refreshing. Aicher's work is an example, but one with dogmatic tendencies that need to be contested.

Here one could turn to the work of another typographer and writer, Jost Hochuli. Working in St Gallen, Switzerland, away from the pressures of the metropolitan centres of Basel or Zurich, Hochuli may be cited as someone who has worked through and out of dogma, while maintaining a strongly principled approach. Though formed in Swiss modernist typography, he has been able, as he developed, to let coexist in his work both this approach and the new traditional approaches of (say) the later Jan Tschichold. A mentor of his, Rudolf Hostettler, also of St Gallen, showed the way along this path. More recently some of Hochuli's book-design work has shown a fusion of both tendencies within one piece. This resistance to dogma was articulated by Hochuli in a lecture of 1991 on 'book design as philosophy'.[28] The argument takes as its motto, the first paragraph of Immanuel Kant's essay of 1784, 'An answer to the question: "What is enlightenment"':

> Enlightenment is man's emergence from his self-incurred immaturity. Immaturity is the inability to use one's own understanding without the guidance of another. This immaturity is self-incurred if its cause is not lack of understanding, but lack of resolution and courage to use it without the guidance of

28. Jost Hochuli, *Buchgestaltung als Denkschule*, Stuttgart: Edition Typografie, 1991. This text was published later in English translation within the book by Hochuli and myself: *Designing books* (Hyphen Press, 1996); in German as *Bücher machen* (St Gallen: VGS Verlagsgemeinschaft, 1996).

another. The motto of enlightenment is therefore: *Sapere aude!*
Have courage to use your own understanding![29]

This critical spirit distinguishes the work of numbers of typographers who have worked free of the ideological polarities that
were present before the 1970s and the onset of postmodernism in
design.[30] In their work, 'principle' tends to mean attention to meaning and to the details of configuration, to production technique and
materials. Thus, as well as producing a stream of exemplary work,
Hochuli has written illuminatingly on 'detail in typography'.[31] Here
is a place of more intelligent, less assuming resistance to the 'current nonsense' against which Otl Aicher inveighed – but against
which he could only finally erect a style.[32] The style-free or style-
indifferent work of these anti-dogmatic but principled typographers
seems to represent, in a microcosm, the spirit of enlightenment:
appropriate means, chosen consciously, without regard to the prevailing spirit.

Talking in public

There is a paradox of typography. While printing is a prime means
of enlightenment and demystification, discussion of it has tended
to be the preserve of specialists. Books about typography are often

29. Hochuli, *Designing books* (1996), p. 11. The quotation here is given
in H. B. Nisbet's translation from: Hans Reiss, *Kant: political writings*,
2nd edn, Cambridge: Cambridge University Press, 1991, p. 54.
30. I attempted to make a small gathering of such work in 'More light!',
Quarter Point, no. 3, 1993, pp. 4–6. This appeared in a short-lived publicity magazine of Monotype Typography, hampered by the usual constraints of such a context. Among the designers whose work was shown
were George Mackie, Jost Hochuli, Karel Martens, Jack Stauffacher, and
Jerry Cinamon. The exercise suggested that one could make a substantial anthology along these lines: though the argument against reproduction might forbid it.
31. Jost Hochuli, *Detail in typography*, Wilmington: Compugraphic,
1987. See also his *Designing books*, Wilmington: Agfa Compugraphic,
1990; material from which was resumed in Hochuli & Kinross, *Designing books* (Hyphen Press, 1996).
32. Jost Hochuli suggests this in some severe remarks on Aicher's
Typographie, in *Designing books* (1996), p. 27.

made to be ostentatious specimens of the art of printing: few copies sold at high prices. The contradiction here becomes more acute the more that use of the means of typography is dispersed into the hands of lay users. Office secretaries can now take decisions about letterspacing, hyphenation procedures, and much else, in the word-processing and desktop-publishing programs that they use. Meanwhile the typography club members talk among themselves. The 'art of fine printing' aura of typography seems only to become reinforced in public perception.

Could typography be a topic of regular and intelligent discussion in newspapers? The typographer Erik Spiekermann set off this hare in his book *Rhyme & reason*, in which he complained that one could never read discussion of typography there.[33] If music, architecture, cookery and gardening have critics and columnists, then why not typography? It is a more fundamental topic than much that is discussed in public places. But it is only when newspapers change their design that one sees any discussion of typography in their pages. Certainly in Britain these redesigns are usually followed by surprisingly passionate letters to the editor, with comments from lay-people about typefaces, column widths, treatment of pictures, and so on. This phenomenon suggests that ordinary people do have a latent consciousness of how they process the pages they read. This is especially true of newspapers, with which one may form a close, sometimes demanding attachment. When a paper gets redesigned, it is as if someone has replaced your familiar soft old shirt by a scratchy new one.

In 1992 the *Guardian* newspaper published a surprising review of a book on René Magritte.[34] The writer, David Hillman, was the designer who in 1988 had given that newspaper its new Continental-European face. Hillman's review was almost exclusively devoted to the design of the book. There was some sort of news story here,

33. Erik Spiekermann, *Rhyme & reason: a typographic novel*, Berlin: Berthold, 1987, at pp. 13–15. The argument appeared first in the original German edition: *Ursache & Wirkung: ein typografischer Roman*, Erlangen: Context, 1982, at pp. 13–15.
34. David Hillman, review of: David Sylvester, *Magritte* (Thames & Hudson, 1992), *The Guardian*, 18 June 1992.

because the book's designer, David King, had been notorious in the 1970s for his vigorous, sometimes strident graphic design, often done for sections of the Trotskyite Left in Britain. Now he was entering the quiet fields of book design. Hillman's discussion was disappointingly thin, and it was not followed up.

In 1993 the typographer John Ryder's book *Intimate leaves from a designer's notebook* was published. It has a chapter on 'The typography critic', in which he starts off with a reference to Spiekermann's idea and to the review by Hillman.[35] Ryder seems to want public typography criticism. He writes about the visual editor – that rare person who can spot a missing ligature, but who also reads for content – and suggests that a typography critic should have such abilities. But after the first page of this essay, we leave behind newspapers and are in the world of limited editions, of the scholar-typographers Stanley Morison and Giovanni Mardersteig, and one knows for sure that one has entered the cosy gentleman's club of rarified typography because Ryder refers to these two men just by their initials, set in judiciously spaced small capitals. John Ryder makes this argument for typography criticism in a book that was printed by letterpress in 400 numbered copies, of which 80 are singled out for special quarter-goatskin binding. The 'ordinary' copies are priced at £85, the special ones at £160.

Ryder's book illustrates the blind alley that typography very often finds itself in. Despite his stated dislike of the book as art-object and his commitment to trade editions, in this instance at least John Ryder condemns himself to the immobility of the deep padded club armchair. But Spiekermann's book suffers another kind of self-limitation. It was first published by a consortium of typesetting houses, then further editions were published by the manufacturing company Berthold. It was not for sale through the book trade. Although *Rhyme & reason* has the aim of explaining principles and subtleties of typography in ordinary language, and with plentiful visual analogies, it may be doomed to stay in the design studio. The form of the book – it is very consciously a nice little object – does not help its argument.

35. John Ryder, *Intimate leaves from a designer's notebook*, Newtown, Powys: Gwasg Gregynog, 1993.

These are stray episodes in a frustrated discussion. Perhaps, on one view, typography needs or deserves to remain a minority pursuit, with correspondingly restricted discussion. It may indeed be like 'chess and other specialist subjects'.[36] Yet it has not attained even the recognized minority status of chess. It is at once entirely widespread in its effects and hidden in its public acknowledgement.

Common sense

The argument made here is that we read in common. Texts become meeting places, grounds for open discussion between people. This line of thought springs from the European Enlightenment, and from the practices and institutions that began to realize these ideals. In his first book Jürgen Habermas described the 'public sphere' – an arena in which the life of a society was openly and freely discussed – as it took shape in Europe through the eighteenth century and in its development into the age of mass communication.[37] There is some risk of building myths about the 'age of Enlightenment', and about the fluid communication that went on in the salons of Paris and coffee houses of London, in the scientific societies, and in the pages of encyclopaedias and of journals of general interest. But one can hold on to certain core Enlightenment ideals without needing to believe in any golden age of the eighteenth century. Or perhaps now one has to put this more minimally: it is still possible to hold beliefs; not everything can be entirely explained as a function of power and self-interest, although there is certainly a lot of that about; absolute relativism is not just terminal – it leads on to absolute cynicism – but is also logically incoherent. The theorists who accept or even advocate a state of complete relativism cannot account for their own position. The out-and-out relativists say 'anything can be said and we can have no grounds for criticism: everything is of equal validity, equal undecidability'. But in saying that they use the use the voice and the tone of reason (it may well be a salaried teacher speaking). They use an instrument

36. This was suggested to me by Michael McNay, arts editor of *The Guardian*, in a letter (4 February 1993), after I had raised the idea of that paper publishing typography criticism.
37. Jürgen Habermas, *The structural transformation of the public sphere*, Polity Press, 1989 [original German-language edition, 1962].

they profess to deny.[38] And, if the idea of the impossibility of common agreement is true, why should we bother to listen to the person who proclaims it? Why should they expect us to respond? Why speak or publish?

Two broad and related ideas live on in the continuing stream of thought and action that flows from the Enlightenment. The first is the critical approach. Kant's simple formulation 'have the courage to use your own understanding' remains. It remains true both in respect of current fashions (that 'meaning is undecidable'), and of now less fashionable beliefs (that meanings can be known and shared). The critical approach questions: and it questions its own assumptions as part of a refusal to take anything unquestioned. There are no beliefs – not of a golden age, nor of transparent communication – that can stand free of these questions and doubts. In this way the critical approach will always live on, never quite satisfied. It is coloured by dissatisfaction, even melancholy: it lives in the contexts in which it finds itself, but questions the terms of those contexts, and is often unhappy with them.

The second still vital part of this stream is the principle of dialogue. Self-interest, coercion, and domination exist, often very powerfully and suffocatingly. But dialogue and free exchange can happen. And there is the possibility of a mutual sharing of views and information, between people. Freely-arrived-at agreement is possible. As illustration, one thinks most readily of small groups of people in discussion. Musical performances in small ensembles can provide vivid metaphors of the dialogue principle. But agreement-through-dialogue can happen in the larger world: democratic constitutions, political treaties and accords are evidence of this – often fragile, of course.

These two connected principles of criticism and dialogue underpin what is argued here for typography. The reproduction and distribution of text is part of the life-blood of social-critical

---

38. Brian Vickers (*Appropriating Shakespeare*, p. 48) traces this contradiction to the poststructuralist muddling of Saussure's 'langue' and 'parole'. The second category (individual acts of speech) is blocked from view by the assumption that 'la langue' (the system of a language) is all that language is.

dialogue. The argument for openness and clarity in typography is made, most importantly, for this reason. It is not a question of 'legibility' or of mere appearance, whether 'traditional', 'classical', 'modern', 'classic modern', or anything else. It is now clear that 'modern' in style came to provide – despite the best professions of the democratic impulse of modernism – an immaculate surface that leaves no room for dialogue.[39] There has to be something – in the text or the image, in the way these are configured and made material – that allows a place for dialogue: a foothold, or perhaps an 'eye-and-hand-hold', in which the reader can grip, and then have a place from which to respond. This refers to the way in which the words are written, to the nature of the images, but also to the qualities of their material embodiment: disposition of information, the visual forms in which it is configured, texture and colour of substrate, the bulk and weight of the object, the way it flexes in your hands, and so on – into innumerable small considerations.

This material dimension of typography, received by the reader through the senses of the body, reminds us of a special meaning of the term common sense.[40] This is the 'common sense' of the human body, which joins together the five distinct faculties by which we gain knowledge of the world. The bodily dimension provides a set of limits and of physical possibilities, which are too little observed in the discussion of reading or viewing. Pages can become simply too big for comfort – or too shiny, too noisy, or even too disconcerting in

39. This thought lies behind an essay I wrote in criticism of notions of value-free design: 'The rhetoric of neutrality', *Design Issues*, vol. 2, no. 2, 1985, pp. 18–30. Later I tried to discuss typography that embodies the critical and dialogic values. See, for example, an article on the work of Karel Martens in: *Eye*, no. 11, 1993 (pp. 87–93 above).

40. The argument here is directly inspired by material published in *Edinburgh Review*, since its new direction under the editorships of Peter Kravitz and Murdo Macdonald, from no. 67/8 in 1985. See especially the Scottish philosophy section in no. 74 (1986), and an essay by Richard Gunn, 'Scottish common sense philosophy', in no. 87, 1991–2, pp. 117–40. Behind these ideas stand the work of George Davie, especially in his book on 'Scotland and her universities in the nineteenth century' with the marvellous title *The democratic intellect* (Edinburgh: Edinburgh University Press, 1961).

their smell. Taste, in the mouth, is perhaps the one sense that is not deployed in our processing of text and images.

The senses of the body have been spoken of as forming a 're-public': a set of equal and distinct members, joined in some federation. It is a little world or microcosm, which only finds its identity in dialogue with others. And here is the other important meaning of 'common sense', already delineated in this essay. Both these understandings – fresh and active – are quite different from the dull 'common sense' that is now deployed as an inhibition, often from the old against the young. So this second idea of 'common sense' can be expanded as follows. We find ourselves through others. Reading in common can be one important path to knowing ourselves, as a human community. The term republic can be applied here too as describing a society in which the principle of critical-dialogue is fully realized.

This way of thinking about the topic of typography lets in some air to often stale debates. Recently, in typography as in the larger culture, there have been discussions over 'high' and 'low'.[41] Are some things higher in cultural value than others? Is John Keats better than Bob Dylan? The same concern has fuelled discussion about the question of a 'canon' of products.[42] Is there a restricted set of material, to which discussion, reproduction and teaching is confined? What then are the biases of this canon? Too many male designers? Too many good self-promoters? Or just too many lazy editors who take over what has already been reproduced? But there is a way through these dilemmas.

In typography, even more clearly than in the 'fine arts', such as music or literature, it becomes clear that there is just one culture and that it is common and ordinary. There are terms of judgement, as suggested throughout this essay, but they are not the received

41. See: Ellen Lupton, 'High and low', *Eye*, no. 7, 1992, pp. 72–7.
42. See: Martha Scotford, 'Is there a canon of graphic design history?', *AIGA Journal of Graphic Design*, vol. 9, no. 2, 1991, pp. 3–5, 13. Scotford reports on her analysis of five books of graphic design history, suggesting that there is some latent 'canon' in what is reproduced. She argues that, if this is a canon, then it needs to be broadened; and that there are more realistic ways of understanding design than to ape the methods of art history.

ones of good or bad design, of beauty or ugliness, of modern or traditional, of innovative or repetitive. Each thing has to be thought out freshly, for itself, in its context. The criteria may be human, physical, social, as well as formal. We will surprise ourselves.

Ordinary people

If typographic design is (should be) a process in which the designer brings critical thought into play, where does the material that is the object of criticism come from? Where is the raw stuff? It is there as content, information, ideas, desires, necessities – which are given form. Typically and traditionally, this raw stuff comes from a client. The designer works in dialogue with that client. And if in this essay the 'critical' component of the process has received emphasis, it is by way of compensation. The figure of the designer has been bathed in an aura carried from the domain of art. The designer is the person who visibly impresses their stamp on the content, conjuring something unique out of what may otherwise be unremarkable. The rhetoric surrounding design is still of 'individuality', 'personality', 'expression', 'creativity'.

In a small, telling instance of this attitude, the designer Jeffery Keedy recently asked in a published letter 'is Piet Zwart considered a good designer because his work was about floor tiles?'[43] (He was referring to the advertisements that Zwart designed in the early 1920s for Vickers House.) Keedy's suggestion is that we can enjoy and admire Zwart's work as 'design' (form) without needing to be interested in its often basely material content. He implies that Zwart was working *despite* his banal content of floor tiles. But Zwart, strongly egalitarian and materialist, worked happily with manufacturers of industrial goods. The spirit of Dutch modernist graphic design of that time – as in their term 'nieuwe zakelijkheid' (new sobriety) – was a celebration of the factual, the everyday, the normative, with a shrug of indifference (or something stronger) at the art-values of unqualified personal expression. In the same letter, Keedy wrote that 'if designers ... pursued only "messages that matter to the reader", we would all need a second job'. In response one can remark that 'messages that matter' – such as floor tiles, indeed – are plenti-

43. Jeffery Keedy, letter in *Eye*, no. 10, 1993, p. 10.

ful. It might take a long time before these are exhausted, and when we arrive at a state in which designers are left only with messages that don't matter, but which allow them an open field in which to exercise their talents.

It is worth trying a brutally simple attitude to design: judge it by its content. This certainly helps to clear the mind – and maybe the shops and museums too. But, having announced the simple criterion of 'content', one then has to explore the ways in which content is mediated by, is inseparable from, the forms in which we find it. So – here I might agree with Jeffery Keedy – we can't merely praise something for good content without considering how that is embodied. We can't know content free of form. But now at least we are not trying to value the embodiment without reference to content. And I would argue that the nature of these embodiments depends on what they are embodying. If, perversely, form runs free of content, that is an escape, but an escape from a relation that sets the terms of the job. All of this can be understood by looking at particular instances and by stepping back to examine the processes by which these things come into the world. The manifestations of design arise out of sets of relationships: of client with designer, of designer with producer, of user with client, and so on. Whatever results can be understood when all these processes, interactions, contexts and histories are understood.

If we no longer want designers to be surrogate artists spreading their touch all over, how can they fit into these processes? In reaction to the supremacy of the designer and, in particular, in reaction to modernist good taste, the attempt has been made at a 'vernacular' in graphic design: a grasping for the 'low' as a rebuff to the 'high'.[44] At its most self-conscious this has involved theoretically sophisticated people speaking graphically – say in an art-exhibition catalogue – to other theoretically sophisticated people, but in the 'graphic language' of the downtown supermarket or the diner (it is

44. Ellen Lupton's article 'High and low' (*Eye*, no. 7, 1992, pp. 72–7) is a critical discussion of some of these issues. See also the publication which accompanied an exhibition that Lupton initiated: Barbara Glauber (ed.), *Lift and separate: graphic design and the quote unquote vernacular*, New York: Cooper Union / Princeton Architectural Press, 1993.

primarily a North American phenomenon). In other, more straight-forward versions of graphic vernacular, one finds high-powered metropolitan design groups devising things – typically in packaging – that pass easily but with just enough differentiation in their desired habitat: say a shop in free-market Poland. All this follows from a failure of modernism, which had dreams of becoming the new vernacular, but which seems now to have given us merely a designer-culture. The public libraries and health centres of the 1930s and 1940s fall into disrepair, are perhaps renovated and regarded as monuments, while smart white restaurants and unlimited matt-black consumer items displace them in our perception of what modernism was or is.

In typography, at least, the game is all but up. The means of design and production are becoming very widely accessible. Designers are losing the place that they had staked out for themselves in the twentieth century, as intermediaries between clients and printers. The obscurantism of deconstructionist design can be understood in this light, as an attempt to hang on to disappearing ground. 'Here are things so difficult and elaborate that only we designers can provide them. Reading is such a complex and indeterminate process that you need us (to make it complex and indeterminate).' And then, in another perhaps opposite move against the threat of redundancy, the fad for vernacular bad taste may be an attempt by designers to survive by blending into the landscape, chameleon-like. These strategies must be doomed – by their own bad faith, if not by public indifference to them.

Typographic and graphic designers do have skills and knowledge that could be useful. These things can find a place in the processes of creation and publication, not as an unveiling of mysteries, but as an open sharing. The calling of our designer bluffs by cheap computing technology may be embarrassing and uncomfortable, but to get rid of illusions is liberating. Then we can see where we are, attend to real issues.

As some evidence for the nutshell summary offered in the first paragraph of this essay, I should cite these ideas in the words of protagonists and apologists of deconstruction within graphic design and typography. For example:

> This work has an intellectual rigour that demands effort of the audience, but also rewards the audience with content and participation. The audience must make individual interpretations in graphic design that 'decenter' the message. Designs provoke a range of interpretations, based on Deconstruction's contention that meaning is inherently unstable and that objectivity is an impossibility, a myth promulgated to control the audience. Graphic designers have become dissatisfied with the obedient delivery of the client's message. Many are taking the role of interpreter, a giant step beyond the problem-solving tradition. By authoring additional content and a self-conscious critique of the message, they are adopting roles associated with both art and literature.[45]

The argument here can be interpreted as follows. Readers are to be put to work in some postgraduate deconstructionist camp, with the promise of a reward at the end of their labour. They 'must' make individual interpretations: as if this did not happen every time a human being perceives the world. Then comes the polarization into either/or extremes. 'Objectivity' is set up as one hard extreme of 'control'; unstable meaning is its opposite. Nothing in between is allowed. So 'objectivity' is then knocked down ('an impossibility, a myth') and replaced. By what? By the designer! Far from being dead, as Roland Barthes and Michel Foucault supposed, the author/designer now becomes a dominating presence. A second apologist adds flesh to this schema:

45. Katherine McCoy, 'American graphic design expression', *Design Quarterly*, no. 148, 1990, at p. 16.

Type design in the digital era is quirky, personal and unreservedly subjective. The authoritarian voices of modernist typography, which seem to permit only a single authorised reading, are rejected as too corporate, inflexible and limiting, as though typographic diversity itself might somehow re-enfranchise its readers. 'I think there are a lot of voices that have not been heard typographically', says Californian type designer Jeffery Keedy. 'Whenever I start a new job and try to pick a typeface, none of the typefaces give me the voice that I need. They just don't relate to my experiences in my life. They're about somebody else's experiences, which don't belong to me.' Another American type designer, Barry Deck, speaks of trading in the 'myth of the transparency of typographical form for a more realistic attitude toward form, acknowledging that form carries meaning'. The aim is to promote multiple rather than fixed readings, to provoke the reader into becoming an active participant in the construction of the message.[46]

Our reporter here rehearses the idea that 'only a single authorised reading' is permitted by an authoritarian modernism. He entertains (sceptically) the possibility that formal diversity 'might somehow' give power to readers. Then the voice of the designer comes in: 'I ... me ... I ... my ... my ... me.' Another designer sets up another absolute ('transparency'), calls it a 'myth', and thus knocks his straw opponent down in two swift moves. This 'unreserved subjectivity' is all for the good: it is for the multiple against the fixed, it is for 'active participation'. But consider the most banal of reading experiences, say that of reading an airline timetable or a listings magazine. What could be more active and multiple than this process? And what fixes unreserved subjectivity more objectively and unchangeably than ink on paper? Now, some new twists to the thesis:

> Legible is easy to read. If it is easy to read it bypasses the visual potential of the message. People prefer the comfort of legibility.

46. Rick Poynor, 'Introduction', in: Rick Poynor & Edward Booth-Clibborn (ed.), *Typography now: the next wave*, Internos Books, 1991, at pp. 8–9.

The passive, comfortable approach and negative visual inter-relationships of type and image were firmly rooted by Stanley Morison in the perpetuation of legibility and the cultural back-water of left to right reading in the 1930s. Reinforced at that time by many, like Bartram: 'Legibility is, of course, the sine qua non of a good type. It should go without saying. It is as elementary and vital a consideration as that the wheels of a car should be round or that a house should have a door.' Well, sadly this still applies today, so that speedreading is seen as a desirable skill; ignoring the visual communication of type and image.[47]

The straw man of 'legibility' is set up, put into stiff 1930s clothing, and pilloried with deadly insults: 'passive', 'comfortable', 'negative'. Even 'left to right reading' comes in for blame: is this another attack on Western metaphysics? In conventional or traditional typography, reading is reduced – accelerated – into 'speedreading'. What is so bad in all this, our radical critic proclaims, is that 'the visual communication of type and image' is ignored. All this fire-breathing polemic seems to lead merely to a plea for graphic designers to be allowed to make their presence known.

You may object that, with these three quotations, I too am mere-

47. Bridget Wilkins, 'Type and image', *Octavo*, no. 7, [1990, pages un-numbered]. The 'Bartram' quoted here is in fact Anthony Bertram, mi-nor 'man of letters' in between-the-wars Britain and occasional prop-agandist for its design movement. The paragraph from which the quotation is taken suggests that the observations I make here about the public obscurity of typography are nothing new. 'The lack of public interest in typography is really astonishing. It is an art with which every-one of us is in daily contact, even if it is only in reading the newspapers or an income-tax form, and yet very few of us are even conscious that it is an art. There is, of course, a fairly large public that expects print to be legible, but they do not go beyond that.' (Anthony Bertram, *Design*, Harmondsworth: Penguin Books, 1938, p. 105.)

As published in *Octavo*, the stew of ideas in Wilkins's text was given appropriate form through a maze-like configuration that certainly gave off an air of 'visual communication'. The next issue of the magazine took further the logic of the maze, or the haystack: a CD, scripted by Wilkins, about multi-media and the future of communication.

ly attacking straw statements, selected only to be knocked down. But I hardly had to select them. They are from the rash of articles published in magazines and anthologies, supporting and explaining the 'new', the 'now', the 'next', and the 'post', in typography and graphic design. And I have not found any more convincing statements than these. So far counter-arguments have tended to occur only in private and public conversation, and to be at the level of 'this new wave stuff is so ugly and polluting'. The deeper arguments about social effects, about the place of the designer, have rarely been made. Paul Stiff has put forward serious objections to this theorizing: that it is another strategy to promote the romance of the designer.[48] But replies have not been forthcoming. An advantage of extreme relativism is its avoidance of the need to argue.

48. In *Eye*, no. 11, 1993, pp. 4–5.

This was published in 1994 as a pamphlet, to accompany a reprint of my book *Modern typography*. A note of acknowledgement explained the sources: 'Some of the material published here was first written for lectures: to the British Computer Society Electronic Publishing Specialist Group conference, Glasgow (September 1993); to the Dr P.A. Tiele-Stichting at the Universiteitsbibliotheek, Amsterdam (November 1993); and for seminars in February 1994 at the Jan van Eyck Akademie, Maastricht, and to the Victoria & Albert Museum / Royal College of Art MA course, London. I am glad now to find the opportunity to thank the people who invited me to these occasions and those who contributed to the discussions that followed. Thanks too to the fellows who read this text in draft and helped it to grow.' The piece was dedicated to Karel Martens; it still is.

In preparing the text for publication in this collection I have left it unchanged, apart from small and mainly bibliographical updatings in the notes.

Acknowledgements & sources

For prompting, commissioning, and publishing these texts, thanks to the following organizations and people: the Bauhaus Archiv (Berlin), the Design Council (London); the organizers of the 'Art in Exile' exhibition (Camden Arts Centre, London, 1986) and of the conferences 'Design & Reconstruction in Postwar Europe' (Victoria & Albert Museum, London, 1994) and 'Ma(r)king the Text' (Trinity College, Cambridge, 1998); and the editors of the journals *Baseline*, *Blueprint*, *Crafts*, *Designer*, *Design History Society Newsletter*, *Design Review*, *Eye*, *The Guardian*, *The Indexer*, *Information Design Journal*, *London Review of Books*, *Octavo*, *Printing Historical Society Bulletin*, *Pts*, *Solidarity*, *The Times Literary Supplement*.

Where they are known, photographers have been credited in captions to pictures. Other sources are as follows, by the page numbers of this book:

58: *Architectural Association Journal*, no. 873, 1963
67: *The Guardian*, 30 August 1994
96: MetaDesign booklet, 1988
115: *The Guardian*, 29 March 1988

Index

This is primarily an index of proper names. Some key topics have been indexed too, where possible grouped into clusters (under 'graphic design' or 'printing', for example). Concentrated discussions are shown with bold page numbers.

Abercrombie, M. L. J, 305
Abrams, Janet, 13
Académie des Sciences, Paris, 351–2
Adams, George, [Georg Teltscher], 60
Adieu aesthetica & mooie pagina's!, exhibition (The Hague, 1995) and book, **207–10**
Adorno, Theodor W, 184–5, 186–7, 190, 196, 287, 289, 300, 306, 307
   Minima moralia, **184–5**, 287
   Notes to literature, 186–7
Adprint, book packagers, London, 22, 60, 305
advertising, 329, 332
Aicher, Otl, 199, 200–6, 354–6, 347
   Schreiben und Wiedersprechen, 354n
   Typographie, 354n, 356, 357n
   Welt als Entwurf, Die, 354n
Aicher-Scholl, Inge, 201
Albatross, publishers, Paris, 179
Albers, Josef, 237, 252, 254, 255
Aldridge, Alan, 178
Aldus Manutius, 118
Allford, David, 66
Alliance Graphique Internationale (AGI), 63
Allner, Heinz Walter, 259n
Alloway, Lawrence, 173
Althusser, Louis, 159, 321
American Institute of Graphic Arts (AIGA), New York, 207
Amsterdam: Universiteitsbibliotheek, 209, 371n; see also: Stedelijk Museum

anarchism, 68, 171, 172, 197, 201, 280, 282, 301
Anarchy, magazine, London, 170
Andere Bibliothek, Die, 190–9
Anderson, Benedict, *Imagined communities*, 345–6
Anderson, Colin, 153; see also: Ministry of Transport
Anderson, Perry, 10, 34, 270n, 306–7, 320n, 322, 340n, 353n
   English questions, 353n
Anhaltische Rundschau, 252n
Apple Macintosh, 14, 86n, 93n, 96; see also: typesetting technics
Arbeiter-Ilustrierte Zeitung, magazine, Berlin/Prague, 304
Architects' Year Book, annual, London, 271
Architectural Design, magazine, London, 59
Architectural Review, magazine, London, 164, 267
Arena, magazine, London, 99
Arjan, *Vítězný život*, 18–19
Arnhem: Hogeschool voor de Kunsten, 88, 89, 104, 106
Arntz, Gerd, 53, 258
'Art in Exile' exhibition (1986), London, 65, 302n, 309
Artists International Association (AIA), 63, 64, 65
Arts & Crafts movement, 69, 148, 187, 207, 255, 282

Arts Council of Great Britain, *Paintings, drawings, and sculpture*, exhibition catalogue, 30

Ascherson, Neal, 286n, 353n
    Games with shadows, 353n

Association of Building Technicians, *Homes for the people*, 24

Attwater, Donald, *A cell of good living*, 167

Aubrey, John, 191

Austen, Jane, 217

Aynsley, Jeremy, 179, 180

Bach, Johann Sebastian, 'St Matthew Passion', 347–8

Baines, Phil, 86

Baker, Steve, 328–9, 332

Balding & Mansell, printers, London & Wisbech, 33, 79

Barker, Paul, 40

Barnett, Anthony, 353n

Barthes, Roland, 319, 322, 324, 328–9, 337, 367
    Mythologies, 328

Bartlett School of Architecture, London, 56

Bartram, Alan, *The English lettering tradition*, 164–6

Basel:
    Allgemeine Gewerbeschule, 73
    Gewerbemuseum, *Planvolles Werben*, 20

Baseline, magazine, London, 129n, 245n

Baskerville, John, 118

Baskin, Wade, 336n

Baudrillard, Jean, 90

Bauer typefoundry, Frankfurt a.M, 255

Bauhaus, Weimer/Dessau/Berlin, 69, 137, 140, 148, 173, 174, 235, 236, 237, 244, 246–63, 293

Baxandall, Michael, 347n

Bayer, Herbert, 137, 139, 237, 239, 247, 252, 254, 255, 256, 260, 261n, 265

Beck, Henry C, 80, 160, 332

Becker, Thomas, 192

Beese, Lotte, 259n

Beethoven, Ludwig van, 70

Bell, Alexander Graham, 69

Belloc, Hilaire, 167

Benjamin, Walter, 185, 287, 289, 350n
    'Über den Begriff der Geschichte', 287, 289

Benn's Sixpenny Library, 179

Benton, Linn Boyd, 144, 235

Benton, Tim, 11

Berger, John, 85, 99, 173
    G, 85
    Seventh man, The, 85
    Ways of seeing, 85

Berlin: Free University, 95

Berlin, Isaiah, 306

Berliner Verkehrs-Betriebe (BVB), 47, 48, 98

Berman, Russell, 338n

Berneri, Marie Louise, 68

Bertelsmann, publishing conglomerate, 199n

Berthold, composing machine & typeface manufacturers, Berlin, 94, 96, 98, 255, 359; see also: typesetting technics

Bertram, Anthony, 369

Best, Alastair, 12

'Best Verzorgde Boeken' competition & exhibition, 211, 212

Bierma, Wigger, 93n

Bildungsverband der Deutschen Buchdrucker, 137, 253

Bill, Max, 9, 175, 256, 282, 283, 284, 291–4, 296, 298, 300
    'Über Typografie', 283n, 290, 291–3, 298

Birdsall, Derek, 33, 34, 40, 58, 79, 89

Blackburn, Robin, 34

Blake, John E, 79

Blake, William, 80, 170
    The marriage of heaven and hell, 207

Bloch, Ernst, 185, 307
Block, journal, London, 321
Blokland, Erik van, **106-9**
Bloomingdale's, department store, New York, 100
Blueprint, magazine, London, 12-14, 63, 65n, 77n, 96, 157n, 169n, 176n, 206n
Bocking, Geoffrey, 68, 279
Boekraad, Hugues, 88, 90, 92
Bohm-Duchen, Monica, 309n
Boijmans van Beuningen Museum, Rotterdam, 92
Bolter, Jay David, *Writing space*, 349n
Bonsiepe, Gui, 323-5
book design, see: typographic design
Book Trust, London, 212; see also: National Book League
Braun, household goods manufacturers, 200
Brecht, Bertolt, 42, 139, 306, 307, 350n
Me-ti, 42-3
Breuer, Marcel, 69, 306
Bridges, Robert, 233
Bringhurst, Robert, 342n
Bristol: West of England College of Art and Design, 70, 83, 173
'Britain Can Make It' exhibition (1946), London, 270
'British Book Design & Production' competition & exhibition, 211-2, 213n
British Federation of Master Printers, London, 212
British Film Institute, London, 85
British Leyland, 62
British Rail, 152
British Standards Institution, London, 308
British Telecom, 105
Brodsky, Joseph, 86
Brody, Neville, 45, 86, **99-100**
Browne, Thomas, 196
Brusse, Wim, 296

Buber, Martin, 71, 172
Building Centre, London, 308
Bulthaup, kitchen manufacturers, 200
Bund Deutscher Grafik-Designer, 94
Burchartz, Max, 256
Burnhill, Peter, 226n
Buruma, Ian, 191

Calvert, Margaret, 65, 66, 153
Calvino, Italo, *If on a winter's night a traveller*, 328
Cambridge University Press, 'Guides for authors and printers' series, 215
Campaign for Nuclear Disarmament (CND), 64, 79
Campbell, Ken, 80, 85
Broken rules and double crosses, 80
Campbell, Peter, 34
Carnap, Rudolf, 55
Carter, Harry, 118, 128, 274
Carter, Matthew, 104
Carter, Sebastian, 208
Twentieth century type designers, **143-9**
Casablanca, magazine, London, 15
Casement, Roger, 196
Cassandre [Adolphe Mouron], 76
Casson, Hugh, 70, 156
Central Lettering Record, London, 166
Central Office of Information, Great Britain, 65; see also: Ministry of Information
Central School of Arts & Crafts [Central School of Art & Design], London, 58-9, 79, 80, 82, 166, 279, 282
Challis, Clive, 85
Chapman, R.W, 217
Charlemagne, 165
Charles, Prince of Wales, 155
Charter 88, 353n

Chartered Society of Designers, 185n; see also: Society of Industrial Arts and Designers

Chelsea School of Art, London, 57, 65

Chesterton, G. K, 167

Christensen, Søren Møller, 199n

Cinamon, Gerald, 89, 179, 185, 357n

Circle (ed. J. L. Martin, Ben Nicholson & Naum Gabo), 265–6

Císařová, Hana, 182

City Limits, magazine, London, 45, 99

Coates, Stephen, 13

Cole, G.D.H, 305

Coleridge, Samuel Taylor, 172

Collins, publishers, London, 194

Collins, F. Howard, *Authors' and printers' dictionary*, 214–7

Coltrane, John, *A love supreme*, 9n

Commercial Art, magazine, London, 265

Communist Party of Great Britain, 279

Conrad, Joseph, 9, 196

Conran, Shirley, 177

Construction School, see: Bristol

Constructivism, 182

Contemporary designers (ed. Ann Lee Morgan), 11

corporate identity, 160

Corriere della Sera, newspaper, Milan, 151

Council of Industrial Design, see: Design Council

Cowper, William, 170

CPNB (Stichting Collectieve Propaganda van het Nederlandse Boek), 211

Crafts, magazine, London, 166n

Crafts Council, London, 86, 166n

Cranbrook Academy of Art, Bloomfield Hills, 15

Crooke, Pat, 59

Crosby, Theo, 57, 59

Crouwel, Wim, 92, 93n, 101, 105, 243, 244

Curwen Press, printers, London, 146

cultural studies, 321–2, 332

Dada, 299

Daily Telegraph, The, newspaper, London, 151

Daulby, George, 82

Davie, George, *The democratic intellect*, 362n

Davis, Miles, *Kind of blue*, 9n

Davison, Ronald, *Social security*, 22–3

Deberny & Peignot, Paris, 73, 74

Deck, Barry, 368

deconstruction, 104, 319, 332–3, 335–41, 344–5, 349–50, 366, 367–70

Deighton, Len, 36

Department of Trade & Industry, Britain, 80

Department of Transport, see: Ministry of Transport

design, theory of, 70, 158–60, 185, 313–27, 364–6

Design, magazine, London, 79, 154, 155

'Design & Reconstruction in Postwar Europe' conference (1994), London, 301n

Design Business Association, 157

Design Council (Council of Industrial Design), London, 79, 155

Designer, magazine, London, 11, 12, 63, 80, 151n, 160n, 163n, 273n

Designers in Britain, annual, London, 269, 271, 272, 273

Designer's Journal, magazine, London, 13

Design History Society, 11, 285n; see also: *Journal of Design History*

Design History Society Newsletter, 11, 181n, 183n

Design Research Unit, London, 65, 270

Design Review, magazine, London, 185n

Deutsche Bundespost (DB), 97

Deutsche Industrie-Normen (DIN), 235, 236, 251, 253, 259, 308–9

Deutscher Normenausschuß, 251, 308–9

Deutscher Werkbund, 94

Dickens, Charles, 98

Didot, François-Ambroise, 352

Directions, newsletter, Harpenden, 67n

Doesburg, Theo van, 243, 250

Dorland, advertising agency, Berlin, 260

Double Crown Club, London, 146, 147, 148

Doubleday, Henry, 67

Downes, Brian, 34

Drexler, Arthur, 200

Dreyfus, John, *The work of Jan van Krimpen*, 208

Drummond, Lindsay, publishers, London, 26, 304

Dutton, Norbert, 271

Dwiggins, W. A, 162

Eagleton, Terry, 320n, 322, 324

Edinburgh Review, journal, Edinburgh, 334n, 362n

editing of texts, 10, 132–3, 143, 204, 213, 215, 218–30 passim

Editions Poetry London, publishers, London, 298

Ehses, Hanno, 325

Eichborn Verlag, publishers, Frankfurt a.M, 191, 194

Einaudi, publishers, Turin, 181

Elek, Paul, publishers, London, 24

Eisenstein, Elizabeth, *The printing press as an agent of change*, 342–3

emigrés, 53–4, 56, 60, 65, 270, 297, 302–9

Emigre, magazine, Berkeley/Sacramento, 15, 106

Empson, William, 10, 12

Encyclopédie, 352

enlightenment, 350–4, 356–7, 361

Enschedé, Joh. & Zonen, typefounders and printers, Haarlem, 207, 208–9

Enschedé Font Foundry, The, typeface publishers & distributors, Zaltbommel, 210

ENSIE (Eerste Nederlandse Systematisch Ingerichte Encyclopaedie), 209

Enzensberger, Hans Magnus, 139, 190, 191, 196, 197

Epps, Timothy, 243, 244

ERCO, lighting manufacturers, 200

Esselte Letraset, typeface manufacturers, London, 129n, 245n

Esterson, Simon, 12–13

European Computer Manufacturers Association, 242

Evans, Christopher, 243, 244

Excoffon, Roger, 76

exile, 173, 184, 304, 309

Eye, magazine, London, 14–15, 61n, 83, 93n, 106n, 110n

Eyton, Audrey, 177

Faassen, Sjoerd van, 207, 208

Faber & Faber, publishers, London, 84, 278

Face, The, magazine, London, 99

Facetti, Germano, 34, 36, 40, 59, 181, 308

Farr, Michael, 79

Febvre, Lucien, & Henri-Jean Martin, *The coming of the book*, 342n

Ferrier, James Frederick, 334

Festival of Britain exhibition (1951), London, 64, 65, 267

'Fifty Penguin years' exhibition (1985), London, **177–81**

Financial Times, The, newspaper, London, 151

Fior, Robin, 85, 89

Flaxman, John, 57

Fletcher, Alan, 58

Fleuron, The, journal, London, 146, 270n

Foges, Wolfgang, 60, 305

Folio Society, publishers, London, 198

font, 113–15, 120; see also: typefaces

FontShop, typeface publishers & distributors, Berlin, 46, 98n, 102, 107

Foot, Paul, 81

Forbes, Colin, 58

'For Liberty' exhibition (1942), London, 65

Forty, Adrian, *Objects of desire*, **158–60**

Foster, Norman, 62, 97, 199–206, 355, 356
    Buildings and projects, **199–206**, 355n

Foucault, Michel, 367

Fournier, Pierre-Simon, 352

Frampton, Kenneth, 88, 185

Frankfurt Book Fair, 186, 190, 191, 199n, 212

Frankfurt School, 287

Frankfurter Allgemeine Zeitung, newspaper, Frankfurt, 151, 186

Freedom Defence Committee, 171

Freedom Press, publishers & printers, London, 172

Friedl, Friedrich, 253n

From Spitfire to microchip (ed. Nicola Hamilton), 284n

Froshaug, Anthony, 9, 10, 32, 40, 58, 63, 68, 69, 80, 84, 141, 271, 279–84, 285n, 293–4, 296, 297, 298, 299, 301, 308
    'Conspectus' (1951), 279, 281, 299
    'Visual methodology', 283

Froshaug, Anthony (ed. Robin Kinross), 285n, 296n

Frutiger, Adrian, 72–7, 241, 242, 243

Fuller, Peter, 167

Futurism, 299

Gaberbocchus Press, publishers, London, 297

Gabo, Naum, 140

Gallimard, publishers, Paris, 181

Galt Toys, London, 80

Garamond, Claude, 145, 161

Garland, Ken, 38, 58, 78–81, 89, 284n
    Graphics handbook, 38–9
    Word in your eye, A, **78–81**

Gasson, Christopher, *Who owns whom in British publishing*, 188

Gatwick Airport, 66

Gennep, Van, publishers, Amsterdam, 198

George, Dorothy, 177

George, Stefan, 136–7, 235, 250, 251

Gesellschafts- und Wirtschaftsmuseum in Wien, 22, 52, 258; see also: Isotype

Giedion, Sigfried, *Mechanization takes command*, 160

Gill, Eric, 77, 123–4, 125, 148, **167–9**, 282
    Art nonsense, 148
    Autobiography, 168
    Essay on typography, 124, 148, 168, 282

Gill, Ethel Mary, 167

Gissing, George, 191

'Glasgow Style' conference (1993), Glasgow, 371n

Glauber, Barbara, *Lift and separate*, 365n

Glazebrook, Mark, 84

Godwin, Tony, 178

Goethe, Johann Wolfgang, 277, 292

Gonsalves, Ron, 347n

Goodhue, Bertram, 118

Goodwin, Paul, 347n

Goody, Jack, 340–1

Gott, Richard, 177

Goudy, Frederic W, 162

Gould, Glenn, 70

Graatsma, William PARS, 107

Grafische Berufsschule, magazine, Munich, 254

Granada, publishing conglomerate, London, 194

graphic design, 53, 255-6, 303, 305, 307, 316, 319, 329
    Britain, 62, 63, 65, 78-9, 80-1, 81-2, 85, 86n
    Germany, 200
    The Netherlands, 87, 106, 109, 212
    Switzerland, 79, 82, 83, 241, 284, 293, 356
    USA, 79

'The Graphic Language of Neville Brody' exhibition (1988), London, 99-100

Graphic Ring, London, 84-5

Graphische Berufsschule, Munich, 254

Graphis Press, printers, London, 309

Grass, Günter, 139

Gray, Nicolete [née Binyon], 127, 131
    History of lettering, A, 131n, **164-6**
    Lettering on buildings, 164
    Nineteenth-century ornamented types, 165, 267

Greater London Enterprise Board, 159

Greisner, Inken, 96

Greno, Franz, 190, 191, 197, 199n

Greno Verlag, Nördlingen, 190-1

Grimbly, Brian, 10

Grimm, Jakob, 135-6, 235, 251
    Deutsche Grammatik, 134, 135
    Deutsches Wörterbuch (with Wilhelm Grimm), 136

Grimm, Wilhelm, 135, 136, 235

Gropius, Walter, 69, 254, 260, 282, 306

Guardian, The, newspaper, London, 55n, 71n, 151, 177, 306, 358, 360n

Guildford School of Art, 70

Gunn, Richard, 362n

Gutenberg, Johannes, 133, 250

Habermas, Jürgen, 352, 360
    Structural transformation of the public sphere, The, 360

Hague, René, 282

Hague, The: Royal Academy, 107

Hall, Stuart, 305, 338n

Hamish Hamilton, publishers, London, 199

Hanser, Carl, publishers, Munich, 198

Harari, Manya, 192

Harling, Robert, 267

HarperCollins, publishers, London, 194

Harris, Roy, 336n

Harrison, Michael, 60

Harrod, L. M, 230n

Hartley, James, 226n

Hart's rules for compositors and readers, 214, 215, 216, 217n, 220-3

Hartz, Sem, 210

Harvill Press, The, publishers, London, 192-9

Hatton, Brian, 13

Havinden, Ashley, 267

Hazlitt, William, *Complete works*, 219, 220

HDA International, design group, London, 62, 306

Heartfield, John, [Helmut Herzfelde], 26, 60, 304-5, 306

Hecht, Ruth, 11

Heineken Prize for Art, 93n

Henderson, Nigel, 58

Henrion, F. H. K, 25, **62-5**, 270, 306, 307, 309

Henrion Design Associates, London, 62

Henrion, Ludlow & Schmidt, design group, London, 62, 306

Herman Miller, furniture manufacturers, 94

Hewetson, John, 68

Hillman, David, 358-9

Hitler, Adolf, 296

Hitchens, Christopher, 81
HMSO (His Majesty's Stationery Office), 273, 274
Hoch, Ernest [Ernst], 28, 270, 307, 309
Hochuli, Jost, 356-7
    Buchgestaltung als Denkschule, 356n
    Bücher machen, 356n
    Designing books, 356n, 357n
    Detail in typography, 357n
Høeg, Peter, *Miss Smilla's feeling for snow*, 197
Hogben, Lancelot, 305
Hollis, Richard, 40, 44, **81-6**, 89
    Graphic design, 246
Holzwarth, Hans Werner, 95
Horkheimer, Max, 307
Hornsey School of Art, London, 70
Hošek, Jaroslav, 18
Hostettler, Rudolf, 356
Howard, Jane, 130n
Hubregtse, Sjaak, 207
Hulse, Michael, 196
Hummel, Robert, 96
Hutt, Allen, 274
Huxley, Julian, 62, 305
Huygen, Frederike, 92

IBM (International Business Machines), 74, 291; see also: typesetting technics
Ideal Home Exhibition (1956), London, 57
Ikarus, type design program, 121
Imprimerie Royale, Paris, 234
Independent, The, newspaper, London, 55n, 151n
Independent Group, London, 59
indexes, 170, **218-30**
Information Design Journal, journal, 10-11, 12, 55n, 217n, 301n, 327n, 328, 329, 333n
information theory, 315-16
Innes, Jocasta, *The pauper's cookbook*, 223

Institute of Contemporary Arts (ICA), London, 59, 63, 82, 173
Institut für Analoge Studien, Rotis, 355
Institut für Sozialforschung, Frankfurt a.M./Los Angeles, 287
Internationales Design Zentrum (IDZ), Berlin, 94
International Socialism, Great Britain, 89
International Standards Organization (ISO), 308
International Union of Architects Congress (1961), London, 57
Isomorph, publishers, London, 294
Isotype, 10, 22, 51-5, 258, 261, 302, 305-6,
Isotype Institute, Oxford/London, 22, 52, 54, 302, 305; see also: Gesellschafts- und Wirtschaftsmuseum in Wien
ITT Industries, engineering and manufacturing conglomerate, 101
Itten, Johannes, 237, 246
Ivins, William M, *Prints and visual communication*, 342

Jaaks, Anke, 96
Jackdaw, book series, 179
Jacobs, Bas, 213n
Jaffé, H. L. C, 296
Janssen, Jacques, 198
Jeffery, Desmond, 283
Jephcott, Edmund, 185, 287
Johnson, Samuel, 217
Johnston, Edward, 123, 152, 165
Jong, Jan de, 210
Journal of Design History, journal, London, 11, 309n
Jung, Carl Gustav, 172

Kamlish, Ivor, 58
Kant, Immanuel, 356-7, 361
Karow, Peter, 121
Keedy, Jeffery, 364-5, 368

Kelfkens, Kees, 89
Kelmscott Press, publishers & printers, London, 144, 145
Kierkegaard, Søren, 172
Kindersley, David, 155
King, David, 45, 82, 85, 359
King, James, *Last modern, The*, **170**–3
Kinneir, Jock, 37, **65**–7, 153–6, 157n, 164
    Words and buildings, 66
Kinneir, Joan, 66
Kinross, Robin
    Modern typography, 15, 149n, 350–2, 371n
Kitzinger, Tony, 179
Klee, Paul, 42
Kloos, J. P, 296
Kluwer, publishers, Dordrecht etc, 88
Knapp, Peter, 83
Knuth, Donald, 121–3
Koch, Rudolf, 162
Kracauer, Siegfried, 185
Kravitz, Peter, 362n
Kreitmeyer, Jens, 95, 96
Krimpen, Huib van, 208
Krimpen, Jan van, 162, **207**–10
    Letter to Philip Hofer, 208
    On designing and devising type, 208
Kropotkin, Peter, 172
Kruk, Raya, 303
'Kunst im Exil in Großbritannien 1933–1945' exhibition (1986), Berlin, 303

Labour Party, British, 64, 178
Lacan, Jacques, 319, 335
Lafayette, Galeries, 83
Lambot, Ian, 200, 201, 204–6
Lampedusa, Giuseppe Tomasi di, 192
Lane, Allen, 177, 178
Lanz, K, 47
Lao-tzu, 172

Large, E. C, *Sugar in the air*, 68
Lasdun, Denys, 31
Lauweriks, J. L. M, 251
Lawrence, D. H, 148
Lawrence & Wishart, publishers, London, 267
Leavis, F. R, 9, 12, 177
Le Corbusier [Charles-Edouard Jeanneret], 69, 181, 236, 296
    Œuvre complète, 204
    Vers une architecture, 279
Lee, S. G. M. & A. R. Mayes (ed.), *Dreams and dreaming*, 40–1
legibility, 155, 362, 368–9
Legros, L. A. & J. C. Grant, *Typographical printing-surfaces*, 114, 120
Letraset, see: typesetting technics
letterforms; see also: typefaces
    bold, 118, 119
    broken (blackletter), 234, 239, 241
    italic, 118, 119, 121
    light, 120
    'modern', 234
    roman, 118, 119, 241
    sanserif, 18, 36, 40, 120, 235, 239, 241, 243, 246, 250–1
Lettergieterij Amsterdam, typeface manufacturers, Amsterdam, 208
LettError, **106**–9
Lévi-Strauss, Claude, 319, 321, 337
Lewis, John, 38
Libanus Press, Marlborough, publishers and printers, 194
Limited Editions Club, publishers, New York, 210
linguistics, 251, 313, 318–20, 325, 336, 337, 339, 340, 345, 346; see also: semiotics
Linotype, composing machine & typeface manufacturers, London, 74, 146, 162; see also: typesetting technics
Lissitzky, El, 250, 265
Lloyd Jones, Linda, 179

Loewy, Raymond, 160
Loghum Slaterus, Van, publishers, Arnhem, 88
Lommen, Mathieu, 207, 210
London College of Printing, London, 63
London Review of Books, journal, London, 149n
London Transport, 160, 303; see also: London Underground
London Typographical Designers, 273, 275
London Underground, 332–3; see also: London Transport; signs map, 80, 160
Loos, Adolf, 137, 252
Lost Boys, new media group, Amsterdam etc, 98n
lowercase, see: typesetting conventions: capitals/lowercase
Lucas Aerospace, 159
Lucky Strike cigarettes, 160
Lufthansa, airline, 200
Luidl, Philipp, (ed.), *Paul Renner*, 242n
Lumitype, composing machine, 73; see also: typesetting technics
Luna, Paul, 151
Lund Humphries, printers & publishers, London & Bradford, 79, 265, 268, 270, 275, 284
Lupton, Ellen, 344n, 363n, 365n
Lussu, Giovanni, 340n

Maastricht: Jan van Eyck Akademie, 93n, 107, 371n
MacCabe, Colin, 85
Godard, 85
MacCarthy, Fiona, *Eric Gill*, 167–9
McCoy, Katherine, 367n
Máčel, Otakar, 182
Macdonald, Murdo, 362n
Mackie, George, 357n
McLaine, Ian, *Ministry of morale*, 267n

McLean, Ruari, 9–10, 274
Jan Tschichold: typographer, 9, 174–6, 265n
McNay, Michael, 360n
Mader, Petra, 96
Maillart, Robert, 294
Majoor, Martin, 102–6, 210
Maldonado, Tomás, 141, 283, 323
Malik Verlag, publishers, Berlin/Prague/London, 304
Mao Zedong, 346
Marber, Romek, 308
Marcuse, Herbert, 306
Mardersteig, Giovanni, 359
Marker, Chris, 85
'Ma(r)king the Text' conference (1998), Cambridge, 199n
MARS (Modern Architecture Research Society) exhibition (1938), London, 62, 267
Martens, Karel, 15, 42, 87–93, 106, 357n, 361n, 371n
Matrix, journal, Risbury, 208
May, Ernst, 258
Mayer, Peter, 177, 178
Mayhew, Henry, 191
Meccano, 91
Médailles de Louis XIV, 233–4
Meermanno-Westreenianum, museum, The Hague, 207
Meisterschule für Deutschlands Buchdrucker, Munich, 254
Mermoz, Gérard, 15
MetaDesign, design group, Berlin, 12, 47, 94–8, 107, 109
Meta-Font, design program, 121–3
Metal Box Company, 271
Meyer, Hannes, 256, 257, 260, 263
Meynell, Francis, 266, 274
Mies van der Rohe, Ludwig, 69, 260
Miller, J. Abbott, 344n
Miller, Jonathan, 347n
Miller, Laura, 189n

Ministry of Information, Britain, 25, 64, 267, 270, 271, 273, 303; see also: Central Office of Information

Ministry of Transport (Department of Transport), Britain, 152–7
  Anderson Committee report on traffic signs for motorways (1962), 66, 153
  Worboys Committee report on traffic signs for all-purpose roads (1963), 66, 153, 155–6

Mitford, Nancy, 191

modernism, 149, 173, 174, 176, 239, 241, 253, 258, 282, 292, 362, 364, 365

modernity, 184, 185, 350–4

Modern Poetry in Translation, journal, London, 86

'modern traditionalism', 102, 104, 105, 106n

Moholy-Nagy, László, 137, 139, 237, 246, 248n, 250, 251, 252, 253, 254, 256, 260, 265, 306–7
  Malerei, Fotografie, Film, 256

Moholy-Nagy: 60 Fotos, (ed. Franz Roh), 291

Mol, Wim, 87

Monde, Le, newspaper, Paris, 151

Monotype Corporation, composing machine & typeface manufacturers, London & Redhill, 74, 79, 145, 147, 148, 208–9, 229, 275, 357n; see also: typesetting technics

Monotype Newsletter, journal, London, 146

Monotype Recorder, journal, London, 146, 273, 274, 281

Moore, Rowan, 13

Morison, Stanley, 74, 98, 139n, 145–6, 147, 148, 155, 162, 163, 164, 165, 168, 208, 210, 266, 267, 268, 270, 274, 359, 369
  First principles of typography, 98, 131–2, 270
  Politics and script, 164

Morris, Charles, 322

Morris, William, 144, 145, 148, 159, 187, 322

Mosley, James, 11, 164, 351
  Nymph and the grot, The, 250n

Moynihan, Rodrigo, 178

Mukherjee, Trilokesh, 60

Mumford, Lewis, 281, 284
  Technics and civilization, 281

Murdoch, Iris, *Under the net*, 36–7

Murray, Peter, 13

Museum of Modern Art (MOMA), New York, 200

Museum of Modern Art, Oxford, 84

Myers, Bernard, 59

Nairn, Tom, 353n
  Enchanted glass, The, 353n

Nash, Paul, 170

National Book League, London, 211–2; see also: Book Trust

National Conference on Art & Design Education (1968), London, 279

National Physical Laboratory, 243

National-Socialism, 138, 149, 174, 175, 184, 241

Neue Frankfurt, Das, magazine, Frankfurt a.M, 258

Neue Linie, Die, magazine, Berlin, 255

Neue Zürcher Zeitung, newspaper, Zurich, 151

Neurath, Marie [née Reidemeister], 22, **51–5**, 60, 258, 302, 305, 306

Neurath, Otto, 10, 18, 22, 51–5, 60, 258–9, 302, 305, 306
  Gesammelte bildpädagogische Schriften, 55

Neurath, Walter, 305

New Left Books, publishers, London, 185

New Left Review, journal, London, 34–5, 353n

News Corporation, publishing conglomerate, 194

New Society, magazine, London, 40, 85

newspapers, 143, **150–1**, 358

'New Spirit in Craft and Design', exhibition (1987), London, 86

'new traditionalism', 145–6, 149, 163, 175, 211, 266–7, 270, 271, 273, 275, 284

'new typography', 24, 148, 174, 175, 181, 234, 235–9, 243, 246–63 passim, **264–85**, 293, 307, 308

Nezval, Vítězslav, *Abeceda*, 182

Nieuwenhuijzen, Kees, 87

Nikkels, Walter, 87, 106

Nonesuch Press, publishers, London, 146

Noordzij, Gerrit, 341–2

Noordzij, Peter Matthias, 102, 210

Norris, Christopher, *Uncritical theory*, 335n

North East London Polytechnic, 69

N R C *Handelsblad*, newspaper, Amsterdam, 151

Nypels, Charles, 106
　　Foundation, 106
　　Prize, 106–7, 109

Oase, journal, Nijmegen, 90, 91, 92, 93n

Octavo, journal, London, 142, 251n, 369n

Offset-, Buch- und Werbekunst, magazine, Leipzig, 237, 252, 254

Olthof, Alje, 87

Olympic Games 1972, Munich, 200

Omnific, design group, London, 40

Open Oog, magazine, Amsterdam, 294–6

Open University, Milton Keynes, 10
　　Institute of Educational Technology, 10

Österreichische Fertighaus, Das, 28–9, 47

Our Time, magazine, London, 279

Oxenaar, R. D. E, 102

Oxford: Brookes University, 213n

Oxford dictionary for writers and editors, 214–7

Oxford guide to style, 217n

Oxford University Press, printers and publishers, Oxford and London, 209, 214, 217

Owen, William, 13

Pais, El, newspaper, Madrid, 151

P & O, shipping company, London, 66, 153

Pandora, journal, Ulm, 139n

Paolozzi, Eduardo, 58

Paris Match, magazine, Paris, 329

Pasternak, Boris, 192

Pearson, publishing conglomerate, London, 177, 178, 199

Peirce, C. S, 313, 319, 322, 323

Pelican Books, 178; see also: Penguin Books

Penguin Books, 36, 40–1, 149, 175, 177–**181**, 277, 308

Penrose Annual, London, 79, 80, 309

Pentagram, design group, London & New York, 84

Pevsner, Nikolaus, 12, 177, 179

Pfäffli, Bruno, 75

Philip, George, 68, 282

Photon, composing machine, 73; see also: typesetting technics

Picture Post, magazine, London, 304, 305

Pitman, Isaac, 233

Plant, Marjorie, *The English book trade*, 225

'Planvolles Werben' exhibition (1934), Basel, 20

Pluto Press, publishers, London, 84, 89

Poetism, 181–2

PoppeKast, computer application, 108

Popper, Karl, 306

Porstmann, Walter, 137, 139, 236, 239, 241, 251, 252
Sprache und Schrift, 137, 138, 235-6, 251, 253
postmodernism, 31, 59, 104, 201, 206, 336
poststructuralism, 322, 335, 361n; see also: deconstruction
Potter, Caroline [née Quennell], 71
Potter, Nic, 71
Potter, Norman, 7, 15, **68-71**, 279, 281, 282, 285n
Models & Constructs, 68, 71
What is a designer, 69, 70, 173, 184, 264n
Potter, Sally, 71
Poynor, Rick, 14-15, 61n, 106n
Typography now, 368n
Practice of design, The, (ed. Herbert Read), 268-9, 270
Pravda, newspaper, Moscow, 151
Presley, Elvis, 59
Preussler, Christoph, 96
Prins Bernhard Fonds, 92, 93n
printing, 132-3, 143-4, 235, 341-6, 350, 358
letterpress, 100, 190, 197, 198
lithography (small-offset), 291
mimeography, 291
transition from letterpress to lithography, 126, 161, 215
Printing Historical Society, London, 11
Printing Historical Society Bulletin, London, 81n, 210n
Pritchard, Jack, 282
Pts, journal, Maastricht, 213n
PTT (Nederlandse Posterijen, Telegrafie en Telefonie), 90, 92, 101-6, 209
Publishers Association, London, 212
Punch, magazine, London, 64
'Purpose and Pleasure' exhibition (1952), London, 275
Pye, David, 165

Quadraat, design group, Arnhem, 46; see also: typefaces
Quarter Point, magazine, Redhill, 357n
Queneau, Raymond, 98

Random House, publishers, New York / London, 199n
Ransmayr, Christoph, *Die letzte Welt*, 191
Rassegna, journal, Bologna, 183
Rathbone Books, book packagers, London, 59
Ravensbourne College of Art & Design, 11
Ray, Peter, 24, 269, 271, 273, 284, 285n
Read, Herbert, 170-3, 268
Art and society, 172
Education through art, 172
Green child, The, 172
Philosophy of anarchism, The, 172
Poetry and anarchism, 172
To hell with culture, 172
Read, Margaret [Ludo], 171
reading, 150, 184, 186, 187, 218, 223, 343, 346-50, 358, 363, 366, 367-70
Reading, University of, Department of Typography & Graphic Communication, 9, 10, 11, 51, 78, 130n, 230n, 258n, 275n, 285n, 302
Reidemeister, Marie, see: Neurath, Marie
Renner, Paul, 239, 254, 255, 260n
Renzio, Toni del, 82
research in typography, 155, 228-9, 263
rhetoric, visual/verbal, 323-6
Rice, Stanley, 95
Richards, I. A, 162
Richards, Vernon, 68, 170
Rietveld, Gerrit, 69, 296
Ring, magazine, Düsseldorf, 250
Ring 'Neue Werbegestalter', 256-8
Road Research Laboratory, Slough, 155, 156

Robbins Report into higher education (1964), 178
Rogers, Richard, 62
Roos, S. H. de, 208
Rose, Gillian, 7
Rossum, Just van, **106–9**
Rot, Diter, 106
Rotha, Paul, [Paul Thompson], 305, 306
    Land of promise, 306
    World of plenty, 306
Royal College of Art (RCA), London, 36, 64, 66, 70, 267, 369n
Royal Cornwall Yacht Club, Falmouth, 70
Royal Institute of British Architects, London, 308
Ruder, Emil, 73, 83
Ruskin, John, 148, 165
Russell, Bertrand, 305
Ryder, John, 359
    Intimate leaves from a designer's notebook, 359
Rykwert, Joseph, 59
Rymans, retailers, Britain, 66

Said, Edward, 7
St Bride Printing Library, London, 11
St George's Gallery, London, 84
Sandberg, Willem, 30, 282, 294–6, 297
Saussure, Ferdinand de, 313, 316, 319, 320, 323, 336–41, 343–4, 345, 361n
    Cours de linguistique générale, **336–41**
Sayer, Phil, 13
Schelvis, Jan-Kees, 102, 104
Schleger, Hans, 268, 270, 307
Schlemmer, Oskar, 246, 254
Schmidt, Joost, 236, 237, 252, 257, 261, 263
Schmoller, Hans, 36, 149, 150, 179, 180, 181, 308
Schnabel, Artur, 70

Schneidler, F. H. Ernst, 21
'Schönste Schweizer Bücher' competition & exhibition, 213
Schuitema, Paul, 83, 256
Schwabe, Benno, printers & publishers, Basel, 276
Schweizer Buchhandel, Der, 213
Schweizer Graphische Mitteilungen, magazine, St Gallen, 290, 292
Schwitters, Kurt, 238, 239, 243, 257, 258n, 265
Scitex, composing machine, 104; see also: typesetting technics
Sciullio, Pierre di, 106
Scope, magazine, London, 279; see also: *Shelf Appeal*
Scotford, Martha, 363n
Sebald, W. G, 191–9
    Austerlitz, 199
    Ausgewänderten, Die [*The emigrants*], 192, 194, 195
    Beschreibung des Unglücks, Die, 191
    Logis in einem Landschaft, 198
    Nach der Natur [*After nature*], 191
    Ringe des Saturn, Die [*The rings of Saturn*], 191, 192, 193–8
    Schwindel. Gefühle [*Vertigo*], 192
Sedley Place Design, design group, London & Berlin, 97
semantic poetry, see: typesetting conventions: semantic
semiotics (and semiology), **313–27**, **328–332**, 337, 340, 341, 344
Serota, Nicholas, 84
Shah, Eddie, 151
Shaw, George Bernard, 167, 233
Shelf Appeal, magazine, London, 271, 279; see also: *Scope*
Shell Transport & Trading, 65
Shenval Press, printers & publishers, London, 267
Sierman, Harry, 87, 106
Sierman, Koosje, 182, 183, 207, 208–9, 210

Sign Design Society, Harpenden, 67n
signs, public, 31, 56–8, 65, 67, 93,
  127, 131, 132, 152–3, 164–6
    Britain: road signs, 37, 66, 132n,
      152–7
    Hongkong & Shanghai Bank, 200
    London: New Scotland Yard,
      56–7
    London Underground, 152
    NEN 3225 [Dutch Standards
      Institute letter], 209
    Paris Métro, 75
    Roissy: Charles de Gaulle air-
      port, 75
    Rome, 132
Simon, Oliver, 266
Slack, William, 58
Sless, David, 314, 317, 323, 327n, 329
Smeijers, Fred, 46, 104, 210
Smets, Edwin, 213n
Smith, Roger, 319, 327n
Smithson, Alison, 57
Smithson, Peter, 57
socialism, 174, 197, 267
Society of Indexers, 230n
Society of Industrial Artists and
  Designers (SIAD), London, 11, 80,
  271, 273, 284, 309; see also: Char-
  tered Society of Designers
Society of Typographic Designers
  (STD), London, 9
Solidarity, journal, London, 173n
Sontag, Susan, 100
Speaight, Robert, *The life of Eric Gill*,
  167
Spencer, Herbert, 30, 79, 271, 272,
  273–5, 283, 284, 297
    Design in business printing,
      275–6, 282, 297
    The visible word, 244
Spiekermann, Erik, 12, 13, 75, **95–8**,
  107, 129n, 130n, 130n, 358, 359
    Rhyme & reason, 98, 358, 359
    Ursache & Wirkung, 12, 98, 358n
Spiekermann, Joan, 107

Stam, Mart, 182, 296
Stamp Machine, computer applica-
  tion, 109
standardization, 18, 20, 33, 53, 74,
  159, 235, 242, 251, 277, 308–9, 354
Stauffacher, Jack, 357n
Stebbing, Susan, 299, 305
    Philosophy and the physicists, 299
    Thinking to some purpose, 299
Stedelijk Museum, Amsterdam, 30,
  92, 180, 181, 183, 296
Steiner, George, 100
Sterne, Laurence, 98
Stiff, Paul, 11, 130n, 275n, 285n,
  289n, 342n, 345n, 370
Stijl, De, 236, 250
Stols, A. A. M, 207
Stölzl, Gunta, 254
Stravinsky, Igor, 286
structuralism, 319–22, 337, 343n
Studio H, designers, London, 62
Studio Vista, publishers, London, 38
Sudjic, Deyan, 12, 185n
Suhrkamp, publishers, Frankfurt
  a.M, 181, 185
SUN, publishers, Nijmegen, 42, 88,
  89, 90
Sun, The, newspaper, London, 151
Suschitzky, Wolfgang, 306
Sutherland, John, 180
'Swiss typography', see: graphic
  design: Switzerland
Sylvan Press, publishers, London,
  277
Sylvester, David, *René Magritte*,
  358–9

Tallis, Raymond, *Not Saussure*, 335n
Tauchnitz, publishers, Leipzig, 179
Taylorism, 137
Teige, Karel, 181–3
'Teige Animator' exhibition (1994),
  Amsterdam, **181–3**
TeleMedia, telecommunications
  company, 101, 104

Telia, telecommunications company, 101

Thames & Hudson, publishers, London, 305

Thatcher, Margaret, 13, 338

Themerson, Franciszka, 297

Themerson, Stefan, 297–9
    Bayamus, 297, 298
    'Semantic sonata', 297

'This is Tomorrow' exhibition (1956), London, 59, 82

Thistlewood, David, *Herbert Read*, 170

Thompson, E. P, 177

Thompson, Philip, 58

Thornton, James, 219

Tillotsons, printers, Bolton, 275

Time Out, magazine, London, 45

Times, The, 127, 150, 151, 155

Times Literary Supplement, The, 100n, 180

Timpanaro, Sebastiano, 320n, 344n

Today, newspaper, London, 151

Tomkins, John, [Julius Teicher], 309

Tory, Geofroy, *Champfleury*, 116

Toscanini, Arturo, 287

Total Design, design group, Amsterdam, 101

Toucan, book series, 179

Tracy, Walter
    Letters of credit, **143–9**, **161–3**, 208

Transformation, book-periodical, London, 26–7

Treebus, Karel, 87

Trevelyan, John, 305

Triest, Jaap van, 93n

Truffaut, Francois, *Les quatre cents coups*, 61

Trump, Georg, 254

Tschichold, Edith [née Kramer], 21

Tschichold, Jan, 9, 10, 20–1, 36, 137, 148–9, **174–6**, 179, 181, 213, 239, 241, 251, 252, 253, 254, 256, 259, 260, 261, 262, 265, 266, 267, 275–9, 281, 283n, 291–3, 308, 356
    Asymmetric typography, 278–9
    'Elementare Typographie', 253, 254n, 252, 256
    'Glaube und Wirklichkeit', 292–3
    Leben und Werk, 265n
    Neue Typographie, Die, 251, 253, 265, 279
    Typografische Entwurfstechnik, 20, 279
    Typographische Gestaltung, 149, 261, 275–9

'Turn Again' exhibition (1955), Manchester, 58

Turner, John, 279

Twentieth Century, journal, London, 279b

Twyman, Michael, 11, 325n

type, 113–15; see also: typefaces

'Type 90' conference (1990), Oxford, 107

typefaces; see also: letterforms
    classification, 353
    concept, 72, 145, **113–29**, 145
    families, 117–18, 120, 122
    instances:
        Advert, 107
        Akzidenz Grotesk, 36
        Avenir, 77
        Baskerville, 115, 117, 118
        Bauhaus, 255n
        Bayer-type, 255
        Bell Centennial, 104
        Bembo, 115
        Beowolf, 107, 108
        Breughel, 75
        Caecilia, 102
        Caslon, 126
        Cheltenham, 118, 120
        Clarendon, 118
        Deutsche Bundespost Hausschrift, 97
        Erik RightHand, 107
        Eurostile, 212

typefaces, *instances (continued)*

Federal, 109

Flipper, 108

Franklin Gothic, 42, 89

Frutiger, 75, 77

Futura, 77, 206, 239, 242, 255, 258

Garamond, 21, 34, 126, 145, 147, 161, 163n, 244

Gill Sans, 36, 102, 120, 124, 148, 169

Grotesque, 215, 36, 93

Helvetica, 34, 97, 99, 241

Icone, 75

Joanna, 169

Just LeftHand, 107

Legende, 21

Lucida Sans, 102

Méridien, 73

Meta, 98n, 102

Modern Extended 8A, 122–3

Myriad, 104

Neue Haas Grotesk, 34; see also: Helvetica

OCR-A, 242

OCR-B, 74, 242

Perpetua, 168, 273

Plantin, 163

Quadraat, 46–7, 104

'romain du roi', 234, 351

Romanée, 210

Rotis, 206, 355

Scala, 102

Scala Sans, 102

Serifa, 77

Sheldon, 209

Stone Sans, 102

Telefont, 102–5

Thesis, 102

Times Europa, 150

Times Roman, 128, 151, 162, 163, 184

Trixie, 107

Univers, 73–4, 75, 76, 77, 101, 120, 241, 243

typesetting conventions

asymmetry, 21, 34, 264, 293, 296

capitals/lowercase, 36–7, 101, 131–42, 235, 236, 237, 246, 247, 251–2, 253, 355

indentation, 34, 83, 89, 226–7

justified, 220, 223, 226, 288, 289, 291

semantic, 226–7, 297–9

symmetry, 21, 100, 175, 223, 296

unjustified, 42, 282, **286–301**, 355

typesetting technics

CRT/digital, 75, 101, 105, 161

desktop publishing, 46, 92, 95, 104, 289, 351

IBM Composer, 74, 89

IBM Executive, 291

metal (hand), 95, 114

metal (machine), 161, 190, 197, 229, 235, 242, 293

photocomposition, 73, 86, 115, 120, 121, 161, 180, 229, 242

rub-down lettering, 42, 86, 89, 127

typewriter, 291, 301, 324

Typographic, magazine, London, 9

Typographica, magazine, London, 275, 297

typographic design

historical emergence, 187, 211, 220, 233

possible contribution of, 227, 229, 343, 344, 366

process of, 85, 87, 204–5, 264

specification in, 264, 265, 271, 275, 279–81, 293, 308

'Typographic Restyling' exhibition (1950), London, 274, 275

Typographische Mitteilungen, magazine, Berlin, 137, 139, 252, 253, 254n

typography

as culture, 363–4

concept of, 144, 350–1

typography (*continued*)
  material dimension of, 87, 187,
    190, 194–5, 362–3
  measurement in, 351–2
Typography, magazine, London, 267
Typography Papers, journal, Reading,
  93n

Ulm: Hochschule für Gestaltung,
  32, 82, 94, 139, 141, 200, 283, 296,
  301, 323
Ulm, journal, Ulm, 32, 283, 323
Unger, Gerard, 98, 101, 244
Updike, D. B, *Printing types*, 119
Uppercase, journal, London, 323
Usborne, T. G, 153

Vachek, Josef, 340
VDU (visual display unit), 215
Verberne, Alexander, 89, 90, 104
Vermaas, Chris, 101
Vermeulen, Jan, 89
vernacular, 201, 365–6
Vickers, Brian, *Appropriating Shake-
  speare*, 335n, 361n
Victoria & Albert Museum, London,
  99, 371n
Vienna Circle, 259
Villiers, Marjorie, 192
Vorticism, 299
Vrij Nederland, magazine, Amster-
  dam, 151

Wadman, Howard, 267n
Wainwright, Alfred, 80
Waller, Robert, 10, 11, 333n, 340n
Ward, Basil, 305
Warde, Beatrice, 145, 147, 275, 279,
  281
Warren, Low, *Journalism from A to
  Z*, 228
Watermark, publishers, Hong Kong,
  202, 204, 206
Weber Nicholsen, Sherry, 186n

Wedgwood, ceramics manufactur-
  ers, 158, 159
Weil, Simone, 71
Weishappel, Theres, 95, 96
'Weiße Rose' group, 301
Wells, H. G, 167
Wendingen, magazine, Amsterdam,
  166, 251
Werkman Prize (1998), 90
Werkplaats Typografie, Arnhem, 93n
Wesel-Henrion, Marion, 65
Westdeutsche Landesbank, 200
Whistler, James McNeill, 194
Whitechapel Art Gallery, London,
  44, 45, 84
Wijdeveld, H. Th, 251
Wilkins, Bridget, 369n
Wilkins, John, 233
Williamson, Hugh, *Methods of book
  design*, 128, 224
Wilson, Vicky, 14
Wingate, Allan, publishers, London,
  269, 272
Wittgenstein, Ludwig, 306
Woestijne, Joost van de, 87
Wolpe, Berthold, 308
Woodcock, George, 68
  Herbert Read, 170
Worboys, Walter, 155; see also: Min-
  istry of Transport
Word & Image, journal, London, 332
Wordsworth, William, 171
Woudhuysen, Lewis, 60, 307
Wordsearch, publishers, London,
  14, 185n
Wouw, Jolijn van de, 101
Wozencroft, Jon, 100
Wright, Edward, 15, 31, 40, **56–61**,
  82, 279, 308
  Codex atorrantis, 60–1
  'Graphic Work & Painting' exhi-
    bition (1985), 60
writing, 143, 341–2